SharePoint® 2010 Disaster Recovery Guide

John L. Ferringer
Sean P. McDonough

Course Technology PTR

A part of Cengage Learning

COURSE TECHNOLOGY
CENGAGE Learning·

Australia • Brazil • Japan • Korea • Mexico • Singapore • Spain • United Kingdom • United States

COURSE TECHNOLOGY
CENGAGE Learning™

SharePoint® 2010 Disaster Recovery Guide
John L. Ferringer
Sean P. McDonough

Publisher and General Manager, Course Technology PTR: Stacy L. Hiquet

Associate Director of Marketing: Sarah Panella

Manager of Editorial Services: Heather Talbot

Marketing Manager: Mark Hughes

Acquisitions Editor: Mitzi Koontz

Project/Copy Editor: Karen A. Gill

Technical Reviewer: J.D. Wade

Interior Layout Tech: MPS Limited, a Macmillan Company

Cover Designer: Mike Tanamachi

Indexer: Larry Sweazy

Proofreader: Sue Boshers

For product information and technology assistance, contact us at
Cengage Learning Customer & Sales Support, 1-800-354-9706.

For permission to use material from this text or product, submit all requests online at **cengage.com/permissions**.
Further permissions questions can be e-mailed to
permissionrequest@cengage.com.

Library of Congress Control Number: 2010920330

ISBN-13: 978-1-4354-5645-7

ISBN-10: 1-4354-5645-9

Course Technology, a part of Cengage Learning
20 Channel Center Street
Boston, MA 02210
USA

Cengage Learning is a leading provider of customized learning solutions with office locations around the globe, including Singapore, the United Kingdom, Australia, Mexico, Brazil, and Japan. Locate your local office at: **international. cengage.com/region.**

Cengage Learning products are represented in Canada by Nelson Education, Ltd.

For your lifelong learning solutions, visit **courseptr.com.**

Visit our corporate Web site at **cengage.com.**

Printed in the United States of America
1 2 3 4 5 6 7 12 11 10

*To Gretchen and Tracy, for their patience,
support, and willingness to tolerate us doing this
all over again . . . and so soon after the last book.*

Acknowledgments

Sean P. McDonough would like to acknowledge the following people and groups:

- Microsoft, for continuing to evolve the SharePoint platform and make it worthy of so many lost hours and long nights.

- My many friends and family, for once again putting up with my half-asleep moaning about countless hours spent writing in the wee hours of the morning.

- Mitzi Koontz, for your patience with a couple of knuckleheads like us. We're not the fastest writers on the planet, but we'd like to think that we're special in our own way. Thanks for bearing with us and admirably handling the situation that landed in your lap.

- Julia Hall and the folks at Idera, for giving us a forum and helping to increase awareness for the cause of SharePoint disaster recovery. Your support of us and our book has been nothing short of fantastic—and I'm not just saying that because I happen to be working for you these days.

- The SharePoint community-at-large. I've greatly enjoyed my interactions with so many of you at SharePoint Saturdays, at user group meetings, at conferences, on my blog, on Twitter, and through all the other mechanisms that bring us together. You remain one of the biggest reasons I keep signing on for this punishment.

- Karen Gill, for once again proving herself a fantastic copy editor and teacher. Although I learned my lesson about ending sentences with prepositions from the last book, you found plenty of other ways to enlighten me this time around. Thank you for patience, diligence, and instruction.

- J. D. Wade, aka "The KB Man," for doing a wonderful job as our technical editor. It wasn't so long ago that I was sitting in your chair, J. D., so I have a special appreciation for the role you filled with regard to this book. Thank you for all of your questions, suggestions, corrections, and support. We simply couldn't have done this without you.

- John Ferringer, a member of the "SharePoint Mr. Clean Team" and my bald-headed partner-in-crime. Thanks for another go-round with the DR Devil. We survived again despite ourselves. Do you think that one of these days we'll learn?

- My mom, Ilene McDonough, who died unexpectedly just before this book went to print. I really wanted to share this book with you. You wouldn't have understood a thing it said, but that wouldn't have changed the excitement and smile on your face when I handed you a copy.

- To my kids, Brendan and Sabrina, who are still too young to read this or understand what SharePoint is. Someday you'll be old enough to comprehend the contents of this book, and I hope that what you see brings smiles to your faces.

- My wife Tracy. Before I even started, you knew that it was going to be another rough ride with overruns, late-night hours, and a worn-down husband, yet you supported me with kindness, patience, and understanding the whole way. As with the first *Disaster Recovery Guide*, I couldn't have possibly done this without you. Thank you. I love you so much.

John L. Ferringer would like to acknowledge the following people and groups:

- My wife, Gretchen, for the unbelievable support, patience, and encouragement she's given me through all of my hare-brained schemes, especially this one.

- My parents, Bernie and Vicki, for the gift of reading and the reassurance that they'll always be there to read to me.

- Enrique Lima, for challenging me to always be better every day, putting up with all my stupid questions, keeping me from going off the deep end, and loaning me the hardware that made so much of my testing and research possible.

- Mitzi Koontz for the limitless guidance and tolerance she's had dealing with a couple of geeks who want to spend every second possible getting it *just* right.

- Karen Gill, for once again making it look like I write so purty, offering encouragement, laughing at all my terrible jokes, and even trying to fool me into thinking that I'm a good writer.

- J. D. Wade, for being a precision technical ace. I've been blessed to work with two incredible technical editors for both of our books, and I know that the value of what we've put into these pages is as much a result of J. D.'s efforts as ours.

- Sean, for a million more things than I'd ever be able to put into words. For keeping me on task, for never settling, for putting himself through this wringer again, for writing incredible stuff, and for being a great friend.

- Piper, for making every sleepless night melt away with smiles, giggles, laughter, and wonder. For being my favorite person in the world to tickle and an incredible blessing; I'm so lucky to have you in my life.

- Gretchen, you are first in this list because you are the most important thing in my life, and last in it because I always save the best for last. Everything I do in this world is for you; you are my heart, my love, my best friend. Thank you for leading me through this journey again. I will always love you.

About the Authors

Sean P. McDonough is a product manager for SharePoint Products at Idera, a Microsoft gold-certified partner and creator of tools for SharePoint, SQL Server, and PowerShell. In his role as a product manager, he is focused on Idera's SharePoint backup and recovery solutions. Sean carries several Microsoft Certified Technology Specialist (MCTS) certifications for SharePoint and other areas, and he is a Microsoft Certified Professional Developer (MCPD). He is also a regular speaker at SharePoint events, a blogger, and a developer of tools that simplify the administration of SharePoint environments.

Prior to joining Idera, Sean served as a solutions architect and SharePoint team lead at Cardinal Solutions Group, an IT consulting and solution provider, where he not only directed internal growth of the SharePoint team, but helped foster and grow Cardinal's partnership with Microsoft. As a consultant, Sean worked with a number of Fortune 500 companies to architect, implement, troubleshoot, tune, and customize their SharePoint environments.

Sean can be reached through his blog (http://SharePointInterface.com), LinkedIn (http://www.linkedin.com/in/smcdonough), or Twitter (@spmcdonough).

John L. Ferringer, a solutions architect for Apparatus, Inc. in Indianapolis, Indiana, with more than six years of experience administering and supporting SharePoint technologies, has spent more than 12 years working in the information technology consulting industry. He coauthored the *SharePoint 2007 Disaster Recovery Guide*, published by Charles River Media, in January 2009. He is an MCTS in the installation and configuration of Windows SharePoint Services (WSS) v3, Microsoft Office SharePoint Server (MOSS) 2007, and Microsoft System Center Operations Manager (SCOM) 2007. He is also a Microsoft Certified IT Professional (MCITP) for Enterprise Project Management (EPM) with Project Server 2007.

John speaks regularly at user groups, SharePoint Saturdays, and other conferences throughout the Midwest. He plans to make his triumphant return to blogging at http://www.MyCentralAdmin.com now that this book is done, besides writing articles and posting at other great SharePoint-related sites throughout the interconnected tubes of the Internet. If you find this book useful, John asks that you send gifts of bacon to Sean down in Cincinnati, because he needs to see the error of his ways. John also administers www.SearchForSharePoint.com, a custom search engine indexing more than 2,000 Web sites of SharePoint content.

If you're looking for inane comments, vented frustrations, or SharePoint wisdom in 140 characters or less, follow John on Twitter at http://www.twitter.com/ferringer.

Contents

Chapter 6
Windows Server 2008 High Availability   117

Chapter 7
SQL Server 2008 Backup and Restore   149

Chapter 8
SQL Server 2008 High Availability 189

Chapter 9
SharePoint 2010 Central Administration Backup and Restore   241

Chapter 10
SharePoint 2010 Command Line Backup and Restore:
PowerShell   299

Chapter 11
SharePoint 2010 Disaster Recovery Development   337

Chapter 12
SharePoint 2010 Disaster Recovery for End Users   375

Chapter 13
Conclusion

Index

Introduction

If you've done any previous research on SharePoint disaster recovery topics, such as content recovery, backup and restore, and high availability, you've probably found quite a bit of information on the subject. That held true for us when we wrote the original *Disaster Recovery Guide* for SharePoint 2007, and it's just as true now with SharePoint 2010. But what we also found was that much of the discussion did one of two things: either it just scratched the surface of SharePoint disaster recovery, or it covered such a narrow focus that it was only applicable in certain situations. So we set out to create a resource for SharePoint disaster recovery that comprehensively examined the ins and outs of the various technical options available to back up and restore your SharePoint environment and highlighted the concerns you need to understand to build an informed and well-rounded disaster recovery plan.

What You'll Find in This Book

Microsoft's SharePoint platform is a complex, diverse technical tool designed to meet a range of business needs and uses. It requires several other platforms and applications for implementation, and it can be integrated with other external lines of business applications. This diversity also applies to the numerous methods, tools, and approaches that can be used to preserve your SharePoint farm if it becomes affected by a catastrophic event. The majority of this book introduces you to those methods, tools, and approaches for backing up and restoring SharePoint. Before covering all the crucial technical aspects of preserving SharePoint with the tools Microsoft provides for it, we introduce you to the key concepts and activities necessary to develop a disaster recovery plan to implement those technical practices. Listed next are some of the main concepts this recovery guide discusses:

- Learning the concepts and terminology of SharePoint disaster recovery planning

- Designing and documenting a SharePoint disaster recovery plan

- Testing and maintaining a SharePoint disaster recovery plan

- Understanding SharePoint-specific disaster recovery concerns and best practices

- Backing up and restoring the foundation of any SharePoint environment, Windows Server 2008

- Understanding how high-availability technologies can aid in SharePoint disaster recovery

- Discussing the role that SQL Server and its backup options play in the SharePoint disaster recovery equation

- Utilizing SharePoint's Central Administration site for backup and restore tasks

- Exploring the new options that are available through PowerShell and SharePoint-specific cmdlets

- Investigating the SharePoint object model and how to employ custom development to meet special backup and restore needs

- Highlighting end user disaster recovery options and the administrative concerns that are tied to them

Who This Book Is For

In general, this book is geared toward readers who are worried about the long-term health and viability of their SharePoint environment and the valuable business information stored in it. It's assumed that readers are at least familiar with SharePoint as end users, and most of the technical content inside is best suited for those who have experience deploying, configuring, and administrating SharePoint. The examples, walk-throughs, and advice in this recovery guide are intended to be general and can be applied to a variety of situations and SharePoint environments.

How This Book Is Organized

Each chapter has relevant visual aids such as screenshots, diagrams, and example documents to guide you through the topics being discussed. You'll also find special breakout sections to call your attention to items of note, tips and tricks, and areas of caution that we have found particularly relevant. Finally, each chapter ends with a series of review questions intended to test your understanding of what you've completed and help you think about some of the chapter's key concepts. Don't worry, though; we're providing answers to those questions in Appendix A, "Chapter Review Q&A." For more information on Appendix A, see the "Companion Web Site Downloads" section that follows.

Companion Web Site Downloads

In addition to the contents of this book, several additional resources are available to you on the Cengage Learning Web site at http://www.courseptr.com/downloads.

- **Bonus Chapter.** This chapter discusses disaster recovery approaches for several common SharePoint environments and farm configurations. These disaster recovery outlines integrate a variety of the concepts and technologies discussed in this book, and they may help you begin thinking about SharePoint disaster recovery plans in your own environment(s).

- **Appendix A.** This appendix contains the answers to the questions that are posed at the end of each chapter in this book. If you want to check your comprehension of each chapter as you read it, be sure to go online to grab the answers in this appendix.

- **Appendix B.** This appendix is an alphabetical list of third-party backup and restore tools that are available for SharePoint 2010 at the time this book was originally published. As much as we would have liked to cover each of these tools in the same depth we devoted to out-of-the-box options from Microsoft, it just wasn't possible given timelines and space constraints we were already up against. But that doesn't mean these tools are unworthy of mention, so in this appendix you'll find a quick synopsis of each tool's attributes as provided by their manufacturer and direction on where you can find out more.

1

SharePoint Disaster Recovery Planning and Key Concepts

In This Chapter

- The Disaster Recovery Plan Context
- Key Concepts and Terms
- Assessment and Planning

This book is written primarily for information technology (IT) professionals; as such, it devotes a significant number of pages to strictly technical concerns. Topics such as high availability, SharePoint farm-level backup and restore operations, SQL Server log shipping, and others are discussed at length. Each of these topics is relevant to the concept of SharePoint disaster recovery, but none of them actually addresses the bigger picture of what constitutes a true disaster recovery strategy and the concerns that drive the construction of an end-to-end SharePoint disaster recovery plan.

If you read *SharePoint 2007 Disaster Recovery Guide*, you may have noticed that this chapter and the two following it were positioned toward the back of the book in Chapters 12 through 14. We did that to encourage readers to first understand the technical aspects of SharePoint disaster recovery, start to think about how to select the right technical approach, and then fit that approach into an effective and complete plan for the entire business, not just SharePoint or the servers hosting it. Since the *SharePoint 2007 Disaster Recovery Guide* was published, we've spent significant additional time working on, researching, and talking about SharePoint disaster recovery. Because of those efforts, we decided that you, the reader, would be best served by an overview of general disaster recovery concepts before, rather than after, a discussion of SharePoint disaster recovery technical specifics.

Disaster recovery is not just the practice of backing up your systems on a regular basis; it's a total commitment to protecting your business's information and documents completely to meet the specific needs of your users. In *SharePoint 2010 Disaster Recovery Guide*, we're starting off with three chapters on general disaster recovery and then diving into the technical mechanics of how to protect your SharePoint environment. We want you to consider each technical solution and think about how it might or might not fit it into your overall disaster recovery plan and business continuity strategy.

In this chapter, the focus is on general disaster recovery planning: what drives a SharePoint disaster recovery strategy, the questions you must answer before you can formulate a technical solution, and other related strategic objectives and concerns. This chapter also focuses on the concepts, terminology, and acronyms with which you must be fluent to speak the language of disaster recovery.

The Disaster Recovery Plan Context

It is certainly true that any reasonable SharePoint disaster recovery strategy is going to enlist hardware and software capabilities from a variety of applications and platforms. To truly understand what drives the process of formulating the disaster recovery plan that employs those capabilities, though, you need to take a step back and understand the context in which a disaster recovery plan is formed.

Although SharePoint is a technical platform, numerous business users use the functions and capabilities it provides in day-to-day operations. Business users of a SharePoint farm depend on it for everything from collaboration and sharing to publication and business process automation. Although those responsible for bringing a farm and its functions online following a disaster might view disaster recovery as a "technical exercise," the restoration of functionality is critical to those who depend on SharePoint for daily operations.

It is in the nature of SharePoint administrators, solutions architects, and those tasked with operational responsibilities to find technical solutions to technical problems. On the surface, a disaster recovery plan looks like such a problem-solution equation. Disaster recovery plans often appear straightforward: a disaster happens, and the disaster recovery plan goes into effect. Operations are shifted from the servers that went down to backup servers that are running in an alternate data center. The previously taken backups are restored. That which is broken is fixed. Once all steps are executed, everything works as it did prior to the disaster. Right?

Unfortunately, this view of disaster recovery and disaster recovery planning is somewhat naive. It's a common mistake for SharePoint professionals and information technology professionals in general to think of disaster recovery in strictly technical terms. Simply take enough backups, buy enough extra hardware, and rent space in an additional data center, and all disaster recovery risks are mitigated. Project teams budget for disaster recovery without having any real idea of what's important, what drives an appropriate disaster recovery strategy, and what a business-acceptable strategy really includes or costs.

In reality, the creation of a disaster recovery plan is driven less by technical requirements and more by the potential revenue losses associated with a system outage, damage to property and materials by the absence of an operational system, the loss of communications represented by a downed system, and other similarly important business factors. For these reasons, a properly considered and well-formed disaster recovery plan is a single piece of a larger business continuity plan that addresses not only the technical aspects of bringing a system back into operation, but all the other challenges that accompany it. These items include procedures for keeping information secure, the changes in day-to-day operations for personnel during a declared disaster, continuity of communications when normal channels are down, compliance measures associated with legal requirements in the event of an outage, and so on.

Key Concepts and Terms

The domain of business continuity planning possesses a somewhat unique set of concepts, terms, and processes. To continue building on the concepts and drivers associated with disaster recovery planning, Figure 1.1 zooms out to look at the larger, more holistic process of business continuity planning and where SharePoint disaster recovery planning fits into it.

Figure 1.1   The stages of business continuity planning.

As illustrated in Figure 1.1, business continuity planning involves three distinct stages:

1. **The risk assessment.** The risk assessment is where disaster recovery planning begins. It entails the analysis of a SharePoint farm and the business processes tied to it from the perspective of vulnerabilities, threats, and general exposures that are introduced simply by having the farm in production and in use by business users. The identifiable risks typically equate to one or more SharePoint functions or usage scenarios. "Collaboration on XYZ project," "business intelligence functions leveraged by executives," and "workflow that is used to approve public communications in the ABC document library" are examples of such functions and scenarios.

2. **The business impact analysis (BIA).** The results of the risk assessment serve as the input to the BIA. The BIA attempts to equate the loss of a particular SharePoint capability or function (such as the loss of business intelligence functions leveraged by executives) with the projected magnitude or expected monetary impact associated with the loss (for example, $10,000 per day in investments). Equating outages to exact losses is difficult at this stage due to all the variables that are typically in play, but the results of the analysis serve as a valuable prioritization tool in the next stage of the business continuity planning process.

3. **The business continuity plan (BCP).** Armed with the results of the BIA, business continuity planners possess the data they need to prioritize and address the risk areas identified during the risk assessment. Risk areas or regions that the BIA identifies as

carrying the largest potential for loss or adverse business exposure are addressed more urgently, whereas those with lesser potential impact are addressed when the opportunity arises or is most cost effective. As described earlier, the BCP that results from this process addresses both the technological areas included in the disaster recovery plan (such as "restore the system and associated databases from backup") and associated business processes (for example, "have the accounts payable team begin using the new repository at URL http://DRAccountsPayable instead of the standard production URL"). A BCP typically includes other prescriptive advice and workarounds to minimize or mitigate the impact of an outage.

As shown in Figure 1.1, a disaster recovery plan is one component of the ultimate business continuity plan that results from both the risk assessment and BIA of identified risks. Of course, the disaster recovery plan does not simply arise from a determination regarding the potential impact of an outage.

The purposes for which a SharePoint farm is used, along with acceptable outage windows in the event of a disaster, ultimately drive the technological aspects of the disaster recovery plan that an organization crafts and implements. Two key concepts determine what constitutes an "acceptable" outage window:

- **Recovery time objective (RTO).** The RTO of a disaster recovery plan defines the amount of time that can elapse between the occurrence of a disaster and the affected system being returned to an agreed-upon level of operational readiness. Put simply, an RTO defines the time you have to get a system back up and running after a disaster. It is typically during this period that the steps of a disaster recovery plan are executed. A highly critical SharePoint system may have a real-time RTO (that is, the failure of a production system immediately results in a backup system taking over). At the other extreme, a farm that handles tertiary business functions may have an RTO that is measured in weeks to support the acquisition of new hardware and the ultimate rebuild of the farm from scratch.

- **Recovery point objective (RPO).** Whereas RTOs are forward-looking, an RPO defines a period of time prior to any disaster where data loss may (and likely will) occur. Crudely explained another way, an RPO defines the maximum amount of data loss that's deemed acceptable in a disaster. Data that existed prior to the point in time defined by the RPO can be restored or recovered, whereas data after that point may not. As you might expect, a highly critical SharePoint system may have a disaster recovery plan with a near-zero RPO that does not accept any form of data loss. Tertiary systems, on the other hand, may have RPOs that are measured in hours or days.

To illustrate the concepts of RTO and RPO, consider the disaster recovery plan profile shown in Figure 1.2. The requirements in this plan are common of less-critical systems, where some amount of data loss and downtime is deemed acceptable in the event of a disaster.

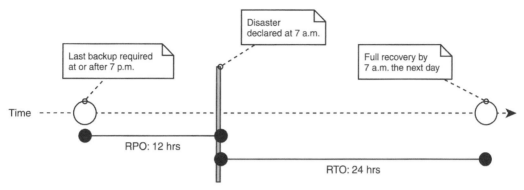

Figure 1.2   RPO and RTO for a SharePoint farm of lesser business significance.

In this disaster recovery plan, a disaster occurs and is declared at 7 a.m. The disaster recovery plan mandates an RPO of 12 hours and an RTO of 24 hours. To satisfy the RPO requirement of this plan, a backup or some capture of relevant data and state must have been performed in the 12 hours leading up to the declaration of the disaster. At the same time, the RTO requirement states that the system must be restored to a functional state (qualified within the disaster recovery plan) within 24 hours of the disaster's occurrence.

Figure 1.3 presents a different set of requirements for recovery when the disaster is declared at 7 a.m. The RTO and RPO shown are more common of a SharePoint farm that is of greater importance to the organization that utilizes it. With an RPO window of one hour and an RTO window of 30 minutes, the potential overall outage window is significantly smaller than the one illustrated in Figure 1.2.

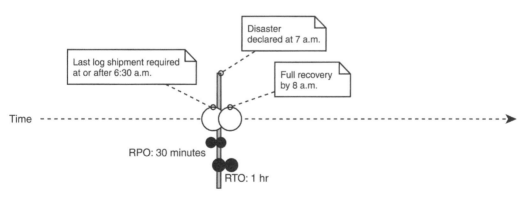

Figure 1.3   RPO and RTO for a SharePoint farm of greater business importance.

As you might imagine, implementing a disaster recovery solution to address the RTO and RPO requirements illustrated by the plan shown in Figure 1.3 carries a different set of challenges than meeting the requirements for the plan shown in Figure 1.2. Technical strategies and supplemental equipment requirements vary significantly between the two.

Note: A discussion of the specific means by which you can address the technical and material requirements of a SharePoint disaster recovery plan takes place next in Chapter 2, "SharePoint Disaster Recovery Design and Implementation."

In a perfect world, all disaster recovery strategies would involve no loss of data (that is, have a zero RPO window) and provide instant failover (zero RTO). Unfortunately, the cost of such strategies for SharePoint farms is exceptional and prohibitive for all but the most critical of business uses. As part of their disaster recovery planning, most organizations discover that as RPO and RTO target windows shrink, the cost of an associated disaster recovery strategy goes up. The challenge then becomes balancing data loss and downtime against the total cost of implementing an appropriate and effective disaster recovery strategy.

Assessment and Planning

The preceding section highlighted the general processes that eventually lead to the formation of a SharePoint disaster recovery plan. It was shown that in the early stages of the business continuity planning process, the bulk of the planning and decision making is driven by business owners and those who are capable of assessing the dollar value of the capabilities and functions that a SharePoint farm provides. Technical owners typically have a part to play in this process, but they don't drive it.

This is not to say that disaster recovery planning should be left entirely to business owners until the process eventually flows downstream to those with technical responsibilities. On the contrary, SharePoint technical owners can undertake numerous assessment and planning activities in advance of their involvement in the business continuity planning process. By staying involved in the planning process, SharePoint administrators can ensure that the finished product is viable from both a business and a technical perspective. Otherwise, business owners may base their decisions on incomplete or inaccurate estimates and place unmanageable burdens upon the architecture or costs of your SharePoint environment.

Finally, it is worth noting that the terms *business owner* and *technical owner* are used primarily to identify roles for planning and usage, not specific identities or groups within an organization. Information technology groups commonly find themselves in the role of SharePoint technical owner, but it is relatively common for IT to also assume the role of business owner when their own processes, data, and intellectual property are stored within a SharePoint environment. In such circumstances, it is reasonable to expect that IT employees would own SharePoint disaster recovery planning from end to end and drive it themselves. A mysterious business owner wouldn't suddenly become involved to ensure that IT remains solely in the role of technical owner.

Discovery and Documentation

In the early stages of disaster recovery planning, the goal for SharePoint technical owners is to fully understand and document the farm or farms they're responsible for. If the SharePoint farm isn't yet in production or is still in the planning stages, the expected operational end state should be the target of activities. This sort of analysis and documentation is a worthwhile objective even without the context of disaster recovery planning, but the knowledge and artifacts delivered by the process are a critical input into the design and implementation phases that are discussed in the next chapter.

Tip: The Unified Modeling Language (UML) is an excellent tool for communicating the information gathered during this phase of the disaster recovery planning process. Created by the Object Management Group (OMG), the UML provides a set of guidelines and standards for the documentation of application architecture and structure. More information is available at the OMG's UML resource page at http://www.uml.org.

Focus discovery and documentation on four key areas: logical architecture, physical deployment, configuration data, and business data.

Logical Architecture

The logical architecture model of a system describes the logical components of the system, the purpose each of the components serves, and how the components interact with one another. It is also common for a system's logical architecture model to identify interfaces and other points of contact between the system and other resources not tied directly to the system.

Whether based strictly on SharePoint Foundation 2010 or SharePoint Server 2010, all SharePoint farms possess a number of architectural aspects that should be documented before disaster recovery planning. Among these are the following:

- Internet Information Services (IIS) application pools
- SharePoint Web applications
- Service Applications, such as Search or Business Connectivity Services (BCS)
- Zones and associated alternate access mappings
- Web application policies
- Content databases
- Site collections (including host-named site collections)
- Sites
- My Sites

SharePoint farms that are based on SharePoint Server (not SharePoint Foundation) have additional architectural aspects that must be considered in addition to those just mentioned. The specifics vary based on the edition of SharePoint Server in use, but many of the enhancements revolve around additional services and applications such as PerformancePoint Services, FAST search integration, and InfoPath Forms Services.

When documenting the logical architecture of your SharePoint farm, direct your focus primarily to the logical components that are present and how they interact with one another rather than the capture of all details associated with settings and configuration. Some amount of configuration data is typically included within the documented model to accurately describe aspects of the logical architecture, but all of the nitty-gritty configuration and setting data is best inventoried separately as part of SharePoint disaster recovery planning.

Physical Deployment

The physical deployment model of a system describes the system's implementation across a specific set of infrastructure components and hardware. Whereas the logical architecture model of a system focuses primarily on the components of a system and how they interact, the physical deployment model of a system gets into the specifics of the environment in which the system resides and operates.

Most physical deployment models have a number of similar characteristics regardless of the system or application being documented, and SharePoint physical deployment models are no exception. Such models commonly include both the hardware that directly constitutes the SharePoint farm and any ancillary hardware that is external to the immediate farm but required for the proper overall functioning of the SharePoint environment. Commonly found elements include these:

- Physical servers that both SharePoint and SQL Server use

- Storage equipment such as storage area networks (SANs) and network-attached storage (NAS) devices

- Switches and other core networking equipment

- Wide area network (WAN) connections and other remote access links

- Firewalls that are between or touched by SharePoint servers

- Hardware load balancers, stand-alone IP address management (IPAM) devices, and other specialty equipment

- Other supporting hardware, such as Windows Active Directory (AD) domain controllers

As with the logical architecture model, you should place greater emphasis on identifying the physical components of the SharePoint farm than on capturing every configuration setting associated with the infrastructure and hardware. Some configuration and setting data is naturally included as part of the physical deployment documentation, but an exhaustive treatment of configuration and setting data takes place in the next section, "Configuration Data."

Configuration Data

Configuration data is any data that is required for proper operation of a system, both internally and within its implementation environment. Applications and systems use and store configuration in a variety of ways, such as via files, databases, and the Windows Registry. Typical SharePoint farms leverage numerous configuration settings and settings storage facilities. Just three examples of the many locations and facilities within SharePoint alone include these:

- Configuration, Search, and Service Application databases

- Web.config files for SharePoint Web applications

- IIS7 configuration files (formerly the IIS metabase)

You can target each of the examples listed with relative ease for automated backup operations. These items represent one type of configuration data you should capture when focusing on SharePoint disaster recovery planning. Documentation should include a description of each item, the location of the item (such as a database name or full file system path), and how the information represented by the item is used.

The second type of configuration data you must capture is data that is critical to farm operations but does not lend itself to easy targeting for backup. This can be data that is stored in multiple locations but must remain synchronized across all locations, data that is difficult to access due to its storage location or form, or even data that depends on or is stored within external systems. Two common examples of data that falls into this overall category are service accounts and passwords that are hashed prior to their storage.

Configuration data that falls into this second category does not lend itself to the same style of capture that was described for data that is easily backed up. Documentation should include the relevant information (such as service account username and password), the purpose of the information, and some indication of how the information is supplied or entered into the SharePoint environment. (The latter might be a reference to the Manage Account page within the Central Administration site where an administrator supplies the account information required to have SharePoint manage the account.)

Note: For reasons of security, many organizations elect to track each of the two types of configuration data separately. Because data falling into the second category typically contains sensitive or restricted information, an organization's computer information security group or personnel operating in a similar role often manage it. At a minimum, control or limit access to this type of data to a defined group of personnel to avoid its misuse.

Business Data

Whereas *configuration data* is information that a system uses to permit it to operate as designed, *business data* is information that flows through the system, is processed by the system, and is often stored by the system during the course of day-to-day operations. Business data is the data that end users care about and that normally has a dollar value attached to it during BIA activities. Business data can also be restricted by an organization's internal policies or governed by laws such as the Sarbanes-Oxley Act of 2002 and Health Insurance Portability and Accountability Act (HIPAA).

Fortunately for disaster recovery planners, SharePoint uses a consistent and centralized storage model for the bulk of the business data it handles. Data going into SharePoint typically ends up in a SQL Server database. In the case of documents and attachments, data is commonly stored in a content database unless the content database has been configured to use a Remote Blob Storage (RBS) provider. In the absence of an RBS provider, the act of documenting content databases, their site collections, and the data that is contained within them arms you with the information you need to guide the development of a recovery strategy for documents and attachments. If you implement an RBS provider, you'll need additional documentation steps to address the location or system this is directed toward.

In addition to content databases, SharePoint 2010 uses many Service Applications for everything from managed metadata to user profile information. These Service Applications commonly utilize SQL databases of their own for business data storage. Documenting the Service Applications that a SharePoint farm exposes and consumes, as well as the databases supporting these Service Applications, is an important step to ensure that business data doesn't fall through the cracks.

Finally, it is worth noting that a SharePoint farm that leverages BCS within SharePoint 2010 may expose and surface business data through SharePoint that actually resides somewhere other than the SharePoint farm. The seamlessness with which external lists and external content types expose data for use can make it difficult to differentiate between SharePoint-resident data and business data residing within external lines of business systems. When documenting business data, it is imperative that you research and clearly identify the system of origin.

Dependencies and Interfaces

Judiciously documenting the four areas just discussed provides an overview of the SharePoint farm and how it operates, the environment it operates in, and how SharePoint-based data is consumed and processed. For SharePoint farms that operate independently of all other systems, this is all the information you need to prepare for the more formal process of disaster recovery design.

Unfortunately, few organizations use only SharePoint. Most organizations using SharePoint also have some combination of e-mail systems, file shares, additional line of business solutions, homegrown applications, and a whole host of additional systems too voluminous to enumerate. Realizing the value of SharePoint when used as a portal or intranet solution, many organizations go to great lengths to integrate SharePoint with these systems.

For purposes of disaster recovery planning, these external integration points represent areas that require special attention. A SharePoint farm that is restored to a fully operational state without external systems and stores it depends on is not going to be viewed as "fully operational" in the eyes of business users. When documenting the logical architecture, physical architecture, configuration data, and business data associated with a SharePoint farm, pay particular attention to interface points with other systems, stores, and services that are leveraged or represented in some form within SharePoint without actually being part of the farm themselves. Examples of such dependencies can include the following:

- Line of business systems that publish data consumed through SharePoint's BCS functionality

- Custom user controls and Web Parts that interface with Web services exposed by other systems

- Service Applications in other farms that the target SharePoint farm consumes

- InfoPath forms that include logic to write portions of submitted form data to a non-Share-Point SQL Server database

- A simple Page Viewer Web Part that provides a browser-based view of a file share

Business users would likely judge a full restoration of the associated SharePoint farm without associated external systems as SharePoint being less than fully functional.

Identifying dependencies and interfaces with other systems goes beyond simply documenting a SharePoint farm. It requires an analysis of the purposes of a farm's site collections, an inventory of implemented features (such as InfoPath forms and BCS connections to line of business systems), and an understanding of the operations being carried out by custom SharePoint solutions and components running within the farm. Often this process ultimately consumes more time than the documentation of the SharePoint farm. Nevertheless, the knowledge gained by the identification of these dependencies and interfaces is critical to any complete SharePoint disaster recovery plan design.

Conclusion

Information technology personnel often regard SharePoint disaster recovery planning as a technical problem that is theirs to solve, but in reality, a disaster recovery plan is just one part of the larger business continuity planning process. If the disaster recovery plan for your SharePoint environment is going to be an effective piece of your organization's overall BCP, you must be ready to invest significant time creating a risk assessment and a BIA. Otherwise, the entire BCP is at risk and fails to provide a necessary and critical service to your business.

Two critical inputs to the disaster recovery planning process come in the form of RTOs and RPOs. These two parameters define the window of available recovery time (RTO) and the window of acceptable data loss (RPO) for a SharePoint farm (or some part of it) when a disaster has been declared. Disaster recovery planners commonly face the challenge of trying to balance downtime and data loss against implementation costs. As RTO and RPO windows shrink, costs associated with appropriate disaster recovery strategies typically rise disproportionately.

A SharePoint disaster recovery design depends on the completion of several business processes to proceed in an informed fashion, but technical owners and those responsible for SharePoint farms can prepare for the design process in a couple of ways. Of greatest importance is the documentation of the SharePoint farm. Detailing the logical architecture, physical deployment, configuration data, and business data aspects of a SharePoint farm provides disaster recovery planners with recovery targets and usage information that are invaluable during the design stage. Also of critical importance in the assessment process is the identification of SharePoint interfaces to other systems and external farm dependencies. Although these non-SharePoint systems may not technically be a part of the SharePoint farm, integration with these systems means that you must address them in some fashion during disaster recovery design.

Having completed this chapter, you should now be able to answer the following questions. As with the other chapters, answers to the following questions appear in Appendix A, "Chapter Review Q&A," found on the Cengage Learning Web site at http://www.courseptr.com/downloads.

1. How do a disaster recovery plan and a business continuity plan differ?

2. What is the difference between an RPO and an RTO?

3. How does configuration data differ from business data?

4. Why are interface points with other systems so important to capture during initial analysis?

5. Name some common interface points between SharePoint and other systems that require special analysis and treatment during disaster recovery documentation.

2 SharePoint Disaster Recovery Design and Implementation

In This Chapter

- Defining Scope

- Planning the Recovery Process

- Documenting and Implementing the Disaster Recovery Design

Many administrators of information technology (IT) systems are all too familiar with that famous axiom known as Murphy's Law, which says, "If anything can go wrong, it will." Although it may sound fatalistic, having the expectation that one day down the road a mishap of one kind or another will happen to your SharePoint environment is an important perspective to maintain when designing and creating your organization's disaster recovery plan. This isn't something you should generate for the sake of crossing an item off your To-Do list or checking a check box in a survey or audit. An effective disaster recovery plan gives you a resource you can use in all situations, regardless of scope or importance. By not losing sight of the fact that this strategy is going to be used and not just gather dust somewhere, you are drastically improving your chances for a successful recovery of your business's crucial SharePoint systems and data when the chips are down.

Now that you've been introduced to the concepts and terminology of disaster recovery in Chapter 1, "SharePoint Disaster Recovery Planning and Key Concepts," it's time to start applying those lessons to your organization's requirements and constraints. This chapter is designed to walk you through the process necessary to design and document your disaster recovery plan. You will gain an understanding of the data you need to collect and maintain in your plan, the parameters necessary for not only its design but its success, and ways to record all that data in a consistent, coherent fashion.

Defining Scope

It's impossible to plan how you will recover your system in the event of an outage or disaster without understanding what your system is composed of and what its critical components are. For many complex environments, it simply isn't feasible to attempt to fully restore every server, application, or database at the same time; trying to do so would add hours, days, or even weeks to the time it would take to complete this vital restoration activity. That is why the first step you must take when developing your disaster recovery plan is to define its scope and to evaluate and select the essential parts of your system that must be restored in the event of a disaster.

Note: It's assumed that you're not designing and developing your SharePoint environment's disaster plan on your own, or only from an IT perspective. As discussed in Chapter 1, a disaster recovery strategy is simply part of a larger business continuity plan (BCP) that's driven primarily by business stakeholders and the cost that is tied to outages in a SharePoint environment. Although you, as an administrator, know what infrastructure components you need to have in place to restore your environment, your users are the ones who should determine which sites are business critical, what content should be preserved at all costs, and what the acceptable levels of downtime are for these items. The results of a business impact analysis (BIA) serve as the primary guide when constructing your disaster recovery plan.

What Are Recovery Targets?

Recovery targets are the critical functions and data of your SharePoint environment that need to be restored following the declaration of a disaster. Seems pretty straightforward, doesn't it? Well, thanks in part to the complex and modular nature of a SharePoint environment, that is not always the case.

Recovery targets are important because not only do they identify the parts of your system that need to be acknowledged and addressed in some way as a part of your disaster recovery plan, but they are the functions and data that must be restored or replaced as part of a successful recovery operation. A set of recovery targets reads like a checklist, and recovery targets are often used in this fashion during disaster recovery testing to gauge the success or failure of a recovery strategy following its execution.

How Are Your Recovery Targets Defined?

Recovery targets are defined through the process of mapping the results of a BIA (that is, the data and functionality that business stakeholders have identified as being critical in a SharePoint farm) to elements within the farm that were identified during the discovery and documentation phase described in Chapter 1. Each result from the BIA should translate to one or more technical functions and data elements within the SharePoint farm.

For example, consider a BIA that identifies a SharePoint site housing online actuarial capabilities as being highly critical to daily business operations. Technical analysis and cross-referencing of the site mentioned in the BIA might yield numerous recovery targets, including these:

- The content database housing the SharePoint site containing Excel spreadsheets
- The Excel Services Service Application providing online calculation functionality

- The physical server that is dedicated within the farm to carry out the processor-intensive Excel calculations

- The unattended service account username and password that Excel Services uses for several trusted data connections

- A custom trusted data provider that is defined within the Excel Services Service Application

- Several legacy line of business systems that are accessed through trusted data connections to supply data for the actuarial spreadsheets

As you can see, a seemingly straightforward business function could lead to a cascading list of technical requirements during the definition of recovery targets.

For large SharePoint farms, the recovery targets that are ultimately selected may comprise only a subset of the farm's total functionality. This is especially true if the recovery time objective (RTO) for the functions and data specified is extremely aggressive and the disaster recovery plan involves a substantial manual effort to carry out.

What Should Be Restored?

As the results of the BIA are mapped to recovery targets, you may begin to see that some technical functions or data within your farm have a higher priority than others and that some pieces of key technical functionality or data are required to make their associated business functions available in SharePoint. It's also perfectly normal for some technical functions to be identified as low-priority components that can be restored once your farm's core content and technical functionality have been fully restored and verified. This kind of triage activity can be beneficial, because it helps you to focus your activities and energy on the most important aspects of your environment without getting distracted by targets of lower priority.

Often this exercise can help you understand that it isn't a good idea to fully restore your production environment immediately after an outage. Another benefit of this analysis is the impact it can have on the architecture, configuration, and governance policies of your SharePoint farm to better position or partition key elements for recoverability based on business value and associated disaster recovery priority. Following are a few other factors that you should keep in mind as you analyze the BIA results and consider the recovery targets that result:

- **Content database distribution.** How are sites and site collections in your farm distributed across content databases? Consider storing high-priority sites in specific or unique content databases to allow more frequent backups to be made on those databases and prevent lesser sites from using resources. Carefully distributing your sites across databases, and even database instances, can make your backup and restore processes much easier to manage and complete.

- **Content.** What types of content or data do users store in different types of sites in your farm? Is the content that users store in their My Sites given the same recovery priority by the BIA as what they store in collaborative team sites? Your organization may already have usage and retention policies that can help to answer these questions about the contents of different types of sites and determine when they should be backed up and restored in the absence of specific directives by the BIA.

- **Service Applications.** SharePoint Foundation uses a number of Service Applications, and SharePoint Server 2010 includes an even greater number. If your recovery strategy involves some form of manual rebuild or reconfiguration, it is important to understand the usage patterns for the Service Applications in your SharePoint farm. In the actuarial example that was mentioned earlier, Excel Services are critical to the restoration of business functionality and would likely receive a high priority for recovery. Excel Services could be run locally within the farm, or the service could be consumed from another farm entirely. Recognizing both the importance of the Service Application and the actual origin of services provided is key in the proper definition of recovery targets.

- **Dependent systems and interfaces.** What applications or configuration items have been identified as recovery targets on your production servers to support the various functions of your SharePoint farm? Some applications provide crucial data or functionality to the users of your SharePoint farm and must be reconnected or restored as part of your farm's restore effort. Other applications are not identified by the BIA as mission critical and are therefore not a priority.

What's Out of Scope

It's just as important to establish what's out of scope for your disaster recovery plan as it is to identify what's in scope. This isn't a simple exercise of listing what platforms, applications, systems, or components are not included in your disaster recovery plan. Yes, such actions are definitely part of the scope definition process, but it's also important to determine what other groups are being expected to support and identify those items deemed to be out of scope for your plan. For example, if database administrators (DBAs) external to your group manage your SharePoint databases, it may be possible to declare the disaster recovery of those databases out of scope to your plan because those DBAs will handle them.

Tip: Establishing external dependencies within a disaster recovery plan introduces risk and is not the "right" of SharePoint technical owners. Prior to portions of a plan becoming dependent on external systems or personnel, discussions with business owners and stakeholders must take place. Although SharePoint technical owners and personnel are ultimately responsible for meeting the recovery objectives identified through the BIA, business stakeholders are the ones assuming the risk and realizing the ultimate impact of a system outage.

What Are the Costs?

As professors of economics are often fond of stating, "There's no such thing as a free lunch." Every choice and decision you make around your disaster recovery plan has a direct impact on how much it will cost to implement that plan. Frequent backups can require extensive storage resources, as well as more time to configure, test, and maintain. Opting to restore every aspect of a farm as quickly as possible is certainly possible, but the hardware, software, and workforce resources necessary to pull off such a plan can prove prohibitively high for all but the largest of enterprises. It's essential to understand the costs inherent in each aspect of a disaster recovery plan so that you can balance and consider them as part of the plan. You may find that the best solution is not always the right solution for your organization once you introduce costs and expenses into the equation.

Planning the Recovery Process

After you've established the recovery targets based on the BIA, it's time to move on to the steps you must take to actually return your system to acceptable levels of functionality. It's time to start determining the people, hardware, software, and other resources that need to be in place before you can start the recovery process.

During the planning and design process, it's common to discover that the level of recoverability that business owners desire isn't possible with the budget allotted to disaster recovery operations. At this stage, bargaining and compromise are common to reach levels of recoverability and cost that are acceptable to both business stakeholders and SharePoint farm owners.

Setting aside issues of cost, there are a number of additional areas to consider as you begin the process of recovery planning and design. Many factors and drivers are commonly uncovered as a plan evolves, and your approach should be flexible enough to respond to them, but at a minimum an effective disaster recovery plan is built with strong consideration for the following three aspects:

- **RTO and RPO.** After reading Chapter 1, you should be familiar with the concepts of RTO and RPO (recovery point objective) and how they impact technical options regarding recoverability. The requirements that are established for each recovery target's RTO and RPO directly affect your plan's design, which must be able to meet those objectives to be effective. RTO and RPO can dictate the type and number of resources you need to have available to execute the plan, the sorts of tools and range of feasible technologies you use to preserve and restore your system, and the way you define your success criteria.

- **Your data.** What content, such as business documents or task lists, must be immediately restored to enable your users to remain productive? How is that data stored within your SharePoint environment, and how easily can it be backed up and restored? These considerations impact your plan, the tools you use to implement it, and the infrastructure you put in place to support it.

- **Physical limitations.** The tangible pieces of your infrastructure, such as your data center, storage, backup technology, and networking configuration, can make a real difference in the options you have available to build into your disaster recovery plan. Can your recovery team directly access your servers in the data center if they need to? Do you have enough storage for your backups? Can you architect enough redundancy into your infrastructure from the ground up to make it highly available? These are just some of the physical limitations you need to keep in mind as you design your disaster recovery plan.

Documenting and Implementing the Disaster Recovery Design

Once you've identified the inputs, requirements, and parameters of your plan's design, you can move on to the fun part: putting it into writing and incorporating its elements into your system. This is where the rubber meets the road—where you must explicitly state how your SharePoint environment is prepared for the declaration of a disaster and how it will be restored after such an event. Thoroughly document your plan and store it in an accessible, visible, and reliable location so it can be quickly accessed by anyone who needs to review, revise, or execute it.

Tip: If your SharePoint disaster recovery strategy includes one or more alternate data centers or facilities, your recovery plan and any associated documentation should be replicated to those facilities to ensure that they are up to date and available in the event of a disaster.

Remember, there's always a chance that the author of the plan (you) is not going to be the person who actually executes it, so make sure the plan contains all the information and instructions required to execute it even if the reader isn't intimately familiar with the plan. The recovery plan should clearly state any assumptions it makes about the executor and that person's knowledge of SharePoint and related systems.

Acquiring Resources

Once you understand your farm's recovery targets and have an appropriate disaster recovery topology, you can start reviewing your available resources and establishing the assets needed to provide or expand your disaster plan. You can also define the resources your plan requires if a disaster is declared and you need to execute your plan. Obviously, it pays to have those items on hand before you actually need them so you can begin to satisfy the requirements of the plan as quickly as possible. The following list outlines the major resource areas you should review for your SharePoint environment and its disaster recovery plan:

- **Determine your physical requirements and resources.** As has already been mentioned, your disaster recovery plan probably identifies some specific pieces of required hardware and infrastructure. Whether the plan's requirements include rack space in multiple data centers, high-speed storage area network (SAN), hardware for hosting virtualized servers, or tape backup drives, you need to enumerate these items as completely and specifically as possible. Review your network requirements and usage, power consumption, available storage, and redundant devices such as load-balancers and Redundant Array of Independent (or Inexpensive) Disks (RAID) arrays.

- **Acquire your hardware.** Once you know what you need, make sure you have it on hand when you need it. Don't put this off for a rainy day or the next fiscal year. Disasters don't happen when it's convenient. You can't afford to lose millions in business and productivity because you saved thousands waiting to procure the hardware required by your disaster recovery plan.

- **Acquire and license your software.** If you have a failover farm, make sure to secure the proper software and licensing for that additional farm to stay in full compliance with your providers. Store copies of any required software or media in a location (or locations) that's accessible in the event of a disaster. Work closely with your software manufacturer's licensing representative. Explain exactly how you're using the software, because the representative often has special provisions (at lower price points) for software running in a failover environment.

- **Review your dependent services.** Most SharePoint installations depend heavily on Active Directory (AD) for user authentication, not to mention service accounts and administrative access to servers. Closely examine the disaster recovery plans for your environment's AD domains, Domain Name Services (DNS), Dynamic Host Configuration Protocol (DHCP) services, Simple Mail Transfer Protocol (SMTP) services, and all other services that your SharePoint environment depends on. If these service dependencies have RPO or RTO targets that are out of alignment with those that your SharePoint environment has identified, you might need to make alternate arrangements and spend more money.

Establishing a Disaster Recovery Baseline

Baselines determine a desired configuration or setup for a given system at a specific point in time and are used as the basis for comparison for subsequent activities in and changes to that system. Establishing a baseline for your SharePoint farm allows you to solidify a specific configuration point and quality of service that your disaster recovery plan should strive to return the system to after a catastrophe. Baselining your system may not be required for your organization, but doing so gives you a defined target for success and goals that you can drive your plan at. You can also repeat the process at regular intervals, allowing you to quantify how your system has grown and changed over time, which can also provide you with valuable data for future updates to your To-Be list. Regardless of whether you baseline your system, you should strive to have a complete picture of its current state and how compatible that state is with your disaster recovery plan.

Documenting Your Procedures for an Outage

Up until now, most of this chapter has focused on the items and details needed for a SharePoint environment's disaster recovery plan to establish the best position possible to deal with the declaration of a disaster. Now this chapter turns its attention to some best practices for actually writing the plan and recording it in a consistent and controlled manner. This is important because the plan must be understandable and complete. Its audience is likely to be under a great deal of pressure when using it and won't have time to spare trying to decipher a dense, ineffective document.

Following Published Standards for Writing

If your organization already has a common set of standards for official technical documents, your disaster recovery plan should follow them. If not, it may be worth the effort to establish them as part of this process. When you're writing a document, it isn't enough to simply outline the steps an executor should take to complete a process. A complete technical document should contain several common types of information, including but not limited to these:

- **Involved parties.** Lists the people associated with the document, such as its author/owner, reviewer(s), and approver(s)

- **Version and revision history.** Details the document's changes over time

- **Effective date.** Records the date that the document became available for use

- **Roles, responsibilities, and capabilities.** Includes a list of the positions that need to be filled to execute the document's instructions, the responsibilities for each of those positions, and the skills a resource must have to fill a position

- **Audience.** Defines who the document is intended for

- **Purpose.** Explains what purpose the document should be used for

- **Scope.** Defines what's in scope and out of scope for the document

- **Covered systems.** Lists the systems or groups that the document applies to

- **Glossary of terms.** Defines common terminology used in the document

- **Prerequisites and dependencies.** Includes any activities or systems that must be completed or in place prior to the document's execution

- **Assumptions.** Details the assumptions the document makes

- **Primary content.** Includes the instructions and procedures the document is intended to cover

- **References.** Lists information, documents, or people external to the document that can be consulted for additional information

- **Training.** Explains how individuals should be trained on the document's content and procedures

Verifying Content

Once you've completed your disaster recovery plan, have a third party review and verify it. If you don't, you risk allowing inconsistencies, omissions, or errors to remain in the document that could directly impact the success of a recovery operation. Consider this book as an example. Every page and every word in it has been reviewed, tested, and verified by at least two separate parties. A copy editor checked it for grammatical consistency and proficiency, and a technical editor checked the technical statements, assertions, walk-throughs, and content written. No matter how much authors check their own work, having outside reviewers drastically improves the quality and accuracy of an author's output. No disaster recovery plan should be allowed to stand without being tested and verified before it's considered complete; otherwise, you chance introducing additional, avoidable risk into your disaster recovery activities.

Lowering the Impact of Recovery

Take whatever precautions you can to lower the impact of your recovery strategy on your SharePoint environment and its users. These steps will vary depending on your situation, but here are two important areas to keep in mind that can make the recovery process go much more smoothly:

- **Securing your crucial disaster recovery resources.** The need for a secure, centralized store for your software installers, license keys, and other associated bits has already been mentioned, but it bears repeating. Ensure that your disaster recovery personnel can access this storage location, and make sure that its contents are backed up and potentially replicated on a regular basis. If your organization lacks a formal disaster recovery department or group, appoint a specific person with the responsibility of maintaining that store and keeping it current. Identify a backup for that person or group in case the primary is unavailable when a disaster is declared.

- **Identifying what to secure.** What items, such as service account identities and passwords, software license keys, or data center access, should be secured and unavailable to public access? What items should be commonly available to all resources? Review your system's assets and the security around them to make sure that you are properly balancing your assets' safety measures against the need to access them quickly.

Tip: As mentioned in Chapter 1, certain types of privileged configuration data are typically stored separately from other types of data. For configuration data that is deemed secure and stored separately, be sure that your disaster recovery plan identifies how (and from whom) such information should be recovered if a disaster is declared.

Defining the Communication Plan

Your disaster recovery plan should also include a plan for communicating information about the declared outage to everyone associated with your SharePoint environment so that you're presenting a uniform, consistent, and informative front to those constituents. The plan should identify the various players and roles in the recovery action, such as data center technicians, database administrators, management, quality assurance, end user advocates, and end users in general. It should also detail the manner in which these various players should be contacted, who should manage and coordinate the communication effort, and the approvals required before a message can be sent. In addition, the plan should inform key personnel of how they can obtain information on their own, via sources such as conference calls, Web pages, and phone trees. It may also be beneficial to designate a specific meeting area that the team can use in perpetuity until the action is completed so that the team always uses a consistent location. Make sure that all key personnel in a recovery action are identified and assigned specific roles to avoid gaps in knowledge and arguments over areas of responsibility.

Determining Success

The last thing your SharePoint disaster recovery plan must provide is a coherent, concrete, agreed-upon list of criteria for a successful recovery. As stated earlier in this chapter, this list is often derived directly from the list of recovery targets.

Define the terms of a successful recovery before you attempt to conduct one so that there are specific goals your team can drive toward and a point where you can declare victory. Keep your business users' needs in mind during this process. As discussed previously, it does little good to deliver a system that may be fully recovered from a technical standpoint but does not allow business users to get their work done. The success criteria and associated conditions must be agreed upon by all stakeholders in your SharePoint environment and with regard to the recovery targets that the BIA identified. Your plan should also identify a person or group that is responsible for verifying that these criteria have been met and approving the completed recovery effort.

Tip: You may find it worthwhile to explicitly include a baseline for your SharePoint environment within your disaster recovery plan and use it as a benchmark for a successful recovery. This allows you to solidify a specific configuration and quality of service for your system that your disaster recovery plan should strive to return the system to after a catastrophe, rather than an assorted list of recovery targets.

Conclusion

Creating a useful, effective disaster recovery plan and documenting it properly is one of the most important aspects of a successful disaster recovery strategy. Documentation isn't one of the more interesting or exciting things that an IT administrator can be tasked with, but it certainly is one of the most crucial. Hopefully this chapter has given you a jump-start on the process.

The goal is for you to use the recommendations and best practices described in this chapter as a starting point for your organization's SharePoint disaster recovery plan. Don't forget that what has been presented may not cover everything that your team needs to meet the unique requirements of your SharePoint environment. Also keep in mind that your plan should, at a minimum, address all the concepts this chapter has introduced. Once you have developed your disaster recovery plan, the bad news is that you're still not done. The good news is that Chapter 3, "SharePoint Disaster Recovery Testing and Maintenance," walks you through the last steps of the process.

Now that you've learned about the importance of an effective disaster recovery plan and what goes into it, you should be able to answer the following questions about a plan's capabilities. You can find the answers to these questions in Appendix A, "Chapter Review Q&A," found on the Cengage Learning Web site at http://www.courseptr.com/downloads.

1. What are recovery targets?

2. What are some items to consider when evaluating what components of your SharePoint environment to restore?

3. What are some of the ways your organization's RTOs and RPOs can impact the design of your disaster recovery plan?

4. What are some examples of resources that must be acquired or provisioned as part of your disaster recovery plan?

5. How do you know when your disaster recovery plan has been completely executed?

3 SharePoint Disaster Recovery Testing and Maintenance

In This Chapter

- Planning Your Test
- Conducting the Test
- Performing Ongoing Maintenance of Your Disaster Recovery Plan

Hopefully it goes without saying that the content covered in this chapter is the next logical step in your disaster recovery planning process: testing and maintaining your plan. These items are natural and important components of any information technology (IT) project or process, but they're all too often given little attention or resources. Given the potential importance of your SharePoint environment and its contents, you can drastically increase your risk factor and decrease the viability of your system if you don't adequately test and sustain your disaster recovery plan.

Obviously, these two items can occur at different stages in the life cycle of your disaster recovery process, but they're related. Most notably, the first maintenance activities of your plan are likely going to happen after you conduct its first test. Testing your plan should produce several lessons learned, valuable data, and necessary modifications. These naturally lead you into the maintenance phase of the process. Likewise, as you continue ongoing maintenance for your plan, you should re-execute your tests to validate all the changes that you've made to the plan.

Planning Your Test

The quality of the testing you do for your disaster recovery plan can be just as crucial to the success of your plan as the quality of its design and contents. If you don't conduct an effective test of your plan, you don't have a comprehensive understanding of how it will be applied and utilized if a disaster is declared involving your SharePoint environment. Testing is the best way to begin identifying potential bottlenecks, weaknesses, and dependencies that you may not have considered during the design process. Testing also provides your team with an outstanding training mechanism. Through execution of the plan, team members are developing a deeper understanding of the plan and gaining realistic experience with it. Testing also helps you to estimate your ability to meet your recovery time objective (RTO) and recovery point objective (RPO) goals, which are of paramount importance to the viability of the disaster recovery plan.

Whenever possible, conduct disaster recovery testing for your SharePoint environment within the context of testing your organization's overall business continuity plan (BCP). Given the interdependencies between technical systems such as SharePoint and the business users who work with them, most of the time it isn't sufficient to simply test your disaster recovery plan in a vacuum. You need to know how your design impacts the rest of the BCP, any consequences the BCP may have for your recovery plans, and any other systems in your organization that depend on the restoration of the SharePoint environment for their own success. This information lets you examine your communication plan and its viability, not to mention allows business users to verify that their expectations and strategies involving the BCP and your SharePoint environment are accurate and realistic. If your testing efforts don't in some way involve stakeholders or resources from the business side of your organization, you should at a minimum convey the results of your testing effort so these key people are informed of your findings.

Defining the Scope of Your Outage

The first step of defining how to create an outage in your SharePoint environment for purposes of testing is to determine the scope of that outage. As with any type of test or activity, the value of your test results is based on how successfully the test covers the key aspects of your system and assesses the effectiveness of your disaster recovery plan. Running a test that doesn't impact SharePoint or isn't likely to actually occur in the real world isn't a productive use of your time and resources. The following list outlines some of the questions you should be asking yourself as you determine what your disaster recovery test will encompass:

- **What are the most likely types of outages your system may experience?** If your SharePoint environment contains mostly read-only content, there may be little reason to test the retrieval of content that was accidentally deleted by end users. If your servers are located in an area of the world prone to certain types of weather patterns or natural disasters (tornados, hurricanes, earthquakes, and so on), does it make sense to simulate one of those events in your test?

- **What are your most valuable recovery targets?** Your test should confirm your plan's ability to restore your system's most important recovery targets. These are likely the items your business users will be looking for first, and your plan must be able to bring them back successfully.

- **What items have minimal RTOs and RPOs?** If you have little time to bring back a resource or need to bring back a resource to a recent state, it's imperative that you test and verify your ability to meet those requirements.

- **What are your most vulnerable recovery targets?** If your SharePoint farm has components that are more likely than others to be impacted by an outage, such as a WAN connection or

Internet-facing servers outside your firewall, you should exercise them during the disaster test.

- **What resources are available for testing?** There may be constraints placed on your test by the resources you have available to execute it with. If your production SharePoint farm contains load-balanced Web front-end (WFE) servers but your test environment doesn't, you won't be able to test that high availability aspect of your disaster recovery plan. This evaluation should also include resources external to your SharePoint environment, such as business representatives, data center administrators, or storage area network (SAN) capacity available to your servers.

- **What components or dependent systems in your SharePoint environment are governed by disaster recovery plans other than your own?** Again, consider testing your plan as part of testing your organization's overall BCP. If you are testing independently of the BCP, your plan may still have dependencies on other plans that you need to examine. In particular, you should be aware of any service-only farms or published Service Applications that your SharePoint farm consumes, because these may tie your recovery plans directly to plans that exist for one or more additional SharePoint environments. It may not be necessary to test these items, but you must verify that these external plans have been tested or are assured by their owners to reduce the risk to your plan.

Organizing Your Resources

The obvious conclusion you may come to when evaluating how to test your SharePoint disaster recovery plan is that your test should, whenever possible, mirror the conditions, configurations, and resources found in your production environment as closely as possible. This is certainly one way to approach your test, but you need to determine if this is the most effective way to test your plan and the most effective use of your resources. Review the requirements and design of your plan, and find an approach for testing that is authentic and challenging without wasting efforts or resources.

Testing Your Systems

Again, your plan's RTO and RPO goals play an important role in deciding what systems or environments to use to conduct your test. If your SharePoint environment is designed to deliver minimal or near-zero RTO and RPO outage windows, it's probably going to involve multiple duplicate systems, such as replicated SharePoint farms in alternate data centers, clustered databases, and redundant storage. In this case, it may make more sense to actually conduct the test by leveraging these failover systems, even though they're in a production environment. This gives you a highly accurate profile of how your system will perform in a disaster by using the actual systems that you'll need to function correctly when something hits the fan. This isn't to say that a duplicate testing environment is a poor solution. Rather, the point is to consider the best testing solution to give you the most accurate and relevant data possible about how your plan, your SharePoint farm, its dependent systems, and all the involved personnel will perform in a disaster. If it makes the most sense for your organization to create a test environment for this activity, by all means do so. But make sure that you think about how your plan, its requirements, and its constituents are best tested, in addition to considering your test's available resources and budget.

Also keep in mind that the physical resources your test requires are not just limited to the Share-Point environment needed to run your test. Just as your production SharePoint environment most likely uses several other systems for monitoring, reporting, networking, and other crucial capabilities, your test environment has equivalent dependencies to consider. For example, if you rely on a monitoring system that generates trouble tickets or pages resources when an outage occurs, make sure that system is also monitoring the SharePoint farm hosting your test. But also configure the monitoring system so that production resources aren't assigned to handle the events generated by your test system during disaster recovery testing, to avoid confusion and service degradation for the production system.

Testing Your People

Whenever possible, make the test as authentic as possible, not just in terms of the IT assets used, but also the team involved in the test. Assign participants to fill each of the key roles dictated by your disaster recovery plan so that the required actions, abilities, and responsibilities of each role can be assessed and evaluated. Also include business owners or their representatives in the test. This can go a long way toward properly setting their expectations in an outage and not only give them an excellent understanding of the communication they can expect when an outage occurs but show them the role(s) they play during plan execution and the overall recovery effort.

Planning for Losses

Seriously consider incorporating certain losses of disaster recovery resources and personnel in your test so that you and your team can understand how to overcome those challenges should something similar occur during an actual outage. Who needs to be informed if the latest set of tape backups is corrupted and an RPO target can't be met? What if a database administrator is on vacation during an outage? Can your plan still be executed to meet its criteria for success without the presence of key resources? By purposely building losses into your test, you can further identify weaknesses and dependencies in your system.

Verifying Checklists and Preparedness

The initial test of your system is also an excellent opportunity to verify or develop any checklists that you may need as job aids for the disaster recovery plan. During the planning phase of any project, it's often difficult to capture every necessary activity down to the smallest detail, but it becomes much more feasible to do so during test execution. Creating task and resource lists can make your personnel more effective during an actual outage, improving your disaster recovery team's efficiency and effectiveness while eliminating common mistakes and missteps. It's also much easier to learn these lessons during a test than during an actual disaster when business owners are breathing down your neck and everything has to be executed without surprises and errors.

Testing your disaster recovery plan with the people who are likely to execute it in a production environment is a great training exercise for these resources and can identify other areas for additional improvement. It also educates your partners and service providers on what you'll be counting on them for in the event of an outage in terms of both services and their delivery windows. Remember that your disaster recovery plan is likely going to encompass a group far larger than just your SharePoint team. The more you can do to ensure the preparedness and responsiveness of all parties involved in a recovery effort, the more effective the recovery effort is.

Conducting the Test

Remember that the more authentic your test is and the more accurately it re-creates an outage of your SharePoint environment, the more value it gives you and the more predictable and effective your disaster recovery plan becomes. The test isn't an excuse to inconvenience your personnel or make unnecessary requests of your external service providers, but all participants should take the test seriously and act as if it's an actual outage. With business representatives and nontechnical personnel from your organization participating, it's even more important to take the exercise seriously to build their confidence in your plan, your team's ability to execute it, and the stability of your SharePoint environment in general.

Encouraging Communication

At all stages of the test, encourage communication among the test's participants and provide them with all the information necessary to fully participate in the test. This starts with the test's kickoff activities, where the participants are introduced to the test SharePoint farm, assigned their roles within it, informed of the outage, and provided with the specific details of the catastrophic event that has occurred in the test environment. All participants must understand their role within the test; otherwise, the test may not be fully implemented or worse, would be executed incorrectly.

Throughout the test, the recovery team should have regular meetings to communicate status and findings. The frequency of meetings can follow the communication requirements of the disaster recovery plan, but you might need to provide updates on a more consistent basis as participants execute, learn, and troubleshoot the plan. Record all the key findings, tips, issues, and communications made during the test so that you can review them once the exercise is completed and incorporate them into the revised plan.

Tip: Because recording information and observations during a test can take a significant amount of time, assign a note-taking observer for each person carrying out some part of the recovery plan. Taking this step ensures that execution of the recovery plan isn't slowed and that the feedback gathered is objective in nature. It also encourages recovery plan participants to stay focused on the work they're doing rather than taking notes.

After the test has been completed, you can take several steps to gather further information about it. Collect any and all notes that participants made during their activities, and survey all contributors to collect general thoughts and responses about the test. Once you've gathered all the data, communicate a summary and findings report to all participants. Make sure that the personnel executing the test are given feedback on their work so they know what they did well during the test and what they need to work on and improve in the event of an actual disaster. Also incorporate the findings into the disaster recovery plan; for more information on maintaining your plan, see the section "Performing Ongoing Maintenance of Your Disaster Recovery Plan" later in this chapter.

Observing the Test

In addition to the notes, thoughts, and data generated by the note-taking observers assigned to each of the test's participants, it's important to assign certain members of your team to observe the overall test as it progresses. These independent observers should especially be on the lookout for items that are not addressed but need to be added to the larger disaster recovery plan, different streams of recovery that may conflict with one another, activities that have some dependency on other activities, timing, or some other outside influence. You may find that you're best served by assigning this task to team members closely familiar with the disaster recovery plan so they can spend their time observing the test, as opposed to constantly referencing the plan to confirm one detail or another. This ensures that your less experienced team members are getting more hands-on time with the plan to build their knowledge and expertise.

Validating the Plan

The nice thing about testing your disaster recovery plan is that it should already provide you with the criteria you need to evaluate whether you passed. Your SharePoint environment's disaster recovery plan should not only define the benchmarks and goals you need to meet for a successful recovery from an outage, but it should inform you of the RTO and RPO goals you're required to meet to fully satisfy your business owners' requirements. Once the test has completed, validate its output against these standards and determine how successful you were at meeting them. If you're unable to meet the RTO and RPO requirements of your plan, you'll need to perform additional analysis to determine how to remedy that issue and update the plan accordingly.

Redesigning the Plan

After you've validated your test and reviewed its output, you may need to redesign your plan based on your findings. Although you can't expect your disaster recovery plan to account for every complication or calamity that may arise during the recovery of your SharePoint farm, an effective test of your plan often results in some valuable information and changes to the plan. Your responsibility, once the test is completed, is to refactor the plan based on those conclusions and then retest it to verify the accuracy of your modifications.

Performing Ongoing Maintenance of Your Disaster Recovery Plan

In life and in IT administration in particular, the only constant is change. One challenging aspect of creating a disaster recovery plan is that the system you're designing against is likely to go through frequent modifications, even during the course of your design process. It is not uncommon that in as soon as six months after your plan is completed and approved, the system you designed it for will have grown, matured, and been updated to the point that the plan is no longer fully relevant. That's why it isn't only important to write your plan in such a way that it can be easily modified and updated, but to re-evaluate and update it on a regular basis to keep it in line with the SharePoint environment it addresses.

Analyzing Your Systems: As-Is/To-Be

One way to anticipate changes that may be required for your SharePoint disaster recovery plan is by creating some key lists that track the current and future state of your environment. Organizations are constantly evaluating their IT systems to determine if they're able to meet their specific needs and learn what modifications, additions, or subtractions they may make to them in the future. Often this analysis is broken into two sections: As-Is and To-Be. As-Is analysis of a system examines the business's current users, processes, and data and compares it to the existing IT system. This comparison is then used to evaluate how well the system serves the needs and actions of the business and to establish a baseline for the future state of the system. The future state is defined in the To-Be analysis. The To-Be list defines the vision for the business's IT systems of the future, prioritizes features and functionality, and establishes goals that upgrades should meet or exceed.

An effective disaster recovery plan is designed to meet the requirements and conditions set forth by the As-Is list of an organization while keeping an eye toward the state described by the To-Be list. A plan must encompass the current system's entire configuration, workflows, and data but also be flexible enough to either handle or be modified to accommodate the projected future state of the system. If a disaster recovery plan can't grow with your SharePoint farm as its role within your organization grows, and thus its IT footprint grows to match, it quickly loses its effectiveness.

If your organization doesn't have official As-Is and To-Be lists that include your SharePoint environment, consider compiling these items before finalizing your SharePoint disaster recovery plan. You need to have a concrete understanding of your system, its strengths and weaknesses, and its projected future state to effectively know what needs to be preserved and restored and how that could yield changes to your disaster recovery plan in the coming years.

Modifying Your Plan

In general, your organization should have procedures that govern the review and update of approved documentation so that all documents are evaluated on a regular basis (for example, every year) and updated accordingly. You may find that, based on how your SharePoint system evolves and grows, your disaster recovery plan requires more frequent care and feeding. Take care to establish certain criteria that can trigger an update to your plan, such as a major release for your system, the deployment of new hardware, or the installation of service packs or version upgrades for your software.

When you do modify the plan, create a new version of its documentation so that you can maintain and track a history of its changes over time. Ensure that the document again goes through a full review and approval process so that all stakeholders are made aware of the changes that have occurred in the system and the disaster recovery plan itself. Allowing the plan to gather dust while the state of your production SharePoint system evolves presents a major risk to the plan's relevance and effectiveness and your ability to actually recover the system in a catastrophe.

Tip: Specialized applications and systems, such as SunGard's Living Disaster Recovery Planning System (LDRPS), exist to serve and address the needs of disaster recovery planners. These applications and systems can greatly simplify the processes of disaster recovery documentation, change tracking, and ongoing plan maintenance. If your organization contains a group with formalized disaster recovery responsibility, check with them to see if you could or should be leveraging such a system for your SharePoint disaster recovery planning purposes. If the decision is in your hands, investigate the use of one of these systems. It can save time, effort, and most importantly, confusion—particularly when disaster strikes.

Expecting and Budgeting for Ongoing Maintenance

To make changes to your disaster recovery plan, you need to expend at least *some* resources in the form of the time necessary to redesign the plan to meet the changing needs of your systems as well as any additional hardware or software that the redesigned plan may require. Be prepared for expenses beyond time if the scope of your SharePoint farm grows, because you'll likely require further physical resources such as expanded storage space or more servers, not to mention the possibility of specialized backup and restore software. All these items can add definitive costs to your budget that you may not necessarily anticipate once the disaster recovery plan is in place, but you should expect them as part of your plan's ongoing maintenance. As economic circumstances fluctuate and available budgets grow and shrink, you must make sure that sufficient resources are made available to support ongoing maintenance of the plan.

Tip: The yearly cost of disaster recovery maintenance is often tied to the disaster recovery design that is implemented for a SharePoint farm. A best practice for most corporate SharePoint farm owners is to calculate and budget for the cost of ongoing disaster recovery maintenance at the same time they prepare a capital asset request for the acquisition of a SharePoint environment and the initial implementation of its disaster recovery strategy and design.

Conclusion

The worst thing you could do once your disaster recovery plan is completed and approved is to put it on a shelf and forget it. As you have hopefully gleaned from this chapter, disaster recovery planning is a process of continuous improvement, not a one-time activity. Just as your users are constantly adding new content, documents, tasks, and more to your SharePoint sites, the system is growing with them, and you need to be confident that you can recover your system in the event of a disaster in spite of those changes.

This may require some vigilance on your part, but there are ways that you can alleviate this burden. Monitor your IT organization's change control process for updates, rollouts, or decommissioning activities that may impact your plan. If your organization doesn't have a defined change control process, implement one as soon as you can. Although this process can create overhead and some extra work for your administrators, it provides an opportunity to review the important changes that are being made to your systems and see how they've changed over time.

Baselining your SharePoint system on a regular basis can also aid in the maintenance of your disaster recovery plan. Comparing a given baseline to the current state of the system allows you to identify changes and additional items that your plan may need to address. It may be best to incorporate a system baseline into your regularly scheduled or triggered maintenance activities for your plan to ensure that it's happening on a consistent basis.

Regardless of how you do it, treat your SharePoint environment's disaster recovery plan as a living document—one in a regular state of modification and improvement like an entry in a wiki, rather than a static resource that changes less than the *Encyclopedia Britannica*. But remember, given the importance of your farm's disaster recovery plan, the quality and accuracy of the information in it should be created, reviewed, tested, and approved more like that of the *Encyclopedia Britannica* than a wiki.

Now that you've seen how to test and maintain your SharePoint disaster recovery plan, you should be able to answer the following questions. You can find the answers to these questions in Appendix A, "Chapter Review Q&A," found on the Cengage Learning Web site at http://www.courseptr.com/downloads.

1. What are some examples of resources that can be removed from a test of your disaster recovery plan to check its effectiveness?

2. What are some of the expected outputs you should have once a test of your plan is completed?

3. Explain the role that independent observers play during a disaster recovery test?

4. Can you describe some of the potential risks of not updating your disaster recovery plan over time?

5. What's the difference between an As-Is and a To-Be list?

4 SharePoint Disaster Recovery Best Practices

In This Chapter

- Getting to Know Yourself
- Getting the Right Tool(s) for the Job
- Putting It All to Good Use

Now that you have a firm grounding in and understanding of the general concepts of disaster recovery, it is time to start figuring out how to apply those concepts to your SharePoint environment. This is where you are finally going to get into the technical aspects of your SharePoint disaster recovery solution and deal with the mechanics of protecting your SharePoint farm. The good news is that this should be somewhat easier for you now that you are thinking about the requirements you need to meet and some of the resources that you should have available to satisfy those requirements. The bad news is that, as much as you would like one, there is not a single, one-size-fits-all, magically handle everything solution for SharePoint disaster recovery (or at least not out of the box with the tools that come with SharePoint and its associated platforms).

The purpose of this chapter is to bridge the gap you may be noticing between general disaster recovery planning and solving the technological pieces of the disaster recovery puzzle. Although there is no one wonderful tool for everyone to use, you can assemble your perfect SharePoint disaster recovery strategy once you answer a common set of questions.

As you read this book's subsequent chapters on the tools that are at hand for protecting your SharePoint environment, bear in mind the concerns posed by this chapter and the ones that come before it. As you read about disaster recovery tools and techniques, consider if and how they pertain to you and your environment. Every SharePoint environment's approach to disaster recovery is unique, and addressing with open eyes the questions and concerns that are posed ultimately helps to lead you to the disaster recovery strategy that is right for you.

The visual examples provided in this chapter were generated in a testing environment using the following platforms and components. Depending on how your environment is configured, your experiences may vary slightly.

- **Operating system.** Microsoft Windows Server 2008 R2 Enterprise Edition (build 7600)

- **Database.** Microsoft SQL Server 2008 Developer Edition with Service Pack 1 (SP1; build 10.0.2740)

- **Web server.** Microsoft Internet Information Services (IIS) 7.5

- **SharePoint.** SharePoint Foundation 2010 Release Candidate 1 (build 4730)

Getting to Know Yourself

One of the reasons SharePoint has seen almost unprecedented adoption by businesses in recent years is its flexibility. Do you need to allow your employees to easily collaborate on business documents? SharePoint can do that. Do you need to find critical information stored in a variety of formats and locations throughout your information technology (IT) infrastructure? SharePoint can do that. Do you need a Web site that your content creators can maintain and manage without having deep knowledge of HTML, CSS, or other Web programming languages? SharePoint can do it yet again.

But that flexibility is not just limited to its functionality. You can also deploy SharePoint's infrastructure components and services in a range of configurations to meet your specific needs and resources. You can deploy SharePoint to something as simple as a single server running Windows Server 2008 Standard Edition and SQL Server Express 2008, all the way up to a global multifarm environment running Windows Server 2008 Enterprise and SQL Server 2008 Enterprise. The inclusion of Service Applications, such as Project Server 2010 and PerformancePoint 2010, can also vastly change the functionality, complexity, and composition of your SharePoint environment.

Your SharePoint configuration has a direct impact on how you plan your environment's protection. You need to take into account several aspects of that configuration before you can begin to fully flesh out the details of how you are going to meet the requirements of your disaster recovery plan and stay within the constraints you have identified. The items in this section highlight several areas that you need to examine in your SharePoint infrastructure to help you make informed decisions about the right way to protect it.

Know Your Scope

As you begin to design your SharePoint disaster recovery solution, the first thing you need to determine is the components or facets of the SharePoint farm you are actually going to protect. This is the process that defines the scope of your disaster recovery solution, but it's not as simple as it may seem. It is not just a matter of declaring a site collection in your disaster recovery plan or deciding to omit a server from it. Yes, you should start by going through something similar to that to determine what's in and what's out, but there's more to it than that. Truly defining the scope of your disaster recovery solution means that you know what you are going to cover, what pieces of your SharePoint environment are more important than others, what potential risks your targets have, and what your restored environment looks like following recovery from a disaster.

What Do You Need to Cover?

This should be the easy part, or at least the most straightforward part of the process: defining the pieces of your SharePoint environment that you must preserve in the event of a disaster. All of it, right? As much as you may like to cover your entire environment, this may not be the best course of action or even something that's necessary. Identify those items within your environment that are mission-critical and those that are not. You should do a large part of this when you establish your disaster recovery plan's recovery targets, but often that process focuses on SharePoint components and content from the end users' perspective, not from an IT or infrastructure perspective. If you have not established your disaster recovery plan's recovery targets, now is the time to do so. Make sure to go back and read the first three chapters of this book, because there is important information within them about the importance of properly defining your recovery targets.

The nature of each of the recovery targets you identify plays a critical role in understanding how you are going to protect and recover those same targets. Now is the time you need to drill into those targets and understand the technical elements and dependencies in your environment that act to support and keep those targets operational. The dependent systems and technologies you identify through this process become recovery targets themselves, and the process of examination and dependency walking continues with them. When followed to its logical conclusion, the process of tracing the chain of technical dependencies ensures that you identify all the elements within your environment that prop up or support the recovery targets originally specified. It is only by addressing each of these items or technologies within the disaster recovery plan that you ensure that the pieces are in place to support the recovery of your original SharePoint targets.

How Is Your Environment Being Used?

The purpose of your SharePoint environment also impacts how you handle it from a disaster recovery perspective, because SharePoint use cases often involve specialized components, platforms, and infrastructure to function properly. In the software industry, *use case* describes how you can use a given tool or application in a certain situation. A large SharePoint Search environment may need a specialized storage area network (SAN) with high disk input/output (I/O) throughput for performance reasons. You need to back up such a SAN differently than you would a hard drive directly attached to a server. A SharePoint extranet solution is likely to use a security platform such as Microsoft's Unified Access Gateway (UAG) and Threat Management Gateway (TMG) products to authenticate users and secure traffic communicating with SharePoint from outside the local network. You must restore a service such as this along with SharePoint to fully return the system to service. On the other hand, you might not need development or testing environments to be protected, because they do not (or at least should not) hold production data and content.

Note: In the past, Microsoft had positioned TMG and its predecessors (primarily the Internet Security and Acceleration server product, or ISA) as its primary platform to secure internal content when clients access it outside the local network, but that has recently changed. A few years ago, Microsoft purchased a company called Whale, which offered an enhanced Web firewall and reverse proxy product. Microsoft has turned that product into the new UAG offering. (Ironically, the Whale product was built on top of Microsoft's ISA platform.) Now Microsoft is recommending that TMG be a firewall as well as a Web proxy and UAG take over the responsibility of securing and encrypting end user traffic to SharePoint as well as other remote access functionality. TMG can still be used for SharePoint publishing in the current release.

What Are Your Priorities?

What is the most important thing in your SharePoint environment? What is the least important? Do these items have the same recovery point objectives (RPOs)? How about recovery time objectives (RTOs)? If they don't, should you spend the same amount of effort and resources to protect both of those items in the same way? If they do, do you need to reexamine these metrics and adjust your disaster recovery plan accordingly? Knowing the highest value targets within your environment is critical, because these are the items you need to focus your protection and recovery efforts on above all else so you can deliver the best possible solution for your organization and your users.

Keep an Eye on Complexity

Prioritization is a good way to make sure you are directing your resources and efforts at the components that need them most, but prioritization does come with a price. As you define your priorities, exercise care to keep them from becoming too granular or narrowly focused. It is all too easy to introduce unnecessary complexity into your disaster recovery solution, which can make your system difficult to manage and easily lead to higher costs and inaccuracies in the delivery of your solution. Some complexity may be unavoidable due to business requirements or constraints; in those situations, it is still important to note and allow for the risk it can pose to the viability of your SharePoint disaster recovery solution.

What Do You Need to Restore?

This might seem like a pretty simple question, but avoid taking the answer for granted. Although it might be easy to just say that you need your collaboration sites or your business intelligence portal restored in accordance with your RPO and RTO targets, there's a great deal more that can go into recovering those resources than just restoring a single backup file. Take into account the dependencies that are tied to your recovery targets, because it is highly likely that recovery from a disaster entails bringing those dependencies back online to fully restore your critical SharePoint content. After you know what you need to restore, you can accurately formulate a plan to preserve it.

Know Your Budget

One of the most eye-opening aspects of a comprehensive disaster recovery solution can be its price tag. Cost is a major consideration when planning how you are going to protect your SharePoint environment. Even though the technical options covered in the following chapters are often available without purchasing additional software licenses, you cannot assume they are cheap to implement.

For example, consider SQL Server 2008's failover clustering capability, a compelling component of SQL Server 2008's Standard and Enterprise licenses. To use failover clustering, you need special hardware in the form of a SAN. This storage resource is necessary so you can share a single storage resource across the multiple member servers in the cluster; however, it does not come cheaply. Although the number of options in this space is increasing and prices are decreasing, purchasing a SAN resource that is capable of providing the performance required to host SharePoint's SQL Server database can come at a considerable cost. When you reflect on failover clustering, consider costs such as these, and evaluate them against your available budget.

The ongoing cost of additional storage to hold backup files, regardless of platform, is the most common cost (and oftentimes one of the most significant ones) that you are going to have to prepare for when you think about implementing a SharePoint disaster recovery solution. Whether your solutions employ tapes, disks, optical media, or other forms of storage, you must factor into your budget the cost of the media and the hardware needed to leverage it.

Defining the cost of your disaster recovery solution is a good exercise and another important reason why disaster recovery planning needs to involve both the technical and business stakeholders in your organization. Every party with a dog in the hunt needs to understand how much it costs to deliver a disaster recovery solution and be able to properly reevaluate and prioritize their requirements to fit them into the budget available for the solution. This is usually not an easy or enjoyable activity, but it is a necessary one nonetheless.

Know Your Infrastructure

To an end user, SharePoint is a great deal like most other Web sites; as long as you know the correct URL and have the right to access the site, it opens in your Web browser just like any other Web page and presents you with a familiar user experience. Just like any other Web site, there is often a great deal more going on behind the scenes to send those SharePoint pages to your Web browser. SharePoint 2010 has specific software needs (Windows Server 2008, IIS 7, SQL Server) and considerable hardware needs (high-performance processors, a great deal of RAM, high-capacity and high-performance storage, and a high bandwidth network), not to mention other optional elements such as load balancers, firewalls, antivirus protection, custom code, and much more. Your SharePoint environment's infrastructure and the details of its configuration directly affect how you should properly protect SharePoint.

What Do You Have?

As a general IT best practice, you should have an inventory of your environment's current infrastructure. You should also be documenting the configuration of the environment. If you are not yet doing these things, it is never too late to start. This data is invaluable in a disaster. Without it, you have little hope of accurately re-creating the proper environment in which to restore service. This documentation also affects how you plan your disaster recovery strategy, because different types of resources you seek to protect often require different solutions. Once you understand what you have, you can effectively begin to prepare to safeguard it against the worst.

In addition, you need to know how much content you are going to protect within your SharePoint environment. You need to know how much content you currently have in your farm, but you also need to know how much is going to be going into it in the future. This can influence your choice of tools to protect your environment with, because some protection options are poorly suited for larger environments. For example, Microsoft recommends against using site collection backups (via PowerShell or Central Administration) with site collections larger than 85GB. Understanding these types of limitations, as well as the amounts and types of data you intend to protect, permits you to make informed disaster recovery planning decisions.

Microsoft has done extensive testing of SharePoint's out-of-the-box backup and recovery tools. It has found that the tools have a much higher rate of failure once certain sizing boundaries, such as the one mentioned earlier, are crossed. If you plan to use SharePoint's PowerShell cmdlets or the Central Administration site for backup or restore activities, keep a close eye on the size of your farm, its content, and its site collections as they grow to ensure that they are staying within Microsoft's sizing boundaries for those SharePoint 2010 tools. If they outgrow the tools, you need to be prepared to consider other options or accept a much greater risk to the viability of your backup operations over time. For more information on this subject, see Microsoft's "Backup and Recovery Overview" page in TechNet at http://technet.microsoft.com/en-us/library/ee663490.aspx. For specifics on those sizing boundaries, see the "Plan for Backup and Recovery" page on TechNet at http://technet.microsoft.com/en-us/library/cc261687.aspx.

What Can You Do with What You Have?

Be as specific as possible when populating your inventory; small details can have a large impact on how you can configure your SharePoint disaster recovery solution. You cannot expect that it is sufficient to know that your environment is using SQL Server, given the complexity Microsoft and other vendors have built into their licensing and provisioning models. Take SQL Server 2008's ability to compress backup files, for example. This is a desirable piece of functionality that can save you a great deal of money on storage costs, but you have to know exactly what release of SQL Server you are using because it is not a feature that is globally available in all licenses for SQL Server. When it was introduced, it was available only with the Enterprise

Edition license for SQL Server 2008 and was not included in any edition of SQL Server 2005. Now, with the recent release of SQL Server 2008 R2, backup compression is available in all licensed versions. This is just one example of how important it can be to know exactly what you have in your environment and what those resources are capable of; thanks to the complexity of SharePoint and its supporting platforms, several cases like this can be an issue if you make incorrect assumptions about the capabilities of your resources.

You need to know what you cannot or should not do with your resources. Do your storage systems have the throughput (disk throughput is measured in input/output per second, or IOPS) necessary to restore a backup to a protected system fast enough to meet your RTO targets? Does Microsoft support the tools or platforms you are using in your environment? If you do not know the answers to these types of questions, you are putting your disaster recovery solution and your overall SharePoint environment at risk.

Consider this from the perspective of one of the IT industry's most valuable and recent technological developments: server virtualization. *Virtualization* is the practice of building a complete computer environment on top of a software platform instead of a hardware one, allowing for multiple "virtual" computers to be run on a single physical host. Virtualization allows for a full server environment to be abstracted into a virtual machine (VM) contained in a set of files on the storage system of its host; many of the modern server virtualization platforms (such as VMware's vSphere and Microsoft's Hyper-V) can easily copy and transfer those files between hosts. This practice, often referred to simply as *copying a VM*, is regularly touted as an excellent backup/restore solution. It offers ease of use and a great deal of flexibility for restoration because the VM abstracts away so much of the hardware layer. Virtualization gives an IT organization flexibility in how it can deploy its resources; often it can provide a definite return on investment by allowing the organization to truly optimize its hardware across all its platforms.

SharePoint runs well when virtualized (in most circumstances; it does not do well in use cases or server roles requiring high IOPS, such as database servers), and Microsoft supports it on multiple virtualization platforms. But the use of VM copies as a disaster recovery solution is not exactly such an encouraging or cut-and-dried story. Why is that? VM copies are pretty straightforward, right? You make a copy of those VM files on the host server's file system, store them in a remote location, and in the event of a disaster just move them to a functional server and turn them back on. That's how it works for most platforms, but you have to remember that SharePoint's architecture makes it a different beast, especially in a multiserver farm scenario.

Part of the problem with using VM copies stems from SharePoint's use of timer jobs to run scheduled activities and functions throughout the farm and on individual servers. SharePoint does not allow you to easily prevent timer jobs from starting, at least not without completely shutting down a server, so the chances of being able to start and stop a VM copy activity with all of a server's SharePoint timer jobs maintaining the same status throughout are low over time. This lack of consistency in creating VM copies of your SharePoint servers introduces an unacceptable level of risk from the perspective of protecting your SharePoint servers. As an extreme example, consider the case of a SharePoint server that is copied while a service pack is being installed. Under such circumstances, the server is in an inconsistent state. If the VM copy that is generated from this server is brought online, will the service pack installation continue? Will the server VM even boot? The result is uncertain due to the inconsistent state of the server when the copy is created.

The companion to this problem is one of overall farm consistency, at least for virtualized multi-server SharePoint environments. Not only are there frequent activities running within a given SharePoint server, but that same server is in almost constant communication with the other SharePoint servers in the farm as well as the SQL Server instance hosting the farm's databases. In fact, SharePoint is so closely tied to its databases that it cannot function without them; they are the glue that holds a farm together. SharePoint's servers are constantly sending and receiving data to and from its databases. For a set of farm VMs to function, those VMs must be created (or copied) for the entire farm at the same time and while the farm is in a consistent state. Failing to copy all members of the farm at the same time—and in a consistent state—introduces risk should you need to restore those farm members.

Now, this is not to say that you cannot use VM copies to capture a SharePoint farm for disaster recovery purposes. Microsoft does recommend one solution: shutting down the target server prior to copying it. This ensures that there are no running processes or network traffic that may not be completely captured because the server is not active during the operation. But is it worth it? This approach requires that you either configure all the servers in your farm to be highly available so the target server's functionality can be delivered by another server in the farm or schedule regular outages during which copies can be created. Neither may be an attractive option, and you must carefully weigh the implications for your IT organization as well as your end users before you decide to go with VM copies.

Ultimately, how you integrate virtualization into your SharePoint environment and its disaster recovery solution is up to you. If you are planning on virtualizing your SharePoint servers, you need to strive to stay up to date on information from Microsoft and the SharePoint community about using virtualization as a disaster recovery solution. Don't assume that VM copies are all you need to protect your environment. At the same time, don't fall into the trap of thinking that things won't change.

How Does the Environment Change?

From the moment you decide to implement SharePoint in your organization, change is occurring. From the time you start deploying servers in a datacenter to the moment the first user opens a SharePoint site in his browser and well beyond, changes are occurring that you have to track. Your disaster recovery solution needs to be able to handle those changes and adapt to account for changes it cannot handle.

Adoption is a major area of concern for anyone who implements SharePoint. Although most of the focus is directed toward encouraging adoption, the growth of your system is the type of change most likely to affect your disaster recovery solution. For example, your RPO and RTO targets may alter to reflect an increased dependence on SharePoint by your users. At the same time, greater usage often results in greater storage use and related demands. Your disaster recovery solution needs to be flexible and extendable to account for these types of potential changes.

That's not all. A major key to a high-quality IT environment is effective change management. *Change management* is the process of changing a system with oversight and control, as well as in-depth documentation and communication. In any IT system, just as in life in general, change is inevitable. It is also something you must manage to prevent your IT infrastructure from becoming unmanageable. It does not matter if you are the only member in your IT organization or if you are a member of a large IT department; you must know about the changes that are being made and document them.

Properly documenting your changes is crucial when it comes to disaster recovery; if you do not know what was done to get your system to its current state, how can you possibly know how to restore it to that state if calamity should strike? Implementing a change management process is something you should have in place for your IT environment in general, but it is absolutely essential if you intend to take disaster recovery seriously.

Know Your Current State

Once you implement a disaster recovery solution, don't think that your work is done. As already mentioned in Chapter 3, "SharePoint Disaser Recovery Testing and Maintenance," there is a great deal of ongoing maintenance and testing you need to plan on performing for your disaster recovery solution once you have put it into practice to ensure its long-term viability. In addition to those activities, you need to stay on top of any supporting infrastructure tied to the disaster recovery solution to make sure that it remains healthy and is functioning properly. Regardless of how you decide to protect your SharePoint environment, there are certain aspects of it that you should always be monitoring to have an accurate understanding of its current state.

In general, strive to have a monitoring solution in place for your SharePoint environment, whether it is Microsoft's System Center Operations Manager, a third-party product such as the Nimsoft Monitoring Solution, an open-source platform built on top of a tool like Cacti, or simply your own custom scripts using the Windows event logs and Windows Performance Monitor. Monitoring is an essential facet of a stable IT environment, and it should keep administrators informed of issues within their systems before users know about them. It also permits administrators to be proactive instead of reactive by identifying trends and patterns within the environment that should be addressed before they become troublesome issues. If you do have a monitoring solution in your environment, make sure it is configured to encompass the components of your disaster recovery solution so that the health and performance of your disaster recovery infrastructure are tracked along with the rest of your systems.

Getting the Right Tool(s) for the Job

Let's be honest. Working in the IT industry does not (usually) require the same kind of physical exertion that is required in more traditional fields such as construction or farming. There are parallels that you can draw between these diverse disciplines, though, especially in the area of tooling. Regardless of whether you get your hands dirty or squint your eyes at an LCD screen all day long, your job is much more difficult if you don't have the right tool for the job at hand.

Does a carpenter use the same saw for every kind of wood he's cutting or every kind of cut he makes? Does a farmer use a garden spade to plant 40 acres of seed corn? No, and these people go out of their way to make sure they avoid situations in which they are forced to make do with subpar solutions. It stands to reason that to effectively protect your SharePoint environment in case of a disaster, you need to have the best possible tools on hand to meet your recovery objectives.

When considering how to protect your SharePoint environment with a disaster recovery solution, realize that no one tool or process is going to address all requirements and recovery targets. Be prepared to implement a tool or strategy to back up your critical SharePoint content. The approach you select needs to fit into an overall disaster recovery plan—not take the place of it. Although the SharePoint platform comes with a set of backup and restore tools, these tools address only a subset of the full range of disaster recovery concerns. These tools also come with their own unique set of idiosyncrasies, limitations, and problems that can directly impact when and how they are used in the event of a disaster.

Remember: it is just as important to know what your tool or strategy *cannot* do as what it *can* do. The harsh reality of SharePoint's dependence on other platforms, such as SQL Server and Active Directory (AD), is that you still have a great deal of work ahead of you to guarantee full disaster recovery coverage in your environment. It is equally important to remember that you do not have to pick just one tool for the job; there is nothing wrong with using multiple tools to independently protect your environment redundantly, especially when those multiple tools allow you to cover gaps in your solution that a single tool may expose.

What Does the Tool Cover?

You absolutely have to know what a tool can back up and restore within your environment. Does it back up your search index? Does it back up customizations that have been deployed to the farm? Does it target SharePoint specifically, or does it protect SharePoint by protecting its supporting systems, such as Active Directory and SQL Server? Answer these types of questions thoroughly, because you don't want to make assumptions about a tool's capabilities only to find out the hard way that you were wrong.

Granularity

When you're establishing your recovery targets, make sure to carefully establish the smallest unit within your SharePoint environment that you are expected to protect and restore within a given amount of time. The more narrowly and granularly you define your targets, the more important it becomes to find the right tool that is capable of providing that granularity. If you need to be able to restore individual documents in a library to a prior state, you need to know if the tool you're going to use can do that automatically for you or if you need to take additional manual steps to make it happen. Many third-party products offer item-level restores, but with Share-Point's out-of-the-box tools, you're still going to have to take some manual steps to do it. If you have granular recovery targets, make sure that your choice of tool is able to be that granular or you have processes in place to fill the gaps left by the tool.

How Does the Tool Provide That Coverage?

A corollary to knowing what a specific tool can cover within your SharePoint environment is the understanding of how it provides that coverage. More succinctly, how does it work? Does it use Microsoft's Volume Shadow Copy services or SharePoint's own backup and restore application programming interfaces (APIs) to back up your farm? Does it require additional hardware, software, or other resources to deliver on its promises? Additional tool requirements and dependencies can add a great deal more cost to your overall solution if you are not aware of them during the planning stages.

Just as Olympic athletes need to know exactly what goes into the food they are eating or mechanics examine every nut, bolt, fluid, and strut they use in a high-performance racing machine, you have to understand how your chosen tool is going to protect your SharePoint environment. What access rights does it need, and how do those requirements impact not only SharePoint, but the rest of your business's environment? Can it schedule backup operations? Is it an easy tool to use, or does it require extensive training for your administrators to operate? You can never ask too many questions about the tools you decide to use as part of your SharePoint disaster recovery solution, because a lack of understanding about them can lead to dangerous assumptions and an increased level of risk to your solution.

What Doesn't the Tool Cover?

It may be even more important to understand what a given SharePoint backup and restore tool *cannot* do than what it *can* do. Again, making incorrect assumptions about the capabilities of your tools can have disastrous effects if those assumptions are not revealed as false until you need the tool for recovery.

A tool's inability to cover one aspect or another of your SharePoint environment is not necessarily the end of the world There is no rule that says you have to use only one device to meet all your needs. Using multiple tools is fine as long as you understand that it does increase both the complexity of your solution and the number of places in your solution where something can go wrong. This means you need to be especially careful in comprehensively training your staff on the use of all tools. You should also implement a monitoring solution that can cover each tool, report on its status, and alert you if something goes wrong with one of them.

Can the Tool Meet Your RTO and RPO Targets?

Even if a single tool can cover everything in your SharePoint environment that you need it to, if it can't do so quickly enough, it is not going to be the right tool for the job. Although the two metrics are not necessarily related, the performance of your backup and recovery tool could be just as important to you as the performance of your overall SharePoint environment. If your disaster recovery solution takes too long to back up or restore some or all of your SharePoint environment, you are not going to be able to meet the RTO and RPO targets you have established in your disaster recovery plan. Because we're talking about both RTO and RPO targets, you need to consider how well the tool completes restore operations just as much as you do backup operations.

You need to consider three factors when evaluating a tool's ability to meet your RPO window targets: the tool's performance capabilities, the size of the components you are backing up with it, and the actual period defined for your RPO target. The interesting thing about these factors is that it's the combination of them that really defines a tool's ability to make or miss your RPO target. If you have a large environment and a tight RPO window, it's going to be much more difficult for a tool to back up everything in a timely fashion. For example, if you have a six-hour RPO target but a tool requires 12 hours to back up your farm, you are guaranteed to miss your target. In this instance, you must either change the RPO target or choose a different tool or strategy.

In the case of restores, it all comes down to one thing: can you restore the targeted functionality and content to your SharePoint environment in time to meet your RTO target? If a tool and any associated recovery process can't restore SharePoint in time to meet the requirements your users have established for the environment, the tool selected isn't the right one for the job. This is a great reason to exercise your disaster recovery solution frequently over the lifetime of your environment, because as it changes and grows, your tools may not be able to grow with it. It is far better to find this out in a test when it doesn't count than in your production environment when it really does.

Usability

Always think about the usability of a tool when deciding whether to make it a key part of your disaster recovery solution. You need to look for some specific things when evaluating options for your disaster recovery solution. Some are pretty straightforward, and others are a little less obvious. What a backup or restore tool can do means little if you can't figure out how to use it—or if you cannot consistently use it correctly every time. At the same time, the easier a tool is to use, the larger the pool of people on your team who can quickly learn how to use it effectively when called upon with little or no notice. You need to keep in mind that the resources using the tool in a time of need may be those who are available instead of those who know it best, so how well they can use the tool may make the difference between a successful recovery and an incomplete or failed one.

Stability

The stability of a tool is its ability to consistently deliver the same result time after time. This is something that is paramount in creating an effective disaster recovery solution. If the tool or tools that you choose are not able to provide consistent stability and predictable usage experience, the level of risk to your environment is going to grow over time as the likelihood of an error increases. Can your tool create a viable backup time after time without errors or inconsistencies? If backup files are compressed, can they be uncompressed every time without loss of data? Are those files always unpacked and restored successfully with every aspect of the environment returned to its original state without change? You need to know that your tool can reliably do the job you need it to time after time after time.

No One Size Fits All

The depth and breadth of your SharePoint environment plays a big role in helping you determine which tool or tools fit best in your disaster recovery solution. The more moving pieces your farm includes, whether it be servers, customizations, or Web sites, the more complex your disaster recovery solution is likely to be to encompass it all. It's going to take a great deal more effort to preserve a farm with four Web front-end (WFE) servers, several dedicated Service Application servers, and clustered SQL Server instances than it will a single server hosting all roles and services for the farm. Keep this in mind as you evaluate tools for your disaster recovery solution, as well as when your environment begins to evolve and expand its scope, so you can properly understand how those changes impact your solution's ability to protect SharePoint.

The amount of content in your SharePoint environment also affects the tools you can and can't use to protect it. In a large environment, a good SharePoint backup or restore tool needs to be capable of handling large amounts of content just as effectively, consistently, and quickly as it does a smaller one. Some tools state up front what they do and do not support when it comes to large environments; pay close attention to whatever limitations and usage guidelines manufacturers place on each tool. You've already seen how you need to take this into account for the out-of-the-box SharePoint backup and restore tools, but it's something you need to watch regardless of the tool you decide to use.

Conclusion

Many technical questions can be answered with two simple words: "It depends." Although this can be frustrating to hear, especially if the answer is delivered sarcastically or flippantly, this response is not given to put someone off or hedge one's bets. These words are spoken because they're true, and there are usually numerous factors that go into a proper answer for complex technical questions. Answering the complex technical questions tied to SharePoint disaster recovery are no different. Finding the right solution and coming up with an answer other than "it depends" is not going to be something as simple as checking a few boxes in a list and getting your perfect match. You need to really consider the factors covered in this chapter, as well as understand the strengths and weaknesses of the tools you're considering, so that you can move from "it depends" to "here's how we're going to do it."

One of the goals in writing this book for SharePoint 2010 was to help you better make that move by adding more information on the proper use cases for the various SharePoint backup and restore tools discussed. As you read the coming chapters, start thinking about how you're going to put each approach or tool to use to best protect your SharePoint environment or a designated aspect of it. Whether that is by making its Web servers highly available, backing up your SQL Server 2008 databases, or backing up SharePoint itself, how you're going to use the information provided is going to be critical. To make that practical application easier, read Chapter 13, "SharePoint Disaster Recovery Case Studies and Sample Scenarios." It explains some of the use cases available for each solution or tool and when one might make more sense for you over another.

The advantage we have in helping you answer the question of "how do I create the right disaster recovery solution for my SharePoint environment" is that by covering so much of the ground out there on the subject, we can introduce you to a range of options and solutions. As you read the following chapters, pay special attention to the usage scenarios discussed, and try to see if they do or don't pertain to your specific set of circumstances. Considering each tool and technology we describe within the context of your environment puts you in the right position to answer that critical question with "here's how we're going to do it" instead of "it depends."

Now that we've started to bridge the gap between general disaster recovery concepts and developing your SharePoint disaster recovery plan, you should be able to answer the following questions about a plan's capabilities. You can find the answers to these questions in Appendix A, "Chapter Review Q&A," found on the Cengage Learning Web site at http://www.courseptr.com/downloads.

1. How do recovery targets factor in the scope of your SharePoint disaster recovery solution?

2. Is it possible to protect every aspect and component of your SharePoint environment from damage or loss in the same manner or with a single tool?

3. What are some of the ways that the amount of content stored in your SharePoint environment can impact the tools in your SharePoint disaster recovery solution?

4. What are some examples of how changes to your SharePoint environment can affect your disaster recovery solution?

5. How is the granularity of coverage that a tool provides going to influence your decision on whether to include it in your disaster recovery toolbox?

5 Windows Server 2008 Backup and Restore

In This Chapter

- Backup Targets
- Before You Begin
- Backing Up Windows Server 2008
- Restoring Windows Server 2008

As discussed in Chapter 4, "SharePoint Disaster Recovery Best Practices," SharePoint is a complex application platform that depends on different services and systems for proper operation. You can envision these services and systems as layers in a software stack—much like a layer cake. The layers sit atop one another, and each layer in the stack depends on the ones beneath it. SharePoint sits at the top, fully dependent on all the layers beneath it.

If SharePoint is the top layer in the stack, the bottommost "foundational layer" of software is the Windows Server operating system (OS). When new hardware is provisioned for use with SharePoint—or any Microsoft application platform—the Windows Server OS is almost always the first prerequisite installation. Without Windows Server and its platform services, SharePoint would not have a way of interacting with the server hardware, network, and other physical devices.

Production installations of SharePoint require an underlying OS that is 64 bit and some version of Windows Server 2008. Valid versions include these:

- Windows Server 2008 R2 (Web, Standard, Enterprise, and Datacenter editions)
- Windows Server 2008 with Service Pack 2 (SP2) (Web, Standard, Enterprise, and Datacenter editions)
- Windows Small Business Server 2008 with SP2
- Windows Essential Business Server 2008 with SP2

SharePoint 2010 is not supported on any Windows Server 2008 Server Core installations, because those installations do not contain some of the components needed to configure and run SharePoint.

Note: Although Microsoft supports the installation of SharePoint Server 2010 and SharePoint Foundation 2010 on 64-bit versions of Windows 7 and Windows Vista Service Pack 1 (SP1) or greater, such installations are intended for development use only.

The important foundational role that Windows Server 2008 plays with SharePoint demands that the OS and the way it works with SharePoint data be understood for proper disaster recovery planning. This chapter examines how SharePoint uses the Windows Server 2008 OS, where SharePoint and the OS store relevant configuration data, and areas you should consider targeting during backup. It also details available backup options, as well as factors to consider while planning a backup strategy. Finally, this chapter presents a walk-through of common backup and restore operations for the OS.

The visual examples provided in this chapter were generated in a testing environment using the following platforms and components. Depending on how your environment is configured, your experiences may vary slightly.

- **Operating system.** Microsoft Windows Server 2008 R2 Enterprise Edition (build 7600)

- **Database.** Microsoft SQL Server 2008 Standard Edition with SP1 (build 10.00.2714)

- **Web server.** Microsoft Internet Information Services (IIS) 7.5

- **SharePoint.** SharePoint Server 2010 Trial (Beta) with Enterprise Client Access License (build 4536)

Backup Targets

To discuss backup and restore in a meaningful fashion, you must first understand the data that you intend to capture and safeguard. As a complex application platform, SharePoint stores business and configuration data in a variety of locations. It should be no surprise that a significant amount of it goes into SQL Server; after all, the first database that is created when a new SharePoint farm is provisioned is the farm configuration database.

Note: SQL Server and its fit into the SharePoint disaster recovery picture are discussed in depth in Chapter 7, "SQL Server 2008 Backup and Restore."

Although SharePoint relies on SQL Server for the storage of data, the services of Windows Server contribute in an equally significant manner to the operation and delivery of functionality within the overall SharePoint farm. Without Internet Information Services (IIS), for instance, Share-Point would not be able to serve Web pages in response to client requests. Without the Windows Registry, SharePoint could not persist and retrieve configuration information that governs farm membership, database connectivity, and more.

As you might expect, each of these constituent services processes data, manages configuration information, and represents one or more targets from a backup and restore perspective. This section examines Windows server as a platform, a subset of its services that are relevant to SharePoint, and aspects of both that are important within the larger SharePoint disaster recovery context.

Customizations

A SharePoint *customization* consists of some combination of files and configuration elements delivering functionality that enhances or in some way alters the out-of-the-box SharePoint experience. Customizations can add new user interface (UI) elements and behavior for users of Share-Point, change the way that SharePoint interacts with other systems, and much more.

Understanding customizations is important within the context of Windows server backup and restore because many of the file and configuration elements that constitute a customization reside in the file system of the Windows server—not within a SQL Server database. For example:

- Web Parts

- XML configuration files, such as Feature or site definition XML files

- List definitions, custom columns, and new content types

- Managed assemblies and other code libraries

- Resource (`.resx`) files

The mechanism by which the files associated with a customization are backed up and restored is determined largely by how the customization elements make it into the file system of the server. For purposes of backup targeting, customizations are classified in one of two ways:

- **Centrally managed customizations.** A customization is centrally managed when all its files and assets are aggregated into a SharePoint solution package and deployed via SharePoint's solution deployment infrastructure. A solution package is a special cabinet (`.cab`) archive file with a `.wsp` extension, and the file and its contents conform to a structure that SharePoint understands. Solution packages, also known as WSPs, are added to a SharePoint farm's solution store, and administrators deploy or retract their contents through Central Administration or PowerShell. SharePoint is fully aware of the changes that a solution package makes; it can reapply and retract those changes as needed.

- **Decentralized customizations.** If a customization is deployed through a mechanism that does not involve the farm solution store, that customization is said to be *decentralized*. This includes the manual copying of files to each of the servers within the farm and the changing of web.config files by hand. It can also include using a third-party installer technology that isn't explicitly designed to integrate with SharePoint. When customizations are decentralized, there is always the potential for SharePoint to overwrite files and modifications that are made for or by the customization because SharePoint simply isn't aware of them.

You should insist upon the use of centrally managed customizations within your farm whenever possible. SharePoint solution packages are widely accepted as a best practice for the deployment of files, resources, and other customization items to the SharePoint farm. In addition, solution packages greatly reduce the manual work required for the backup and recovery of customizations. When a solution package is added to a SharePoint farm via the Add-SPSolution Power-Shell cmdlet, for example, the contents of the package are copied to the farm's solution store within the configuration database. You can capture such solutions through both SharePoint and SQL Server backup mechanisms. Solutions that are present in the farm solution store are also viable targets for configuration-only backup and restore.

The backup and restore picture for decentralized customizations is significantly less attractive. Although you can generally automate the backup of the associated files, restoration of the items captured by those backups is more challenging. New files that are added to the file system for a customization can generally be restored in-place directly from a backup, but changes to shared configuration files such as a web.config cannot be directly restored because such a restoration could overwrite existing configuration elements needed by other features and solutions. In such circumstances, manual application of changes to affected files is the safest approach, albeit a tedious one. Decentralized customizations underscore the need for thorough change management procedures and associated documentation, as described in Chapter 4.

The constituent files that are deployed through a customization end up in three possible areas within the server file system.

SharePoint Root

When installed in Windows Server 2008, most applications create a directory for use within the Program Files directory. (This directory is the location pointed at by the %PROGRAMFILES%PATH variable in the server's system drive [typically the C: drive].) See Figure 5.1 for an example. This directory usually contains the executables, libraries, and configuration files necessary for the application to run on the server. SharePoint follows this convention, but only to a point. After you install SharePoint, you should see a directory named Microsoft Office Servers within the Program Files directory. An examination of its contents reveals several files necessary to run SharePoint. Generally speaking, the contents of the Microsoft Office Servers directory are relatively unchanging.

Where SharePoint strays from the conventional approach to the Program Files directory is in its use of a directory known as the SharePoint Root.

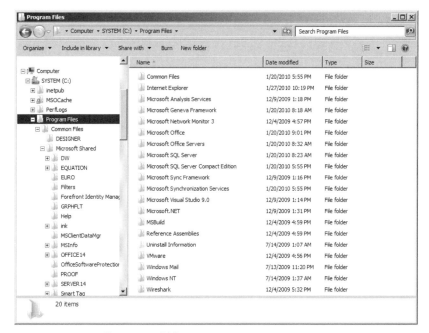

Figure 5.1 The `Program Files` directory in a Windows Server 2008 installation hosting SharePoint 2010.

The SharePoint Root is also located within the `Program Files` directory, but it is nested within several other folders that other Microsoft applications sometimes leverage. As shown in Figure 5.2, the SharePoint Root resides at `%COMMONPROGRAMFILES%\Microsoft Shared\Web Server Extensions\14\` within the server file system.

Note: The SharePoint Root has not always been widely known as such. In Windows SharePoint Services (WSS) v3 and Microsoft Office SharePoint Server (MOSS) 2007, the directory was labeled as `12` rather than `14` and was commonly referred to as the *12 Hive*. Prior to that, with WSSv2 and SharePoint Portal Server (SPS) 2003, the folder was labeled as `60` and oftentimes referred to as the *6 Hive* or *60 Hive*.

So what is in the SharePoint Root? The short answer is "Quite a bit." By default, the directory contains a number of applications, libraries, and resources that are crucial to SharePoint's operation: .NET assemblies that house the compiled code that is the SharePoint platform, a variety of different diagnostic logs, out-of-the-box image files, ASP.NET application and administrative pages, and SharePoint Features to name just a few.

In addition to its role as the central hub for many out-of-the-box SharePoint files, the SharePoint Root plays an important role for customizations. When farm-wide assets such as administrative

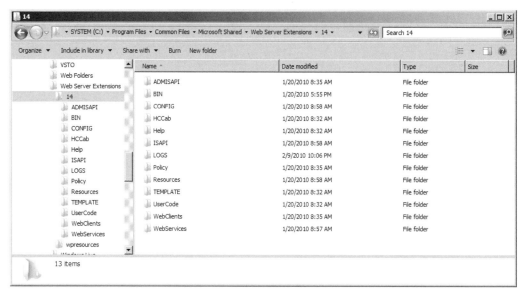

Figure 5.2 The SharePoint Root directory in a Windows Server 2008 installation.

pages, site templates, and shared images are packaged into a customization, they are normally deployed to one or more folders within the SharePoint Root.

For centrally managed customizations, PowerShell or Central Administration handles the addition of new files and changes to the SharePoint Root automatically during solution package deployment. You can easily check the installation and deployment status of centrally managed customizations within the farm within Central Administration using the Solution Management page shown in Figure 5.3. If a centrally managed solution package is later retracted, SharePoint takes care of removing the files and changes it made earlier. No manual intervention is required on the part of the administrator.

The SharePoint Root is just as important to decentralized customizations, but administrators must manually carry out file copies, file removals, and configuration changes within the Share-Point Root. SharePoint isn't aware of the changes being made in this fashion, and there is always a risk that additions and changes that are made by other administrators—or SharePoint itself, for that matter—could conflict with one another.

If decentralized customizations are used within your farm, the SharePoint Root is a mandatory backup target. Without a copy of the SharePoint Root, you risk losing part or all of the files that comprise your customizations. In the case of centrally managed customizations that are deployed using SharePoint solution packages, though, a backup of the SharePoint Root is secondary. Backing up the SharePoint Root is still recommended for the sake of redundancy, but the primary point of capture, management, and deployment for solution packages is the solution store within the SharePoint farm configuration database.

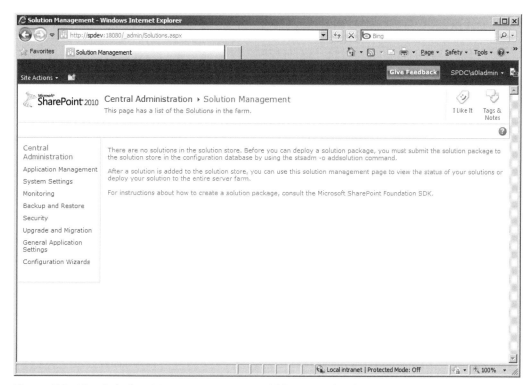

Figure 5.3 The Solution Management page within Central Administration.

Inetpub

The Web Server (IIS) server role is a required role on any Windows server that runs SharePoint. When this role is enabled on a server, an `Inetpub` folder is created to house much of the file and configuration data that IIS uses to serve up Web sites and carry out associated operations. By default, the `Inetpub` folder is located at `C:\inetpub` within the server file system, as shown in Figure 5.4. The actual location of the folder may vary, though, depending on how IIS has been configured.

Each of the Web applications within a SharePoint farm possesses one or more folders within the `Inetpub` directory of each farm member, where the Microsoft SharePoint Foundation Web Application service is running. To be more specific, a Web application has one Web site folder for its Default zone mapping. For each zone beyond the Default zone that the Web application has been extended to, an additional Web site and associated folder exists within `Inetpub`. For example, a Web application that has been extended to the Internet and Extranet zones possesses three folders within `Inetpub`—one folder for the Default zone, one folder for the Internet zone, and one folder for the Extranet zone.

The root folder for each of the Web sites that map to a SharePoint Web application is located within the `Inetpub\wwwroot\wss\VirtualDirectories` directory by default. Each of the

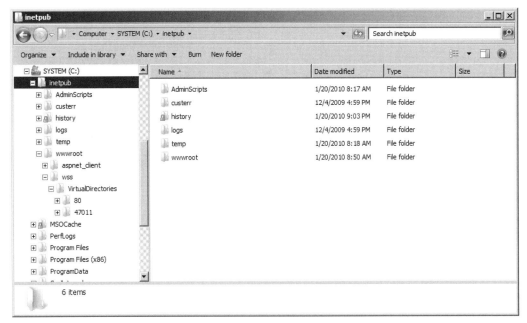

Figure 5.4 The `Inetpub` folder in its default location.

folders is named according to the host header that is applied to the zone of its corresponding Web application within SharePoint. If no host header is in use, the listener port of the associated Web application is employed instead.

Of course, you can specify a nondefault path for the folder that is actually used when you create the SharePoint Web application. Changing the contents of the Path text box in the IIS Web Site section of the Create New Web Application dialog box instructs SharePoint to use your desired path as the Root folder for the Web application rather than the default.

Note: The one exception to the naming convention described is the Central Administration Web application's Default zone Web site. Regardless of the port assigned to the Central Administration site collection during provisioning, the folder name applied corresponds to a random high port that SharePoint selects.

Figure 5.5 illustrates the contents of a SharePoint Web application that is mapped to the default Web site on the server.

Customizations contribute to and affect the contents of the SharePoint Web application `Inetpub` folders in a handful of ways. First and foremost, each of the folders has a `web.config` file that governs many of the configuration and operational aspects of its associated Web application. Customizations that are scoped at the Web application, site collection, or Web level usually

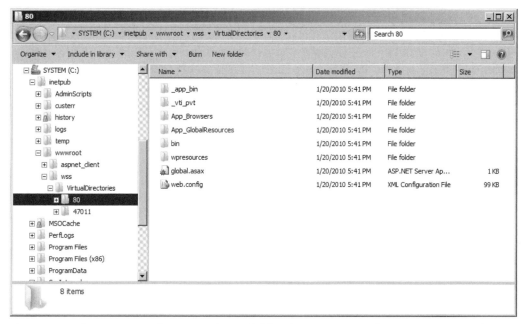

Figure 5.5   The contents of an IIS Web site folder that maps to a SharePoint Web application.

require modifications to a Web site's `web.config` file for proper operation. These configuration changes can permit the execution of code present in non-SharePoint .NET assemblies, add new application settings, wire up new `HttpModule` and `HttpHandler` entries, and more.

Changes to the `web.config` files of a Web site occur most frequently, but they are not the only changes that a customization may make or require within the `Inetpub` directory and its subdirectories. Other examples include these:

- The addition of .NET assemblies to the `bin` subdirectory

- Navigation changes to the sitemap file(s) within an `_app_bin` subdirectory

- Web Part definition and resource file additions to various subdirectories

The guidelines for backup and recovery of the `Inetpub` folder are much the same as those for the SharePoint Root folder. Centrally managed customizations normally affect required changes on the `Inetpub` folder when they are deployed through SharePoint Central Administration or PowerShell. When they are retracted, those changes that solution packages have made are also retracted. Backup of the `Inetpub` folder is a good practice, but it is redundant when considered alongside solution packages that properly deploy and retract their own `Inetpub` files and settings.

Decentralized customizations require that the `Inetpub` folder and all its contents be backed up. Failure to do so results in the loss of all files and changes that have been made in the event of a disaster or failure of the server. In addition, recovery in a disaster scenario is a tricky proposition. As mentioned, many customizations modify the contents of the Web site folders used by each of SharePoint's Web applications. This is especially true for the `web.config` file used by each SharePoint Web site within IIS. During recovery operations that involve decentralized customizations, it is an administrator's responsibility to ensure that all necessary changes to `web.config` files (and the rest of the `Inetpub` area) are properly applied and nonconflicting.

Global Assembly Cache

Every Windows operating system with one or more installed versions of the Microsoft .NET Framework possesses a Global Assembly Cache, or GAC. The GAC is a protected operating system location where .NET assemblies are located and shared for use by multiple applications. Within the Windows Server operating system, you can find the GAC at `%WINDIR%\Assembly`, as shown in Figure 5.6.

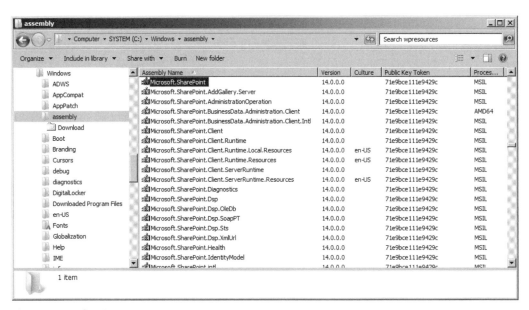

Figure 5.6   The GAC.

.NET assemblies that are placed within the GAC behave differently from those that are located elsewhere within the file system of the server, including those that are placed within the `bin` folder of a Web site within the `Inetpub` area. Here are some important differences:

- Assemblies within the GAC are fully trusted.

- The GAC supports the installation of multiple versions of the same assembly.

- The .NET assembly resolver checks the GAC before looking elsewhere, such as in a `bin` folder.

Being a .NET application platform itself, SharePoint makes extensive use of the GAC. Many of the assemblies that SharePoint uses are within the GAC. By extension, many customizations choose to place assemblies in the GAC. In some cases, such as customizations that include feature receivers, placement of assemblies within the GAC is mandatory.

As with the SharePoint Root and Inetpub folders, centrally managed customizations handle the placement and retraction of assemblies within the GAC directly through the SharePoint solution deployment framework. Backup of the GAC is a recommended action for centrally managed customizations, but only as a step that is redundant with SharePoint farm or SQL Server backups.

In the case of decentralized customizations, placement of assemblies within the GAC is a manual affair—or, at the very least, one that SharePoint doesn't control. As a result, the GAC must be targeted for backup operations to ensure that the assemblies supplying runtime functionality for such customizations are captured and preserved in the event of a disaster.

IIS

IIS receives requests for SharePoint pages and hands rendered pages back to client browsers and applications. This description is a gross oversimplification of the role that IIS plays, but it serves as a good starting point to understanding the ways in which IIS serves and interacts with Share-Point. Interaction with IIS is commonly carried out through its management application, as shown in Figure 5.7.

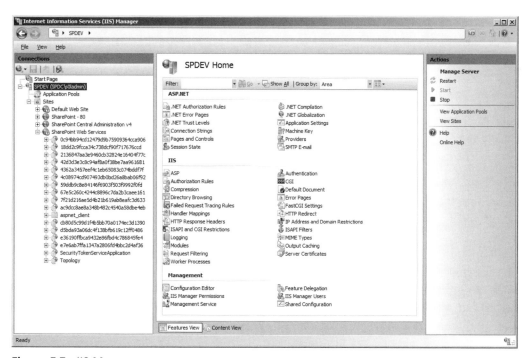

Figure 5.7   IIS Manager.

As a Web server, IIS faithfully carries out many duties on behalf of SharePoint—too many to fully describe here. Some of the more well-known ones, though, include the following:

- Managing one or more instances of the SharePoint application process

- Hosting Service Applications and the communications between them

- Enforcing security at the transport layer

- Providing static and dynamic compression for outgoing data

IIS is enabled through the Web Service (IIS) role within Windows server, and mechanisms within SharePoint afford a great deal of control over IIS and how it operates, both directly and indirectly. It is not possible to manage all facets of IIS from within SharePoint or PowerShell, though. A number of settings and configuration items tied to IIS must be addressed and targeted separate from SharePoint for disaster recovery purposes.

Configuration

As a complex set of services in its own right, IIS depends on a significant amount of configuration data to govern its own operations. In IIS6 under Windows Server 2003, this configuration data was maintained in a database known as the IIS Metabase. With Windows Server 2008 and IIS7, the Metabase has been replaced by a set of XML configuration files that are located in the `%WINDIR%\System32\Inetsrv\Config` folder. The following three files primarily govern IIS operations:

- The `ApplicationHost.config` file houses configuration data for each of the Web sites and applications that IIS manages and serves. The contents of this file are updated each time a configuration change is made within IIS.

- The `Administration.config` file contains settings that relate to the management of IIS itself, including data that governs management modules for the IIS Manager application. In most cases, the contents of this file are static.

- The `Redirection.config` file is employed when IIS is being run in shared configuration mode. Because the shared configuration feature of IIS is not supported with SharePoint, this configuration file is of little practical use on SharePoint servers.

Regular backups of the configuration folder and subfolders are a best practice, because they afford you the opportunity to roll back any IIS changes that may adversely affect the operation of Web sites, Web services, and SharePoint Service Applications. You can back up the configuration folder and subfolders directly, or you can make a more targeted backup directly using the AppCmd.exe tool that is described later in this chapter.

Even if you don't make regular backups, IIS itself affords a certain degree of resiliency through its configuration history feature. As changes are made to IIS, the contents of the `ApplicationHost`.

config file change. By default, IIS checks for changes to the ApplicationHost.config file every two minutes. If a new version of the file is found to be in effect, IIS takes a snapshot of the file and places it in the %SYSTEMDRIVE%\inetpub\history folder. IIS keeps up to 10 historical versions of the ApplicationHost.config file in this way.

Tip: You can alter or even turn off the operation of the configuration history feature by editing the system.applicationHost/configHistory <sectionSchema> element within the iis_schema.xml file located within the %WINDIR%\system32\inetsrv \config\ schema\ folder.

Although the configuration history feature doesn't protect IIS against catastrophic server failure, it does support the rollback to a previous IIS configuration if problems are encountered following changes to IIS.

Secure Socket Layer Certificates

IIS uses Secure Socket Layer (SSL) certificates to establish secure channels of communication between clients and the Web server. In the context of SharePoint, "clients" refers not only to end user Web browsers, but to Service Applications communicating in an intra- and inter-farm capacity. Clients also include any other requestors directing HTTPS traffic to the SharePoint server(s).

An SSL certificate supports secure Web server communications in two important ways. First, the SSL certificate provides the evidence a client requires to validate that the server responding to the client's Web requests has the authority to do so. Once this validation has occurred, the SSL certificate allows the Web server and client to establish a shared key that can symmetrically encrypt communications between the client and the Web server.

Although IIS uses SSL certificates directly, the certificates are neither stored within Web sites nor captured when an IIS configuration backup is performed. SSL certificates that IIS uses are stored within the server's local machine certificate store and managed through the Certificates Microsoft Management Console (MMC) snap-in, as shown in Figure 5.8.

You should back up the contents of the certificate store anytime you change it—through the addition, update, or removal of certificates. In the event of a disaster, restoring the configuration of IIS without the associated certificates it might need can adversely impact secure communications with clients. As mentioned earlier, this can include interactions between client browsers and the Web server as well as secure communications between SharePoint farm Service Applications.

Windows Registry

The Windows Registry is a repository that stores configuration data for the Windows Server 2008 operating system, its hardware, and much of the software installed on it. Although the

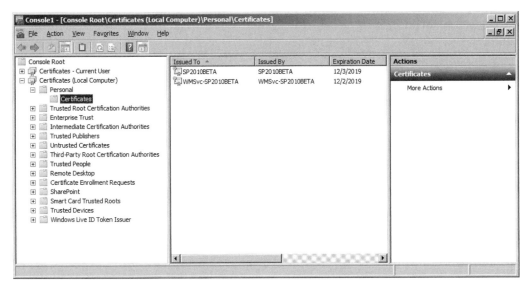

Figure 5.8   The Certificates MMC snap-in.

role of the Registry is not as all encompassing as it was prior to the advent of XML and the many configuration files that leverage it, you can still think of the Registry as the configuration database for Windows.

A SharePoint farm stores much of its configuration data within the farm configuration database, but many of the services and components that constitute the SharePoint platform use the Registry for settings and configuration storage. The SharePoint Timer service and some of its Registry-resident settings appear in Figure 5.9.

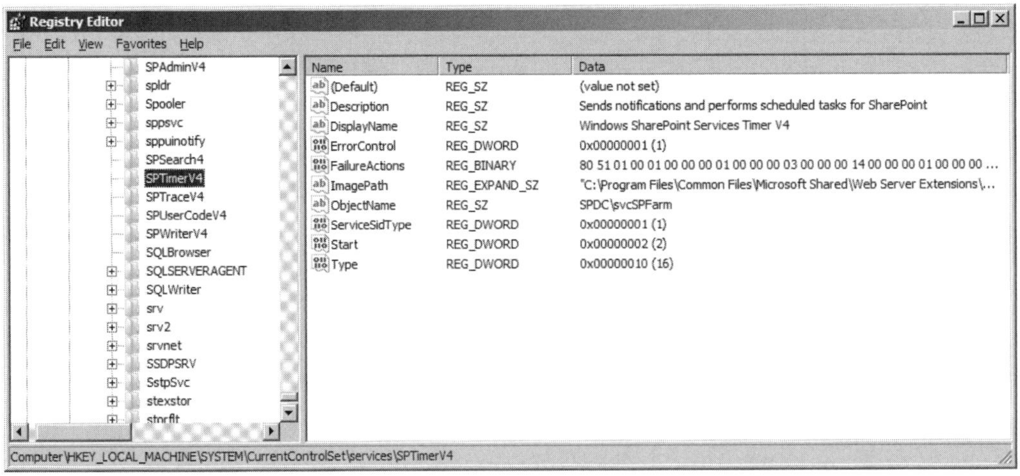

Figure 5.9   SharePoint Timer Service Registry settings.

In addition to SharePoint's services and components, many applications associated with SharePoint store settings and other configuration data within the Registry. Any Windows server backup strategy that you employ must account for the Registry and capture its contents.

Providers and Additional Dependencies

This final category of backup target is the catchall for any services, components, applications, and other software that is not covered within the SharePoint platform itself but must be addressed at the Windows server level for purposes of disaster recovery. Following are some examples of items in this category:

- Decentralized customizations that require the placement of files, settings, or other data outside of the SharePoint Root, GAC, or `Inetpub` areas

- Drivers, clients, and connection information for database technologies other than SQL Server upon which some aspect of SharePoint operations depend

- Nonstandard authentication providers that SharePoint Web applications leverage

- Custom IFilter and Protocol Handler additions to extend SharePoint search functionality

You must formulate a backup and restore strategy for each of these items, and other items within this category, on a case-by-case basis.

Before You Begin

Now that you possess an understanding of those items within the server operating system that you should back up as part of a disaster recovery plan, it is important to pause and consider how to address the backup targets this chapter has discussed. What are the tools you have at your disposal? What approach should you take? Are there any questions you should be asking yourself before diving headlong into the backup process?

At a minimum, it is important to simply recognize the need for backing up your Windows Server 2008 servers; if you don't currently have a backup plan, you should seriously consider implementing one for your entire organization's servers, not just your SharePoint resources. Without server backups of some sort, a disaster recovery plan must include provisions for the rebuilding and configuration of Windows servers. Such rebuilds are commonly a time-consuming procedure—one that can quickly limit your ability to meet aggressive recovery point objective (RPO) and recovery time objective (RTO) requirements.

The pages that follow outline how to prepare for and create a server backup using some of the tools included with Windows Server 2008, as well as how to individually back up some of the components previously mentioned that SharePoint depends on for key functionality.

Selecting a Backup Approach

After you decide to conduct backups, the next most logical question is, "Which approach is right for me?" A point this book states repeatedly is that there is no one-size-fits-all approach to disaster recovery; that notion holds true for the subtopics of server backup and restore as well.

Instead of trying to exhaustively describe every possible option for data protection and recovery available on the Windows Server platform, this chapter discusses two general approaches to data protection. Each has its strengths, weaknesses, and associated toolsets, and both play an important role in any comprehensive strategy that may be assembled to address your specific disaster recovery needs.

Full Server Backup

A full server backup is a complete backup that captures the entire contents of the server, including the operating system, installed applications, server configuration, and any data housed on the server. If any software component of the server is corrupt, damaged, or deleted, you can typically restore or recover it in some way using the full backup.

The true strength of the full server backup is not its component-level restore ability, though, but rather its support for full recovery of the server in catastrophic disaster scenarios. In the event of a complete server failure through the loss of its hard drives, for example, the full backup can restore the server's operating system, configuration, applications, and other data on new hard drives. Even if you lose the entire server, hardware and all, you can restore a full backup onto identical hardware to essentially bring the server back online.

Although this type of bare-metal backup and recovery was technically possible prior to Windows Server 2008 using the built-in Windows NTBackup and its Automated System Recovery option, it was not for the faint of heart. Backup and restore was overhauled and streamlined with the Windows Server Backup functionality in Windows Server 2008, however, and it is now much easier to perform backups, establish a backup schedule, and carry out recoveries when needed. Multiple avenues of access to the server backup functions exist, including an MMC snap-in (used individually or through Windows Server 2008's Server Manager), the wbadmin command line tool, and numerous PowerShell cmdlets.

The new Windows Server Backup includes a significant number of backup-related enhancements, but they are not the entire story. Enhancements in backup coverage are matched on the recovery side of the equation by the Windows Recovery Environment (Windows RE). If Windows Server 2008 becomes corrupt or cannot be started for some reason, the stand-alone Windows RE can be started to conduct a recovery. Based on the Windows Preinstallation Environment, Windows RE possesses its own graphical user interface (GUI) and comes with a set of recovery-oriented tools that greatly speed and simplify the process of system recovery. You can even conduct bare-metal recoveries with the aid of the Windows RE restore wizard.

Individual Component Backup

The strength of Windows Server Backup is its support for full server protection and recovery in true disaster scenarios, and this makes it the logical choice for disaster recovery scenarios where entire servers must be protected. In situations where it is desirable to protect specific subsystems and components within the overall operating system against user-induced outages, administrative misconfiguration, and other related problems, one or more specific protection strategies may be appropriate for individual components and backup targets.

The good news is that Windows Server 2008 includes a number of different tools to address each of the backup targets that have been discussed thus far:

- AppCmd.exe for IIS configuration

- InetMgr.exe and the Certificates MMC snap-in for SSL certificates

- Windows Server Backup for the GAC and other file system targets

- RegEdit.exe for the Windows Registry

The strength of a component-based backup approach is that it is typically narrower in scope and easier to use within an individual backup target. If you need to roll back a server's IIS configuration to a previous state, for instance, it is quicker, easier, and less invasive to use the AppCmd.exe utility than to execute a full server recovery.

Of course, narrow backup approaches such as these come with a number of limitations. One downside to backing up individual components is the lack of cohesion between the tools that are used. Some are driven from the command line, others have a GUI, and no two are alike. In addition, the tools themselves are part of the operating system and cannot be employed unless the server is operational. These limitations mean that per-component backups alone should generally be considered as an addition to full server backups, not as a replacement for them.

Other Options

In addition to tools that play a direct role in Windows Server backup and restore, Windows has additional features and functions that you can leverage to provide some measure of protection against outages, corruption, and other service disruptions. For example, the Shadow Copies of Shared Folders option gives you the capability to recover accidentally deleted or overwritten files within file shares. This feature, and others like it, are not strictly for disaster recovery use but can be employed as part of disaster recovery strategy in certain limited scenarios. You are encouraged to explore the Windows Server platform to learn about this feature and others like it to see if it may be useful to you in your overall disaster recovery strategy.

Although the focus of this chapter is on tools that are included with Windows Server 2008, they are by no means the only options you have available to you. Many third-party tools extend native OS functionality or present disaster recovery options that go well beyond those that are available out of the box. If you're interested in reviewing third-party backup and restore tools for Windows Server 2008 and SharePoint in general, be sure to look at Appendix B, "Third-Party Tools," found on the Cengage Learning Web site at http://www.courseptr.com/downloads.

Backup Prerequisites

Prior to attempting any form of full server or component-specific backup, you need to address a few prerequisites.

Enabling the Windows Server Backup Features

Although Windows Server Backup is included with Windows Server 2008, it is not enabled by default. Attempts to launch the Windows Server Backup application from the Administrative Tools menu or WbAdmin.exe from the command line yield the window seen in Figure 5.10.

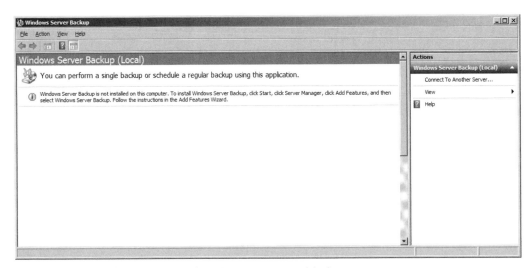

Figure 5.10 Windows Server Backup Feature not enabled.

Enabling Windows Server Backup on the server is a straightforward process:

1. Ensure that you are logged onto the server as an administrator capable of making server feature changes.

2. Click the Start button, and navigate to Administrative Tools, Server Manager, as shown in Figure 5.11.

3. After the appropriate snap-in has been added and the Server Manager has enumerated each of the roles that are active on the server, you are presented with a Roles Summary screen. In the left-hand tree view, select the Features node under the Server Manager root. Doing so displays a summary of active features on the server, as shown in Figure 5.12.

Figure 5.11 Launching the Server Manager.

4. Select the Add Features link along the right side of the Features Summary. Doing so displays the Add Features Wizard. Within the list of available features, scroll down and locate the expandable node labeled Windows Server Backup Features. Expand the node and place check boxes next to both the Windows Server Backup and Command Line Tools options, as shown in Figure 5.13, and then click the Next button.

Note: The Windows Server Backup option actually installs the MMC snap-in, services, and the WbAdmin.exe command line tool. The Command Line Tools option, on the other hand, simply enables the creation and management of backups using PowerShell. The Command Line Tools option is strictly optional but depends on the installation of the Windows Server Backup option.

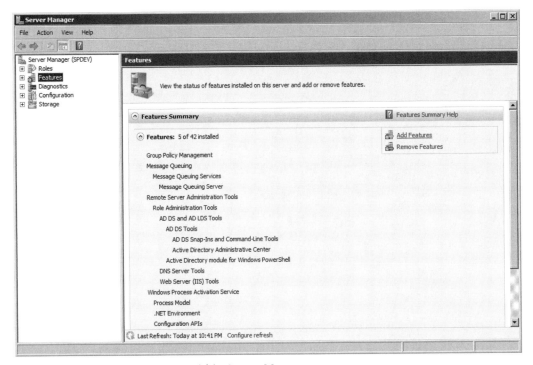

Figure 5.12   Features Summary within Server Manager.

5. A confirmation dialog appears, as shown in Figure 5.14. Click the Install button to carry out the feature installation.

6. As the installation of the feature is carried out, a progress bar keeps you apprised of the status of the install, as shown in Figure 5.15.

7. Once the Windows Server Backup Features have been installed successfully, as shown in Figure 5.16, click the Close button to finish the process and close the Add Features Wizard window. After the Add Features Wizard window has closed, you can also close the Server Manager window.

Once these steps are complete, the server is capable of carrying out full server backup and restore operations using Windows Server Backup.

Path Considerations

Enabling the Windows Server Backup Features as just described addresses prerequisite concerns for both full server backup/recovery and targeted file system backup/recovery if you employ individual component backups. For the bulk of the remaining tools that are used for individual component backup and restore operations, prerequisites do not exist. You can easily launch the tools from the Run dialog box that you open from the Start menu.

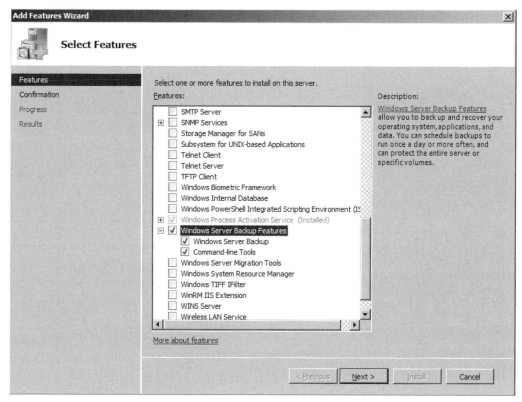

Figure 5.13   Selecting the Windows Server Backup Features.

The one tool requiring a bit of preparatory action is the AppCmd.exe tool that backs up and restores a server's IIS configuration. AppCmd.exe resides in the %WINDIR%\System32\inetsrv directory, which is not one of the default paths included within the server's Path environment variable. As a result, attempts to execute AppCmd.exe from anywhere other than the %WINDIR% \System32\inetsrv folder fail, as shown in Figure 5.17.

Note: By default, the %WINDIR% folder translates to C:\Windows in most server environments. Examples and screenshots that reference the %WINDIR% path for the remainder of this chapter assume this translation.

There are two ways to address this limitation. The obvious approach is to ensure that attempts to call AppCmd.exe from within the PowerShell and command line environments are done so with full path information. Although this certainly works, typing C:\Windows\System32\ inetsrv\AppCmd.exe every time AppCmd.exe is referenced is laborious to say the least.

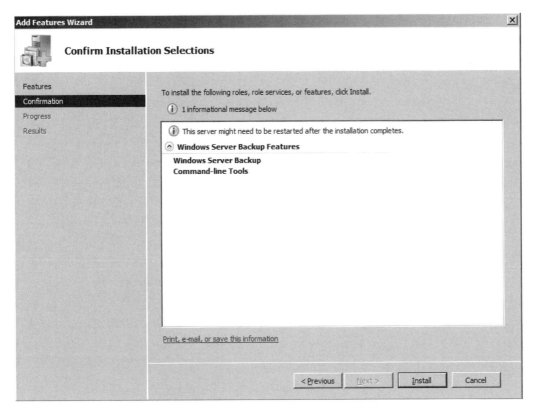

Figure 5.14   Confirming the installation.

The more viable long-term approach is to modify the server's Path environment variable to include the `C:\Windows\System32\inetsrv` path. You can easily accomplish this through a few simple steps.

1. Ensure that you are logged onto the server as an administrator capable of making server environment changes.

2. Open the Start menu and navigate to the Control Panel. Once the Control Panel has opened, select the System and Security link, and then select the System link. Doing so opens the server's System window, as shown in Figure 5.18.

3. Select the Advanced System Settings link near the top left of the System window. Once selected, the System Properties tabbed dialog box opens. Ensure that the Advanced tab is selected, as shown in Figure 5.19.

4. Click the Environment Variables button near the lower-right corner of the System Properties dialog box. Once you've done this, the Environment Variables dialog box

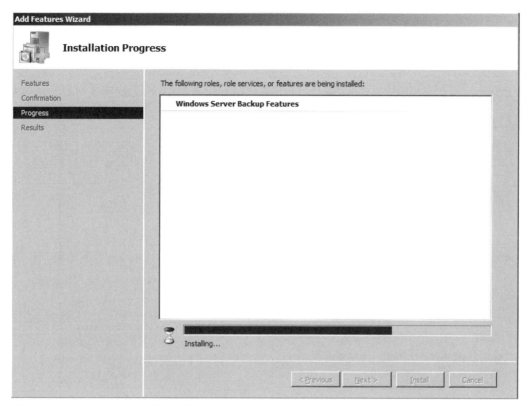

Figure 5.15   Installation of the feature.

opens. The top portion of the dialog box shows per-user environment variables, whereas the lower half of the window shows environment variables that apply system wide. Scroll through the System variables in the lower half of the window and locate the Path variable, as shown in Figure 5.20.

5.   With the Path variable selected, click the lower Edit button. Doing so opens the Edit System Variable dialog box. Enter the Variable Value text box, and scroll as far to the right (that is, the end of the line) as possible. When you reach the end of line, add a trailing semicolon (if one is not present) and the path `C:\Windows\System32\inetsrv\`, as shown in Figure 5.21.

6.   Click the OK button on the Edit System Variable dialog box, the Environment Variables dialog box, and the System Properties dialog boxes to accept changes and close them. With the dialog boxes closed, close the System window.

7.   Confirm that the Path variable changes have been accepted and incorporated into the environment. To do this, open a PowerShell window by opening the Start menu and

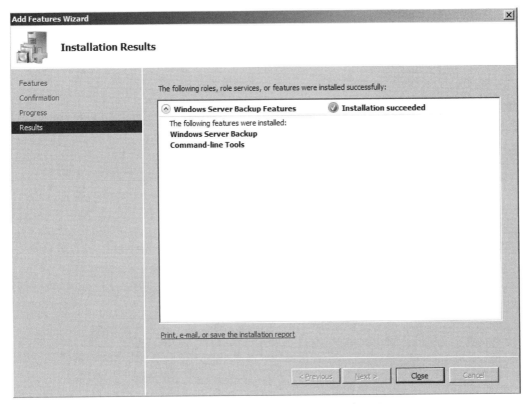

Figure 5.16   Successful installation of the Windows Server Backup Features.

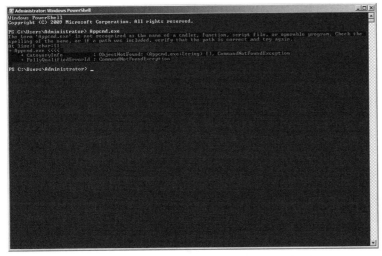

Figure 5.17   AppCmd.exe called without path qualification.

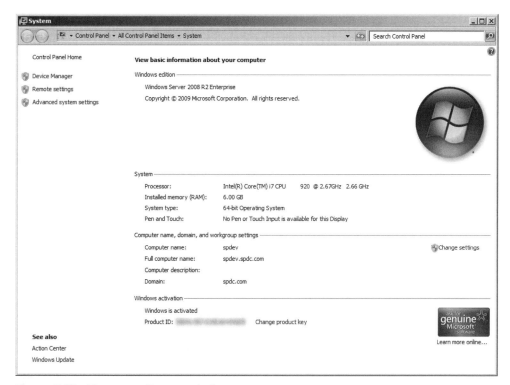

Figure 5.18   The server System window.

navigating to All Programs, Accessories, Windows PowerShell, Windows PowerShell. When the PowerShell window has opened, type AppCmd.exe and press Enter. Instead of your seeing the error that appeared previously in Figure 5.17, the AppCmd.exe application executes, and you are presented with something that appears similar to Figure 5.22.

With the environment variable change in place, you can call AppCmd.exe interactively without path information in both command line and PowerShell environments. This path support extends to PowerShell scripts and command line batch files.

Choosing a Storage Location

Where you choose to back up your data is a decision you should make with the same care and deliberation as selecting the data to back up. If you choose to store your backups on the file system of a server you are trying to protect, for instance, your ability to recover data in the event of catastrophic server failure may be severely limited unless you take additional steps to move or copy the backups to a more accessible location prior to the disaster.

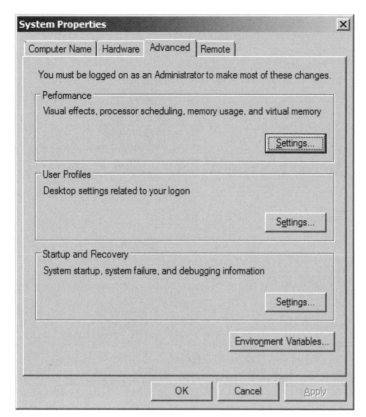

Figure 5.19 The System Properties tabbed dialog box.

Full server backups that utilize Windows Server Backup can use four different storage locations or types. Each has benefits and disadvantages associated with it:

- **Remote shared folders** can be used as a storage location for both scheduled backups and one-time backups. The use of a shared folder on another server is ideal for full server backups given that such backups are commonly used in the event of catastrophic server failure. If the server that is backed up fails, the backup is unaffected and available for recovery operations through the shared folder. The primary limitation associated with remote shared folders is that such folders can store only one backup per server. If you need more than one backup, or you must maintain a backup history in some form, remote shared folders alone may not be suitable.

- **DVD/optical/removable media** can be used as a storage location only for one-time backups of a server. Many types of optical and other removable media can also be slower, write-once in nature, or of limited capacity when compared to other disk-based media types.

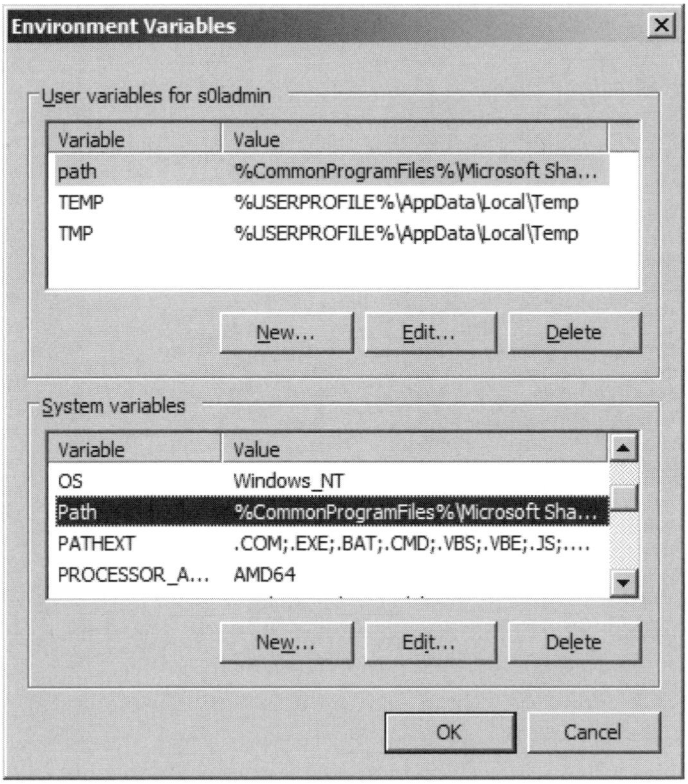

Figure 5.20 The Environment Variables dialog box.

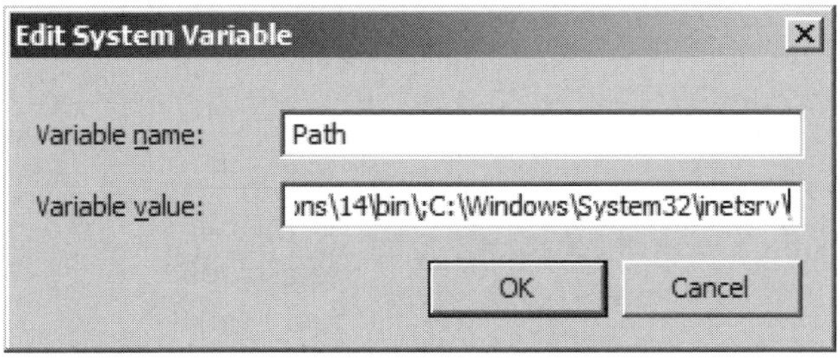

Figure 5.21 The Edit System Variable dialog box.

Considering these limitations, backups made on such media are generally impractical for disaster recovery scenarios.

■ **Internal hard disks** can be used as a storage location for both scheduled backups and one-time backups. Unlike remote shared folders, internal hard disks can house multiple backups of the server to which they are attached—ideal in scenarios where backup history or

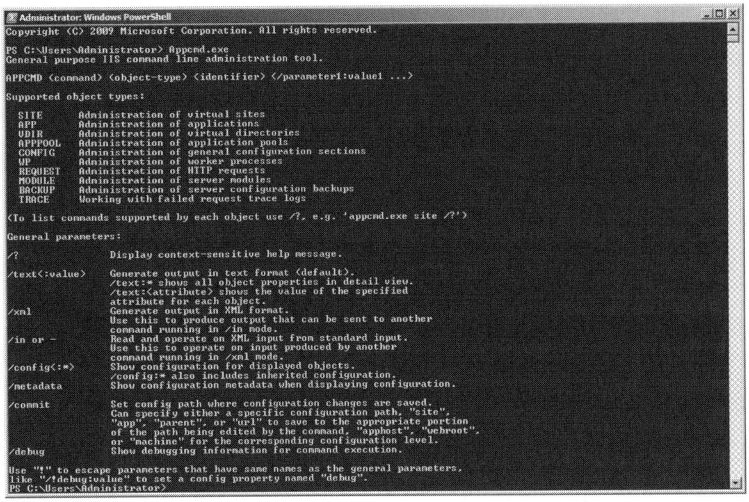

Figure 5.22 Successful execution of AppCmd.exe following Path variable modification.

versioning is desired. The single greatest shortcoming associated with internal hard disk backups is the fact that they are directly attached to the server that they are protecting. You must make provisions to relocate backup data regularly to prevent it from falling victim to disaster events impacting the housing server.

Note: Many network-attached storage (NAS) and storage area network (SAN) options allow hard disk storage that is external to the server to actually present itself as if it were internal to the server. Although normally more expensive than simple internal disks, NAS and SAN options oftentimes afford additional benefits such as data replication, additional redundancy, and versioning. These benefits can make such options extremely attractive for disaster recovery and backup purposes, provided your budget can accommodate their extra cost.

- **External hard disks** can be used as a storage location for both scheduled backups and one-time backups. External hard disks possess the same set of advantages and disadvantages as internal hard disks with one notable distinction: they can be detached and physically relocated more easily. Generally speaking, though, this only translates into a significant disaster recovery benefit if such disks are on some form of physical rotation into and out of the data center.

Tip: If internal or external hard disks are used as a backup storage location, it is highly recommended that such disks be dedicated for use solely with Windows Server Backup. Dedicating a disk for Windows Server Backup usage precludes the disk from being used for other types of file storage, but it affords several benefits relating to recoverability and input/output (I/O) performance. See the "Backing Up Your Server" section of the Windows Server Backup help file for additional details.

Despite the fact that Windows Server 2008 includes tape drive support, Windows Server Backup does not support the targeting of tape drives for backup operations. You cannot place backups on USB flash drives or pen drives, either. Backup operations must target one of the four storage types.

When weighing the decision of the type of storage to use with Windows Server Backup, be sure to consider the following points:

- Windows Server Backup cannot back up files and folders that total more than 2040GB (roughly 2TB) per volume. This limitation is based on the fact that a virtual hard drive (VHD) file is created at the backup destination for each volume that is backed up, and VHD files themselves are limited to no more than 2040GB in size.

- Because Windows Server Backup employs shadow copies for versioning, you must format backup storage locations with NTFS. You cannot use FAT32 on storage targets for backup operations.

- Microsoft recommends that storage locations that support multiple backup versions be at least 1.5 times the size of the data being backed up to enable the storage of a couple of backup versions. Additional storage naturally allows for a greater number of backup versions.

- Windows Server Backup does not support backing up data from or storing backups on Clustered Shared Volumes. Data on such volumes must be handled with something other than Windows Server Backup.

Because full server backups are typically performed to provide recovery options in the event of a catastrophic server failure or similar disaster scenario, the storage of backups on direct attached storage is contraindicated. For Windows Server Backup, this means you should strongly consider the use of remote shared folders for your server backups to guarantee that backups are not lost when a server becomes unavailable or is impacted by a disaster.

If the limitation of a single backup per server per remote folder is too constraining, a process that begins with a backup to an internal or external hard disk supports the storage of multiple backup versions per server. This increased flexibility comes with greater complexity, however. To ensure the availability of required recovery data in a disaster scenario, it is necessary to copy captured backups to a network location or replicated storage each time a backup is taken. You can perform such copies by scheduling custom scripts or using third-party tools.

The storage location equation is balanced somewhat differently for individual component backup and restore. With the notable exception of AppCmd.exe the tools that are tied to the backup and recovery of individual components have relatively similar profiles and trade-offs when it comes to addressable storage locations:

- **AppCmd.exe.** Limited to generating IIS configuration backups within the local `%WINDIR%\System32\inetsrv\backup` directory.

- **InetMgr.exe.** Can target both local and network locations for SSL certificate export and import. Supports mapped drives and Universal Naming Convention (UNC) paths.

- **Certificates MMC snap-in.** Can target both local and network locations for all certificate exports and imports. Supports mapped drives and UNC paths.

- **Windows Server Backup.** Supports local and network locations as described earlier.

- **RegEdit.exe.** Local and network locations can be targeted for the export and import of registry settings. Supports mapped drives and UNC paths.

Placement of backups on local storage is generally more convenient and quick than using network storage, but it limits recovery when the server is down. Because the majority of the backup and recovery scenarios that are tied to individual components depend on applications that are part of a functional server and file system anyway, the choice of whether to back up and restore from local storage or network storage is really one of preference. The only strong recommendation is that the backup location or locations be communicated clearly and applied consistently across servers to reduce confusion if a restoration must be performed.

Backing Up Windows Server 2008

The tools that you have available to you out of the box, the targets that are of interest, and the major considerations related to backup planning have all been discussed. It is time to integrate each of these topics and actually carry out some backup operations.

Full Server Backup

This section takes you through the process of establishing a daily full server backup schedule that targets a remote shared folder. This backup scenario is a relatively common one, and it addresses many of the basic requirements that exist for disaster recovery scenarios involving server recovery from a catastrophic event.

Before attempting the following series of steps, you must address the following prerequisites:

1. Ensure that Windows Server Backup Features are enabled, as described earlier in the section titled "Enabling the Windows Server Backup Features."

2. Make sure your account is a member of either the Administrators group or Backup Operators group on the local server being backed up.

3. Create a service account that is used when executing the backup jobs that are created. This account should also be a member of either the Administrators group or the Backup Operators group on the local server.

4. Have a remote shared folder that is online, possesses sufficient free space for your backup data, and is accessible via UNC path for reading and writing by both your account and the service account created in step 3.

5. Ensure that clustered shared volumes (distributed-access file system volumes that are new to failover clustering in Windows Server 2008 R2) are neither the source nor the destination for backup data.

If you have addressed these concerns, you are ready to proceed.

1. Log on to the server that is to be backed up using your account credentials.

2. Click the Start button and navigate to Administrative Tools, Windows Server Backup. Doing so brings up the Windows Server Backup MMC snap-in, as shown in Figure 5.23.

Figure 5.23   The Windows Server Backup MMC snap-in.

3. Click the Backup Schedule link under the Actions menu on the right side of the menu to launch the Backup Schedule Wizard. After a few moments with a progress bar, the Getting Started page of the Backup Schedule Wizard appears with some basic information about the wizard. Click the Next button to continue.

4. The Select Backup Configuration page appears. As shown in Figure 5.24, you should select the Full Server (Recommended) option to capture all data on the server within the backup.

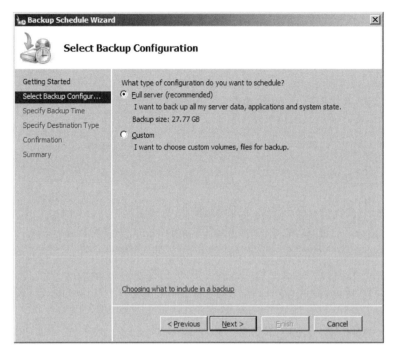

Figure 5.24   Selecting the server's entire contents for backup.

Selecting the Full Server (Recommended) option affords you a great deal of flexibility in the event of a disaster. With a full server backup, you could choose to recover the entire server, only certain volumes on the server, system state information, or any combination of these items and more. Click the Next button to continue to the next wizard page.

5.   On the Specify Backup Time page, you select the time or times at which you want Windows Server Backup to launch a backup operation. Figure 5.25 demonstrates configuring a single daily backup that is executed at 2 a.m. each day.

If Windows Server Backup represents the primary mechanism through which server data protection is achieved, RPO targets that have been established for the server environment should directly drive the frequency with which you perform backups. You can typically use a single daily backup to meet a 24-hour RPO target for server data, two evenly spaced daily backups to meet a 12-hour RPO target, three evenly spaced daily backups to meet an 8-hour RPO target, and so on.

Of course, you must balance the frequency with which you take backups against the impact of running such backups. Conducting backups during normal business hours can adversely impact server availability and network utilization, so many organizations choose to run backups during nonbusiness hours.

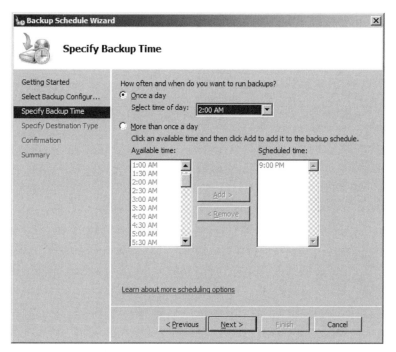

Figure 5.25 Establishing a 2 a.m. daily backup schedule.

In addition, backups do not complete instantaneously; they may take hours to run. You must consider this backup run time when determining the frequency with which to perform backups to avoid overlap between adjacent backups.

Click the Next button to continue once you have specified your backup frequency and execution time(s).

6. The Specify Destination Type page appears and prompts you to select the storage location type used to store your backups. Because this walk-through places backups on a shared network folder, the Back Up to a Shared Network Folder option is selected, as shown in Figure 5.26.

Note: As shown in Figure 5.26, the wizard recommends that a dedicated hard disk, either internal or external, be utilized as a storage location for backups. Dedicating a disk permits multiple backup versions and removes the dependency of a functioning network, but it does not offer a built-in mechanism for offloading or migrating backup data in the event of a catastrophic server failure. If you elect to take the dedicated disk route, your implementation should also include a custom script or migration strategy to transfer backups to a safe location in accordance with your disaster recovery strategy and larger business continuity plan (BCP).

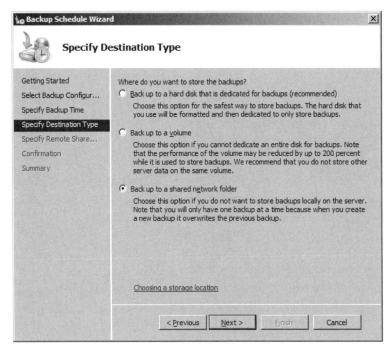

Figure 5.26   Selecting a shared network folder for backups.

7.   Once you have specified the destination type, click the Next button to continue. A message box appears to warn you that each backup to a remote shared folder erases any that were previously present. Click the OK button to continue.

8.   The Specify Remote Shared Folder page appears and prompts you for the UNC path of the remote shared folder to create backups. It is here that you supply the predetermined file share location, as shown in Figure 5.27.

Tip: Because the backup is performed to a remote share, the only Access Control option is Inherit. This means that anyone with access to the file share where the backup data is written can see the data, work with it, and even delete it. Therefore, it is strongly recommended that the backup destination location be locked down to just a select group of administrators and the service account under which the backup jobs are executed.

---

9.   Once you have specified the backup location, click the Next button. The Register Backup Schedule dialog box appears to prompt you for the credentials under which the backup jobs should be run. It is here that the service account credentials, which were created in prerequisite step 3, are supplied.

Once you have supplied the backup service account credentials, click the OK button to continue.

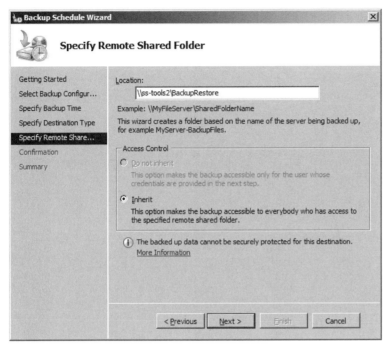

Figure 5.27   Specifying the backup location.

10.   The Confirmation page of the wizard appears, as seen in Figure 5.28. Confirm that the details are correct, and click the Finish button.

11.   The Summary page appears, and the wizard establishes and schedules a recurring backup job according to the parameters supplied. When it has finished its actions, click the Close button to close the wizard.

12.   Once you have closed the wizard, the Windows Server Backup snap-in updates to reflect that a backup schedule has been created, as shown in Figure 5.29. Note the addition of the Scheduled Backup pane at the bottom of the main window, as well as the change in status under the Next Backup area in the middle of the window.

The completion of step 12 means that your server has been set up to run daily backups on the schedule specified. An actual backup has not yet been run, though. Ideally, you should validate that a backup can be run given all the configuration data that was just supplied to create the scheduled task.

With a scheduled backup, it is a simple matter to go through the Backup Once Wizard within the Windows Server Backup snap-in, indicate that you want to run a single backup using the parameters you just supplied through the Backup Schedule Wizard (as shown if Figure 5.30), and execute a one-time backup task to perform validation by clicking the Backup button.

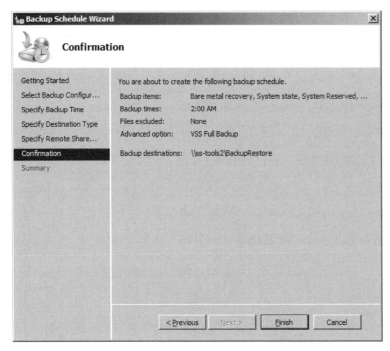

Figure 5.28 Confirming the backup schedule parameters.

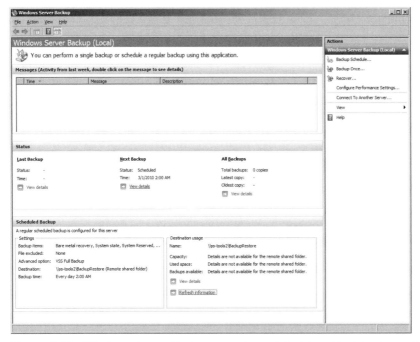

Figure 5.29 Windows Server Backup snap-in updated to reflect backup schedule.

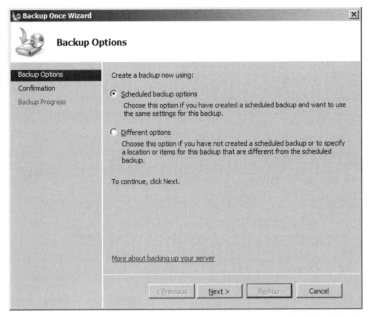

Figure 5.30   Launching a one-time backup using scheduled backup options.

After you have started the one-time backup, the display of the Backup Once Wizard changes to provide a detailed status for monitoring the backup operation, as shown in Figure 5.31.

You can close the Backup Once Wizard after the backup is complete or at any point prior to completion. If you close the wizard prior to backup completion, the backup simply continues to run in the background until it is complete.

Independently of the Backup Once Wizard, the Messages window within the Windows Server Backup snap-in updates to reflect both the backup job's progress and its ultimate success or failure. The Status displays below the Messages window also change to incorporate the status of the most recently attempted backup operation.

Assuming the backup job completes successfully, you have the data needed to fully recover the server in the event of a catastrophic failure.

Individual Component Backup

Whereas full server backups capture the contents of an entire server to provide recovery options in the event of a catastrophic failure, the scope and benefits of an individual component backup are more specific in nature. These backups commonly provide some form of rollback support and guard against unwanted configuration changes should something go awry during an operation such as an upgrade, a patch cycle, or the rollout of new solution packages to the farm.

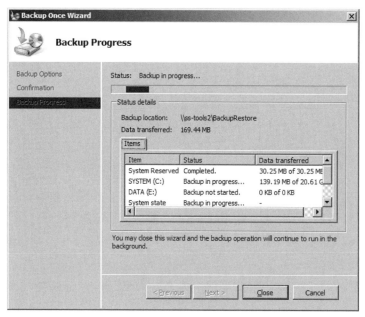

Figure 5.31   Monitoring the backup job from the Backup Once Wizard.

Individual component backups, and their associated recovery operations, usually require that the server already be operational and in good general health. This precondition is assumed for each of the backup procedures that follow.

Files and File Folders

Backing up files and folders on the server entails using the Windows Server Backup snap-in and a process that is similar to the one described previously for a full server backup. The prerequisites for a full server backup apply here, as well, but with one notable exception: no service account is needed, as described in prerequisite 3.

Note: Although this specific walk-through details a one-time backup of files and folders on the server, it is certainly possible to establish a scheduled backup for these items. Anytime a scheduled backup is established, it is considered a best practice to run the scheduled job within the context of a service account. For one-time backups, however, backup operations are conducted directly from the context of your user account.

Once you have addressed all prerequisites, you are ready to proceed.

1.   Log on to the server that is to be backed up using your account credentials.

2. Click the Start button and navigate to Administrative Tools, Windows Server Backup. Doing so brings up the Windows Server Backup MMC snap-in, as shown previously in Figure 5.23.

3. Click the Backup Once link under the Actions menu on the right side of the menu to launch the Backup Schedule Wizard. After a few moments with a progress bar, the Getting Started page of the Backup Schedule Wizard appears with some basic information about the wizard. Click the Next button to continue.

4. The Backup Once Wizard appears as shown in Figure 5.30. If one or more scheduled backup jobs exist, the Scheduled backup options selection is available. The selection of interest for this exercise, however, is the Different Options selection. Choose this option button and click the Next button to continue.

5. You are prompted to select either a Full Server or a Custom backup, as shown in Figure 5.32. Select the Custom option to specify a subset of folders and files, and then click the Next button to continue.

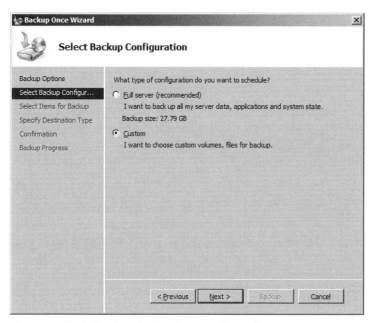

Figure 5.32   Selecting the backup configuration.

6. The Select Items for Backup page appears as shown in Figure 5.33. It is here that files and folders are selected as backup targets. Initially, no files and folders are selected. Click the Add Items button to begin the selection process.

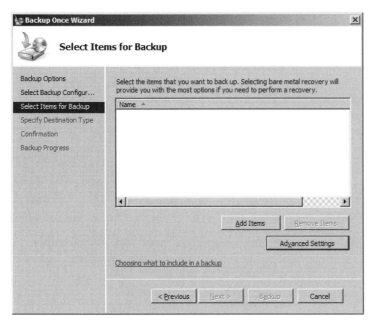

Figure 5.33   Items that are selected for backup.

Note: The Advanced Settings button affords you some additional control over the backup operation, including the option to specify backup exclusions and the ability to indicate how application log files should be handled by the Volume Shadow Copy Service (VSS) during the backup operation. The default settings for these options are sufficient for one-time backups, but investigate the Advanced Settings if you desire greater control for the areas mentioned.

7. The Select Items dialog box appears, as shown in Figure 5.34. It is here that you can specify files, folders, system state, and additional backup targets. In this example, all the files in the GAC (at `C:\Windows\assembly`) are selected for a one-time backup. Once the GAC has been selected, the OK button is clicked to continue.

8. The Select Items dialog box closes, and the Select Items for Backup page (Figure 5.33) becomes active again. At this point, the list of items for backup now includes the `C:\Windows\assembly` folder. Click the Next button to continue.

9. You are prompted to select one of the local drives or a remote shared folder as destination for the backup, as shown in Figure 5.35. Select the Remote Shared Folder option, and click the Next button to continue.

10. The Specify Remote Folder dialog box appears. It is here that a network share is specified as a destination for the backup. In addition to selecting a remote folder, you must

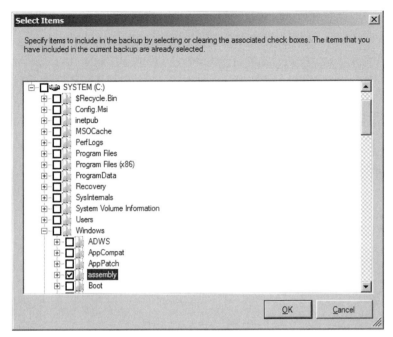

Figure 5.34   Selecting items to be backed up.

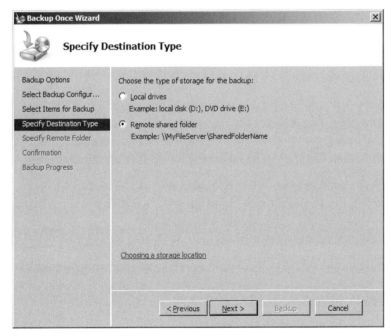

Figure 5.35   Specifying the backup destination type.

specify one of two Access control options. The Inherit option is selected by default, and it leaves the permissions of the remote share and created subfolders intact during the backup. If the Do Not Inherit option is selected, Windows Server Backup attempts to restrict access to the WindowsImageBackup subfolder that is created within the specified location to a single user account. For the purposes of this exercise, the default Inherit option is selected, along with the remote share (as shown in Figure 5.36). Click the Next button to continue.

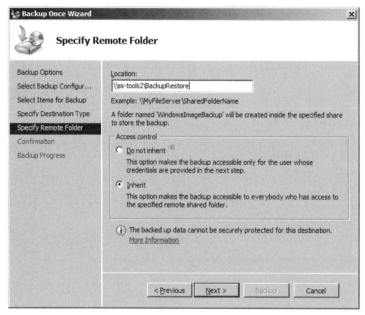

Figure 5.36   Specifying the remote share for backup.

11.   If the remote share already contains a backup for the current server, either scheduled or one-time, a warning dialog box appears to inform you that the backup operation that is about to be performed will overwrite the existing backup. Click the OK button to continue.

12.   The Confirmation page of the Backup Once Wizard appears, as shown in Figure 5.37. Validate the selection you have made, and click the Backup button to begin the backup process.

13.   A Backup Progress dialog box similar to the one shown in Figure 5.31 appears. As the backup operation runs, the progress being made is reflected on the form. You can close the dialog box at any time during the actual backup operation, or you can wait until the backup has completed in its entirety before closing it. If the dialog box is closed prior to the completion of the backup operation, the backup continues in the background until it completes.

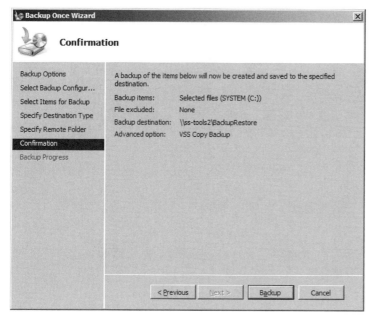

Figure 5.37   Confirmation of backup selections.

IIS Configuration

Creating a backup of the IIS7 configuration files is a relatively straightforward affair provided the Path environment variable has been updated to include the %WINDIR%\System32\inetsrv path, as described earlier in "Path Considerations" under the "Backup Prerequisites" section.

1. Open a PowerShell window by opening the Start menu and navigating to All Programs, Accessories, Windows PowerShell, Windows PowerShell.

2. Type appcmd.exe add backup "<name>", where <name> is replaced by the name you want to give the backup file set. After you have entered the full command, press the Enter key to execute the backup.

3. When the backup is complete, you are presented with a status message similar to the one shown in Figure 5.38.

4. Close the PowerShell window by typing exit and pressing the Enter key.

The backup that you have created can be left in place or moved to an alternate location as needed. By default, the backup is in a directory within the %WINDIR%\System32\inetsrv \backup folder that matches the name you specified in step 2. Figure 5.39 demonstrates this for the example shown earlier.

Figure 5.38 Successful execution of an IIS configuration backup.

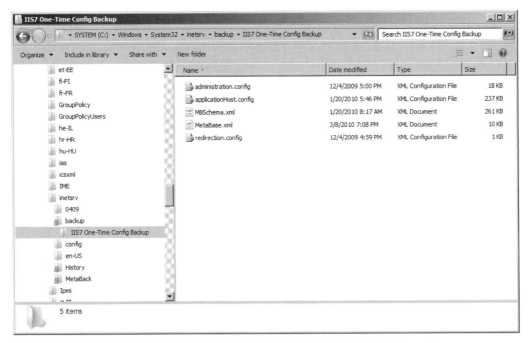

Figure 5.39 IIS7 configuration backup folder and contents.

Note: Microsoft's TechNet documentation for SharePoint 2010 recommends against using "metabase backup" to protect IIS settings. Instead, Microsoft recommends manual documentation of all IIS configuration settings or the use of a tool (such as Microsoft System Center Configuration Manager) to automate the process. Because IIS7's configuration backup files are XML, they are still largely human-readable—meaning that even if you elect not to use them for direct restore purposes, you can still examine them to extract a significant quantity of configuration information. At the end of the day, simply make sure you have a plan in place for how you intend to use your backup files, and test that plan regularly.

SSL Certificates

SSL certificates are commonly backed up in visual fashion using either the Certificates MMC snap-in or the IIS Manager snap-in. The example that follows demonstrates the latter approach, although both lead to the same endpoint.

1. Start the Internet Services Manager by opening the Start menu and navigating to Administrative Tools, Internet Information Services (IIS) Manager.

2. When the IIS Manager starts, locate the `Start Page` root node in the Connections Tree-View control on the left side of the snap-in. Select the node representing the current server that appears just below the Start Page node. In the example shown in Figure 5.40, the current server is SPDEV.

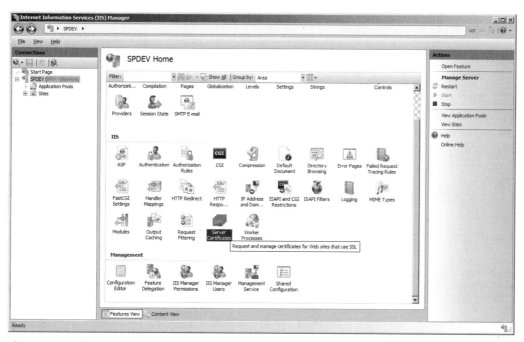

Figure 5.40   The IIS Manager snap-in.

3. When the current server node is selected, the central task pane in the snap-in is populated with various ASP.NET, IIS, and Management Features. Locate the Server Certificates Feature under those listed for IIS, and double-click it.

4. The central task pane shifts to display Server Certificates, as shown in Figure 5.41. Each line in the central task pane represents an SSL certificate that is installed and available for use by IIS7. Select the one that you want to back up by clicking on it, and then click the Export link that appears under Actions on the right side of the snap-in.

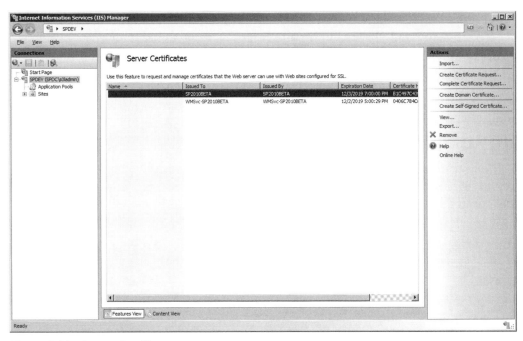

Figure 5.41 Server Certificates.

5.   The Export Certificate dialog box appears, as shown in Figure 5.42, and you are prompted to select a file name and a password for the exported certificate. Specify these values, and then click the OK button to execute the export.

Figure 5.42 Specifying the certificate export parameters.

Note: You are prompted for a password, because the certificate you select is exported with its private key data. Any server possessing the private key for a certificate may act and respond as the server named by the certificate, so naturally it is important that any certificate export that contains private key data is protected.

6. The export executes and completes without confirmation. To verify that the export succeeds, browse to the location you selected for your export, and verify that the appropriate certificate export file is present, as shown in Figure 5.43.

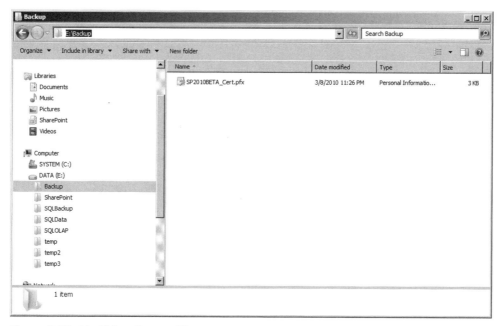

Figure 5.43 Verifying the certificate export.

Windows Registry

You accomplish exports of the Windows Registry using the Registry Editor tool. This example exports the HKEY_LOCAL_MACHINE branch of the Registry to the local file system.

1. Open the RegEdit.exe tool by clicking Start and selecting Run. When the Run dialog opens, type regedit.exe and click the OK button.

2. The Registry Editor tool appears, as shown in Figure 5.44. Locate the HKEY_LOCAL_ MACHINE node under the Computer root node in the left TreeView control, and select it by clicking on it.

Figure 5.44   The Registry Editor tool.

3.   Click on the File menu at the top of the Registry Editor window and select the Export option. A dialog box pops up, as shown in Figure 5.45.

Figure 5.45   Specifying export information for the selected Registry branch.

4. Specify path and file name information for the export file, and click the Save button. The Registry Editor carries out the requested export without confirmation or an indication of completion. To verify that the export was successful, browse to the specified destination, as demonstrated in Figure 5.46.

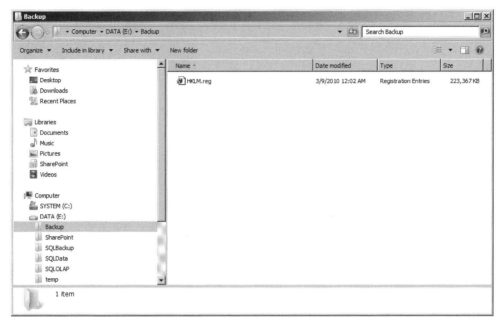

Figure 5.46 Successful Registry export.

Restoring Windows Server 2008

When questioned, most administrators indicate that they perform some type of server backup on a regular basis. When that same group of administrators is asked if they frequently test their recovery operations for the systems being backed up, the percentage of those responding "yes" tends to drop to an alarmingly low level.

Simply put, it is not enough to execute backups and hope that recovery proceeds without issue in the event of a disaster. The time to discover that recovery is not possible or that a backup strategy is insufficient is not when you need recovery. Test recovery operations regularly to ensure that they work when needed.

Full Server Recovery

This exercise assumes the catastrophic loss of the server that was fully backed up in the previous "Full Server Backup" section. This section walks you through the recovery of that server using the backup that was created.

First, a word of caution: the Windows RE greatly simplifies the process of bringing back a server following catastrophic failure, but full server recovery is an inexact science. Oftentimes there are hardware differences between the server that was backed up and the server upon which recovery is being attempted. For example, hard drive counts and capacities may vary, RAID controllers may differ, network cards may be different, and more. Potential hardware differences and other variations may require you to adapt the full recovery process described next. At a minimum, be sure to practice the recovery of your servers at regular intervals and accurately document the details of the restoration process.

Before you attempt any sort of full server recovery, you must address a number of prerequisites:

1. You must have a test server with characteristics that are "very similar" to the server that was fully backed up. Ideally, the test server should have hardware that is identical to the server that was backed up. Some differences can be tolerated fairly well, such as the test server possessing hard drives of greater capacity than those in the source (backup) server. Other differences are not tolerated at all, such as trying to restore an x64-based backup to x86-only hardware. As a rule of thumb, the greater the number and type of differences between the source server and the backup server, the greater the likelihood of encountering problems during recovery.

Tip: Virtual machines can be used to great effect when testing recovery plans. Windows Server 2008 includes Hyper-V for virtualization. If you are not familiar with Hyper-V, consider checking it out.

---

2. You must possess account credentials that can be used to access the remote shared folder where the target server backup is stored.

3. You must have access to a Windows Server 2008 installation DVD, a bootable installation thumb drive, or some other bootable mechanism that affords you access to the Windows RE. If you are attempting to recover an x64 environment, you must use the x64 version of the Windows RE. By the same token, x86 recoveries require the x86 Windows RE.

4. Ensure that clustered shared volumes are neither the source nor the destination for any backup data.

If you have addressed these concerns, you are ready to proceed with recovery.

1. Start your server and boot from the media containing the Windows RE. Your server should automatically go into the Windows Is Loading Files screen with a progress bar at the bottom shortly after booting. If this does not occur, or the server attempts to boot from another source (such as a residual hard drive image), you may need to access the one-time boot menu option that is commonly available on servers. Using such a boot menu allows you to specify the server's boot location, be it a DVD, a USB location, or something else.

2. After the server has booted from the desired media, you are presented with the Install Windows screen. Ensure that you select the desired installation language, time and currency formats, and input method before clicking the Next button to continue.

3. You are presented with the window shown in Figure 5.47. Although the Install Now option is front and center in the window, the area of interest is in the lower-left portion of the window. Click on the Repair Your Computer link to continue.

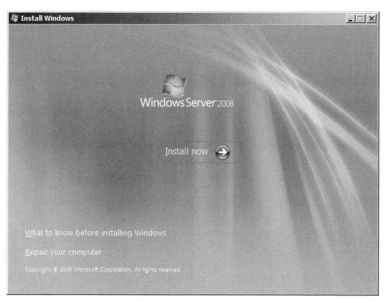

Figure 5.47   The Install Windows screen.

4. You are presented with the System Recovery Options dialog box shown in Figure 5.48. Ensure that the Restore Your Computer Using a System Image That You Created Earlier option is selected, and click the Next button to continue.

5. Neither an internal nor external hard drive containing a system image is attached to the server, so you are warned that a system image cannot be found on the computer. Click the Cancel button to dismiss the dialog box.

6. Because a system image isn't available locally, the only option that is available on the Re-Image Your Computer dialog box (shown in Figure 5.49) is Select a System Image. Click the Next button to continue.

7. You are prompted to select the location of the backup you want to restore, as shown in Figure 5.50. Because you need to point the Windows RE at the remote share housing your system image, you need to click the Advanced button in the lower-left portion of the screen to guide the tool to a network-based image.

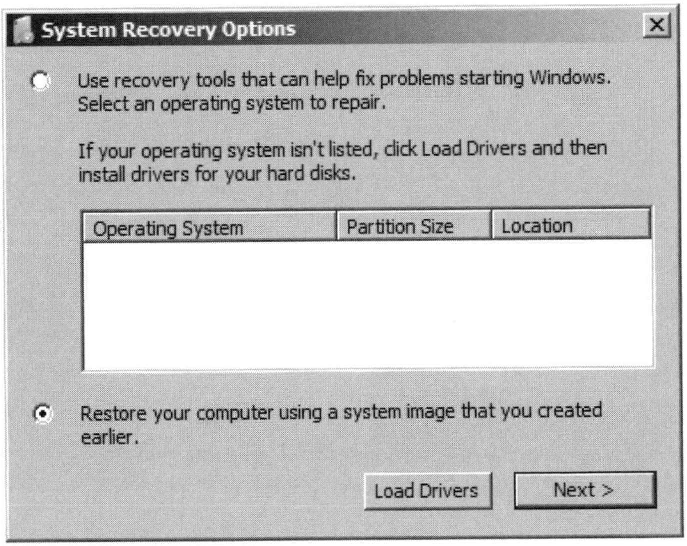

Figure 5.48   System Recovery Options.

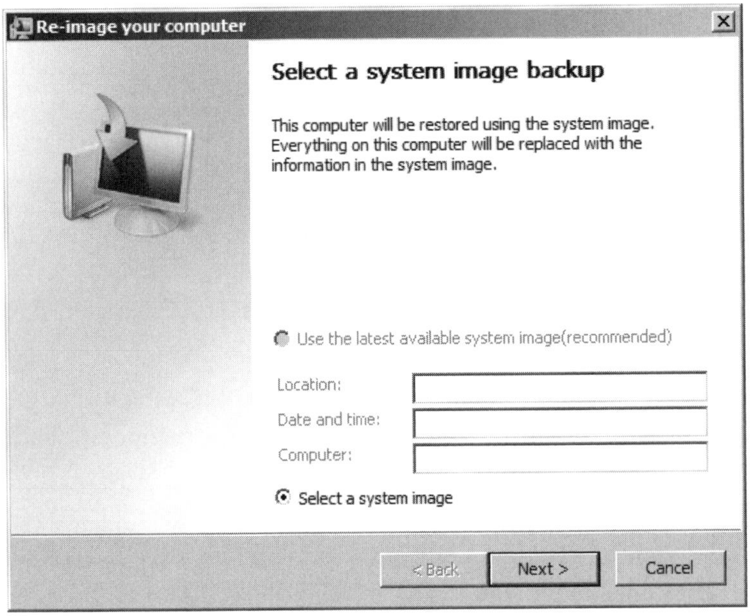

Figure 5.49   The Re-Image Your Computer dialog box.

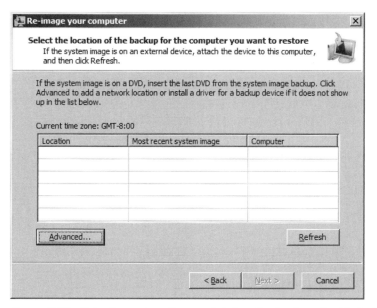

Figure 5.50   Selecting a location containing the backup that is to be restored.

8. The dialog box shown in Figure 5.51 appears. Select the Search for a System Image on the Network option to continue.

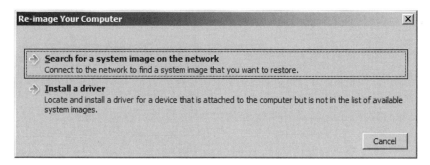

Figure 5.51   Specifying a system image on the network.

Note: Although the Windows RE contains drivers for a significant number of network adapters, you may discover that you are unable to browse or specify a network location without first loading drivers for your server's specific adapter or adapters. If this is the case, select the Install a Driver option and follow the instructions to load drivers for your network adapter or adapters before attempting to proceed.

---

9. You are warned that connecting to a network may leave your server vulnerable, and you are asked to confirm the connection. Click the Yes button to confirm and continue.

10. You are prompted to specify the network location where the system image that is used for restoration resides. As shown in Figure 5.52, specify the UNC path to the image that was previously created during the full server backup process, and click the OK button to continue.

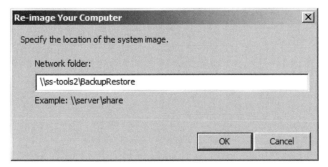

Figure 5.52 Supplying the UNC path to the recovery image.

11. You are prompted to supply the credentials of the account you want to use when accessing the remote share specified in the previous step. Supply the username and password desired, ensuring that you include a domain qualifier (in the form of *domain\username* or *username@domain*) for the username if needed. Once you have supplied the credentials, click the OK button to continue.

12. The backup location dialog box reappears, as shown in Figure 5.53. Provided the network location specified previously in step 10 contained a recognizable system image, the grid in the dialog box now contains a populated row. Ensure that the row is selected, and click the Next button to continue.

13. You are prompted to select the date and time of the system image you want to restore. Because a remote shared folder can house only a single image per server, just one entry is available for selection, as shown in Figure 5.54. Select it and click the Next button to continue.

14. The restore options dialog appears, as shown in Figure 5.55. For a server with unformatted hard disks or with hard disks that do not have system volume information matching the system image that is being restored, the Format and Repartition Disks option is selected and grayed out as shown. Because a full recovery is being performed and it is desirable to restore all data volumes in addition to the system drives, ensure that the Only Restore System Drives check box remains unchecked. Click the Next button to continue.

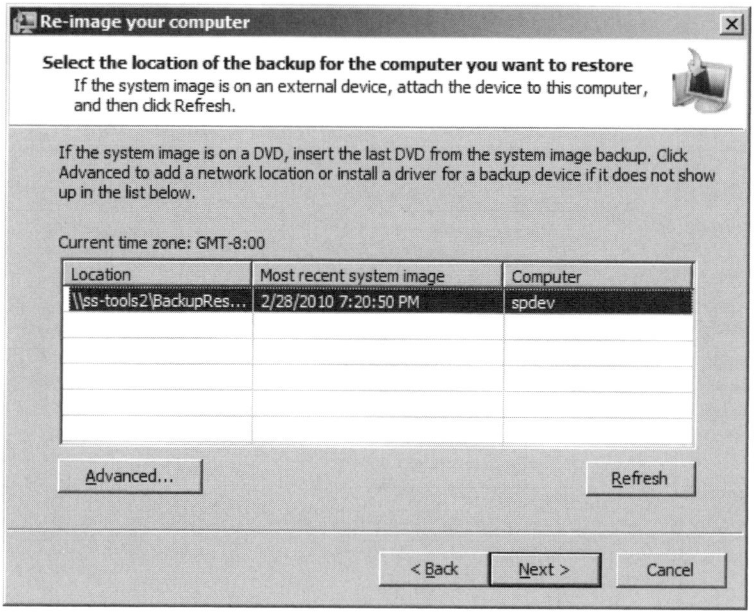

Figure 5.53   Backup image available for recovery.

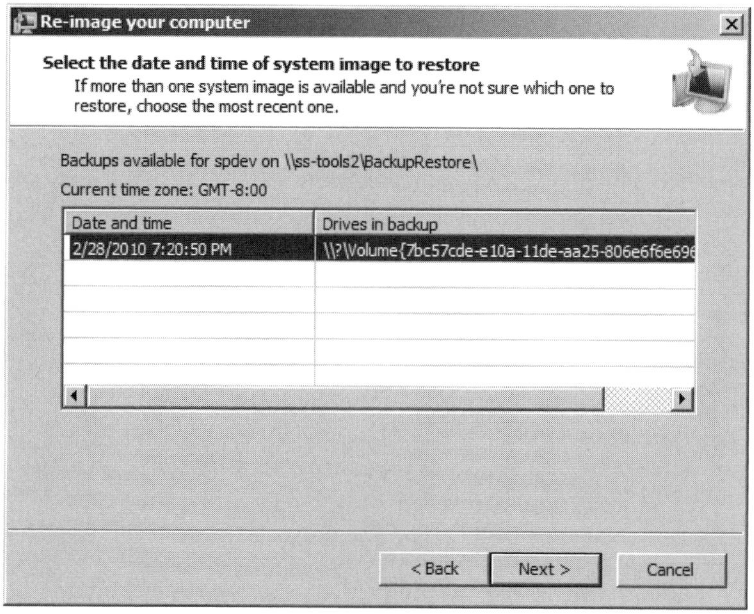

Figure 5.54   Selecting the available system image.

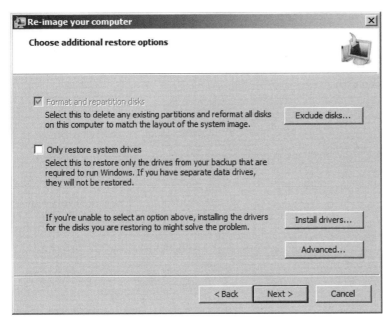

Figure 5.55 Choosing additional restore options.

Note: Similar to step 8, there is a possibility that you may have to load additional drivers for Windows RE to see all the hard drives attached to your system. If this is the case, click the Install Drivers button, and follow the instructions presented before attempting to advance from the Choose Additional Restore Options dialog box.

---

15.   A basic confirmation dialog box appears so that you can verify your recovery selections. Click the Finish button to continue with the recovery.

16.   A message box pops up to warn you of the impending hard drive reformatting. Click the Yes button to acknowledge the warning and continue.

17.   The recovery process begins, and a message box tracking the progress of the restoration appears, as shown in Figure 5.56. As stated in the message box, the recovery operation may take anywhere from a few minutes to a few hours. The amount of time taken depends on the amount of data to be restored, the speed of your network connection, the speed of your server's hard drives, and a number of other factors.

18.   Once the recovery operation has completed, the restart dialog box appears, as shown in Figure 5.57. If you take no action, the server automatically restarts after a minute and boots into the restored operating system.

As stated earlier, full server recovery is an inexact science. If the recovery operation fails the first time for unforeseen reasons, consider trying it again with slightly different recovery parameters.

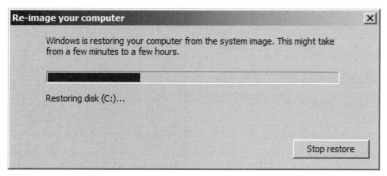

Figure 5.56   Tracking the progress of the recovery.

Figure 5.57   Restarting the server following recovery.

Sometimes reformatting hard drives, restoring only the system drive on the first pass, or perhaps excluding an extra disk from within the restore options dialog box can make the difference between a restoration error and a successful recovery operation.

Restoring Individual Components

Each of the recovery activities described here assumes that you have completed its corresponding backup activity. For example, the IIS Configuration restore utilizes the folder of files created in the IIS Configuration individual component backup exercise.

Files and File Folders

Restoring files and folders on the server entails using the Windows Server Backup snap-in and a process that is similar to the one described previously for a full server recovery. The prerequisites for a full server recovery apply here; you must also ensure that your account has read access to the backup files you intend to restore.

Once all prerequisites have been addressed, you are ready to proceed.

1.   Log on to the server that you intend to restore files to using your account credentials.

2. Click the Start button and navigate to Administrative Tools, Windows Server Backup. Doing so brings up the Windows Server Backup MMC snap-in, as shown previously in Figure 5.23.

3. Click the Recover link under the Actions menu on the right side of the menu to launch the Recovery Wizard. After a few moments with a progress bar, the Getting Started page of the Recovery Wizard appears with some basic information about the wizard. You are also prompted to indicate whether your backup files are stored on the server or in another location. Because the backup is stored on a remote share, select the second option, as shown in Figure 5.58, and then click the Next button to continue.

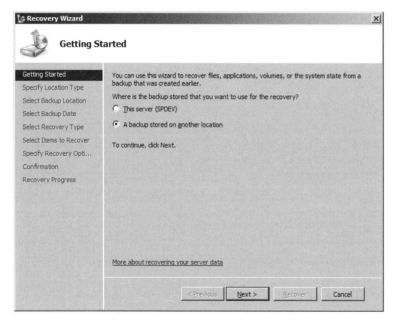

Figure 5.58 Specifying a backup storage location for restore operations.

4. The Specify Location Type page of the wizard appears, and you are prompted to indicate whether the target backup is stored on a local drive (internal or external) or a remote share. Select the Remote Shared Folder option, as shown in Figure 5.59, and click the Next button to continue.

5. You are prompted to select the remote share where the backup file set is located. Specify the UNC path to the backup share, as shown in Figure 5.60, and click the Next button to continue.

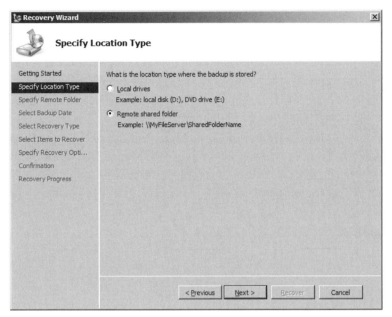

Figure 5.59   Selecting the backup location type.

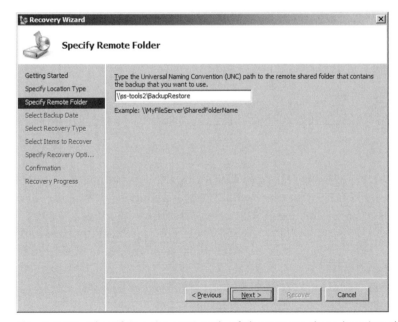

Figure 5.60   Identifying the UNC path of the remote share housing the backup files.

Note: If you are presented with a dialog box prompting you to specify the credentials of a user who has read access to the network share, it means that your account doesn't possess the rights needed to access the location. Either supply the credentials of an account that does have access to the location, or verify that you have specified the proper remote share information.

6. You are prompted to select the date and time of the backup set that will be used for restore operations, as shown in Figure 5.61. Because remote shares can be used only to store a single backup set per server, only a single date and time will be available for selection. Click the Next button to continue.

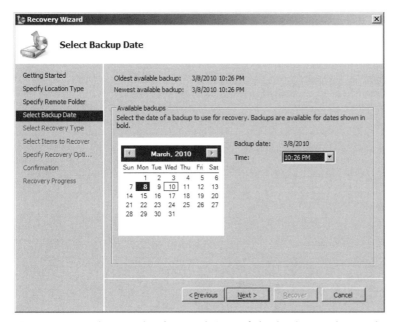

Figure 5.61   Selecting the date and time of the backup to be used.

7. The Select Recovery Type page of the Recovery Wizard appears, as shown in Figure 5.62, and you are presented with the option of restoring either specific files and folders or an entire volume. The remaining two options are grayed out because application and system state information was not captured by the original backup operation. Because only the GAC was backed up, select the first option (Files and Folders), and click the Next button to continue.

Note: The option to restore an entire volume is somewhat deceptive in the case of the backup that was performed. If this option is selected, you are eventually told that only a subset of files had been backed up and that only they can be restored. The restore operation obviously cannot recover files that were not part of the original backup.

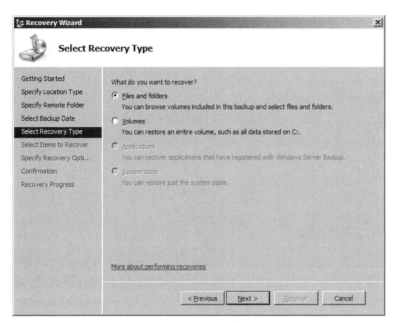

Figure 5.62   Specifying the type of recovery to perform.

8. On the Select Items to Recover page, you are given the option to specify the files and folders you want to restore during the recovery operation. You select a folder under the Available Items pane on the left, and that folder and all its files and subfolders are selected for recovery on the right. In the case of Figure 5.63, you can see that three different folders were captured during the backup operation and are selected for recovery.

Note: "Wait a minute," you might be saying, "Only the GAC was selected during the backup operation. Why do I see additional folders besides the C:\Windows\assembly folder listed for possible recovery?" Good question! The GAC is actually a special folder, and it operates somewhat similarly to the new libraries that are available in Windows Server 2008 R2 and Windows 7. When you are looking at the GAC within Windows Explorer, you are actually looking at a listing of .NET assemblies, native images, policy files, and other elements that exist in a variety of different locations within the file system. Many of the items are located at the C:\Windows\assembly path as you would expect, but some of the listed items are located in application directories and other locations within the Windows folder. While backing up the GAC, Windows Server Backup was "smart" enough to pull in all the files that were reflected through the GAC. Pretty neat, huh?

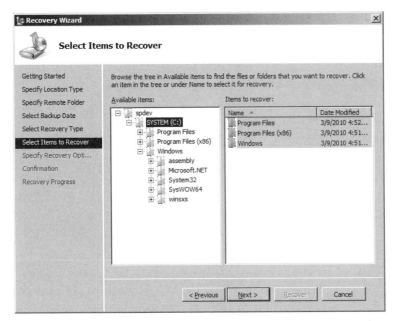

Figure 5.63 Selecting the files and folders that will be recovered.

9. You are prompted to indicate how the recovery should proceed on the Specify Recovery Options page, as shown in Figure 5.64. When recovering individual files and folders, you do not have the option to automatically restore to the original location from which

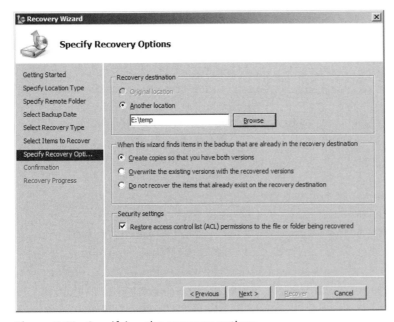

Figure 5.64 Specifying the recovery options.

the files and folders were captured. You need to specify the actual path where restored folders and files are placed.

Tip: Although you cannot choose to automatically have the Recovery Wizard place the restored files back in their original locations, there is generally no barrier to using the Browse button to manually select the appropriate top-level folder to force the files back to their original locations. This generally works without issue, but exercise care for system directories and some application directories where some target files may be locked or nonwritable.

You also have control over how potential file collisions are handled and whether file and folder permissions are applied from the original backup location or inherited from the recovery destination.

10.   Before the recovery begins, you are asked to review the recovery selections you have made on the Confirmation page, as shown on Figure 5.65. When you are satisfied with the selections, click the Next button to begin the recovery.

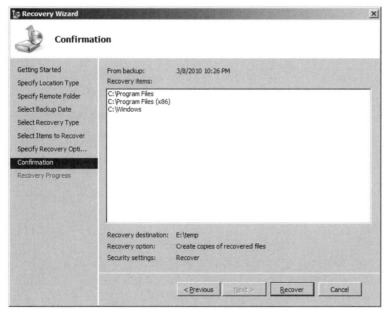

Figure 5.65   Confirming the recovery selections.

11.   The page changes to allow you to monitor the progress of the recovery operation, as shown in Figure 5.66. You can close this wizard at any time prior to or after the

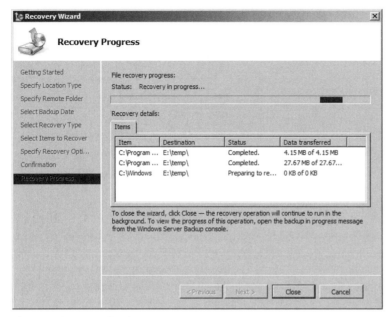

Figure 5.66   Monitoring recovery progress.

completion of the recovery by clicking the Close button. If the Recovery Wizard is closed prior to completion, the recovery continues in the background.

12.   Upon completion of the restore operation, the files and folders that were selected for recovery are found under the E:\temp path, as specified in step 9. As shown in Figure 5.67, the folder structure under E:\temp mirrors the folder structure of the GAC and the referenced locations that were captured as part of the original backup.

With files recovered in E:\temp, you are free to copy them to their original locations on the server or use them elsewhere as needed.

IIS Configuration

Restoration of a previous set of IIS configuration files is incredibly easy as long as the desired backup folder is placed in the %WINDIR%\System32\inetsrv\backup folder—either manually or through the action of the IIS configuration backup described earlier and shown in Figure 5.39.

If the backup is present in the aforementioned folder, use the following steps to restore it:

1.   Open a PowerShell window by opening the Start menu and navigating to All Programs, Accessories, Windows PowerShell, Windows PowerShell.

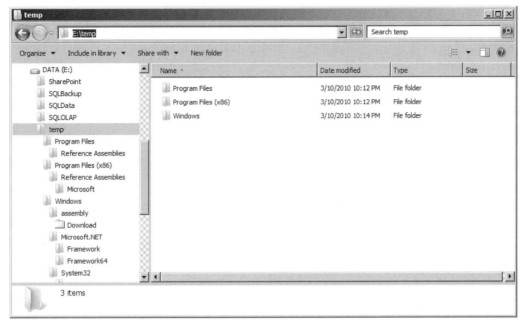

Figure 5.67   Recovered folders and files.

2. Type `appcmd.exe restore backup "<name>"`, where <name> is replaced by the name of the configuration file backup set that is being restored. After you have entered the full command, press the Enter key to execute the restore.

3. When the restore is complete, you are presented with a status message similar to the one shown in Figure 5.68.

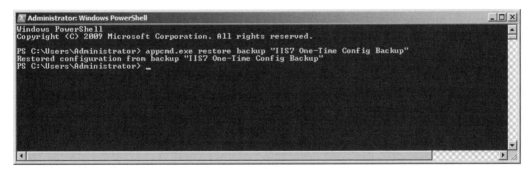

Figure 5.68   Successful restoration of an IIS configuration.

4. Close the PowerShell window by typing `exit` and pressing the Enter key.

SSL Certificates

As with the SSL certificate backup process, restorations are typically carried out using either the Certificates MMC snap-in or the IIS Manager snap-in. The restoration example that follows demonstrates the latter approach and assumes that you carried out the SSL certificate backup process illustrated earlier in the chapter.

1. Carry out steps 1 through 3 as described in the SSL certificate backup example to arrive at the Server Certificates window, as shown in Figure 5.41.

2. Click the Import link under the Actions options on the right side of the window. This brings up the Import Certificate dialog box.

3. Specify the fully qualified path to the certificate file you are importing, and provide the password that was supplied at the time of certificate export. When the fields have been filled out as demonstrated in Figure 5.69, click the OK button to continue.

Figure 5.69 Populating the Import Certificate dialog box.

Note: Unless you have specific security concerns or reasons for blocking future exports of the SSL certificate, it is recommended that you allow the check box for certificate export to remain checked. This is the default. Unchecking the box means that you are no longer able to export the certificate and have to rely on external backup copies in the event that you want to copy the certificate, migrate it, reinstall it, or take some action that would involve bringing the certificate outside the certificate store.

---

4. The import executes and completes without confirmation of any sort. To verify that the import has succeeded, simply verify that the certificate is present in the main pane of the Server Certificates window in Figure 5.41.

Windows Registry

The easiest way to restore exported Registry settings is to double-click a Registry export file and click the Yes button on the warning dialog that appears, as shown in Figure 5.70.

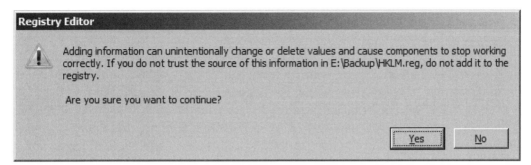

Figure 5.70   Warning that appears when merging a .reg file with existing Registry settings.

Tip: An alternative to double-clicking the file is to right-click on it and select the Merge option from the context-sensitive menu that appears.

Once you select Yes, a merge is performed in the background. When the merge action is complete, you are notified with a dialog box indicating whether the operation was completed successfully or encountered issues.

Conclusion

The Windows Server 2008 operating system is the foundation of your SharePoint environment. Every server in your farm must be running it as its base operating system. You need to preserve the key elements of your SharePoint farm stored within the operating system to have a solid, comprehensive disaster recovery solution for your organization's SharePoint resources. If you don't take care to include these items in your backup and restore plans, at a minimum you're incurring additional time and resources spent to re-create them. Or, even worse, you may not be able to re-create them and stand to lose valuable configuration details and resources.

A common theme that runs through the topic of SharePoint disaster recovery is the notion of layered protection, and this concept extends to the Windows server operating system as well. You can achieve catastrophic protection of the server and its contents using the Windows Server Backup Features that are built into Windows Server 2008. Windows Server Backup provides end-to-end protection, and together with the Windows RE can be used to perform a bare metal restore of a server.

In addition to Windows Server Backup, the operating system includes a number of tools you can use to provide additional protection against common occurrences such as file deletions, misconfiguration, and other noncatastrophic issues. The list of tools includes the Registry Editor, IIS Manager, and AppCmd.exe among others; you can use each tool to back up and restore a specific type of data or target within the operating system. These tools augment Windows Server Backup rather than replacing it.

Another best practice previously mentioned in this guide that is especially relevant to this topic is the creation, maintenance, and review of a detailed change log for the servers in your SharePoint environment. It can quickly become difficult, if not impossible, to build an accurate picture of what has been installed, modified, or removed from your servers if you don't record those updates. Although a full server recovery can return a server to a predefined point in the past, such a recovery is seldom carried out unless a total system failure is encountered. Having an accurate change log can be an invaluable asset when you are attempting to restore a server's configuration or data with tools that target individual components and through means other than a full server recovery.

You should also keep in mind that a current change log does you little good unless you know where individual components backups and other assets are stored. Although it is all too easy to store these files wherever you please or just delete them when you're done with them, this can pose a serious risk to your system in the event of a disaster. You should store these crucial files in a controlled, centralized location so that you know exactly where to find them and exactly which version to use to redeploy the correct update. Make sure that the proper personnel can access the location as needed when you must carry out recovery operations.

Now that you've learned more about backing up and restoring SharePoint-related items within Windows Server 2008, you should be able to answer the following questions. You can find the answers to these questions in Appendix A, "Chapter Review Q&A," found on the Cengage Learning Web site at http://www.courseptr.com/downloads.

1.   What is the SharePoint Root?

2.   Can the Windows Server Backup Features write backups to tape devices?

3.   What is the Windows RE?

4.   How can you back up the IIS configuration files?

5.   What is a bare metal restore?

6

Windows Server 2008 High Availability

In This Chapter

- Load Balancing
- High Availability

In the mid-1970s, the United States Air Force (USAF) introduced a new aircraft designed to provide U.S. forces on the ground with close-in air support, the A-10 Thunderbolt II, affectionately known as the "Warthog." The A-10 is not a sleek, sexy fighter jet like the F-22 Raptor or F-15 Eagle, nor is it technologically advanced like the B-2 Stealth bomber. It isn't pretty, but it's effective. The A-10 is slow, as least compared to burners like the Raptor, and it's far less maneuverable. This means it's exposed to counterattacks for longer periods than its fighter brethren, and these attacks come in a much higher volume, meaning that the highest priorities in its design were reliability and durability. Every system in the A-10 critical to keeping it in the air has redundant backups available in case of an error or failure. This is just one aspect of the thought that has gone into keeping the A-10 safely in the air for as long as possible. The approach works; A-10s have been hit by missiles and hundreds of shells and kept on ticking on countless occasions. They've even flown home missing half a wing and survived.

You may be asking yourself, "What does this have to do with Windows Server 2008 high availability (HA)?" Hopefully, the brief description of the A-10's redundant design and durability has gotten you thinking about the steps you could take to introduce similar attributes into your SharePoint environment. What sort of redundant systems do you, or should you, have in place if a key component of your system should fail? In Chapter 5, "Windows Server 2008 Backup and Restore," you were introduced to some of the ways you can back up and restore items in Windows Server 2008 that are crucial to SharePoint. This chapter outlines several ways you can create redundant systems for your SharePoint environment so that if a hard drive, server, or more should fail, your users can still access, modify, and work with their business-critical SharePoint content.

HA is not a term that this book has discussed in great detail yet, but it's an integral part of a comprehensive disaster recovery system. HA refers to the ability of a technology platform, system, or environment to remain online and available in the face of outages or failures by one or more of its constituent subsystems.

It is pretty much physically impossible and all too often financially unrealistic for a system such as your SharePoint environment to be 100 percent available all day, 365 days a year. Designing and engineering for HA means that the system is built to be fully available for a given percentage of time, such as 95 percent, 99 percent, or 99.999 percent (also referred to as having *five nines* of uptime) and withstand unplanned situations such as a hard drive failure, a network outage, or a power outage rendering an entire datacenter inoperable.

HA is not something that is easy to implement, nor is it a problem you can solve by a single hardware or software solution. It requires comprehensive analysis, planning, and design of your information technology (IT) infrastructure from the ground up, not to mention careful consideration of your service and uptime requirements, the budget you have available to meet those requirements, as well as the staff needed to manage and implement your HA processes. Although uptime numbers such as the "five nines" may be attractive to you and your management, the overhead associated with providing that kind of service is often prohibitive to all but the largest of enterprises. The important thing to do is to review the options discussed in this chapter, determine the HA solution that best fits your needs and budget, and then make sure your service levels are clearly defined and communicated to your customers.

If you take away one thing from this chapter about Windows Server 2008 HA, keep this in mind: there is no one solution that is going to make your SharePoint environment and its infrastructure highly available from top to bottom. It takes a combination of hardware, software, configuration, repeatable and stable procedures, and maintenance to achieve this goal for most platforms, and SharePoint is no different due to the flexibility of how you can configure it and its general overall complexity. You need to handle different pieces of the puzzle with different solutions, whether its load-balancing the Web servers hosting content for SharePoint's users or implementing a redundant storage solution to store SharePoint's data.

Note: It's a well-known fact that SharePoint puts the majority of its content and data into its back-end SQL Server databases. Although this chapter does not make direct mention of SQL Server HA (mainly because Chapter 8, "SQL Server 2008 High Availability" covers this in depth specifically for SQL Server), the information in the "Storage" section later in this chapter is still relevant for SQL Server hosts just as much as the servers that SharePoint is installed on.

The visual examples provided in this chapter were generated in a testing environment using the following platforms and components. Depending on how your environment is configured, your experiences may vary slightly.

- **Operating system.** Microsoft Windows Server 2008 R2 Enterprise Edition (build 7600)
- **Database.** Microsoft SQL Server 2008 Developer Edition with SP1 (build 10.0.2740)

- **Web server.** Microsoft Internet Information Services (IIS) 7.5

- **SharePoint.** SharePoint Foundation 2010 Release Candidate 1 (build 4730)

Load Balancing

One of the best ways to ensure that your SharePoint farm's content is always available to your users is by spreading the responsibility for serving that content across multiple SharePoint servers via a practice known as *load balancing*. Load balancing is most commonly applied to servers in a SharePoint environment that is assigned the Microsoft SharePoint Foundation Web Application role (in SharePoint 2007, these were often referred to as Web front-end [WFE] servers; you may notice that term used again here for simplicity's sake), but SharePoint 2010's new Service Application architecture introduces a new approach that allows other critical aspects of a SharePoint farm to be distributed across multiple points of failure, such as Search or Business Connectivity Services. Interestingly, the implementation and configuration of load balancing of these Service Applications are built into the SharePoint product, but load balancing of the WFEs that deliver SharePoint to your users is not. The next two sections address the ins and outs of configuring load balancing for your WFEs, followed by an examination of each server role that is available in SharePoint 2010 and how (or if) they can be made highly available.

SharePoint is designed to allow for the use of multiple WFEs in a load-balanced configuration, serving up content to users on a single host name. Even though users may be making complex requests to SharePoint, the servers are able to answer those requests in a uniform manner, even if during a single session end users are directed to multiple servers for their content. You can load-balance by installing a hardware or software solution in front of your SharePoint WFE servers that forwards a Web request directed at a single host name to one of the WFE servers. If one of the servers in your load-balanced pool is overwhelmed and crashes, the load balancer can redirect traffic away from the affected server to the other members of the pool, ensuring a higher level of service continuity than what is possible with a single server.

Load-Balancing Software

Load-balancing software is pretty easy to describe: by installing and configuring an application on the SharePoint WFEs that you want to load-balance, you can distribute client requests across all those servers. It requires no special hardware and usually comes with a lower price tag than hardware-based solutions. In fact, the most common load-balancing software solution for SharePoint, Windows Network Load Balancing (NLB), is available as a Windows Server 2008 Feature, meaning it can be added free of charge to any server running Windows Server 2008, at any time. This section guides you through enabling and configuring an NLB cluster to load-balance the HTTP traffic directed at your SharePoint farm's WFE servers, as well as discusses the challenges of using NLB with SharePoint. It is by no means the only way you can use a software product to load-balance SharePoint, but it is the most prevalent option available.

Caution: Even though NLB and the Windows Server 2008's failover clustering (formerly known as Microsoft Cluster Service or MSCS in Windows Serve 2003) feature share some of the same terms and concepts, they are two distinct technologies intended to provide solutions for different problem sets. Failover clustering is best suited for applications that require transactions to occur in a synchronous order and be aware of their position within that order, referred to as the application's *state*. Applications that need to frequently update large amounts of data in a specific sequence, such as SQL Server, are excellent candidates for clustering via failover clustering. NLB is targeted at applications that operate primarily in a "stateless" manner, such as IIS Web servers. The transactions used by these applications generally have no knowledge of the transactions that came before or after them; each one is treated as an independent operation. Keep in mind that Share-Point's Web traffic isn't always stateless, in fact, it often isn't, which is why some NLB settings, such as affinity (discussed later in the chapter), are used differently for SharePoint than they may be for other Web-based applications.

About Windows Network Load-Balancing Services

Windows NLB is designed to be a scalable, reliable, high-availability solution for applications that communicate via the Internet Protocol (IP). It allows up to 32 servers to be placed into a server farm cluster to avoid outages or performance losses for a single host name. To configure an NLB cluster, a single host name and its IP address serve as a "virtual" IP that receives all traffic directed at the application and reroutes it to one of the member servers within the NLB cluster. If a member of the cluster fails, NLB automatically removes the server from the cluster and distributes its load among the rest of the servers in the cluster until service is restored on the affected server.

NLB does not require special hardware to configure or use its functionality. No hardware devices or storage area network (SAN) configurations are required. For optimal use, the member servers in the NLB cluster should have two network interface cards (NICs), but you can certainly use NLB if the servers have only one NIC. Configure each member server to allow network communication with the server via IP, because NLB relies on this protocol to communicate with the cluster and direct traffic through it.

What's New in Windows Server 2008 and Windows Server 2008 R2

Although Windows Server 2003 was usually the operating system (OS) of choice for SharePoint 2007 deployments, the 2010 release of the SharePoint platform runs only on Windows Server 2008 or Windows Server 2008 R2. The 2008 release, as well as the R2 release, of the Windows Server OS brought with it several enhancements and new features for NLB. It is important to understand if the environment you're working with in SharePoint 2010 is using Windows Server 2008 or Windows Server 2008 R2, because there are important differences between what each OS can and cannot do. The two sections that follow summarize the changes made to NLB in both releases.

NLB Enhancements and Additions in Windows Server 2008. The following key components or functions have been significantly updated or added to NLB's feature set by Microsoft with the release of the Windows Server 2008 OS:

- **Networking.** NLB now fully supports IPv6 for traffic between servers and offers enhanced driver performance and scalability through its support of the Network Driver Interface Specification (NDIS) v6.1.

- **Multiple network addresses.** NLB now supports the clustering of multiple dedicated IP addresses per node in the NLB cluster.

- **WMI enhancements.** The *MicrosoftNLB* namespace within Microsoft's Windows Management Instrumentation (WMI) has been updated to support NLB's IPv6 and multiple IP address enhancements.

- **Enhanced interaction with Forefront TMG.** When used in conjunction with Microsoft's Forefront Threat Management Gateway (TMG) 2010 Enterprise Edition, NLB offers better notification of potential attacks and management of multiple IP addresses per node.

NLB Enhancements and Additions in Windows Server 2008 R2. With the release of the Windows Server 2008 R2 OS, Microsoft has updated its NLB solution with even more new or improved features, including these:

- **Improved affinity.** NLB's affinity functionality (see the "NLB Session Affinity and Share-Point" section that follows for more information on NLB Affinity) has been updated to allow for relationships between nodes and clients to be held longer, even if they are disconnected.

- **PowerShell support.** The PowerShell scripting language now allows for the scripting of NLB's configuration and management activities.

- **Flexible upgrades.** Existing NLB clusters created on Windows Server 2003 can be upgraded all at once to Windows Server 2008, or member servers can be upgraded one at a time, a process known as rolling upgrades.

- **Health monitoring.** Microsoft has released an NLB-specific management pack for use with its enterprise monitoring product, System Center Operations Manager (SCOM) 2007.

NLB's Operational Modes

You can configure NLB to operate in two modes: Unicast and Multicast. You must set all the member servers within an NLB cluster to the same operational mode, regardless of whether Unicast or Multicast is selected.

- **Unicast.** In Unicast mode, the Media Access Control (MAC) address assigned to the NIC for clustered traffic is overridden by a virtual MAC address that the NLB generates. Each server in the cluster uses the same MAC, which means that each member server receives all traffic directed at the cluster. Unicast mode can cause conflicts with network-switching hardware, leading to dropped traffic to and from the cluster or to the switch being flooded by traffic it can't redirect.

■ **Multicast.** In Multicast mode, a second MAC address is added to the NIC of each member server in the cluster, and the original MAC address for the NIC is retained. The NLB-generated MAC address sends and receives traffic directed at the NLB cluster's virtual IP address. The original MAC address sends and receives traffic directed specifically at the member server on its own IP address. With Multicast mode, your network administrators can create static entries in the cluster's network switch that point to the ports used by the cluster, removing the risk of flooding your switch. Windows Server 2008 also introduces a new Multicast option—Internet Group Management Protocol (IGMP) multicast—which enables IGMP support for limiting switch flooding by limiting the NLB cluster's traffic to only those ports on the switch serving the cluster hosts and not all its ports. If you are using IPv4 addresses in your network, you can only use Class D IP addresses (that is, addresses in the 224.0.0.0 to 239.255.255.255 range) as your clustered IP address with the IGMP multicast cluster operation mode.

Although Unicast mode is enabled by default when creating an NLB cluster, Multicast mode is the operating mode often recommended for NLB clusters. Multicast mode provides more functionality when only a single NIC can be used on member servers in the cluster; it avoids the issue of switch flooding as long as static entries are created in the switch to properly map the cluster's address to the ports being used by the cluster. Unicast, on the other hand, does not function well (some would say it doesn't function at all) if your server has only one NIC, and it causes switch flooding no matter what you do. If your networking hardware does not allow for the creation of static port entries, Unicast is the route you should take. But, if your networking hardware does allow it, and most modern hardware is now Multicast-compatible, Multicast is the way to go.

Tip: When planning how to configure your NLB cluster, make sure to consult and involve your organization's network administrators. Not only can they provide details on how your network is configured and how that impacts your design, but they can also give you valuable recommendations and constraints based on their knowledge of the network that your SharePoint environment uses.

Caution: There has been a dramatic increase in the use of virtualized servers in IT environments in recent years, and with good reason; virtual machines (or VMs) offer a number of compelling features, such as quick deployment, optimization of physical resources, and flexibility of management. If you are implementing NLB on VMs in your SharePoint environment and plan to use Unicast mode as your cluster's operational mode, there are additional considerations you need to make for the configuration of your virtual network resources, both NICs and switches. VMware has published an excellent white paper (http://www.vmware.com/files/pdf/implmenting_ms_network_load_balancing.pdf) that we recommend you review for more detailed information on the subject and how you need to configure your virtual environment for NLB and Unicast.

How to Configure Windows NLB Services

The following instructions detail the steps necessary to install and configure NLB to create a cluster containing two physical servers. Each server has two NICs installed, but the cluster is going to be configured to operate in Multicast mode so that only one NIC on each server is used for the cluster. The user executing these steps must be a local administrator on each of the servers in the cluster. The member servers in the cluster have unique IP addresses assigned to each of their NICs, and an IP address is available to serve as the cluster's "virtual" address.

1. Log on to the server you want to add to an NLB cluster as an administrator.

2. Open the Server Manager if it is not already open, and click on the Features item in the left menu. The Network Load Balancing Feature should be enabled on the server, as shown in Figure 6.1. If it is not enabled, add the Network Load Balancing Feature to the server before continuing.

3. Click the Start button and navigate to All Programs, Administrative Tools, Network Load Balancing Manager.

4. This opens the Network Load Balancing Manager application, as shown in Figure 6.2.

5. From the Cluster menu, select the New option to open the New Cluster : Connect window (see Figure 6.3) and create a new NLB cluster.

6. When the New Cluster : Connect window opens, enter the IP address and subnet mask for the first host to be added to the cluster, and click the Connect button. The NLB Manager searches for the server based on the IP address entered, and if found displays the names and IP addresses of any NICs on the target server that are available to be added to the new cluster in the Interfaces Available for Configuring a New Cluster list. Select the row for the NIC to be added to the cluster in the list, and click the Next button to continue. Figure 6.3 depicts the New Cluster : Connect window after a host to be added to the cluster has been located and a NIC on the server has been selected.

Caution: In a Multicast configuration such as the one this process describes, you should leave at least one of a server's NICs out of the NLB cluster. This NIC is needed to enable traffic to directly reach the server on its own unique address; adding it to the cluster would not permit the Multicast configuration to function properly.

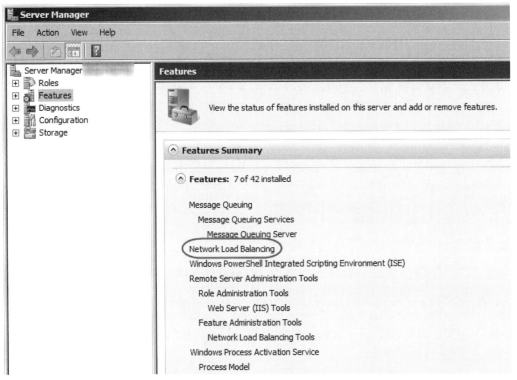

Figure 6.1 The Windows Server 2008 Server Manager, with the Network Load Balancing Feature enabled.

7. When the New Cluster : Host Parameters window opens (see Figure 6.4), if you want to add additional host IP addresses to the cluster, click the Add button to open the Add IP Address window (shown in Figure 6.5). In this window, enter the required information for the server's dedicated IP address, and click the OK button. You can enter IP addresses in IPv4 format, or IPv6 format as long as your network is set up to use that implementation of the Internet Protocol. (If it is not set up for IPv6, this option is disabled.) After entering the dedicated IP address for the server, click the Next button to continue. If you want, you can continue without adding additional IP addresses. If you want to have multiple hosts participating in this cluster, though, you must add them in this dialog box.

8. The New Cluster : Cluster IP Addresses window is now opened, as shown in Figure 6.6. IP addresses added in this window are the target addresses that client computers use to access your SharePoint sites that are then load-balanced between the hosts in the NLB cluster. The IP address you enter here is the shared address that you should direct your users to use to access your load-balanced SharePoint site; the cluster takes the

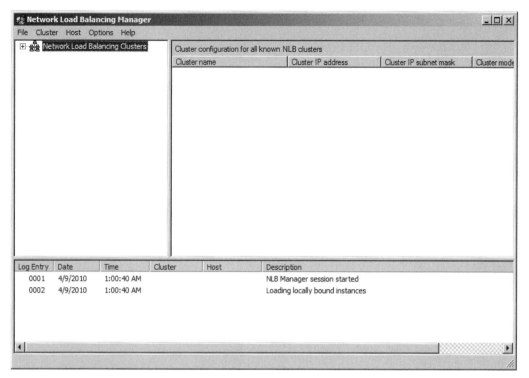

Figure 6.2   The Network Load Balancing Manager.

traffic to this IP address and redirects it to individual server nodes within the cluster. To add an IP address, click the Add button to open the Add IP Address window (identical to the Add IP Address window shown for Host IP Addresses in Figure 6.5). In this window, enter the required information for the clustered IP address, and click the OK button. The IP address entered must be a static IP address; NLB disables the Dynamic Host Configuration Protocol (DHCP) settings on each NIC it configures, which is why static IP addresses are required. You can enter IP addresses in IPv4 format, or IPv6 format as long as your network is set up to use that implementation of the Internet Protocol. (If it is not set up for IPv6, this option is disabled.) After entering the IP address for the cluster, click the Next button to continue.

9.   The New Cluster : Cluster Parameters window opens, as shown in Figure 6.7, allowing you to configure the shared Uhostname for the new cluster you are creating and select the cluster's operation mode. Enter the host name for the load-balanced host name of your SharePoint sites in the Full Internet Name text field; select the radio button for the desired cluster operation mode, which in this case is Multicast; and then click the Next button to continue.

10.   The New Cluster : Port Rules window is now opened, as shown in Figure 6.8. By default, a single rule has already been created to encompass every TCP and UDP port

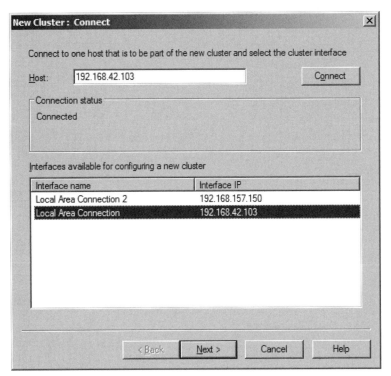

Figure 6.3   The New Cluster : Connect window.

on the clustered IP address. If you want to modify that rule, click the Edit button to open the Add/Edit Port Rule window (shown in Figure 6.9). In this window, you can apply the rule to the entire cluster or a single IP address if there are multiple in the cluster, change the range of ports included in the cluster for the IP address, select the Internet Protocol that the cluster uses, set its Filtering Mode, set its Affinity, or disable the selected range of ports for the cluster. To accept the defaults for the rule, click the Finish button to initiate the configuration of the cluster.

Note: An NLB cluster's Affinity setting configures how "sticky" a session is between a client and a host within the cluster. If None is selected for a cluster's Affinity, each client session is directed by the load balancer to the next available host in the cluster, regardless of whether the client previously was communicating with a specific host. Selecting Single sets a client to always be directed to the same host within a given session, regardless of its traffic load. The Network option directs requests from the same TCP/IP Class C address range, such as clients using multiple proxy servers to access the cluster, to a specific host in the cluster. For more information about NLB Affinity settings and SharePoint, see the "Windows NLB and SharePoint" section later in this chapter.

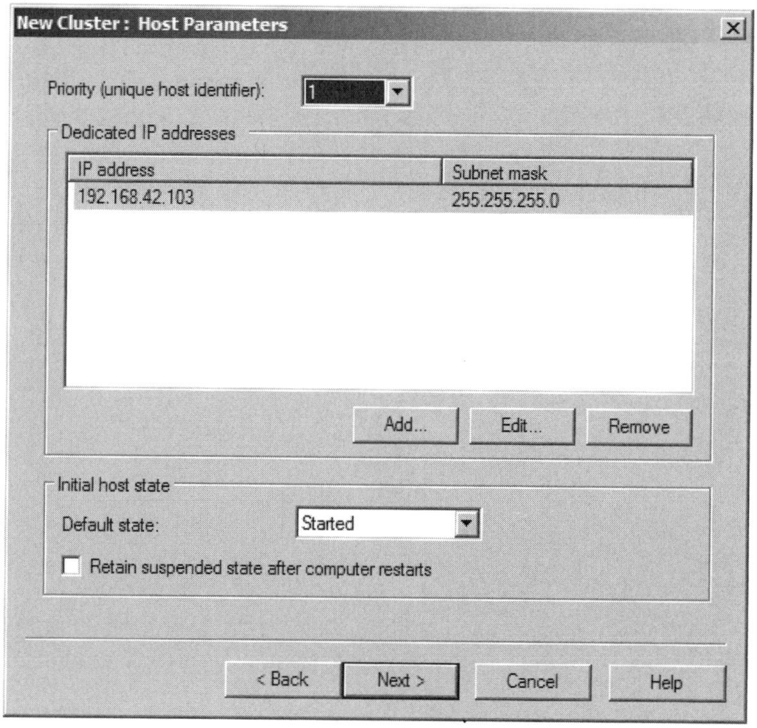

Figure 6.4   The New Cluster : Host Parameters window.

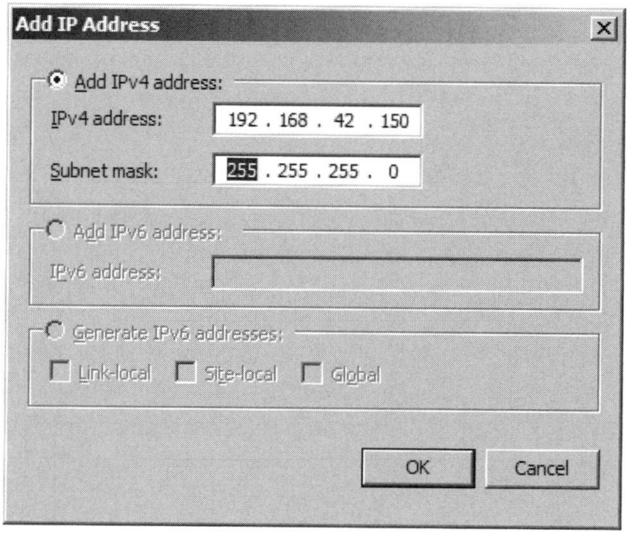

Figure 6.5   The Add IP Address window.

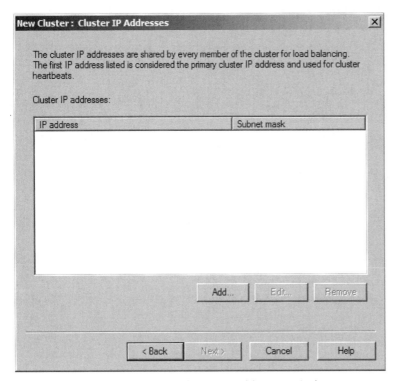

Figure 6.6   The New Cluster : Cluster IP Addresses window.

11.   When the cluster configuration operation completes, the cluster is shown in the Network Load Balancing Manager screen in the left window pane under the Network Load Balancing Clusters entry (see Figure 6.10). To add hosts to the cluster, right-click on the new cluster's name and select the Host Properties option from the menu. This opens the Host Properties window for the cluster (see Figure 6.11), allowing you to complete step 7 to add subsequent hosts to the cluster.

Caution: As you add servers to the cluster, remember that you must assign each server a unique identifier determining its priority within the cluster. Also, you can configure affinity individually for each host, giving you greater opportunities for both flexibility and complexity within the cluster.

Windows NLB and SharePoint

When implementing Windows NLB with SharePoint, you need to keep in mind and consider two main issues: operational mode and session affinity. You can configure each of these items in different ways, and your choices can have a definite impact on the functionality and performance of your SharePoint environment.

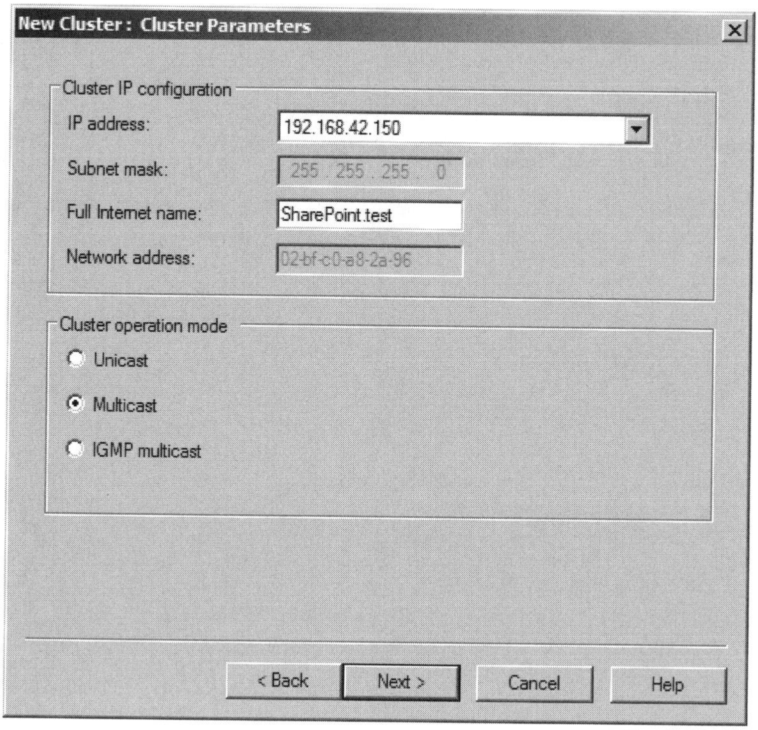

Figure 6.7   The New Cluster : Cluster Parameters window.

NLB Operational Mode and SharePoint. You are most likely to decide between Unicast and Multicast based on the configuration of your environment's networking hardware. If your servers in the NLB cluster are configured with multiple NICs and flooding your switches is not an issue, Unicast is the best-fitting operational mode. If your servers have only one NIC or switch flooding impacts the performance of your network, Multicast makes the most sense. If you are building your servers from the ground up, the recommended approach is to install more than one NIC and go with Unicast, but these recommendations are based on general situations, and your specific requirements and environment may dictate otherwise. Regardless of the operational mode you select, make sure to apply this setting uniformly across all servers in the NLB cluster; each node must use the same setting, or you'll encounter errors.

Note: If you use Multicast in your cluster, make sure that your network's hardware is compatible. Specifically, your hardware must be able to accept the Address Resolution Protocol (ARP) replies generated by the multicast nodes in the NLB cluster or allow administrators to create a static ARP entry to properly resolve the addresses that the cluster is using. Although most modern networking hardware is now compatible with the functionality and settings required to make NLB work, you may still encounter legacy or niche hardware that is not compatible. You need to confirm that your infrastructure meets the needs of your solution and thoroughly test the full configuration before using it in a production environment.

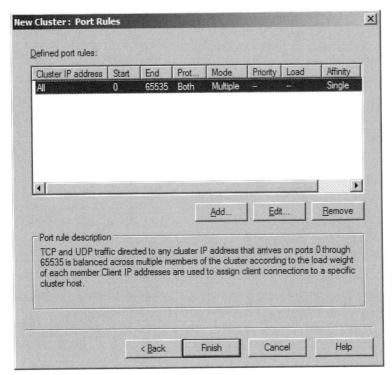

Figure 6.8   The New Cluster : Port Rules window.

NLB Session Affinity and SharePoint. Internet traffic, by design, is intended to be stateless. That is, each transaction between a client and a server is supposed to be self-contained and unconnected so that it can be routed by the most efficient means possible regardless of how communication operated in the past. Some SharePoint sites, such as public-facing sites using SharePoint's Web content management functionality, are truly stateless, and each host within an NLB cluster should be set to None to take advantage of that stateless nature and focus on using the cluster to improve performance and stability.

But the reality of the situation is that not all traffic over a network, even a big network like the Internet, is stateless. And, although SharePoint is in many ways a typical stateless Internet application, this is not always the case. Some functionality, such as workflows or InfoPath forms, is prone to errors in load-balanced SharePoint environments where clients can communicate with any WFE server at any point in time. To avoid these errors and place a greater emphasis on data integrity, each node in your NLB cluster should have Affinity set at Single so a client's repeated traffic becomes "sticky" by being directed back to the same WFE server for each trip. This ensures continuity in these transactions that do require the persistence of state for proper operation.

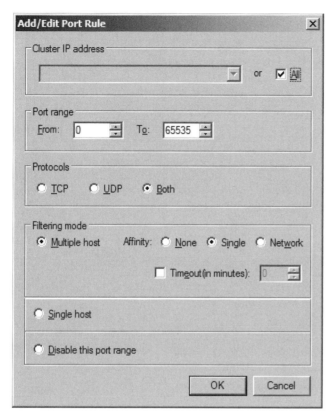

Figure 6.9   The Add/Edit Port Rule window.

Advantages of NLB and SharePoint. The most obvious advantage of using Windows NLB is cost. Because SharePoint requires the Windows Server operating system, you already obtained the right to use NLB when you purchased your Windows Server licenses. NLB does not require the additional purchase of expensive, proprietary hardware to enable HA for serving up your SharePoint content. Windows NLB also allows administrators to manage the NLB configuration by logging into your SharePoint servers, providing a central location for the administration of your environment's critical platforms.

Drawbacks of NLB and SharePoint. Windows NLB is not a sophisticated load-balancing solution. It can require specific or at times unusual networking hardware to function effectively. Its network bandwidth requirements make it a poor choice for load balancing across diverse locations for geographic redundancy. For a single NLB cluster to be spread across two datacenters, the connection speed between those datacenters must have response times of 500 milliseconds or less, a capability that could be difficult over extremely long distances and in certain wide area network (WAN) situations. (Your network must be capable of supporting a subnet that can span across a WAN connection.) Another possible solution for multiple sites is to create a separate

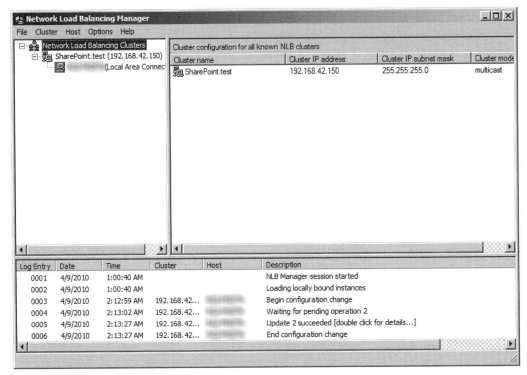

Figure 6.10   A cluster shown in the NLB Manager application's window.

NLB cluster in each location and direct traffic to one or the other via a Domain Name Services (DNS) round robin solution, but this approach does not truly distribute traffic loads between the sites.

Perhaps NLB's biggest drawback is its inability to detect when a host within a cluster is no longer serving live content. If the IIS Web server in one of your SharePoint WFEs has crashed and is no longer sending Web pages to requesting clients, the NLB cluster continues to direct traffic to the Web server until its service is restored or the host is manually removed from the cluster. This can have a definite impact on your environment, because some end users are going to see intermittent errors while that downed server is still being used by the cluster—and that can be difficult to troubleshoot. It also requires manual intervention by an administrator, not only to remove the affected server from the cluster, but to determine which server is displaying the errors in the first place. Differentiating between load-balanced servers can be difficult when each is generating the same content, adding additional challenges to your ability to provide stable and consistent service via NLB.

Load-Balancing Hardware

Hardware load balancers are specialized networking applications designed to route traffic to certain individual servers in a network. You can configure hardware load balancers to distribute

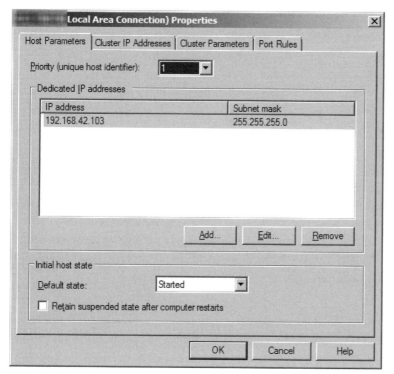

Figure 6.11   The Host Properties window of a newly created NLB cluster.

network traffic across multiple servers based on a variety of conditions such as connection volume, bandwidth utilization, processor utilization, and overall server performance. Software load balancers add an additional task load to the servers in the cluster on top of their normal tasks, such as generating the load-balanced content. Hardware load balancers, on the other hand, are specialized hardware devices whose sole responsibility is distributing traffic to their constituent servers according to their configuration. They are designed, engineered, and tested to efficiently and flexibly spread network traffic across the servers clustered beneath them.

The most obvious benefit to the use of a hardware load balancer is the reduction of workload on your servers compared to Windows NLB. Because the servers are not responsible for establishing and managing the NLB cluster, those free cycles can be allocated to other responsibilities, such as generating and serving content. Hardware load balancers also offer a variety of configuration and management options, although options do vary from manufacturer to manufacturer. Traffic destinations can be determined by affinity, server workload, bandwidth availability, geographic location, and several other factors. Clusters can span network subnets or even datacenters. Servers can be automatically or manually removed from active service depending on a range of criteria such as failure to respond or errors being displayed in requested content. Hardware load balancers are offered by several network hardware vendors, including Cisco, F5, Juniper, Coyote

Point Systems, Barracuda Networks, and many more. Each vendor has its own feature sets, capabilities, and limitations. You should work with your organization's network administrator(s) to determine the hardware solution that is the best fit for your needs if you decide to use a hardware load balancer.

Load-Balancing Hardware and SharePoint

Much like Windows NLB, hardware load-balancing is going to be most effective for a SharePoint farm when its affinity settings are configured to meet the farm's most prevalent usage pattern, such as making sessions sticky when data needs to be maintained across server calls or stateless when transactions are anonymous. This is a universal requirement that should be tested and implemented (when testing shows that it is beneficial) whenever possible. One difference between hardware load balancers and Windows NLB is that the Unicast/Multicast operating modes are functions unique to NLB; there may be hardware solutions that offer similar functionality or drawbacks. You should review their documentation and conduct your own testing to determine the behavior of that functionality.

SharePoint is supported on most, if not all, hardware load-balancing solutions, so it is ultimately up to you and your network administrators to determine which solution is right for you. When evaluating a hardware load balancer, do not make your choice simply based on the load-balancing functionality of the devices. Also consider each candidate's manageability and flexibility, because networking administration (especially for Web server-based solutions like SharePoint) is a fluid and ever-changing responsibility. Your hardware load balancer should be able to quickly enable configuration changes, effectively identify status changes in the servers beneath it, and make your life as a SharePoint administrator easier, not harder.

As SharePoint's sales and popularity have grown, so has the need to deliver it to end users efficiently and consistently. This has not gone unnoticed by the manufacturers of hardware load balancers; several have begun to provide information, guidance, and configurations specifically geared toward the load balancing of SharePoint content with their products. This is great news for SharePoint administrators, because it means that the manufacturers have taken care of the extensive testing and monitoring activities necessary to find the configuration sweet spot for running SharePoint behind their devices. This allows you to quickly and often drastically improve the performance of your SharePoint environment with reduced risk to your service quality.

You should still exercise caution when considering a hardware load-balancing device optimized for SharePoint, because the gains in stability and functionality offered by these products can vary drastically depending on the configuration of your SharePoint environment and its network. If your SharePoint servers and the client workstations accessing your SharePoint site have high-bandwidth connections, you may not see performance gains worth the cost of implementing a SharePoint-optimized load balancer. This is because many manufacturers have focused on situations where network configurations lead to smaller or slower pipes for data to flow through, such as WAN connections. Connection speeds for WANs, which often use public communication links to connect local area networks (LANs) across multiple geographic locations, can pale in comparison to LANs.

It is easy to understand, given the connection limitations WANs face and the amount of network traffic that an active SharePoint site can generate, why this is a main area of focus for manufacturers. But if your network does not use or include WAN connections, you may not see large performance gains when using a SharePoint-optimized load-balancing device. Does this mean you shouldn't use such a device in your network? Not at all. It's just that you need to evaluate the reasons and requirements for load-balancing devices, along with the possible avenues of growth your network might follow, and select your resources accordingly. If your environment is not likely to include WAN connections and there is a more affordable device available that offers all the load-balancing capabilities you need, it is probably a better choice than an expensive purchase for technology that you are not going to see much benefit from.

Advantages of Hardware Load Balancing and SharePoint. Because hardware load balancers usually run on computing devices specifically devoted to providing load-balancing capabilities to a network, they are generally more stable and reliable than NLB. NLB has to run on your SharePoint WFE servers, so it is using computing resources that are tasked with a variety of functions. This in turn can lead to contention and impact the performance of an NLB cluster. But because hardware load balancers do not face the same competition for resources, they are more stable and offer better performance.

Hardware load balancers also offer a much wider range of functionality and features than what's available in NLB. Depending on what the manufacturer of a specific device decides to include in it, you may have options for securing, compressing, or caching traffic sent through the device, not present in NLB. Also, hardware load balancers often can better identify and respond to errors, such as routing traffic away from failed nodes without an outage, or enabling a predetermined static error page should all of a cluster's nodes become unavailable.

Drawbacks of Hardware Load Balancing and SharePoint. Just as cost is an advantage for NLB, the high cost of purchasing specialized hardware is a definite drawback for hardware load balancing. The good news is that this is a diverse marketplace with offerings filling a broad range of price points, and feature sets to match those costs. For some budget-minded organizations, it might be awfully difficult to get away from a comparison of potentially high costs against NLB's price tag of $0.00.

Adding a hardware load balancer to your environment also means that you need to integrate yet another component from yet another manufacturer into your environment, adding to its overall complexity and making it more difficult to manage. Manufacturers often implement unique, proprietary hardware components and setups to add to their ability to differentiate their products and lock customers into their solutions. These dependencies can make it more difficult to manage your SharePoint environment in general, not to mention your HA solutions in particular.

Finally, not all hardware load-balancing options offer the advanced error detection and handling capabilities mentioned earlier, which means your environment could face the same kind of risks NLB clusters do because they lack this functionality. Regardless of the load-balancing solution you choose, make certain that you understand exactly what it can and cannot do; optimally, you'll be able to mitigate those risks via other tools or procedures, but at a minimum you need to be aware of what they are.

Load Balancing and SharePoint Farm Topology

Implementing load balancing to distribute traffic across multiple resources within your Share-Point farm can positively impact the performance of your servers and, most importantly, the end user experience. It can also ensure that your environment can withstand the loss of a server within the farm by sharing the load between multiple resources. But you don't achieve that benefit simply by adding more servers to your environment, installing SharePoint on them, and adding them to an NLB cluster. You need to understand not only the areas within your Share-Point farm where load balancing can be advantageous, but where it provides little to no value and where it can actually be detrimental to the health of your system. Not only that, but Share-Point 2010 introduces a new approach to scalability with the Service Application model (which replaces the SharePoint 2007 concept of Shared Service Providers, or SSPs); allowing you to architect a much more highly available solution for your entire SharePoint environment, not just your Web servers or SQL Server instances.

The WFE Role

The most obvious item within your farm that benefits from load balancing is the WFE role, which is responsible for serving SharePoint's Web pages, content, and functionality to your end users. If you have a large user base who frequently visit your SharePoint sites or you need to make sure that your content is always online and available, you will most certainly want to load-balance your WFEs.

One interesting thing that Microsoft discovered in SharePoint 2007 about load-balancing WFE servers is that there is a point where the performance of your environment flattens as you insert additional WFEs to scale out the farm. Microsoft conducted extensive testing of how SharePoint 2007 performs under extremely heavy loads, for a variety of typical use cases. Although Micro-soft has made a great deal of information about the product available well ahead of its release, the problem with SharePoint 2010 being such a new product is that there just has not been enough time to do the same kind of capacity performance testing with the final version of the product.

To its credit, Microsoft has been working to deliver this content with the launch of SharePoint 2010, but it is not fully released for all of SharePoint's numerous use cases. At the time this book is being written, Microsoft has released case and lab studies that examine the performance metrics of large-scale SharePoint environments focused on collaborative activities, SharePoint's most common use. Much as in SharePoint 2007, these studies show that in a SharePoint 2010 collaborative environment, there is a definitive point where performance gains flatten out as new WFEs are added to a load-balanced farm. The flattening tends to occur when a fourth WFE is added to a farm. After that point, there was no value in adding additional WFEs. Beyond the fourth WFE, performance was being constrained by CPU utilization on the SQL Server instance hosting SharePoint's databases, not SharePoint itself. If you would like more information on Microsoft's testing approach and findings with SharePoint 2010's capacity and performance limitations, head to the Capacity Management for SharePoint Server 2010 Resource Center on TechNet, at http://technet.microsoft.com/en-us/sharepoint/ff601870.aspx. It is an outstanding repository that is sure to have new content on the subject of SharePoint 2010 capacity planning added on a regular basis and well worth a look.

If you are planning a large implementation of SharePoint, test your configuration on its own so that you can determine your performance baseline and whether it's going to meet your needs. Performance may vary depending on a variety of factors, as follows:

- **Network configuration.** The unique configuration of your network and its hardware may provide you with performance metrics that vastly differ from Microsoft's.

- **Hardware configuration.** The unique configuration of your server hardware may also provide you with performance metrics that vastly differ from Microsoft's.

- **Caching configuration.** Configuring your farm's servers and content to leverage caching functionality can drastically improve the performance of your Web servers.

- **Farm usage scenarios.** A farm intended for internal collaboration and knowledge sharing by authenticated users is going to perform differently from a farm intended for Web content management and anonymous users.

Adding More Servers to a SharePoint Farm

Because load balancing is common for SharePoint to improve performance, Microsoft has made the process to add additional servers to a SharePoint farm easy and straightforward. The SharePoint installer should be run on the server to be added to the farm, using the same accounts and configuration as the rest of the servers in the farm, making sure to do a Complete Advanced installation. Once the installer finishes, the SharePoint Products and Technologies Configuration Wizard starts up. Walk through the wizard, making sure to select the Connect to an Existing Farm option, and then connect to the configuration database for the existing farm. Confirm that the server is not set to host the farm's Central Administration site (unless you have a specific requirement to create a redundant site), and complete the wizard. Log into the Central Administration site, and configure the server with the WFE role that it should play in the farm.

Note: Adding a server to a farm within SharePoint does not automatically add it to the pool of load-balanced servers for Windows NLB. You must still perform this configuration step in the management tools for the load-balanced cluster, not in SharePoint, for end users to reach the server via the load-balanced URL.

Service Applications

In Microsoft Office SharePoint Server (MOSS) 2007, Microsoft introduced the concept of SSPs, applications within a farm designed to provide specialized services—such as My Sites, Search, and User Profiles—to multiple Web applications within the farm. SSPs were helpful in that they allowed common functionality to be used consistently across sites and Web applications in the farm, but the approach was not without its drawbacks. SSPs were often difficult to manage, especially in large farms, and they were a challenge to protect from a DR standpoint. In the case of Search specifically, SSPs represented a single point of failure because only a single server could be designated for operation in the Index Server role for a given SharePoint Search index.

Microsoft has revamped its approach to these types of applications in SharePoint 2010 by retiring the concept of an SSP and introducing the Service Application model. It also applies to both SharePoint Foundation 2010 and SharePoint Server 2010 instead of just the server product. Microsoft has designed the Service Application model to build on the direction taken by the SSP approach while addressing some of its shortcoming and drawbacks. Service Applications are designed to provide scalability to your SharePoint farm, give administrators greater control over which services are delivered to SharePoint resources, and allow third-party vendors to create their own custom Service Applications to enhance and extend the functionality available through a SharePoint environment.

The big reason that Microsoft's change from SharePoint 2007's SSP model to SharePoint 2010's Service Application model makes such a difference is in how it handles load. With SharePoint 2007, applications within the SSP were often difficult to scale out as usage increased. Some applications, such as Excel Services, required careful consideration and configuration to set up for large environments or high availability. Search in SharePoint 2007 was an even more frustrating story: the Index server role could not be spread across multiple servers, making it a single point of failure.

In a multiserver SharePoint 2010 farm, Microsoft recommends that Service Applications are hosted on dedicated application servers (giving the farm a three-tier hierarchy, with the other tiers consisting of WFEs and SQL Server hosts). These application servers host the Service Applications and respond to requests made by the client applications hosted by the farm's WFEs to deliver their functionality. If the farm has multiple application servers, it is not necessary to configure a load-balanced cluster (via NLB or a hardware load balancer) as it would be for a farm with multiple WFEs. Instead, Microsoft has built a simple round-robin load balancer into its Service Application Framework that distributes traffic across each application server automatically.

Search Roles

The one piece of SharePoint most impacted by the new Service Application model in SharePoint Server 2010 is Search. SharePoint's Search capabilities have always been a highly touted aspect of the platform, and that's no different in 2010, featuring lots of new features and functionality for end users. But with this new release also comes a much better story around the idea of making SharePoint's Search infrastructure pieces highly available. This simply wasn't possible in MOSS 2007 due to the inflexible nature of the Index server role, but SharePoint Server 2010 gives you a great deal of flexibility and scalability.

Note: The content in this section focuses almost entirely on the Search functionality of SharePoint Server 2010. Although SharePoint Foundation 2010 does now allow for the presence of multiple Search servers within a farm, those servers cannot be deployed redundantly. Each Search server must be configured to crawl and index different content databases within the farm, so you cannot configure the farm so that if one Search server goes down its load is distributed to the other servers. If one Search server goes down, its indexed content is unavailable. There are also three other search products related to or for SharePoint 2010 from Microsoft: Search Server Express 2010, Search Server 2010, and FAST Search Server 2010 for SharePoint. These products may be worth your consideration, but this book focuses on covering and protecting SharePoint's core functionality. Please review the documentation for the products mentioned to determine if and how they can be made highly available.

SharePoint servers in a farm can serve a few different roles to add performance and functionality to the farm's search capabilities. The two listed server roles affiliated with searching in a SharePoint farm are the Crawl server role (known as the Index server in MOSS 2007) and the Query server role. Crawl servers are responsible for generating the farm's search index by crawling the target content sources and building the index with the results of that crawl. Query servers are tasked with the processing required to execute all requested queries against a copy of the farm's search index stored locally on the Query server. In SharePoint 2010, you can assign both the Crawl server and Query server roles to multiple servers within a farm, allowing for redundancy and load distribution of SharePoint's Search functionality.

A Crawl server must be associated with a single Crawl database; this database specifies the content that the Crawl server must crawl to build its assigned index. This relationship allows for Search indexing to be constructed for both redundancy and scalability, as desired. You can add redundancy to a farm's Search crawls by associating multiple Crawl servers with a single Crawl database so that if one Crawl server becomes unavailable, a replacement is available to continue indexing the Crawl database's designated content. If you want to improve the performance of the crawl activities, you can create additional crawl databases. This allows you to separate the crawl content between databases so that multiple Crawl servers can process and crawl it in parallel.

Query servers respond to search queries submitted by end users on WFE servers and return results using the Search index generated by the farm's Crawl servers. If a single server in the farm is configured with the Query role, a copy of the entire index is stored in the Query server's file system. If a farm has multiple Query servers, each Query server receives an index partition, or a portion of the overall index. By default, the distribution of index partitions is based on the number of Query servers in a farm, but administrators can manually specify the number of index partitions that are created and how they are distributed. In the case of two Query servers, for example, each server stores an index partition equal to half the index. If there are four Query servers, each server stores an index partition containing 25 percent of the overall index. This approach allows for redundancy (if one of many Query servers in a farm goes down, the index partitions can be redistributed to cover the outage) and may improve performance as additional Query servers are added to a farm.

Caution: Although the new Search architecture in SharePoint Server 2010 overcomes a number of the problems administrators faced with redundancy and scalability in MOSS 2007, it still has components that you can't duplicate within a farm. Each farm requires a Search Administration component that can only be deployed to one Crawl server in a farm, and only one Search Administration database can be associated with that single Search Administration component. The database can only be made redundant if database mirroring or clustering is implemented (see Chapter 8, "SQL Server 2008 High Availability" for more information); the Search Administration component itself cannot be made redundant. The impact of losing these pieces would be minimal and mainly affect an administrator's ability to manage the Search functionality; the farm's Search service would still be available but could not be modified.

This new Search architecture also allows for entire SharePoint Server 2010 farms dedicated to crawling content and responding to search queries. This is typically only a consideration in large, often global, SharePoint deployments, but it does add versatility in search scenarios that were often troublesome in MOSS 2007.

High Availability

Load balancing your Web servers is by far the most obvious and effective way to ensure continuous uptime for your SharePoint environment, but it does not necessarily represent a complete HA solution. Because SharePoint requires such a wide range of infrastructure and systems to function, you need to configure these systems redundantly so they can be as highly available as your load-balanced SharePoint components. The failure of a hard drive or network connection can just as easily impact SharePoint's service levels as the more obvious candidates for HA, SharePoint, and SQL Server. Luckily, the IT industry has been hard at work for years to develop and create stable, redundant infrastructure components that address those problems.

Storage

Let's face it: it's impossible to have a server running Windows Server 2008 and not have some sort of storage device attached to it. Hard disk drives, commonly known as hard drives, have been used in computers for more than 50 years and have evolved and improved as much as processors have over the years, albeit with much less fanfare. Modern hard drives are designed not only to store large amounts of data (manufacturers are now producing drives with capacities measured in terabytes), but to make reading, writing, and transmission of that data happen as quickly as possible. But one thing hasn't changed: drives still fail.

That is not to say that manufacturers have ignored the reliability of their products. That statement could not be further from the truth. Today's hard drives are made to last longer while still withstanding the heavier workloads that interconnected, data-driven computer systems place upon them. They are being made to use less power and reduce noise and to handle sudden movements such as those that could impact the hard drive of a laptop computer. But real-world experience has shown that hard drives are still prone to failure for a variety of reasons.

To expect otherwise is foolhardy, if not irresponsible. Want proof? Consider the findings offered by Google, probably one of the largest consumers of hard drives in the world. In a white paper published in February 2007 (http://labs.google.com/papers/disk_failures.pdf), Google presented data based on analysis of hundreds of thousands of hard drives. It found that, despite the best efforts of manufacturers and system administrators, hard drives are prone to failures caused by a variety of sources, especially as the drives become older. Age is not the only reason for hard drive breakdown, and Google is careful to point out that it should not be the only determining factor. But it's important to keep in mind that as a drive gets older, it is more likely to fail.

When it comes to the business-critical data stored on your servers and in your SharePoint environment, we recommend that as a part of an effective disaster recovery plan, you should not only back up your data on a regular basis, you should also configure the systems you store that data on as redundantly as possible. This helps to make certain that your data is still available if a hard drive fails, and it avoids any outages that may be experienced while a backup is being retrieved from storage and restored. The good news is that modern IT systems have some effective solutions available to them to redundantly store their data.

RAID

A Redundant Array of Independent (or Inexpensive) Disks, more commonly known as a RAID array, is a storage solution that uses two or more actual hard drives to create a reliable storage option for servers. The multiple disks in a RAID array are configured to be presented to a server as a single device, providing a redundant solution that can either copy or distribute data across the disks in the array.

Note: Because there are so many hardware vendors and configurations for RAID arrays on the market today, be sure to review any documented performance metrics for your RAID solution, and if possible do your own testing, to better understand how quickly it can do the various types of disk operations you plan to use it for. As shown next, in general, different RAID configurations work best for different types of operations, but technological and design advances may prove differently for specific products.

There are several types of RAID arrays, each providing different attributes and drawbacks to be considered. Some of the most common are listed here:

- **RAID 0.** With RAID 0, data is "striped," or broken down into blocks, and each block is written to different disks in the array. RAID 0 requires at least two hard disks to implement, and its primary advantage is its ability to read and write data to the disk much more quickly than a single disk. Because data is not duplicated across multiple disks in the array, RAID 0 does not provide fault tolerance for high availability.

- **RAID 1.** In this configuration, data is "mirrored" across each disk in the array so that it is preserved if a drive in the array fails. Writing to the array takes slightly longer than a single disk, because the array is writing to multiple drives (a problem more often seen in software-based RAID solutions than in hardware-based ones). The available storage in the array is also limited to the size of the smallest disk in the array.

- **RAID 5.** This combines a minimum of three disks and ensures that the data on one disk in the array is duplicated on at least one of the other disks in the array. It provides fault tolerance (it can withstand the loss of one disk in the array), and reading data from a RAID 5 is similar in performance to a RAID 0. Writing to a RAID 5 array is a different story, because it generally takes considerably more time to determine what should be written and where it should be written within the array. The total storage capacity of a RAID 5 array is the sum of all disks in the array but one.

- **RAID 6.** This is similar in configuration to RAID 5, but it offers additional fault tolerance, allowing the array to survive the loss of two disks in the array. Read performance is equal to that of RAID 5, but writes can take even longer. The total storage capacity of a RAID 6 array is the sum of all disks in the array but two.

- **RAID 10 (also known as RAID 1+0).** RAID 10 is a combination of RAID 1 and RAID 0. With RAID 1+0, drives in the array are paired, data is mirrored across the pairs, and the data is striped throughout the array. RAID 1+0 can also experience the loss of up to 50 percent of the drives in the array and still maintain data integrity. RAID 1+0 offers faster read and write operations than RAID 5.

Beyond the configuration of the RAID array, there are two ways to implement an array: software and hardware.

- **Software RAID.** Some operating systems, including Windows Server 2008, can create RAID arrays by creating logical disks that are then mapped to the physical disks attached to the server. Using a software RAID configuration can reduce costs, but managing the array can impact a server's performance—particularly in the case of computationally expensive RAID configurations, such as RAID 5. More importantly, manual intervention is required to fail over the array if there is a hard disk failure within the array, leading to service outages.

- **Hardware RAID.** Hardware RAID controllers are specifically built to manage and operate RAID arrays and can be implemented as expansion cards installed in the server or built into the server's motherboard. They offer numerous advantages over software solutions, such as no use of a server's processing power, onboard caching, better failover options, and better error handling, but they can be expensive.

It's difficult to advocate a specific RAID array configuration for your SharePoint farm, because everyone's requirements, budget, and infrastructure are unique, and these factors influence the decision. Because server roles within a farm use their hard drives in various ways, you may end up with different RAID array configurations within your farm. If your organization has a standard configuration for RAID arrays in its datacenters, review those settings to confirm that they meet your requirements. The list that follows outlines several items you should keep in mind when designing your RAID configurations.

- **Use hardware RAID controllers when possible.** Hardware RAID controllers offer so many advantages over software-based controllers, especially where RAID is being used to ensure fault tolerance in disaster recovery solutions. They are more expensive to implement, but they may prove to be worth the investment if they end up saving you big bucks by avoiding productivity-killing downtime for your SharePoint environment.

- **Right-size solutions for WFEs.** WFEs do not necessarily need big-time RAID 1+0 arrays to store their data. In most situations, RAID 1 or RAID 5 is sufficient to provide data preservation and fault tolerance in case of a failure, because SharePoint WFEs do not read or write as much data from and to their disks as SQL Server 2008 does.

- **Right-size solutions for SQL Server 2008.** As you will see in Chapter 7, "SQL Server 2008 Backup and Restore," SharePoint's SQL Server databases mean everything to the farm's survival. Moreover, SharePoint is pretty hard on its databases, performing countless reads, writes, and deletes to them every second under load. It makes sense to use the most fault-tolerant, high-performing array configuration you can afford for the hard drives of your SQL Server.

- **Use quality hard drives.** An easy way to ensure good performance for your RAID arrays is to use hard drives with fast access times and large amounts of cache memory built in.

- **Use enough hard drives.** Adding disks to your arrays is another easy way to improve RAID performance. This gives the array another drive to store content on, provides additional redundancy within the array, and can increase the available disk space (depending on the array configuration).

SAN

The other storage option available (besides just using hard drives in your servers) that makes sense to use with SharePoint is storage area networks, or SANs. SANs let you attach remotely located storage to a server so that the operating system displays and treats the storage as if it were local. SANs are usually best suited to large enterprises due to their high costs to implement, but smaller organizations can also purchase managed SAN storage products from hosting providers if desired.

SANs can be a viable disaster recovery solution based on their ability to make storage resources available to servers in multiple locations. SANs are also a good way to make large amounts of storage available in a configurable fashion; this makes them appealing as a storage location for SharePoint's SQL Server databases. As Chapter 8 explains, SAN storage is also required to enable Windows failover clustering, a tool that can be important in making SQL Server 2008 highly available.

Although SharePoint's SQL Server databases definitely lend themselves to being stored in a SAN, most of SharePoint's additional storage needs do not map particularly well to a SAN solution. In most cases, the benefits of a SAN are outweighed by the high cost of using such a resource for the relatively small-in-comparison hard drives of a SharePoint server, especially when there are other ways that the data stored there can be backed up or made highly available.

Windows Server 2008 and Server 2008 R2 Storage Improvements

In addition to some of the hardware considerations for storage that you need to be aware of, keep in mind that the server operating system that you run SharePoint 2010 on may also be able to do some new things to help make your systems more highly available. Windows Server 2008 now offers several features not found in Windows Server 2003 that can help keep your server's storage healthy and functioning properly, such as these:

- **Self-healing NTFS.** Prior to Windows Server 2008, if a Microsoft server OS detected corruption in the file system of a New Technology File System (NTFS) storage volume (the most commonly used format for drives attached to computers running Microsoft operating systems), the volume had to be taken offline to correct the errors that had been found. With Windows Server 2008, the operating system is able to run a process in the background to repair and isolate damaged regions without taking the full storage volume offline.

- **S.M.A.R.T error detection.** The Self-Monitoring, Analysis, and Reporting Technology (S.M.A.R.T.) monitoring system for computer disks has been around for a while in monitoring systems like Microsoft System Center Operations Manager 2007 (SCOM), but Windows Server 2008 is the first time that S.M.A.R.T. detection techniques are being used within a Microsoft server OS to identify and warn administrators of drive failures before they may arise.

- **Enhanced management of storage networks.** Microsoft implemented the Internet Storage Naming Server (iSNS) protocol in Windows Server 2008, which allows the OS to manage disks attached via the Internet Small Computer System Interface (iSCSI) just as it would disks attached to the server via Fibre Channel (such as SANs). This makes management of those iSCSI devices much simpler and more effective.

- **Disk resizing on the fly.** With Windows Server 2008, administrators can now resize hard disk partitions without shutting down the server hosting the partitions, even if the target partition is the system drive. Although this does not apply to striped drives (such as drives configured in a RAID-0 array), it does allow for greater flexibility when managing your servers' storage.

In October 2009, Microsoft made available a second release of Windows Server 2008, known as Windows Server 2008 R2. (Microsoft is clever with its naming standards for this product, isn't it?) This updated release contained a wide range of new features and functionality for Microsoft's flagship server operation system, but not enough to warrant incrementing the product's version number. The R2 release had two updates that were pertinent to server storage:

- **Storage fault tolerance.** If a server running on Windows Server 2008 R2 has multiple paths connecting it to a storage device, the OS can switch to an alternate path to the device should the primary fail or become unavailable. The OS also allows for the configuration of the priorities for these paths to your storage device for better flexibility in configuration.

- **Storage configuration backups.** Windows Server 2008 R2 allows administrators to take snapshots of their storage configuration settings, such as its iSCSI setup, so that the server can be quickly restored to a functioning state should the configuration fail or change unexpectedly and affect the availability of a server's storage.

Server Clustering and SharePoint

The most common element of SharePoint to make highly available via a clustering tool such as Windows failover clustering is its SQL Server databases. The topic of Windows failover clustering and SQL Server is covered extensively in Chapter 8.

Networking and Infrastructure Planning

The other element of your SharePoint environment that is vulnerable to hardware failures and outages is your networking hardware and infrastructure. If your network or a component within it should fail, is your environment redundant enough to keep lines of communication open between your users and your SharePoint farm? What about between your SharePoint farm and its database servers, domain controllers, and other crucial remote resources? Don't overlook the vital components that provide the key lines of communication into and out of your environment when planning for high availability.

Work with your network administrator(s) to confirm that the switches, routers, load balancers, and other pieces of the network are redundant, so that the connection to the network remains active if one of those items should fail. Regularly test your network to confirm that communications are being quickly and efficiently routed from point A to point B, and to make sure that all address mappings and configurations are correct so that traffic can get to where it is supposed to.

Your servers can be configured with additional NICs, a setup that can offer a lot of additional benefit to your system. Not only do multiple NICs allow for the use of the Unicast operating mode with Windows NLB, but you can establish specific channels for communication, restricted to a specific IP subnet, between your SharePoint servers and their database instances. This is beneficial to performance, because it gives your farm a network location solely devoted to its own database traffic, the foundation of SharePoint's publishing process. It also provides important security to the process by restricting access to the IP subnet to only the servers using it. Multiple NICs can also be teamed, opening up greater bandwidth into and out of your server for content to flow through, as well as making it possible to add greater redundancy and failover capabilities to your servers should a NIC fail.

Conclusion

As a SharePoint administrator, it is all too easy to become locked onto the SharePoint or SQL Server components of your environment. But from the perspective of disaster recovery and high availability, that just isn't enough. SharePoint depends on many systems, devices, and processes to function effectively. As an administrator, it is your responsibility to make sure that those constituent items are just as robust, redundant, and available as your SharePoint systems are. How you are able to accomplish that depends a lot on the kind of operating budget you have available and your existing resources. The good news is that SharePoint and its constituent systems are pretty flexible, so you have flexibility and options. Oftentimes, the hard part is sifting through those options to determine which is best for you.

A point that we have consistently stressed throughout this book is the importance of testing and monitoring everything within your environment. It is far better to know ahead of time when a system is failing or needs repair or modification, because that way you have more time to plan the right solution and put it in place—not to mention that it's a much easier conversation to have with your supervisor and customers than the alternative.

The concepts and information in this chapter are designed to get you thinking about the foundational systems of your SharePoint environment and what you can do to make them highly available. The best solution for you depends on your organization and its needs, but whether you have a single SharePoint Foundation 2010 server that is accessed by 10 users or a global organization with multiple SharePoint Server 2010 farms and thousands of users, implementing some, any, or all of the concepts in this chapter can only benefit your SharePoint environment.

After completing this chapter on Windows Server 2008 High Availability, you should be able to answer the following questions about their capabilities. You can find the answers to these questions in Appendix A, "Chapter Review Q&A," found on the Cengage Learning Web site at http://www.courseptr.com/downloads.

1. Do you need to purchase a separate license for Windows NLB?

2. What is the difference between Unicast and Multicast operating roles for NLB?

3. What SharePoint server roles can be load-balanced?

4. How does RAID 1+0 differ from RAID 5?

5. What new storage management features were introduced in Windows Server 2008 R2?

7 SQL Server 2008 Backup and Restore

In This Chapter

- SharePoint's Database Options

- How to Back Up a SQL Server 2008 Database

- SharePoint and Backing Up SQL Server 2008

- How to Restore a SQL Server 2008 Database Backup

- SharePoint and Restoring a SQL Server 2008 Backup

It seems these days that the majority of applications, whether they are used by the largest of corporations or the average Joe User, rely heavily on back-end databases to retain the information associated with the applications. Tools such as Oracle PeopleSoft and Microsoft BizTalk, as well as Web sites such as Amazon.com, Salesforce.com, and Microsoft.com, store large quantities of data in databases that they could not function without. In SharePoint, you have yet another excellent example of an application platform built on top of back-end databases, using those databases to store content, user profile data, configuration settings, and much more.

But SharePoint is also somewhat unique in how much it depends on its back-end databases. An overwhelming majority of the data and settings associated with SharePoint are actually stored in SharePoint's databases, not the file system of the SharePoint servers in a farm. It can be quite a surprise to a first-time SharePoint administrator to learn that the documents in a library are actually stored in SharePoint's back-end database; this is not a fact easily explained or grasped until you really start to examine the platform. In fact, by default SharePoint does not save content on a server's file system. It inserts all content into a SharePoint content database in SQL Server and retrieves it as requested to be displayed to the user in a Web browser. Whenever SharePoint loads a page for a user, it makes calls to its databases to determine what goes on the page and how it is displayed. Granted, SharePoint also uses the template files and application code stored on its servers when rendering a page, but it's a good bet that if you have unique content on a SharePoint site, it's being retrieved from a database.

The same goes for the configuration settings and details for your SharePoint environment. The majority of such information is not saved in a configuration file or the Windows Registry on your SharePoint servers. Instead, SharePoint has a specific configuration database designed to house the configuration settings for your environment as well as details on every server and Web application in it. Saying that SharePoint is somewhat dependent on its databases to operate is like saying that you somewhat need oxygen to live; if SharePoint's databases go down, it cannot display documents, content, or even the simplest of pages without an error message. That means if you want your SharePoint environment to be up and running 24 hours a day, 7 days a week, 365 days a year, you had better take a close look at your SQL Server installation and how to keep it up and running, because if it goes down, it makes no difference what SharePoint's status is.

Initially in this chapter, we cover the basics of how to back up and restore your SQL Server databases. Once we've set the stage with the nuts and bolts of SQL Server backup and restore, we'll dive into the specifics of how you can, should, and should not protect your SharePoint databases using SQL Server's built-in tools. Be warned: this chapter is intended to outline the mechanics of how to configure Microsoft SQL Server to support SharePoint in the event of a catastrophic occurrence. It does not go into great detail about the architecture and administration of Microsoft SQL Server for general, non-SharePoint catastrophic operations. We encourage you to discuss and review the concepts and practices in this chapter with your database architects or administrators (DBAs) so they can be integrated with any disaster recovery activities that those parties may already have in place or are planning for your database servers. If you are also directly responsible for the administration of the SQL Server environment used by your SharePoint farm, you may want to consider obtaining an additional resource on SQL Server disaster recovery to further supplement the information in this chapter.

SharePoint's Database Options

As you have hopefully already encountered by this point in your journey with SharePoint, SQL Server in some shape or form is required to successfully install the SharePoint platform. Both SharePoint Foundation 2010 and SharePoint Server 2010 can run with several variations of SQL Server as their back-end database but cannot use other non-SQL server database platforms such as Oracle, MySQL, or even Microsoft's Access in that role. This requirement can be frustrating and limiting if your organization favors a database platform other than SQL Server, but it is not something that can be worked around or hacked to use a different type of database. If you implement SharePoint, you are also going to be installing some incarnation of SQL Server; it is just that simple.

As absolute as that constraint is, you are not without some options in exactly what flavor of SQL Server you choose to use as your SharePoint database provider. The list that follows outlines the six most common SQL Server variants that can host SharePoint 2010's back-end databases:

- **SQL Server 2005.** Microsoft supports SharePoint 2010 on the 64-bit version of SQL Server 2005 SP3 with Cumulative Update (CU) package 3. Any available edition of SQL Server 2005

(Developer, Workgroup, Standard, and Enterprise) is supported with SharePoint, subject to the edition's limitations (for example, the Developer SKU cannot be used in a production environment), as long as it is 64 bit. Although it isn't the latest and greatest database product available, SQL Server 2005 provides a stable database platform for SharePoint, analysis services, graphical and command line management tools, and much more.

- **SQL Server 2005 Express.** Much like the Microsoft SQL Server Desktop Engine (MSDE), SQL Server 2005 Express is a free edition of SQL Server 2005 distributed by Microsoft for use in small applications or environments. Express is constrained by three major limitations: the size of its databases (limited to 4GB of storage), its ability to use only a single CPU, and its ability to address only up to 1GB of RAM. Express can be managed via an available graphical management tool or the command line. SQL Server 2005 Express should be patched to the same version as SQL Server 2005's full editions, SP3 with CU3.

- **SQL Server 2008.** Microsoft supports SharePoint 2010 on the 64-bit version of SQL Server 2008 SP1 with CU2, CU5, or any CU greater than CU5 applied. Any available edition of SQL Server 2008 (Developer, Workgroup, Standard, and Enterprise) is supported with SharePoint, subject to the edition's limitations, as long as it is 64 bit. SQL Server 2008 is the latest full release of Microsoft's enterprise database platform, offering several functional improvements over SQL Server 2005, such as improved performance, spatial data types, backup compression, and much more.

- **SQL Server 2008 Express.** SQL Server 2008 Express is a free edition of SQL Server 2008 distributed by Microsoft for use in small applications or environments. Express is constrained by three major limitations: the size of its databases (limited to 4GB of storage), its ability to use only a single CPU, and its ability to only address up to 1GB of RAM. Express can be managed via an available graphical management tool or the command line. If you choose the all-in-one, or Basic, installation option for SharePoint 2010, the setup program installs SQL Server 2008 Express by default as the back-end database provider. You should patch SQL Server 2008 Express to the same version as SQL Server 2008's full editions, SP1 with CU2, CU5, or greater.

- **SQL Server 2008 R2.** Microsoft supports SharePoint 2010 on the 64-bit version of SQL Server 2008 R2. Any available edition of SQL Server 2008 R2 (Developer, Workgroup, Standard, and Enterprise) is supported with SharePoint, subject to the edition's limitations, as long as it is 64 bit. SQL Server 2008's R2 release adds even more functionality to the platform, including business intelligence tools such as PowerPivot, improved administrative features, and tighter integration with SharePoint.

- **SQL Server 2008 R2 Express.** SQL Server 2005 Express is a free edition of SQL Server 2005 distributed by Microsoft for use in small applications or environments. The major change to the Express edition for SQL Server 2008 R2 is that databases are now limited to 10GB of storage instead of just 4GB.

Note: One adjustment to the list of database platforms for SharePoint 2010 that you should take note of is the retirement of the use of SQL Server 2005 Embedded Edition (also known as the Windows Internal Database or WID). In Windows SharePoint Services (WSS) v3, the WID was automatically used as the back-end database host for all-in-one installations, but SharePoint Foundation 2010 now uses SQL Server 2008 Express as its database host for all-in-one installs, just like SharePoint Server 2010 does. This does make it easier to keep all of the installation options for SharePoint 2010 straight, but it is worth keeping in mind because it does mean you are facing a hard cap on the size of your Share-Point databases due to the limitations of the Express license.

Since the release of SQL Server 2008, Microsoft has made a large amount of information and data available regarding its benefits over the previous SQL Server 2005 release, both in general terms and specifically regarding SharePoint. Use of SQL Server 2008 can offer an improved administrative experience, backup compression functionality, richer analysis of business intelligence data, and much more. In addition to these benefits, SQL Server 2008 is expected to offer a much longer period of support coverage from Microsoft than SQL Server 2005 given its more recent entrance into the marketplace. Finally, it is worth mentioning that SQL Server 2008 was the database platform used by Microsoft during the development of SharePoint 2010, allowing the SharePoint product team to take full advantage of SQL Server 2008's feature set rather than targeting the less advanced SQL Server 2005.

The material covered in this chapter primarily discusses the use of SQL Server 2008 in a Share-Point environment. Much of the content also applies to SQL Server 2005, but there are cases when it doesn't. If you are looking for content specifically pertaining to SQL Server 2005, you should look into purchasing *SharePoint 2007 Disaster Recovery Guide*, which offers two chapters specifically devoted to backup/restore and high availability for that database platform.

The visual examples provided in this chapter were generated in a testing environment using the following platforms and components. Depending on how your environment is configured, your experiences may vary slightly.

- **Operating system.** Microsoft Windows Server 2008 R2 Enterprise Edition (build 7600)

- **Database.** Microsoft SQL Server 2008 Developer Edition with SP1 (build 10.0.2740)

- **Web server.** Microsoft Internet Information Services (IIS) 7.5

- **SharePoint.** SharePoint Foundation 2010 Release Candidate 1 (build 4730)

How to Back Up a SQL Server 2008 Database

The following steps walk you through the process necessary to back up a database in SQL Server 2008 through the SQL Server Management Studio GUI tool. These steps are designed to give you an idea of what you need to consider when backing up your own databases and how you

Figure 7.1 Enter the connection information for the target SQL Server database instance to connect to it via SQL Server Management Studio.

could go about the process. As covered later in this section, this is not the only way to back up your SharePoint databases through SQL Server, and it may not be the best option for you to choose, but it is a starting point from which you can better understand how SQL Server handles database backups.

Note: The user executing the backup must, at a minimum, have been granted the db_backupoperator security role within the target database server to back up a database.

---

1. Open SQL Server Management Studio and connect to the SQL Server database instance hosting the database you want to back up. Figure 7.1 depicts the connection dialog box shown when opening SQL Server Management Studio.

Note: SQL Server Management Studio is the graphical user interface (GUI) client management tool provided with SQL Server 2008 to administrate database instances and databases running on the platform. It is installed by default on all servers hosting SQL Server 2008 and can be individually installed on client computers to allow for connections to remote SQL Server hosts.

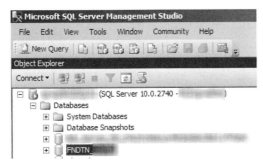

Figure 7.2 SQL Server Management Studio with a database selected for backup.

2. Once SQL Server Management Studio connects to the target database instance and opens, the contents of the instance are displayed in the tree view of the Object Explorer pane (which, by default, opens on the left side of the window). Expand the Databases entry in the Object Explorer, and find the name of the database targeted for backup. See Figure 7.2 for an example.

3. Right-click on the name of the database, select the Tasks option when the menu opens, and then click on the Back Up option (as shown in Figure 7.3) to open the Back Up Database dialog box.

4. The Back Up Database dialog box opens, allowing you to customize the backup operation to meet your needs. On the General page (see Figure 7.4), you can configure the source database for the backup and determine the backup type, the components to be backed up, the backup set associated with the backup, and the destination for the file(s) created by the backup operation. The Options page (see Figure 7.5) allows you to configure settings for overwriting existing backup files, backup reliability testing, and handling of transaction logs and tape drives by the backup operation. After you have configured the backup settings according to your requirements, click the OK button to start the backup operation.

Note: The Script drop-down menu (see Figure 7.6) at the top of the Back Up Database dialog box allows you to create a Transact-SQL (T-SQL) script that can be executed to back up your database without the GUI interface described in these steps. The script created by this process uses the same configuration settings that you selected in the dialog box. This allows you to configure your database backup using a user-friendly tool and convert those settings into a format that an experienced database administrator can use to automate the backup process.

---

5. As the backup runs, the Progress box in the lower-left corner of the dialog box (see Figure 7.7) displays a percentage indicating how much of the backup operation has been

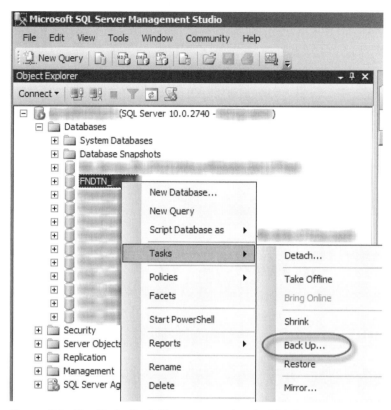

Figure 7.3 The Tasks Back Up menu option in SQL Server Management Studio.

completed. There is also a link displayed below the Progress indicator allowing you to cancel the operation.

6. After the backup is finished, a message box stating The backup of database <your database's name> completed successfully is displayed (see Figure 7.8). Click the OK button to return to the SQL Server Management Studio main window.

Before moving on to how to restore the target database from the backup file you just created, take a moment to review the configuration options available for your SQL Server backups. As noted in step 4, you have quite a few options available for configuring your database backup to meet your specific needs. If possible, it's a good idea to discuss these options with your database administrator before implementing them to confirm the correct course of action to take for your system.

Database Recovery Models

SQL Server offers three types of recovery models for each database it hosts: Full, Simple, and Bulk-Logged. The main differentiating factor between the three recovery models is how the

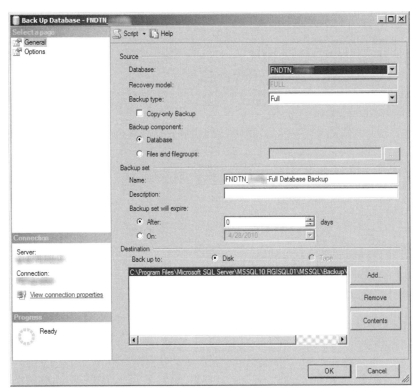

Figure 7.4   The General page of the Back Up Database dialog box.

transaction logs for a database are managed and backed up. By default, a database uses the same recovery model as the SQL Server system-level "model" database, which should be Full if the setting is not changed after installation. Of course, SharePoint is a bit of an exception to that rule. Because SharePoint's installers and tools create its databases, those databases follow a different set of rules than databases created directly in SQL Server. Each section that follows notes which SharePoint databases are created with the related recovery model. If you want to change the recovery model of a SharePoint database once it is created, you can modify it in the SQL Server Management Studio via the database's properties or via a T-SQL command.

Full Recovery Model

As its name implies, the Full recovery model protects data about every transaction made in the database by requiring that a backup of the database's transaction log be made along with one of the database. By including a backup of every transaction for the database, the Full recovery model is the only model that allows for a database to be restored to a specific time in its history. You should use the Full recovery model if your data is mission critical and you need the ability to restore backups to a specific point in time. For the Full recovery model to be completely

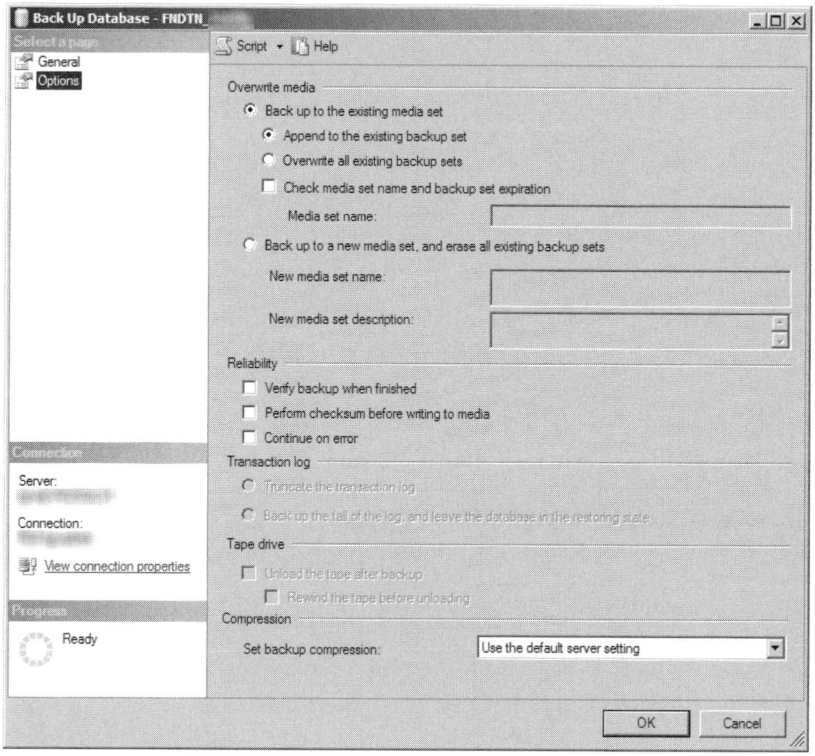

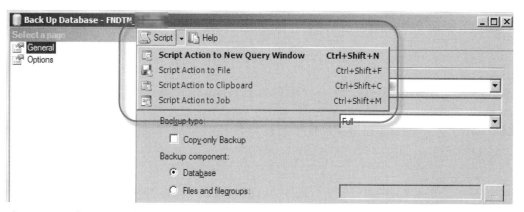

Figure 7.5   The Options page of the Back Up Database dialog box.

Figure 7.6   The Script drop-down menu of the Back Up Database dialog box.

effective, you must make regular backups of both your database's data and log files. By default, SharePoint's Configuration database, the databases associated with the Central Administration site, and any content databases created through Central Administration, PowerShell, STSADM, or the SharePoint object model are set with the Full recovery model.

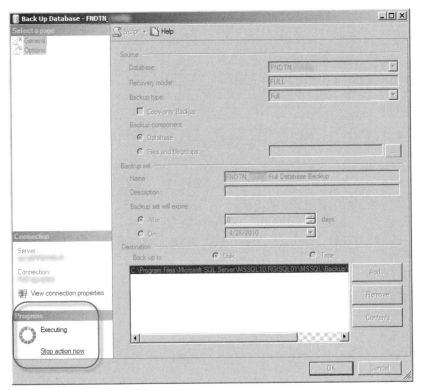

Figure 7.7   The Progress indicator shows the status of the backup operation as it runs.

Caution: When evaluating recovery models, keep in mind the storage implications of choosing one model over another, in addition to what backup and restore data is being retained. Because the Full recovery model allows you to record every transaction executed in a database by also backing up the transaction log, it requires a great deal more space to store that data within the database's transaction logs. You may find that you are prevented from using the Full recovery mode due to a lack of available storage, in which case you must keep in mind the impact that has on how you can restore your databases.

Simple Recovery Model

The Simple recovery model retains the least amount of information about the database being backed up. No transaction logs are backed up, meaning that the database can only be restored to the most recent full or differential database backup, not to a specific point in the database's transactional history. The Simple recovery model is ideal when your data is not critical (such as a development environment), is not subject to frequent change (not a likelihood for a SharePoint database), or is not a requirement to recover all transactions since the last backup. By

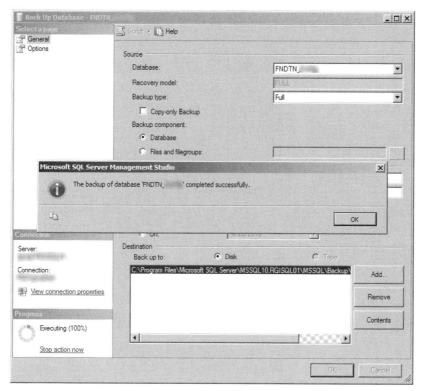

Figure 7.8 When the backup operation is completed, SQL Server Management Studio displays a completion dialog box.

default, databases associated with SharePoint Service Applications, such as the Search databases, are set with the Simple recovery model.

Bulk-Logged Recovery Model

The Bulk-Logged recovery model represents a middle-ground option between the Full and Simple recovery models. Like the Full recovery model, the Bulk-Logged recovery model requires the database's transaction log to also be backed up, allowing it to track transactions made in the database. The Bulk-Logged recovery model is designed to reduce the logging of bulk operations such as data imports and index management actions to a minimum, providing some of the performance benefits of the Simple recovery model. Microsoft recommends only using the Bulk-Logged recovery model in specific circumstances, switching to it prior to bulk operations and then returning to the Full or Simple models once the bulk operations are completed.

Database Backup Types

SQL Server 2008 offers several types of backups that can be made for the databases hosted in an instance: full, differential, partial, and transaction log. Each option is designed to provide a unique set of benefits to meet a variety of needs and use cases, but each comes with its own unique set of drawbacks as well. When considering which backup type to use for each of your SharePoint databases, consider these attributes in conjunction with the use of the specific database. Some databases may need to be restored quickly, for example, in which case it may make sense to use full backups on a frequent basis. On the other hand, differential backups typically require less storage space than full backups, but they often take longer to restore. This is just one example of a trade-off you must consider. The selection and application of backup types in your environment can have serious implications on the effectiveness and cost of your SharePoint implementation.

Note: SQL Server 2008 stores a database in the file system of a host server across a set of files. You can group these files into collections known as *file groups* for ease of allocation and administration. Each database must have at least one data file and one log file, although it can possess more than one. If you use multiple files for a SharePoint content database, Microsoft strongly recommends that you protect it with SQL Server's backup and restore tools instead of SharePoint. SharePoint's restore tools cannot restore a database with multiple files as effectively as SQL Server's tools can.

The list that follows defines each backup type within the context of SQL Server and discusses its common use cases.

- **Full.** A full database backup backs up the entire database, including its full data files and the transaction log components necessary to allow the whole database to be recovered. Because a full backup encompasses everything associated with a database, its output requires the most storage space. Additionally, a full backup of a database is required before any other type of backup can be made for that database.

- **Differential.** A differential backup of a SQL Server database only includes the data in the database that has changed since the last full backup was made of the database. Differential backups can be requested for a database or one of its files or file groups. The biggest advantage of a differential backup is that it doesn't take up as much space as a full backup and can be completed more quickly. As noted in the previous bullet, you must first perform a full backup of a database before the differential option becomes available.

Note: To restore a differential backup, you must first restore its associated full backup set or include that full backup set in the requested restore operation.

- **Partial.** Partial backups are designed to provide a smaller and faster backup alternative for large databases with multiple file groups. Partial backups always include the database's primary file group and any other file groups set as writeable. If a database is set to be read-only, a partial backup of that database includes only the primary file group. The partial backup option was originally designed for read-only databases using the Simple recovery model, but you can also use it with read-write databases and the Full and Bulk-Logged recovery models.

- **File.** You can back up a database's data file (or files) individually. If a single file is corrupted or deleted, backing up the individual files can allow for a speedier recovery because only the affected file has to be restored. This can become complex if your database has a large number of files associated with it or overdo it if you have only one file for your database, so you should only use it in when your database environment has specific needs or requirements for file backups.

- **Copy-only.** Most types of SQL Server backups have an actual impact on the source database, affecting how the backup (as well as subsequent backups) are restored. One method that is an exception to this is the copy-only backup, which is specifically intended to not modify the target database in any way when the backup is made—hence the use of the term *copy*. Usually, making a backup changes the database and affects how later backups are restored. Normal backup types change a database's log archive point, which creates a need to properly sequence backups so that you can properly apply transaction logs when restoring these backups. Copy-only backups remove the need for that sequencing, so if it or the ordering of the backup files for it is interrupted, you can still restore the database.

- **Transaction log.** A transaction log backup creates a backup copy of the log files detailing all the modifications that have been made to a database over time. Transaction log backups are available only with the Full and Bulk-Logged recovery models; because the Simple recovery model does not offer the ability to recover to a specific point in time, there is no need to track changes that have been made to a database. Transaction logs are also important to preserve because of the role they can play in other SQL Server high availability (HA) functionality, such as database mirroring and log shipping. Additionally, transaction log backups play a vital role if you are using the Full recovery model for your database; to do a full recovery with that model, you must have completed a full backup *and* at least one transaction log backup of your database. Performing frequent transaction log backups also keeps the database's transaction logs from taking up too much space on the database because they are truncated as part of the backup process, allowing SQL Server to delete them and reclaim disk space.

Note: SQL Server writes all its actions to a database's transaction logs immediately after the actions are requested, before changes to the database are actually completed. This ensures that the requested changes to the database are recorded and preserved in the transaction logs should a system failure or data corruption occur during execution.

Backup Expiration Settings

In the Backup Set section of the General page in the Back Up Database dialog box, you can configure specific expiration settings for your database backup. Depending on the radio button you select, your backup can expire after a specified number of days or on a specific date. The option button for the After option is selected by default in the Back Up Database dialog box, and the Days field value is set to 0. You can modify this default value by configuring the media retention setting within SQL Server's configuration options. If you are backing up your database via a maintenance plan or regularly scheduled backup, specifying a value for this setting prevents SQL Server from overwriting your backup file until the number of days or date threshold has been met.

Caution: Setting an expiration value for your backup does not prevent it from being overwritten by applications or users outside of SQL Server. You can still delete the files through the file system or overwrite them in their storage location.

Backup Destinations

Unlike SharePoint, SQL Server can back up its databases directly to a tape storage location attached to the server in addition to a server's hard disk. In the Destination section of the General page in the Back Up Database dialog box, you can enter up to 64 paths by clicking the Add button and navigating to the desired storage location. This allows you to simultaneously create multiple copies of your backup files without manual intervention. You can also remove a backup path from the list by selecting it and clicking the Remove button. Selecting a path and clicking the Contents button displays summary information for the backup and a list of the backup sets associated with it.

Note: The location you select for your backup media set must be associated with or available from the server hosting the SQL Server instance that you are connected to. So if you are running SQL Server Management Studio on your workstation and connecting to a remote database instance, you are only able to save the backup to a file system directory or attached tape drive on the database host server, not on your local workstation. Once the backup is created, you can copy it to your local workstation if you desire, but you cannot create backup files on your local workstation through the backup operation.

Overwrite Existing Backup Media

The Overwrite Media section of the Options page in the Back Up Database dialog box allows you to determine how SQL Server handles any existing files in the backup storage location that were created by a previous backup operation. (See Figure 7.5 for an example of the Options page.) You have the option to add your current backup's data to the existing backup media set or create a new backup media set and have SQL Server erase the previous files. If you chose to use the current media set, you still can decide whether to append your data to the existing files in the media set or overwrite it. You are also given the option to have SQL Server look for potential naming and expiration date conflicts between the media sets by selecting the Check Media Set Name and Backup Set Expiration check box and entering a media set name in the text field. If you chose to create a new media set, you must enter a new name for the media set in the associated text field.

Reliability Checks

SQL Server 2008 also offers the ability to check a backup media set when the operation is finished to confirm that the output of the operation is viable. In the Reliability section of the Options page in the Back Up Database dialog box, you have the option to require SQL Server to verify the backup files when the operation is completed as well as to request a checksum verification of the backup before it is written to its storage media. The backup file verification confirms that the media set has been written to its storage media without error. The checksum verification confirms that the data within the backup media set is consistent with any checksums associated with the database to ensure that valid data is being written to the storage media and has not become corrupted.

Caution: As with almost every decision an information technology (IT) professional must make throughout the course of a day, there are potential drawbacks to performing reliability checks that must be taken into account. Specifically, these checks can have a significant negative impact on the database's throughput while they are being performed and utilize a great deal of the host server's available CPU processing power, both of which can cause a serious degradation of the database's performance. It is important to determine how necessary it is to perform reliability checks on your database's backup and when these activities are occurring if requested so that conflicts with periods of high user activity can be avoided.

Database Snapshots

Originally introduced with SQL Server 2005, database snapshots offer administrators another option for creating a point-in-time view of a database on top of SQL Server's normal backup functionality. Database snapshots capture a fixed viewpoint of a target database, including all of its state and content except for any uncommitted transactions. Database snapshots are attractive because they can take up much less storage than a backup file by only tracking the changes made to a database after a snapshot is made, but this is not always the case, especially for databases that are frequently updated (such as heavily trafficked SharePoint collaboration content databases). According to Microsoft, snapshots are best used as a reporting resource (creating a view of the database at a specific point in time for later analysis) or for immediate protection of a database prior to a major update, but not as a regular or scheduled backup solution.

Note: SQL Server's database snapshot capability is available only in Developer and Enterprise Edition SKUs for SQL Server 2005, 2008, and 2008 R2.

Unlike previous versions of the platform, SharePoint 2010 includes native support for SQL Server database snapshots. You can explicitly create, delete, and manage snapshots through PowerShell and custom code that is written against the SharePoint object model. In addition, a number of platform functions include support for leveraging database snapshots in their operations.

For example, the `Backup-SPSite` PowerShell cmdlet includes a `-UseSqlSnapshot` switch that allows you to perform a site collection backup against a snapshot of a content database rather than the actual database. Using a snapshot for this operation removes the need to lock the site collection to prevent update and write operations to the database when the backup is being performed. When the backup operation is complete, the cmdlet takes care of cleaning up the database snapshot that was used. The net effect is that users can continue to operate as they normally would without interference from the backup operation.

Snapshots are not a replacement for backup and restore operations, but you can leverage them to enhance or improve the overall administrative experience associated with these types of tasks.

Mirrored Backup Media Sets

Another feature only available in the Enterprise SKU for SQL Server 2005, 2008, and 2008 R2 but relevant to the topic of disaster recovery is mirrored backup media sets. Mirrored backup media sets allow a database to be backed up to multiple backup storage locations with a single operation, adding greater redundancy to backup operations and protection from storage hardware failure. Mirrored backups can use either disk or tape as the target storage medium, but the same type of hardware must be used for all mirrored targets in a given operation. A single operation can include up to four mirrors of the database, and restoration of mirrored backup sets allows for every mirror within the set to be used as the source for the restore. Mirrored backup media sets provide an additional option for increasing the redundancy of your SQL Server DR solution, but they can easily come with an additional cost, thanks to the requirement for additional storage media, not to mention the SQL Server Enterprise Edition license.

What's New in SQL Server 2008 Backup

Microsoft added several new features and enhancements to the SQL Server platform with its 2008 release. These include spatial data types for integrating geographical data into applications, the ability to manage multiple SQL Server 2008 hosts from a single location using policy-based management, and data compression to reduce the amount of storage database files need and improve disk input/output (I/O) and memory utilization. This chapter is about SQL

Server 2008 backup and restore, though, so let's focus on what's new in that area: backup compression.

Backup compression is a feature completely new to SQL Server 2008. It was not possible in SQL Server 2005 to compress database backups in any way with the out-of-the-box tools available for SQL Server. In SQL Server 2008, backups can be automatically compressed when they are created without impacting the targeted database. Compression is available for all types of database backups, including log backups. Additionally, when a compressed backup is restored into SQL Server 2008, the data stored in it is automatically uncompressed. This means that the restore process for compressed backups is no different from the restore process for uncompressed backups.

It may seem that the biggest advantage of this backup compression feature is its ability to use less storage space to retain a backup, allowing you to reduce your storage usage and costs. Although this is definitely a benefit, there is another gain that can be equally valuable to your environment, if not greater: reduced disk I/O. When you compress the backup file, it takes less time to write the backup file to your disk and frees up that I/O for more critical activities, such as writing uploaded documents into a SharePoint content database or updating a Search crawl database. Depending on the resources available for your database servers, this can positively affect your performance over uncompressed backups. This is true especially if, once these smaller files are created, you can transfer them more quickly than uncompressed backups via a network connection that may have restrictions on its bandwidth, such as a local area network (LAN), WiFi, or a wide area network (WAN), to a remote storage repository.

Keep in mind, though, that this new feature in SQL Server 2008 has some drawbacks. First and foremost, a performance trade-off happens during compression: although your disk I/O impact is reduced, the CPU utilization that is necessary increases to allow the server to perform the compression function. The good news is that, overall, the usual result from backup compression is better overall performance, but you need to keep an eye on CPU and disk performance metrics in your environment to understand exactly what the benefits of using backup compression are for your SharePoint databases and if they are worth the cost.

Tip: You can also mitigate some of the risk that backup compression presents to your CPU performance by taking advantage of another new feature in SQL Server 2008: the Resource Governor. With the Resource Governor, you can limit the utilization of your server's CPU resources by the backup process so that it does not affect other more important processes during peak loads.

To enable compression of a backup for a database, locate the Compression section on the Options page of the Backup Database dialog box, and select the desired option from the Set Backup Compression pull-down menu. For an example of the Compression section, see the bottom of Figure 7.5. By default, compression is not enabled for databases in SQL Server 2008. You must select to compress the database in the dialog box's Options page, configure it as a setting in a T-SQL backup script, or change the default setting for the entire SQL Server instance if you want to use the function.

Finally, you should note some limitations to the use of backup compression prior to implementing it in your environment. Make sure you closely review the list that follows and understand how its points can apply to your SharePoint environment and its use of SQL Server 2008 before you take advantage of backup compression.

- **SQL Server 2008 license.** Backup compression is available only with the Enterprise SKU for SQL Server 2008. The good news is that if you are running SQL Server 2008 R2, backup compression is available with both the Standard and Enterprise SKUs.

- **Backups lack compatibility with previous versions of SQL Server.** You cannot restore compressed backups created with SQL Server 2008 into older versions of SQL Server such as SQL Server 2005 or 2000.

- **Lacks compatibility with Transparent Data Encryption (TDE).** If your database has TDE enabled, you cannot compress its backups.

There is another new feature in SQL Server 2008 that may not seem to be directly related to the topic of backup and restore, but it does provide some interesting implications and circumstances to consider in your disaster recovery planning for your SQL Server 2008 databases: Remote Binary Large Object (BLOB) Storage, or RBS for short. The direct implications of RBS are discussed in the "What Cannot (or Should Not) Be Backed Up" section that follows, but it is important to first set the stage with a description of this feature.

A BLOB is commonly backed by a variable-length SQL Server column data type that allows for large amounts of binary data, such as a Microsoft Word document or an encrypted file, to be stored directly in a SQL Server database table rather than in a file system directory. Traditionally, SharePoint has made heavy use of BLOB columns in its database tables, storing documents uploaded into a site directly in these columns. SharePoint 2010 is no different in that regard. BLOBs offer much flexibility so that SharePoint can handle a range of file types and sizes, but they can also consume a great deal of storage space and computational resources on a SQL Server instance.

To try to alleviate the pressure that BLOB usage can place on SQL Server, Microsoft introduced the RBS feature with SQL Server 2008, which allows BLOB data to be stored in a remote location but still be accessed via SQL Server. RBS enables SQL Server to designate external content addressable stores (CAS) as dedicated storage repositories for BLOB data that still present to client applications, such as SharePoint, as if it were stored in a database table directly. RBS uses a flexible provider model so that different storage solutions can be chosen to meet the specific requirements of your environment. SQL Server provides its own RBS provider, the SQL FILE-STREAM provider, for use with SQL Server 2008, but third-party providers such as Metalogix's StoragePoint, EMC, and AvePoint's DocAve Extender are also available. RBS can be used with any edition of SQL Server 2008, but a storage solution other than storage locally attached to the host server can be used only with the Enterprise edition. The FILESTREAM provider is included with SQL Server 2008 at no additional cost, but it does have some limiting factors to consider: it can only work with a SQL Server host's local drives, it doesn't support database snapshots or mirroring, and it doesn't support TDE, just to name a few.

In the case of SharePoint 2010, awareness of SQL Server's RBS capability was added as a new feature. This allows SharePoint to be configured consistently regardless of how SQL Server's storage is configured; at the same time, it allows SharePoint administrators and DBAs to have some flexibility in how SharePoint uses its storage. Although it may seem like this is a feature that would appeal only to the largest of enterprises, it also provides smaller organizations with appealing flexibility. One major change to the database situation for SharePoint 2010 is that it is no longer possible to create databases of unlimited size using the free Windows Internal Database included in a basic install of Windows SharePoint Services (WSS). The only free database option for SharePoint 2010 is SQL Server Express, but its databases are limited to 4GB (SQL Server 2005 and 2008 Express) or 10GB (SQL Server 2008 R2 Express). You can overcome that size limitation with the use of RBS because content stored with RBS does not count against the total size of the database.

Tip: The use of RBS as a way to overcome the sizing limitations of SQL Server Express is likely to be most applicable when upgrading a WSS v3 environment using the Windows Internal Database to SharePoint Foundation or Server 2010. If the size of one or more of the databases in your Windows Internal Database instance is larger than your new target SQL Server Express instance, you are not going to be able to migrate it unless you purchase a full SQL Server license or implement RBS.

If you are thinking about using SQL Server Express and RBS because of database sizing issues, in general it is a good idea to seriously consider using a full SQL Server license for your SharePoint environment instead. SQL Server Express is a good platform, but it does not provide the same overall scalability, coverage, and functionality of a purchased version of SQL Server. Also, there are some performance limitations on SQL Server Express. (It is limited to only one core on a server, and there isn't good data available at this time on how RBS performs with SQL Server Express.) If you're considering it as a temporary or short-term part of your migration strategy, that's great. But it probably isn't the way to go if you aren't including a plan to move to a paid version of SQL Server in your migration.

SharePoint and Backing Up SQL Server 2008

The steps at the beginning of the previous section show you one method by which you can create a backup of a database in SQL Server 2008; you can use them to back up pretty much any database hosted in a SQL Server 2008 database instance. There are other more complex ways to create database backups in SQL Server 2008, such as T-SQL scripting and maintenance plans, but as mentioned earlier, it is best to leave those more involved approaches to the experts. Because you now have a starting point for backing up your SharePoint environment via SQL Server, it is important to start thinking about the issues and restrictions specific to SharePoint that you need to address when moving forward with the process.

Tip: For the best results when backing up your SharePoint databases, plan on executing the backup operations during periods of reduced user activity in your SharePoint environment, such as after normal business hours or during planned maintenance periods. Also, avoid scheduling them against other scheduled activities within the farm itself, such as search crawls or usage log processing. This ensures that a minimal number of changes are being made to your databases while the backups are being created; in addition, it prevents your end users from experiencing performance issues when attempting to access SharePoint. SQL Server backup operations can be resource intensive for their host instances, and you should try to avoid impacting SQL Server's ability to serve its data to SharePoint as much as possible.

If you need to back up a SharePoint database with SQL Server during normal business hours or when there is regular or elevated user activity in the sites within that database, consider applying a read-only site lock for affected site collections in the SharePoint Central Administration site or with PowerShell prior to executing the backup. This action can ensure that your users do not encounter degraded performance when accessing the site during a backup operation, as well as prevent them from tying up the database when the operation is also trying to use it. This is not required for a backup operation but can reduce the time a backup takes to complete and the number of support calls that may be made regarding poor performance. If you are making a backup through the Central Administration site or via a PowerShell cmdlet, SharePoint automatically sets the targeted site collection to read-only, but with SQL Server, you must manually configure the site collection before backing it up.

What Can Be Backed Up

Above all else, the most important aspect of your SharePoint environment, the reason it is so important to your business, is what your end users put into it. The contents of your SharePoint sites, whether they are documents, lists, forms, or some other form of knowledge capital, are most likely to be the first and foremost item that your organization needs replaced should disaster strike your SharePoint environment. Happily, you can easily back up SharePoint's content databases and restore them at a later date using SQL Server's tools, using either the steps described earlier or the other options that SQL Server offers.

Note: The location you select for your backup media set must be associated with or available from the server hosting the SQL Server instance that you are connected to. So if you are running SQL Server Management Studio on your workstation and connecting to a remote database instance, you are only able to save the backup to a file system directory or attached tape drive on the database host server, not on your local workstation. Once you create the backup, you can copy it to your local workstation if you desire, but you cannot create backup files on your local workstation through the backup operation.

In addition to your SharePoint content databases, don't overlook other databases in your SQL Server environment that may contain critical information for your SharePoint environment, even if they are not explicitly SharePoint databases: SQL Server's system databases. Every SQL Server instance is created with several default databases that are required to store critical data about the state of the instance, such as its MASTER, MSDB, MODEL, and TEMPDB databases. You can also back up these system databases if you want to preserve the most recent state of your SQL Server instance. It may not be necessary to do so, depending on your requirements for data preservation and your ability to rebuild the instance, so you should validate your plans with your SQL DBA, if possible. Of those databases, the MASTER, MSDB, and MODEL databases are potential candidates that you should consider backing up; the TEMPDB is re-created every time a SQL Server instance is restarted.

What Cannot (or Should Not) Be Backed Up

Much like the out-of-the-box backup tools provided with SharePoint, SQL Server cannot back up your SharePoint environment's IIS Web server settings, custom code or site templates, the SharePoint Root directory (also known as the 14 Hive), or any other items located in the file system of your SharePoint servers. Because these items are not stored in a SharePoint database in SQL Server, it stands to reason that they cannot be backed up. Nonetheless, it is important to keep this fact in mind when developing your comprehensive disaster recovery plan so that you are aware of what holes you need to fill with alternative tools or approaches.

If your SharePoint content is being stored in an RBS-enabled content database, you are not directly backing up BLOB data when you back up your database; you are simply backing up pointers that are understood by the RBS provider that is associated with the database. To protect the BLOB data that is tied to the content database, your backup strategy must incorporate your RBS provider; more specifically, you must ensure that the storage location or locations that the RBS provider uses are protected by some data protection strategy. This makes the total protection of SharePoint data stored in RBS-enabled content databases more difficult, and any plan depends on the nature of the RBS provider.

It is important to understand the details of this constraint. It only pertains to backups performed using SQL Server's tools, any other backup tools that operate directly against the databases, or any non-Microsoft RBS solutions. If you are backing up an RBS-enabled content database with SharePoint backup tools in the Central Administration site or PowerShell via the FILESTREAM provider, the database and its associated BLOBs are backed up together in a single operation because SharePoint's application programming interfaces (APIs) hide RBS implementation details from the applications that use them. If you are using a third-party RBS provider, Share-Point 2010's backup tools do not include those BLOBs; you must manually back them up.

The two major aspects of a SharePoint environment that we haven't covered yet are its configuration (specifically its configuration database) and its Service Applications. Although you can back up your SharePoint 2010 farm's configuration database and the databases associated with its Service Applications using SQL Server's tools, you also need to understand how to use the backups of those items. With Service Applications, you can restore a backup of their associated database, but you must have taken a backup of the Service Application through the Central Administration site or PowerShell and restored that into a farm before you can restore its database. In most cases, SharePoint's built-in tools or a third party backup tool is going to be a better option for protecting those items in case of a disaster. There can be utility in creating SQL Server backups of the Service Application databases, but it is more as a point of reference or referral than for disaster recovery protection.

With the SharePoint farm's configuration database, you can't restore directly back into a live farm; there's just no supported way to do it with SQL Server's tools. The good news with Share-Point 2010 is that this is not the end of the discussion. SharePoint 2010 introduces several new tools in the area of backup and restore. Interestingly, one of those tools changes what you can now do with SQL Server backups of a farm's configuration database. One of SharePoint 2010's new PowerShell cmdlets, `Backup-SPConfigurationDatabase`, allows you to generate a configuration database backup of a configuration database attached to your current farm, a separate farm (assuming the account running the script has the proper rights in that farm), and most importantly, a configuration database that is not attached to a farm.

This means you could take a SQL Server backup of your configuration database and restore that database to a SQL instance in the event of a disaster. You could then extract the details of the database's configuration using `Backup-SPConfigurationDatabase`. You can then use this backup like you would any other configuration database backup created via the PowerShell cmdlet, except that you preserved the data in it via SQL Server's tools instead of SharePoint's. For more information on the new backup and restore tools in the Central Administration site and PowerShell, see Chapter 9, "SharePoint 2010 Central Administration Backup and Restore" and Chapter 10, "SharePoint 2010 Command Line Backup and Restore: PowerShell."

Note: This aspect of SharePoint 2010's new configuration backup functionality is only possible via the PowerShell cmdlet; the Central Administration site can only take configuration database backups of the farm it governs.

Database Sizing

As with any SQL Server backup operation, the size of the SharePoint database you are backing up directly influences the amount of time that the operation takes to complete: the larger the database, the longer it takes to finish. As your databases grow larger, you need to continually evaluate the timing and approach you take when backing them up so you can minimize the impact of your backup operations on your SharePoint environment's ability to serve its users. You may find that after a certain point you are no longer able to complete full backup operations quickly enough to meet your desired schedule. When this happens, consider using differential backups or moving some site collections to new content databases to shorten your backup periods. Monitoring and managing the size and usage of your SharePoint databases should already be a part of your operational SharePoint maintenance plan, but these activities become even more important when you start considering disaster recovery.

Tip: There is no hard, fast limit on how large a SharePoint site collection should be. In some cases, SharePoint site collections and their associated SQL Server content databases have grown to be hundreds of terabytes (TB) large and still been viable for end users. But just because this is possible does not make it feasible, especially from a disaster recovery perspective. Microsoft recommends limiting your content databases to 200GB and an individual site collection in a database to 100GB unless it is the only site collection in a database, but these are not absolute. Discuss this topic with your organization's SQL Server DBA, because this person often has preferences for general database size limits that need to be observed.

The good news is that SharePoint can be quite flexible when it comes to its content databases, allowing you to associate one to many of them with a single Web application. The main limitation is that you cannot divide a site collection across content databases, which means that if a single site collection grows beyond your size restrictions, you must split it into two collections or have content removed to comply. SharePoint administrators also have several commands available, such as the `Move-SPSite` PowerShell cmdlet, to help them move site collections from one content database to another.

Another less obvious item to consider is how the site collections within your SharePoint databases are utilized. If numerous users access the site, collaborate on documents, or update content at the same time, it can directly impact your backup and restore planning. These activities lead to SharePoint reading and writing to its databases with increased frequency, which in turn means SQL Server is writing a large amount of data to the transaction logs associated with these databases. Because a full backup of a SQL Server database includes the database's active transaction logs, heavy usage of your sites adds to the time it takes to back up (and restore) the databases associated with them. If you find that this is negatively affecting your ability to preserve your SharePoint farm's databases, you may need to reevaluate your farm and site hierarchies to better distribute use traffic across databases.

Note: The previous database sizing issues have a similar impact on SQL Server restore operations. One reason it is important to test both your backup and restore strategies is so that you have an accurate estimate of how long each activity should take in expected conditions. If your restore operations are taking hours to execute due to the size of your databases and your system needs to be available as soon as possible, you are better served by finding that out through testing rather than the first time you execute your disaster recovery plan during an outage that is costing you real money every second.

How to Restore a SQL Server 2008 Database Backup

As with the previous walkthrough of how to back up a database in SQL Server 2008, the following steps give you a general idea of what is involved in restoring a backup of an existing database through the SQL Server Management Studio. This is not the only way you can restore a database in SQL Server and is not necessarily going to be the best approach for you to take with your SharePoint environment and its specific needs. These steps are intended to get you thinking about the needs and requirements for your environment and the information you need to have on hand before you execute a SharePoint database restore through SQL Server.

Caution: If the database being restored is not currently hosted in the target database instance, the user must have `CREATE DATABASE` permissions in the instance to restore the database. If the database already exists in the target database instance, the user must be assigned the `sysadmin` and `dbcreator` server roles in the instance or be the owner (also known as the *dbo*) of the database. If a password has been assigned to the backup media set being used in the restore operation, that value must be provided for SQL Server to execute the restore.

---

1. Open SQL Server Management Studio and connect to the SQL Server database instance to which you want to restore the database backup.

2. When SQL Server Management Studio connects to the target database instance and opens, the contents of the instance are displayed in the tree view of the Object Explorer

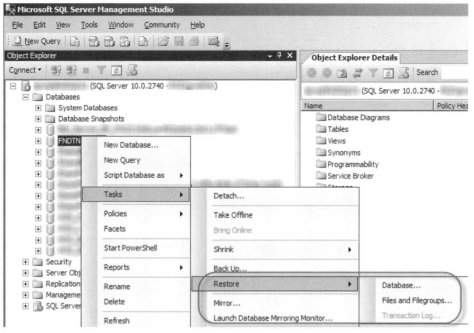

Figure 7.9   Select the Restore, Database option from the Tasks menu.

pane (which by default opens on the left side of the window). Expand the Databases entry in the Object Explorer, and find the name of the database targeted to be over-written with a previously created backup.

3. Right-click on the name of the database, select the Tasks option when the menu opens, select the Restore option, and then click on the Database option to open the Restore Database dialog box. See Figure 7.9 for an example.

Tip: This action automatically takes the target database offline and prevents other applications or processes from accessing it. Whenever possible, attempt to undertake a restore operation during a period of advertised or regular downtime for your SharePoint environment.

---

4. The Restore Database dialog box opens, allowing you to customize the restore operation to meet your needs. On the General page (see Figure 7.10), you can configure the database to be restored, determine the source of the backup set used in the restore operation, and select the specific backup set used to restore the database. The Options page (see Figure 7.11) allows you to configure settings for overwriting the existing database, preserve replication settings, prompt before each restore activity, restrict

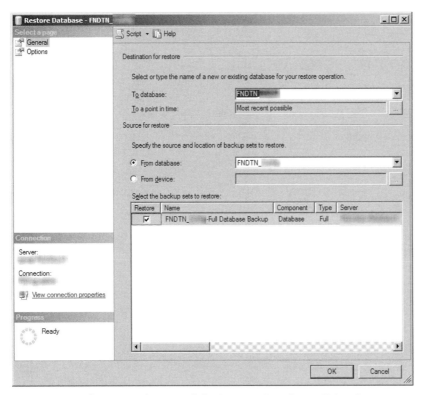

Figure 7.10   The General page of the Restore Database dialog box.

access to the database once it is restored, configure where the database's files are restored on the server's file system, and determine the type of recovery state the database is placed in when the restore operation is completed. After you have configured the restore according to your requirements, click the OK button to start the restore operation.

Note: As with the Back Up Database dialog box, the Script drop-down menu at the top of the Restore Database dialog box allows you to create a T-SQL script that you can execute to restore your database without the GUI interface described in these steps.

---

5. As the restore operation executes, the Progress box in the lower-left corner of the dialog box displays a percentage indicating how much of it has been completed. There is also a link displayed below the progress indicator allowing you to cancel the operation.

6. Once the restore is finished, a window stating The restore of database <your database's name> completed successfully is displayed (see Figure 7.12). Click the OK button to return to the SQL Server Management Studio main window.

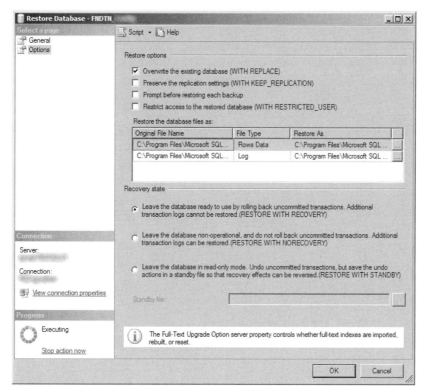

Figure 7.11   The Options page of the Restore Database dialog box.

Similar to database backups through SQL Server Management Studio, several configuration options are available in the Restore Database dialog box. You can use these options to specify the backup set that is used for the restore, where the backup is restored to, the state the database is placed in when the restore is finished, and much more. Again, discussing these options with your database administrator is highly recommended so that you can determine the best configuration to use with your environment.

Restore Destination Options

The first section of the Restore Database window's General tab, titled Destination for Restore, not only allows you to select where the backup is restored within the target database instance, but allows you choose a specific point in time where you want the database restored. In the To Database field, you can select a database from the drop-down menu to be overwritten by the backup, or you can type the name of an existing or new database as the restore target. By default, the database displayed in the field is the database you right-clicked on to open the Restore Database window. The drop-down menu is populated with all the databases hosted by the database instance.

The next field, To a Point in Time, is grayed out (disabled) by default and contains the text Most recent possible, indicating that the database will be restored to its condition when the backup

Figure 7.12   When the restore operation is completed, SQL Server Management Studio displays a completion dialog box.

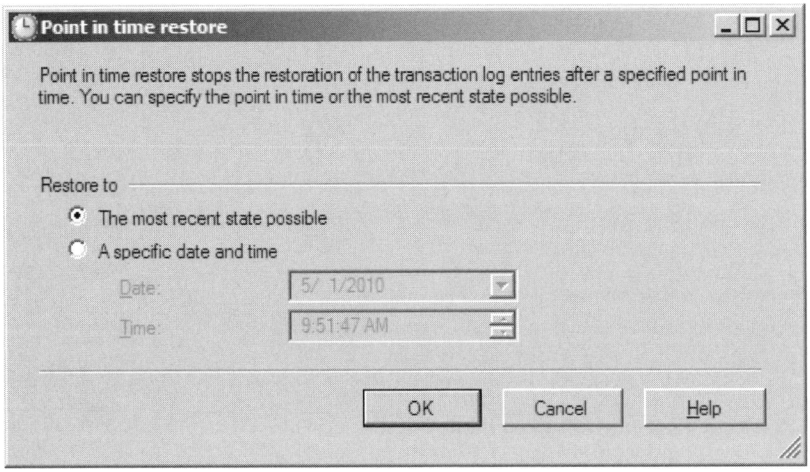

Figure 7.13   The Point in Time Restore dialog box.

set was created. To change this setting, click the ellipses (…) button to the right of the disabled text field. Doing so opens the Point in Time Restore dialog box (see Figure 7.13).

Note: The Point in Time Restore option is not available for databases configured to the Simple recovery model.

In this window, the option The Most Recent State Possible is initially selected, and the Date and Time fields are disabled. To select a specific point in time for the database to be restored to, select the A Specific Date and Time option button, which enables the Date and Time fields. Clicking the Date drop-down menu displays a calendar control (see Figure 7.14), where you can navigate to the specific date desired. You can update the Time field by either typing the desired value for each digit of the time or using the Up and Down arrows to the right of the text field to select the correct numerical value.

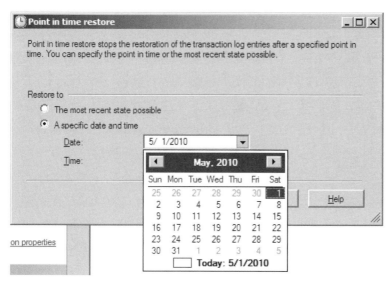

Figure 7.14   The Date drop-down menu of the Point in Time Restore dialog box.

Note: Selecting a date more recent than the date the target backup set was created, or a date that lies in the future, results in the database being restored to the most recent possible state.

Restore Source Options

In the Source for Restore section of the Restore Database window's General tab (see Figure 7.10), you can specify which backup set is used to restore your database. By default, the From Database option button is selected, and the drop-down menu next to it is populated with the name of the database you right-clicked to open the Restore Database window. This menu is populated with the databases hosted in the instance that have previously had backup sets created for them; if a database has not been backed up, it does not appear in this list. If the target database has not been backed up with SQL Server before, this field is blank. Selecting a different database in the From Database drop-down menu results in the Select the Backup Sets to Restore list box being updated to show the backup sets associated with the selected database. If the Select the Backup Sets to Restore list box displays more than one backup set, you can select the desired backup set by clicking its check box.

Selecting the From Device option button disables the From Database drop-down menu and the Select the Backup Sets to Restore list box. To select a device as the source of the backup, click the ellipses (...) button to the right of the disabled From Device text field. This opens the Specify Backup dialog box (see Figure 7.15), where you can select a file, tape, or device to be used as a backup source for the restore operation. You select your type of device from the Backup Media drop-down menu (File, Tape, or Backup Device, depending on the types of devices that are

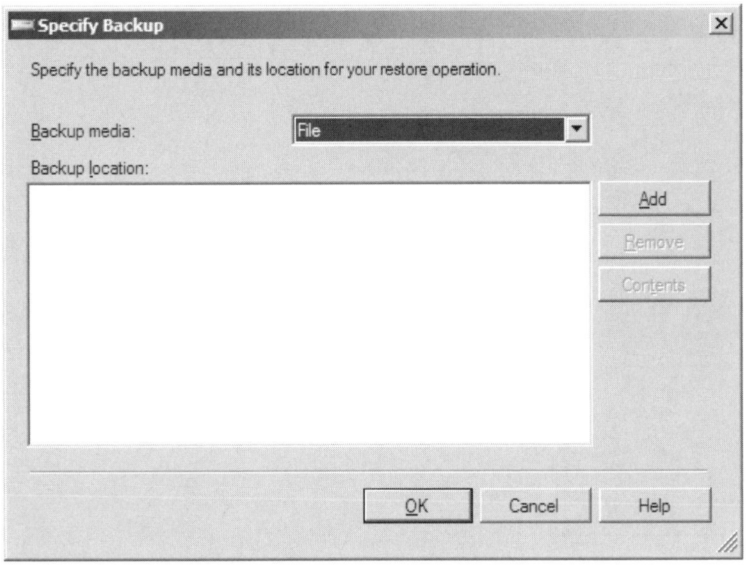

Figure 7.15 The Specify Backup dialog box.

attached to your system) and then click the Add button to add an instance of the selected device type. A dialog box opens, allowing you to select the desired backup from a list. See Figure 7.16 for an example of the Locate Backup File window. After selecting a backup, click the OK button to close the window and return to the Specify Backup window with your selected backup displayed in the Backup Location field. You can remove the backup selection by clicking the Remove button, and you can view the items in the backup by clicking the Contents button. Clicking the OK button saves your configuration and returns you to the Restore Backup window, where your selected backup is now shown in the Select the Backup Sets to Restore list box.

Note: Keep in mind that you must store the backup files to be used in the restore operation in a location you can access from the server hosting the target database instance. If you store the files on an unconnected device, such as your local workstation, you must copy the files to the server, map a connection on the host server to your local workstation, or place the files in a server-accessible network location.

Restore Options

The first section on the Options tab of the Restore Backup window, Restore Options, contains four check boxes that you can select to configure different aspects of the requested restore operation. By default, all four check boxes are unchecked.

- **Overwrite the Existing Database.** When you select this option, the restore operation completely overwrites an existing database and its associated files if its name matches the database listed in the To Database field on the General tab.

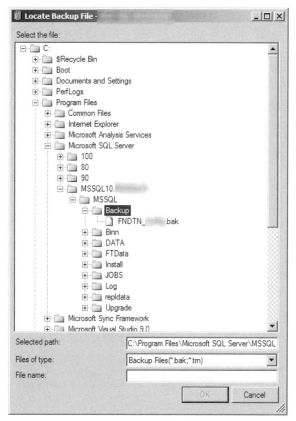

Figure 7.16   The Locate Backup File window.

- **Preserve the Replication Settings.** This option allows you to keep the original replication settings of the database in the backup set when restoring it to a server different from the server the database was backed up on. If the new server hosting the database has different replication settings than the original host, selecting this option prevents the server from overwriting the restored database with its local settings. It can be used only when the Leave the Database Ready to Use by Rolling Back the Uncommitted Transactions option is selected in the Recovery State section.

Note: Microsoft does not support the use of SQL Server 2008's replication functionality with SharePoint.

- **Prompt Before Restoring Each Backup.** This option prompts the user for confirmation prior to restoring each backup set requested by the restore operation, which can be helpful when you need to pause the restore operation for activities such as swapping backup tapes.

■ **Restrict Access to the Restored Database.** Selecting this option limits access to the database when the restore operation has completed to the following SQL Server security roles: db_owner, dbcreator, or sysadmin.

Below the four check boxes is the Restore the Database Files As list box. This list box displays each of the database files associated with the database in the backup set, showing the full path and name of the file as it existed when the backup was created and the full path and name that it has when the restore operation is completed. You can modify the destination path and name of any file in the list box by clicking the ellipses (...) button to the right of the Restore As column for the file you want to change. This action opens a window titled Locate Database Files, which is similar in appearance to Figure 7.16's Locate Backup File window. Select the desired destination location in the window's tree directory, and click the OK button to return to the Restore Database window.

Recovery State

The Recovery State section of the Options tab contains three radio buttons that determine what condition the database is in once the restore operation is completed.

■ **Leave the Database Ready to Use by Rolling Back the Uncommitted Transactions.** This option is selected by default and allows for the restored database to be immediately used once the restore operation has completed. This option is also known as Restore with Recovery.

■ **Leave the Database Non-Operational and Do Not Roll Back Uncommitted Transactions.** This option keeps the database in a restoring state after the requested restore operation has completed, which is useful when restoring a database with multiple transaction logs or when restoring a sequence of backups to a database (such as a full backup followed by a differential backup). You cannot use the database until a subsequent restore operation using the first option in this list has been completed. This option is also known as Restore with No Recovery.

■ **Leave the Database in Read-Only Mode.** This option allows a database to remain in a restoring state but makes read-only access to the database available when the requested restore operation is completed. This option creates a standby file on the local file system of the server hosting the database instance to allow for the actions of the restore operation to be undone. This option is also known as Restore with Standby.

Below the three option buttons is the Standby File text field, which is enabled only if the Leave the Database in Read-Only Mode option button is selected. To change the location of the standby file, modify the text in the text field or click the ellipses (...) button to the right of the Standby File text field. Doing so opens a window titled Locate Rollback Undo File, similar in appearance to Figure 7.16's Locate Backup File window. Select the desired destination location for the standby file in the window's tree directory, and click the OK button to return to the Restore Database window.

Note: The standby file is simply a copy of the existing database. If the file group for the target database is 20GB, for instance, the standby file requires an additional 20GB of available disk space. If there is not enough storage space for the standby file in the file system at the location specified, the restore operation fails.

SharePoint and Restoring a SQL Server 2008 Backup

Unfortunately, restoring a SharePoint database is not as simple as executing the previous steps to restore your environment. Because SharePoint is constantly accessing, reading from, and updating its databases, you must take certain precautions to avoid inconsistent or corrupted data. The following sections detail the steps you must take, depending on the restore situation, as well as some other considerations when planning your restore strategy for your SharePoint databases.

Overwriting SharePoint with a Restore of a SQL Backup

Although not many additional steps are required to restore a SharePoint database in SQL Server for an existing and operational SharePoint farm, the following steps are important to ensure the integrity and stability of the data in your system:

1. One important step to take before making changes to your environment is to lock down any affected SharePoint site collections so that users do not receive inconsistent or incorrect data during the restore, or lock up resources that may need to be accessed or written by the process. Although it may seem attractive to set site collections within a targeted database to Read-Only or No Access, this can be time-consuming through the Central Administration site, especially if the database has several site collections. It is going to be far simpler to use a PowerShell script leveraging the Set-SPSite cmdlet and its LockState input parameter or to completely remove the content database from the farm via the Manage Content Database page in the Central Administration site. Regardless of how you do it, initially you should make sure that users cannot tie up items with affected site collections to ensure the best experience for you and your users during the process.

2. Microsoft recommends that if the SharePoint 2010 Timer service on the SharePoint server hosting your farm's Central Administration site is running, you should stop it via the Services management console snap-in on the server before proceeding with the database restore. Don't restart the Timer service until the database has been fully restored. This is a good practice, but it may affect what your end users experience if they are using your farm while the Timer service is stopped. Consider communicating with

your users regarding a potential outage, and understand how this action in general might impact any service-level agreements (SLAs) that you have in place.

3. Open SQL Server Management Studio and the Restore Database window for the target SharePoint database to be restored in SQL Server.

4. When the Restore Database window opens, confirm or modify the destination and source data, and then select the Options tab to open it.

5. Unless you have specific requirements or needs for your SharePoint environment, the Overwrite the Existing Database check box is the only Restore option that you should select.

6. In the Recovery State section, select the Restore with Recovery radio button if you are including all the database's transaction logs in the current restore operation. If you need to restore additional transaction logs after this operation, select the Restore with No Recovery option button. You should not use the Restore with Standby option when restoring a SharePoint database.

7. Click the OK button to initiate the restore operation for this database.

8. Once you've restored the database, review its settings to ensure that the farm database access service account is assigned as the Database Owner. You can check this in SQL Management Studio by right-clicking on the database and choosing Properties. In the General tab, under the Database section, see the Owner property. If it is not assigned, use the `sp_changedbowner '<domain/username>'` Transact-SQL command to update the database owner (http://msdn.microsoft.com/en-us/library/ms178630.aspx). Making the farm database service account be the database owner assigns this account the `DB Owner` security role.

9. If there are additional databases in your SharePoint environment that need to be restored, repeat steps 1 through 8 as needed.

10. Once all databases have been restored properly, unlock their site collections or reattach the databases to the farm to re-enable end user access for those items.

11. Finally, restart the SharePoint 2010 Timer service on your farm's Central Administration site host server.

Restoring a SQL Backup to a New SharePoint Environment

One of the great things about SharePoint's reliance on its databases is that it makes the data in your SharePoint farm much more manageable and portable. In steps that are described next, you can move or copy a content database full of sites from one SharePoint farm to another without losing content or configurations within a site. This is especially useful if you want to move a site collection from a quality assurance (QA) environment to a production environment, or you want to create a copy of a given site collection in a new farm without having to re-create all of its contents from scratch.

You need to consider some prerequisites prior to executing a SQL Server restore of a SharePoint content database backup in a new environment:

- **The new SharePoint farm must already be built.** The restore steps in this section assume that a new SharePoint farm has already been installed, configured, and is ready to receive the restored content database.

- **Patch levels and versions must be equivalent (or greater).** The new SharePoint farm must be running the same version and patch level or a more recent version of SharePoint as the farm that the database backup was created in. If the restore farm is at a more recent version of SharePoint, the platform updates the database to the correct database schema for the farm's version automatically.

- **All installed custom code and files in the original farm must be present in the new farm.** The new SharePoint farm must have all the same solutions, features, site definitions, workflows, and any other custom code or files installed and configured as the original farm.

- **Only restore content databases.** This process cannot be used to restore a configuration database to a new farm; content databases for one or more site collections can be restored into a new farm using this process, as well as databases associated with Service Applications as long as the Service Application for the database has already been restored or created in the new farm.

- **Use SharePoint 2010's Unattached Content Database option if you are restoring a database to its original farm and not overwriting the existing database.** Accessing a restored content database from its original farm as an unattached content database is the only way to avoid data integrity issues and globally unique identifier (GUID) conflicts throughout your farm without overwriting the database, even if you give it a new name in SQL Server. For more information on accessing unattached content databases in your SharePoint farm, see Chapter 9.

To restore a SQL Server database backup of a SharePoint content database to a new farm, execute the following steps:

1. Restore the database in the SQL Server database instance for the new farm. If the database does not previously exist in the instance, you can create an empty database in the instance and overwrite it with the backup or type the name of the new content database into the To Database field in the Restore Database window. Don't overwrite existing content databases for the new farm.

2. After you've restored the database, review its settings to ensure that the target's farm database access service account is assigned as the database owner. You can check this in

SQL Management Studio by right-clicking on the database and choosing Properties. In the General tab, under the Database section, see the Owner property. If it is not assigned, use the `sp_changedbowner '<domain/username>'` Transact-SQL command to update the database owner (http://msdn.microsoft.com/en-us/library/ms178630. aspx). Making the farm database service account the database owner assigns this account the `DB Owner` security role.

3. If there is not already a Web application in your farm that you want to associate the site collection(s) in the restored database with, create one. Open the new farm's Central Administration site in a browser, click the Application Management link, and then click the Manage Web Applications link in the Web Applications section of the page.

4. When the Application Management page opens, click the New button in the Web Applications section of the Central Administration site's Fluent user interface (UI) (also known as the ribbon).

5. When the Create New Web Application window opens (see Figure 7.17), select the desired configuration settings for the new Web application and click the OK button to create it.

6. When the new target Web application has been created to receive the restored content database, you can delete its initial content database because the site content you are interested in resides in the restored content database. Return to the Application Management page in the Central Administration site, and click the Manage Content Databases link in the Databases section.

7. When the Manage Content Databases page opens (see Figure 7.18), if any content databases exist for the Web application, click the linked name of the content database for the Web application to open its Settings page. If no content databases currently exist for the Web application, proceed to step 9.

Caution: Be sure to confirm that the correct Web application is listed in the Web Application drop-down menu in the upper-right corner of the page. If it is not, click the arrow for the drop-down menu and select the Change Web Application option. When the dialog box opens, navigate to the correct Web application and select it.

---

8. When the Manage Content Database Settings page opens (see Figure 7.19), check the Remove Content Database check box, which causes a confirmation window to be displayed (see Figure 7.20) if the content database contains existing site collections. If the confirmation window is displayed, determine whether you can remove the content database from the farm. If you can, click the OK button in the confirmation window and click the OK button to remove the content database.

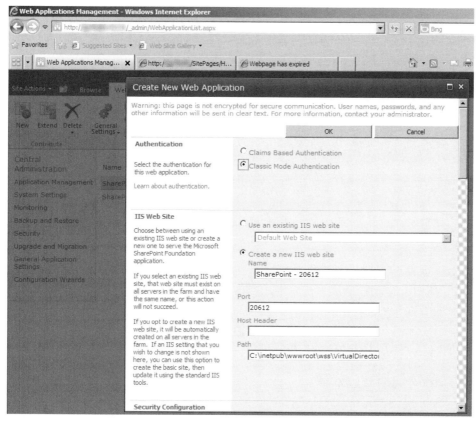

Figure 7.17   The SharePoint Central Administration site's Create New Web Application window.

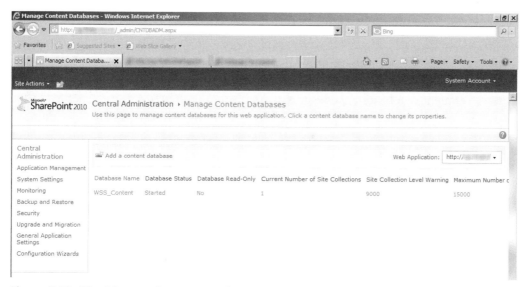

Figure 7.18   The Manage Content Databases page.

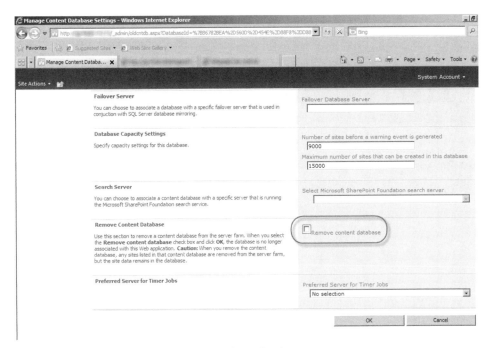

Figure 7.19   The Manage Content Database Settings page.

Figure 7.20   The confirmation window displayed when a user clicks the Remove Content Database check box warning him of the implications of the action.

9.   After all content databases have been removed from the Web application, return to the Manage Content Databases page for the target Web application and click the Add Content Database button in the upper-left corner of the page.

10.   In the Add Content Database page (see Figure 7.21), enter the name of the database instance hosting the restored content database in the Database Server field and the name of the restored content database in the Database Name field. Confirm the other settings for the content database, and click the OK button to add the database.

Note: If you are more comfortable using PowerShell, see Chapter 10 for information on how to add the restored content database to your new farm with it.

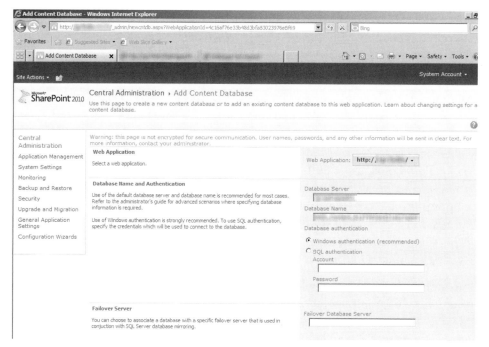

Figure 7.21   The Add Content Database page.

11.   After the content database has been added to the Web application, review the contents of the database through SharePoint to confirm that the addition of the database was successful. View the Web application's new site collection(s) through the Central Administration site to confirm that they are properly listed, and open them directly through a browser to verify that all their contents and settings were correctly restored into the new environment.

Tip: You may need to reset the Internet Information Services (IIS) Web servers hosting your new farm for these changes to be visible to end users.

Conclusion

Like SharePoint, Microsoft provides several options for backing up and restoring your SQL Server databases to meet the specific needs of your organization. The procedures discussed in this chapter merely scratch the surface of what is possible with SQL Server's backup and restore options, and the advent of a new version of SQL Server brings with it even more opportunities for ensuring the security and long-term viability of your business-critical data. None of this takes into account the third-party tools available to enhance, extend, or replace SQL Server's backup and restore tools. (For an introduction to some of these tools, see Appendix B, "Third-Party

Tools," available on the Cengage Learning Web site at http://www.courseptr.com/downloads.) With the information in this chapter, you should be able to start compiling a backup and restore strategy for your databases, selecting the configuration and procedures that best suit the needs of your organization and infrastructure.

Keep in mind that although backing up your SharePoint databases is a good start on preparing your SharePoint farm for the possibility of a catastrophic event, that's all it is: a start. How SharePoint relies on and uses its databases is far from normal and, as you have seen, this means you must make special considerations and plans when backing up and restoring those databases. Again, like SharePoint, using SQL Server's tools to back up and restore your Share-Point database is unlikely to be a complete disaster recovery solution for your organization. Making that assumption leaves you vulnerable and most likely unable to quickly recover your system in the event of a disaster, if at all. Restoring a backup can be a time-intensive process and can cost your enterprise countless man-hours of lost productivity as your users wait for Share-Point to be brought back online.

Thankfully, backup and restore is not the only method available with SQL Server for restoring and, just as importantly, maintaining service to your farm's databases. Chapter 8, "SQL Server 2008 High Availability," introduces you to the concept of high availability (HA) and some of the paths you can take to help your SQL Server environment withstand an outage or disaster. These practices are invaluable to your business, because they are intended to minimize the duration of an outage as much as possible so your SharePoint farm can remain available to your end users.

SQL Server backup and restore can be a powerful asset in your SharePoint disaster recovery toolkit, but as has been shown with so many of the other tools you have at your disposal, it does not necessarily stand well on its own for SharePoint. As you continue through this book, start to think about how you want to put together all this information to construct your own SharePoint disaster recovery solution. You are not quite finished learning the various tools and platforms you need to consider, but you are getting there.

After reading this chapter, you should be able to confidently answer the following questions about SQL Server's backup and restore tools:

1. What is the difference between a database backed up using the Full recovery model and one backed up with the Simple recovery model?

2. What types of storage media can you use to store SQL Server database backups?

3. What SharePoint databases should not be backed up with SQL Server? Why?

4. What are the performance implications for your SharePoint farm when backing up and restoring large SharePoint databases?

5. What state can a database be placed in when it is restored to a SQL Server database instance?

8 SQL Server 2008 High Availability

In This Chapter

- Log Shipping
- Database Mirroring
- Database Clustering

High availability (HA) is a term that we covered for components of SharePoint 2010 and the Windows Server operating system in Chapter 6, "Windows Server 2008 High Availability," but there is another integral part of SharePoint 2010's ecosystem that has the ability to be highly available: its SQL Server databases. Because SharePoint is so dependent on the availability of its databases to serve content to its users, a good case can be made that your SQL Server database instance(s) should be the first area of your farm that you review when planning for HA. Microsoft has wisely recognized the importance of making SQL Server highly available and provides several options and tools to assist in that endeavor. In addition, several third-party tools are available that you can use to support your SQL Server HA configuration and execution.

The first step you must take in planning and designing your SQL Server HA architecture is to evaluate your environment's HA requirements and available budget. SQL Server HA can have a high cost associated with it, which you must consider when determining exactly how to implement it and establish the amount of uptime you are expected to provide for your SharePoint environment.

Three built-in options are available for SQL Server HA (depending on the type of SQL Server license in use): log shipping, database mirroring, and clustering. Each of these options can be a viable solution for your SharePoint environment, but determining which one best fits the needs and limitations of your organization and environment is an important activity that you need to be sure to include early in your SharePoint design process. After all, your decision has lasting implications and is not easily changed without affecting SharePoint. This is yet another item for discussion that you should cover with your database administrator. Your administrator's insights and expertise are invaluable for not only selecting an HA solution but also implementing it and supporting it over time.

Note: Each of these HA solutions may require the purchase of additional Windows Server, SharePoint, and SQL Server licenses and hardware to implement, adding definitive costs to your environment, regardless of what licenses or hardware approach you decide to take. Microsoft states that passive SQL Server installations configured for HA do not require additional licenses unless they process queries. You should contact your Microsoft licensing or sales resources for specific information about how to properly license your HA resources. You may also be able to leverage virtualization products from Microsoft or VMware to reduce hardware costs by creating multiple virtual servers on a single physical host, but you must carefully evaluate the performance and support implications of this option. Furthermore, these solutions can involve the use of separate datacenters to host the servers used to make SQL Server highly available, allowing your SharePoint databases to keep serving content because they can fail over to servers in a completely different geographic location. Although this can be valuable, it adds infrastructure costs and solution complexity and can introduce the potential for latency as data is transferred between the datacenters.

The visual examples provided in this chapter were generated in a testing environment using the following platforms and components. Depending on how your environment is configured, your experiences may vary slightly.

- **Operating system.** Microsoft Windows Server 2008 R2 Enterprise Edition (build 7600)

- **Database.** Microsoft SQL Server 2008 Developer Edition with Service Pack (SP) 1 (build 10.0.2740)

- **Web server.** Microsoft Internet Information Services (IIS) 7.5

- **SharePoint.** SharePoint Foundation 2010 Release Candidate 1 (build 4730)

Log Shipping

Originally introduced as a supported feature with SQL Server 2005, log shipping is an available HA feature in every SQL Server edition except Express. Log shipping takes advantage of the platform's backup functionality that was covered in Chapter 7, "SQL Server 2008 Backup and Restore" and uses it to create a second iteration of the target (or primary) database in a separate database instance. It creates a secondary copy of the primary database by taking a transaction log backup from the primary database and copying it to a secondary database. The transaction log copy process needs to occur regularly to keep the secondary database synchronized with its primary source in case a disaster occurs and it is needed. One advantage of log shipping is that once the backup of the transaction log is created in the primary database instance, the remainder of the process occurs in the secondary database instance, allowing the primary instance to return to normal activities.

The Server Components of Log Shipping

Log shipping requires at least two servers—a primary and a secondary—and allows the use of an optional third server to monitor the log-shipping operation.

- **Primary.** This is the database you want to back up to a SQL Server instance on a separate server. All configuration of the log-shipping process must occur on this server. You must back up the primary database using the Full or Bulk-Logged recovery models for the backups to be used with log shipping; log shipping is not available when the target database uses the Simple recovery model. A target database can have only one primary server, but you can ship its logs to multiple secondary servers for redundancy.

- **Secondary.** This is the database that functions as a separate backup copy of your primary database. You must initially restore the secondary database from a full backup of the primary database using either the Restore with No Recovery or Restore with Standby options before you can update it with transaction logs via log shipping. A single secondary server can host multiple databases backed up via log shipping.

- **Monitor.** This server lives up to its name by tracking all the activities of the log-shipping process, such as transaction log backup dates, secondary server transaction log copy and restore dates, and information on any failures or errors that may occur. A monitor server is not required to use log shipping, but if you do decide to use it, you should host it somewhere other than your primary or secondary server. A single monitor server can track multiple log-shipping configurations.

Log-Shipping Jobs

SQL Server executes four distinct SQL Server Agent jobs as part of the log-shipping process:

- **Backup.** The SQL Server Agent executes this job on the primary server to back up the target database, log the action to the local server (as well as the monitor server), and clean up any old backup files or logs created by previous iterations of the job. This job kicks off the log-shipping process; when it is finished, SQL Server initiates a Copy job on the secondary server and returns the target database to normal processing. By default, Backup is configured to run every 2 minutes, but you can configure it to run more or less frequently based on your requirements.

- **Copy.** The SQL Server Agent executes this job on the secondary server to copy the transaction log backup from the primary server to the secondary server. Its actions are logged on the secondary server and reported to the monitor server, and then it deletes any old backup files or logs.

A Warning About the Size of Your Transaction Log Files Be careful to monitor the size of any database and its transaction logs if you are using log shipping. As these files grow, so does the amount of data that you need to send over the network from your primary server to the secondary server. The larger the transaction log, the longer it takes for it to be copied from the primary to the secondary and the more bandwidth that is being tied up over your network.

The good news is that solutions are available to make the transfer of large log files more efficient and better performing. Compressing transaction log backups, a feature now available in SQL Server 2008 (see Chapter 7 for more information on SQL Server 2008's backup compression), can reduce the size of the files that are sent over the network. Other methods are also available to improve the act of copying the files from point A to point B, such as the Windows Distributed File System with Active Directory Domain Services, which can increase the throughput of the copy activity.

- **Restore.** The SQL Server Agent executes this job to restore the copied transaction log to the secondary database and bring it in line with the content of the primary target database. Its actions are logged on the secondary server and reported to the monitor server; then it deletes any old files or logs associated with the job.

- **Alert.** If a monitor server is configured for the log-shipping process, this job is created on the monitor server and shared by all servers using the monitor server. The SQL Server Agent executes this job to raise alerts when any job within the log-shipping process fails to run successfully to completion. Additional configuration must be completed for SQL Server to deliver these alerts to an operator. If a monitor is not configured, alert jobs must be configured individually on the primary and secondary servers to report the result of the jobs run on each server.

How to Configure Log Shipping

Your environment must meet the following requirements to enable log shipping for one or more of your SQL Server databases:

- **Servers.** In addition to the server hosting your primary SQL Server database instance, you must have a second database instance hosting on a separate server to function as the secondary server. A third monitor server is optional.

- **File share.** A network file share must be available to store the backed up transaction logs. Microsoft recommends, but does not require, that this file share be located somewhere other than your primary or secondary server in the interest of enhanced availability for your data.

- **SQL Server license.** All servers participating in the log-shipping process must be running one of the following versions of SQL Server: Server 2008 or 2008 R2 Workgroup Edition, Server 2008 or 2008 R2 Web Edition, SQL Server 2008 or 2008 R2 Standard Edition, SQL Server 2008 or 2008 R2 Datacenter Edition, or SQL Server 2008 or 2008 R2 Enterprise Edition. Log shipping is not available with SQL Server Express Edition.

- **Case sensitivity.** All servers participating in the log-shipping process must have the same SQL Server case sensitivity configuration.

- **Recovery model.** You must back up the database targeted for log shipping using the Full or Bulk-Logged recovery models.

- **SQL Server Agent.** The SQL Server agent service must be running on each server for the associated jobs to execute. In most cases this service is active by default, but if it is not running, the log-shipping process is not fully functional.

The following steps provide an example of how to enable and configure SQL Server log shipping with a primary and secondary server:

1. Open SQL Server Management Studio and right-click on the database you are targeting for log shipping. Select the Properties item from the menu.

2. When the Database Properties dialog box opens (see Figure 8.1), click the Transaction Log Shipping link in the left pane.

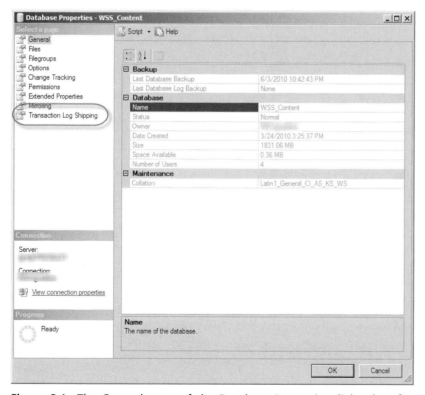

Figure 8.1 The General page of the Database Properties dialog box for a selected database in SQL Server Management Studio.

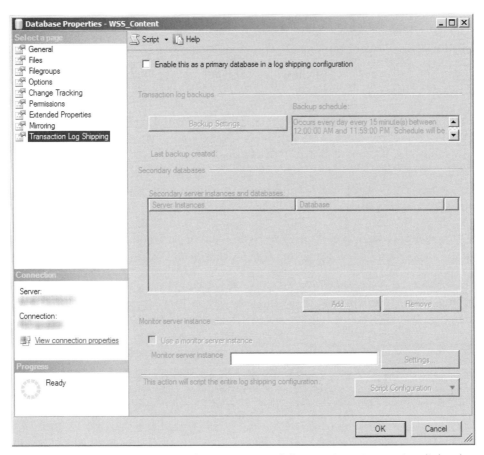

Figure 8.2   The Transaction Log Shipping page of the Database Properties dialog box.

3.   This action opens the Transaction Log Shipping page (see Figure 8.2) with most of its options disabled. Click the Enable This as a Primary Database in a Log Shipping Configuration check box to enable the other fields, buttons, and items in the page.

4.   To open the Transaction Log Backup Settings dialog box (see Figure 8.3), click the now enabled Backup Settings button.

5.   In the Network Path to Backup Folder text box, enter the Universal Naming Convention (UNC) path for the network share you have designated as the storage location for the backed up transaction logs. If you have chosen to use a local folder on the primary server, leave this field blank and enter the path to that directory in the If the Backup Folder Is Located on the Primary Server, Type a Local Path to the Folder text box.

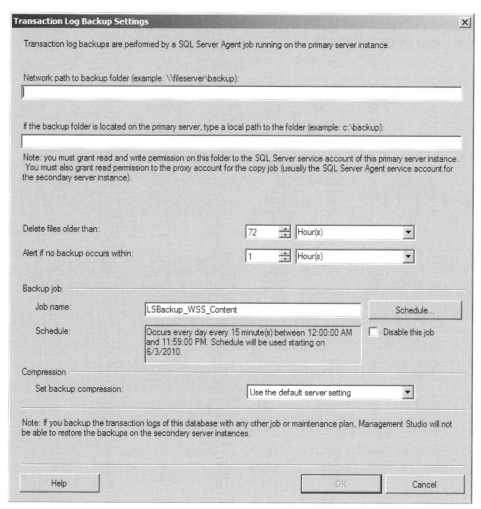

Figure 8.3 The Transaction Log Backup Settings window allows you to set the storage location of the transaction log backups, manage the deletion schedule for those backups, and set operator alerts in the case of errors.

Note: Regardless of its location, the primary server's SQL Server service account must have read and write privileges for the directory provided. In addition, the secondary server's SQL Server Agent service account must have read privileges in the directory.

6. Configure the Delete Files Older Than and Alert if No Backup Occurs Within fields according to the needs and requirements of your system. The first field helps to keep your transaction log backups from overwhelming your storage system, whereas the second warns your database's operators if its transaction logs are not being backed up on a regular basis.

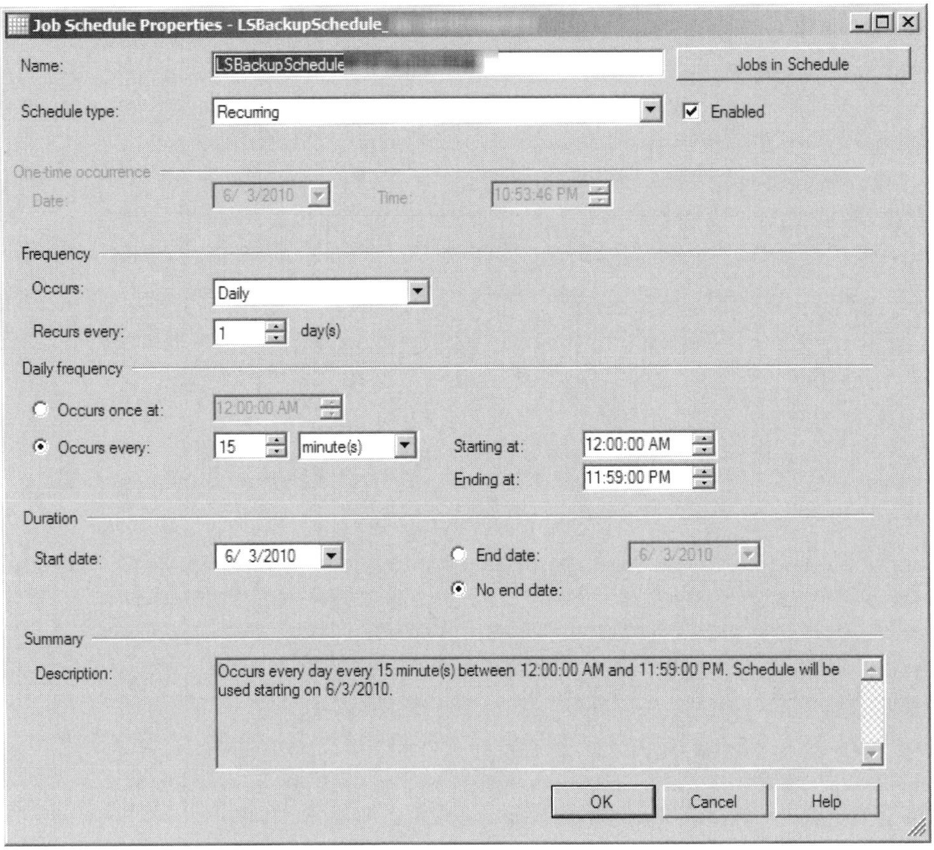

Figure 8.4 The Job Schedule Properties window.

Tip: Be careful not to set too small of an interval on the deletion of your backup files, or they may be deleted before the log-shipping Copy job can create a copy of the files on the secondary server.

---

7. In the Backup Job section, you have the option of renaming the job used to back up the target database if the default name provided is not sufficiently descriptive. More importantly, clicking the Schedule button opens the Job Schedule Properties dialog box (see Figure 8.4), allowing you to configure how frequently the database's transaction logs are backed up and sent to the secondary server. You can modify the various schedule settings for the backup in this window; be sure to closely review the Summary text field to confirm that the settings match your preferred schedule before clicking the OK button to save your changes.

Tip: As with any other scheduled activity within your farm, such as SharePoint backups, search crawls, or other regular activities, be careful about when you decide to have the transaction logs backed up and shipped to the secondary server. These processes could incur some (if not considerable) overhead for your environment and have the potential to impact the experience for your end users, especially if there are other resource-intensive activities running at the same time. It may be difficult, but at a minimum you need to be aware of the possibility for contention with these and other scheduled activities.

8. To save your changes to the Transaction Logs Backup Settings, click the OK button. This returns you to the Transaction Log Shipping page of the database's Properties window.

9. Now that you have configured the backup of the primary database's transaction logs, click the Add button in the Secondary Databases section to select a secondary server to receive the backed up logs.

Note: You must enter a storage location for the transaction log's backups in step 5 for the Add button to be enabled.

10. This opens the Secondary Database Settings dialog box (see Figure 8.5). By default, most of the items are disabled when this dialog box first opens; you must connect to the secondary server to be able to modify them. Click the Connect button to open a SQL Server login screen, and enter the connection data for the secondary server's database instance to proceed.

11. The Initialize Secondary Database tab is now enabled, allowing you to select whether you want the secondary database initialized by a fresh full database created by the log-shipping process, by an existing full backup that has already been taken, or to inform SQL Server that the database has already been initialized. Select the option button next to the correct option for your system, configure any necessary Restore Options, and then click the Copy Files tab.

12. In the Copy Files tab (see Figure 8.6), you must provide a destination directory on the secondary server for the transaction log backup files copied from the primary server. (The window's OK button is not enabled until you enter a value in this field.) You can also configure how long these log files are retained, when operators should be alerted in case of an outage, and the schedule by which the log files are copied from the primary server to the secondary server. After you have completed the Copy Files configuration, click the Restore Transaction Log tab to continue.

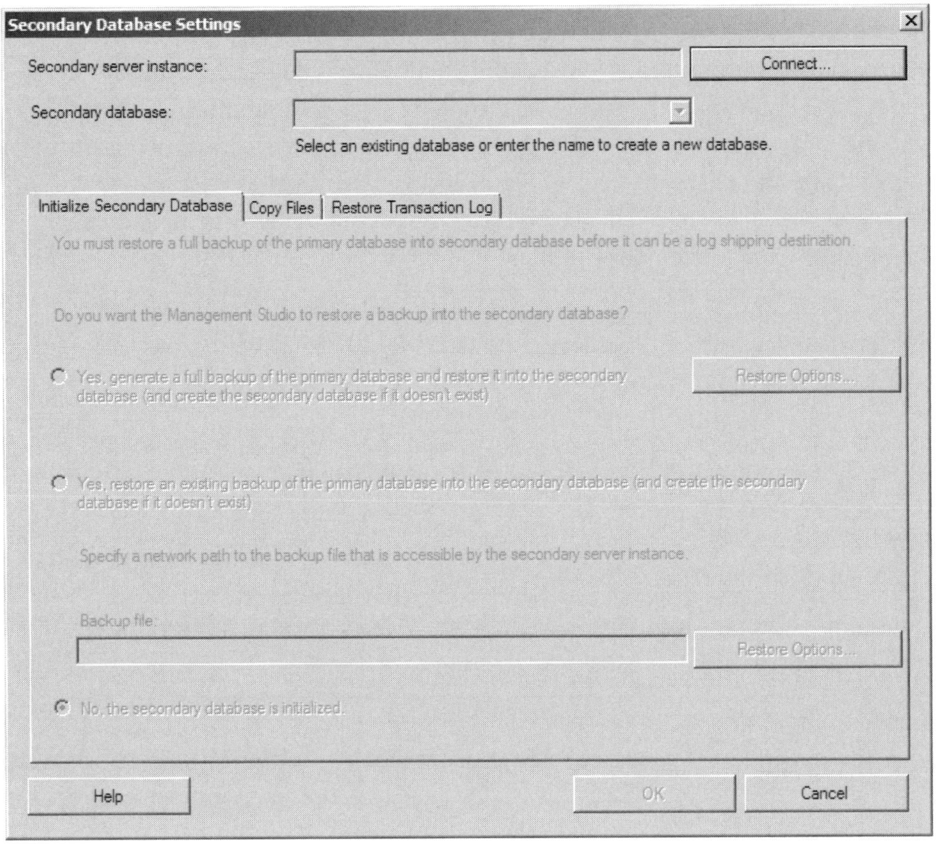

Figure 8.5   The Secondary Database Settings dialog box prior to connection to the secondary server.

Tip: The schedule for copying files to the secondary server should match the schedule for transaction log backups as closely as possible. Copying the files with a greater frequency can result in the same data being copied multiple times, whereas a lesser frequency can result in the loss of transaction data if backups are overwritten or deleted before they can be copied.

---

13.   In the Restore Transaction Log tab (see Figure 8.7), you must select the state that the database is in while restoring backups. The No Recovery Mode option is selected by default, but you can also opt to place the database in Standby Mode. The tab also allows you to delay a restore, alert an operator if a restore cannot be run, and change the schedule for restore operations.

14.   After you have completed your Secondary Database Settings configurations, click the OK button to return to the Database Properties dialog box.

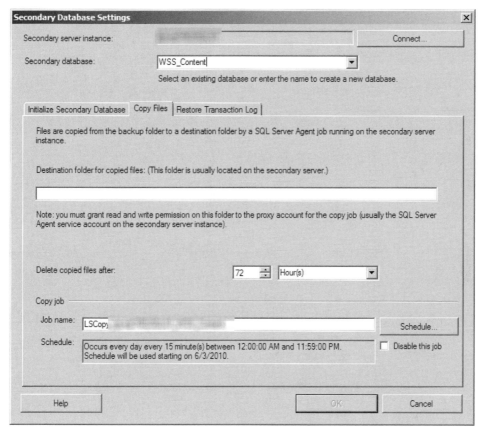

Figure 8.6 The Copy Files tab of the Secondary Database Settings dialog box.

15. If you want to configure a monitor server for the log-shipping process, select the Use a Monitor Server Instance check box in the Monitor Server Instance section. This enables the Settings button in that section; click it to open the Log Shipping Monitor Settings dialog box (see Figure 8.8.).

16. When the Log Shipping Monitor Settings dialog box opens, click the Connect button to open a SQL Server login screen and enter the connection data for the monitor server's database instance to proceed. In this dialog box, you can also configure which account is used to connect to the monitor server, how long the monitor server retains history data, and when alert jobs are scheduled to run. After you have completed your configuration, click the OK button to return to the Database Properties dialog box.

17. After you have completed the log-shipping configuration for the database, click the OK button in the Database Properties dialog box to commit your changes.

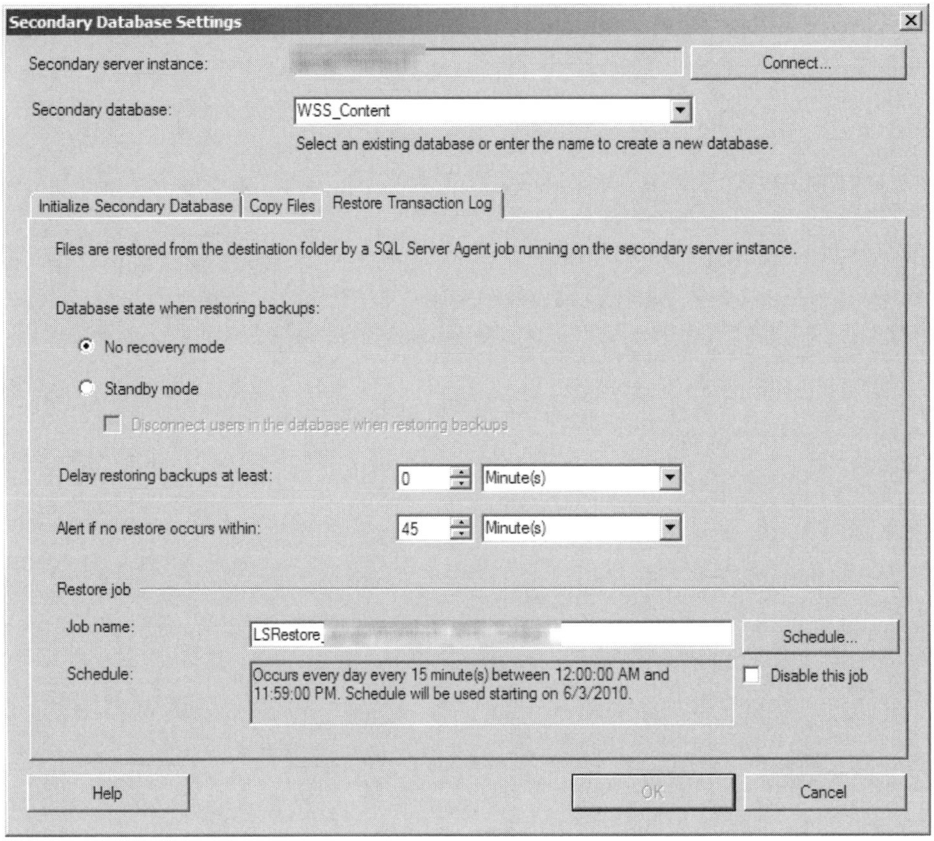

Figure 8.7 The Restore Transaction Log tab of the Secondary Database Settings window.

18.   To verify that the log-shipping configuration was completed successfully, review the status of the SQL Agent jobs on each server and confirm that they are running as expected and without error.

SharePoint and Log Shipping

As with SQL Server database backups in general, several types of SharePoint databases *cannot* be preserved via SQL Server log shipping. The following list addresses each type of database and whether it can be made highly available via transaction log shipping.

- **Configuration database.** You should not log-ship SharePoint configuration databases; configuration databases are farm specific. A configuration database is intended to be used only with the original farm it is attached to.

- **Search databases.** Because search databases are tightly integrated with the index files stored on the file system of a SharePoint crawl server, you should not log-ship them. The time it takes to transfer log files between primary and secondary servers can result in inconsistencies

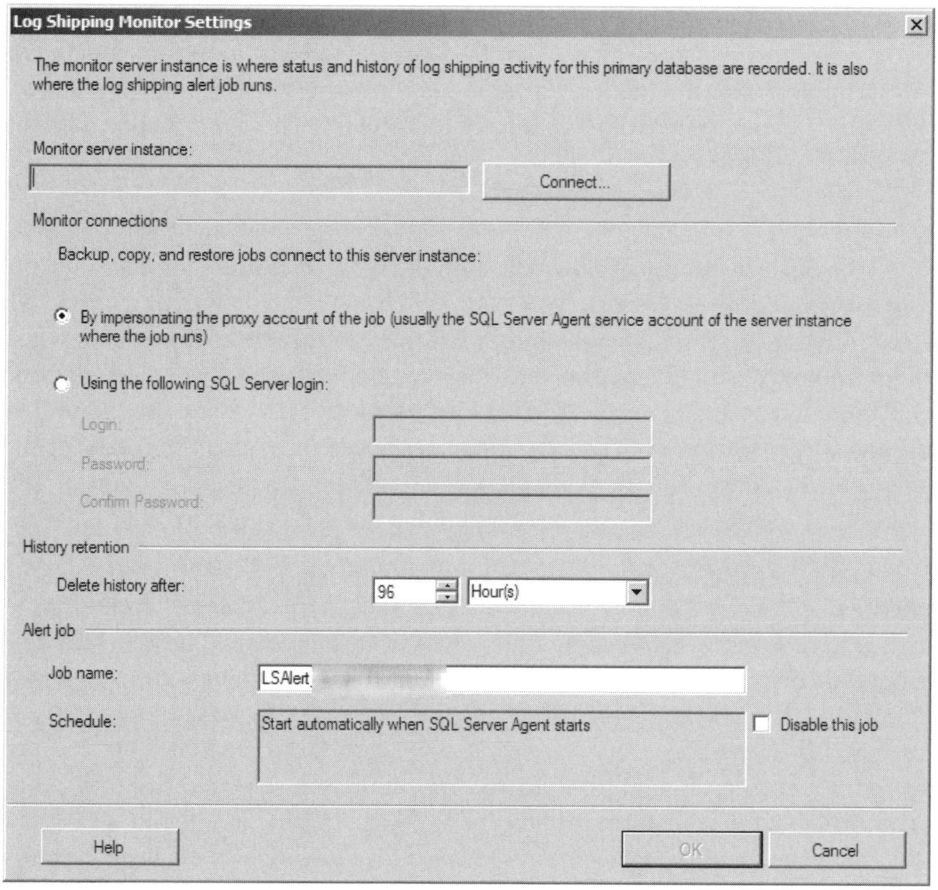

Figure 8.8 The Log Shipping Monitor Settings dialog box.

between the database and the indices. In the case of a disaster, it is likely a better option to re-create the indices from scratch or back them up using the Central Administration site or PowerShell than a SQL Server backup. If the SharePoint content databases that are being log-shipped are attached to a standby farm, you can use that farm's search components to crawl and index them.

■ **Some Service Application databases.** It is difficult to succinctly identity exactly what databases for SharePoint 2010 Service Applications cannot be log-shipped because of the large number of Service Applications available as well as the fact that the Service Application Framework is extensible and supports the creation of custom Service Applications. For a good list of what Service Application databases can and cannot be log-shipped, as well as general criteria for making the distinction, see http://technet.microsoft.com/en-us/library/ff628971.aspx. Also, review any documentation available for each Service Application to determine its specific availability for log shipping or lack thereof.

- **Content databases.** You can log-ship SharePoint content databases to a secondary server. You can also attach them to a standby SharePoint farm for limited read-only viewing, if you restore them in Restore in Standby mode. Depending on how the standby farm is set up, some functions such as search, user profiles, and people search may not be available without some extra configuration efforts.

As you can see in the list, not every type of SharePoint database is highly available through SQL Server log shipping. This directly influences how you should use log shipping to implement HA for your SharePoint farm's databases, because you can't simply switch over to your secondary log-shipped databases if your primary databases are lost. You can take two approaches when using SQL Server log shipping with SharePoint: creating standalone secondary clones of your Service Application and content databases or creating a full standby SharePoint farm based on your log-shipped Service Application and content databases. Because you cannot make your configuration and search databases highly available via log shipping, you must build a new farm to host the log-shipped Service Application and content databases to restore your environment to its users.

The first option means that you are not going to build a new farm until a disaster occurs, but it does reduce your startup time because the content is preserved in a separate database host and ready to be reintroduced back into the farm. If an outage hits a single database, it gives you a running resource to add back into your farm. The fact that this option takes more time to use in a recovery scenario does then require that you have greater leeway in terms of your recovery time objective (RTO) for your SharePoint farm. The second option allows you to have a full, up-to-date replacement available for your farm in the case of a catastrophic event, shortening the time that your environment is unavailable to your users and allowing you to meet a much smaller RTO window. Although the specifics of implementing the first option have already been covered in the chapter, you need to take additional steps to create a full standby SharePoint farm using log-shipped databases.

Building a standby SharePoint farm provides a system for the log-shipped Service Application and content databases to be integrated into and gives you a fallback option if a disastrous event should befall your primary production SharePoint farm. It also gives you a read-only environment where users can view data or run reports without impacting the performance of your production farm. (Keep in mind that this may influence how the platforms in your standby farm are licensed.) You can use the following steps as a guide to build your own standby Share-Point farm.

1. Configure log shipping for each database selected to be replicated into the standby farm using the Restore to Standby mode.

2. Install SharePoint in the standby farm, using the SQL Server database instance hosting the log-shipped databases as the database host for the standby farm.

Note: If possible, use PowerShell (you can also use VBscript or another compatible script-ing language, but others are not as … powerful … as PowerShell, if you get our drift) to script the installation and configuration of both your primary and standby SharePoint farms. This gives you a much higher probability of creating identical deployments in both environments, which in turn gives you a higher probability of success for your log-shipping configuration. In general, take special care to apply the same patches, hotfixes, or updates to the operating systems, SharePoint, and SQL Server in the standby farm as have been applied to your production farm. You must build the standby farm to the same SharePoint version as your production farm. If your production farm has any custom code or language packs installed, also install them to the standby farm.

3. Configure the standby farm to match the setup of the production farm. (SharePoint 2010's new configuration-only backup and restore functionality may be helpful here; see Chapter 9 "SharePoint 2010 Central Administration Backup and Restore" and Chapter 10, "SharePoint 2010 Command Line Backup and Restore: PowerShell" for more information.) If you have a Service Application configured in your production farm, you must either create a new Service Application to match it or restore a backup of the Service Application from the production farm into the standby farm so you can be certain that the configuration matches exactly. (See the previously referenced document on Microsoft's TechNet Web site for information on how to configure specific Service Applications, as well as the product document for the Service Application itself.) Although you should conduct a search in the standby farm, disable any search crawls unless you specifically need them. Confirm that the standby farm's MySite configura-tion matches that of the production farm's.

4. To build the new standby Web applications for each Web application in your produc-tion farm, execute steps 2 through 11 from the list in the "Restoring a SQL Backup to a New SharePoint Environment" section in Chapter 7, adding the log-shipped content databases to each new Web application.

5. In the standby farm, configure an alternate access mapping (AAM) that points to the URL of your production farm; see Figure 8.9 for an example of the Add Internal URLs page.

6. On the file system of all the Web front-end (WFE) servers in the standby farm, open the server's Hosts file (typically located at `%WINDIR%\system32\drivers\etc\`). See Figure 8.10 for an example. Then add an entry pointing the production farm's URL at the server's local loopback IP address, 127.0.0.1. This ensures that any requests for the production farm that originate on the local server are directed back to the local server, not a server in your production farm.

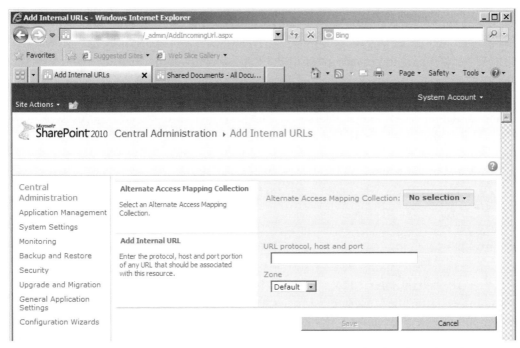

Figure 8.9 The Add Internal URLs page in the SharePoint Central Administration site.

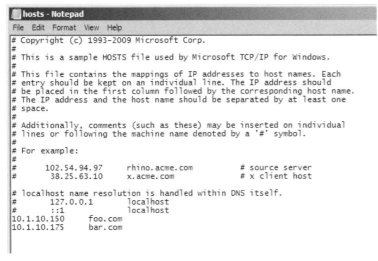

Figure 8.10 An example of the Hosts file on a Windows server.

7. If you are using SharePoint Server 2010, Search Server 2010, or Search Server 2010 Express, in the standby farm open the Search content source named "Local Office Server SharePoint Sites" for editing. Remove any URLs that refer to local servers in the standby farm or the URL of the standby farm, and replace them with the URL of the production farm.

Tip: Unless you have a specific need to make search queries in the standby farm, try to ensure that no crawls are scheduled to run in the farm until it is needed in the case of a failover. This reduces the resources that the standby environment uses and makes it easier to configure search for the proper targets should a failover occur.

---

8.   Your standby farm is now ready to be used as a read-only copy of your production farm that can be failed over to in case of an outage or disaster.

Caution: Once your standby farm is created, be careful to duplicate every configuration change or update that you make to your primary SharePoint farm to your standby farm. If the two environments are not kept in sync, you risk displaying inconsistent content to your users or worse, breaking your standby farm entirely when it attempts to use your modified Service Application and content databases that are log-shipped into it.

Although using SQL Server log shipping as your HA solution has several benefits, it also has quite a few drawbacks that you must consider when evaluating the approach. This is not to say that log shipping is or is not a good solution. Our main caution is that you pay close attention to the items that follow and determine how they relate to your environment, needs, and limitations. You may find that log shipping fits you like a glove, or you may find that one of the other HA solutions in this chapter is what you need to bring long-term stability to your database environment.

Log-Shipping Pros

Log shipping may be the right HA solution for your environment for a variety of reasons. The following list outlines its positive attributes. Take a look to see if it meets your needs.

- **Independence.** The jobs used to log-ship a database are not tied to SharePoint, nor are they impacted by any other processes in the SQL Server database instance. This means that changes to your SharePoint configuration or its databases do not directly impact or harm your log-shipping procedures.

- **Cost effectiveness.** Unlike some other HA solutions (such as clustering), log shipping does not require high-priced components and (as noted earlier) can be implemented for the costs that may or may not be associated with provisioning and licensing an additional SQL Server instance.

- **Highly configurable nature.** As described earlier, a large number of options and configurations to be set for log shipping allow it to meet the needs of your environment.

- **Read-only availability.** If you want, you can create a read-only version of your SharePoint environment using its log-shipped content databases for research or reporting purposes to reduce the load placed on your primary farm.

- **Low impact on performance.** Once the transaction logs of your SharePoint database are backed up, the log-shipping process is executed on the server(s) hosting the secondary database and has no affect on the performance of your primary database server.

- **Unlimited use.** You can log-ship as many databases in an instance as you want; the platform imposes no hard limit. (Keep in mind that you may still encounter limits imposed by the capacity of your hardware or network infrastructure.)

- **Use of backups.** The transaction log backups that the log-shipping process uses to update the secondary database can restore the primary database to a previous point in time as necessary. This means that you can make your database highly available and implement a backup/restore solution for it at the same time, an option not available with SQL Server's other HA solutions. In this situation, it is still necessary to perform full backups of your transaction logs over time, otherwise restore operations are going to take much longer to implement all of the differential backups back to the original full backup, but completely feasible.

- **Capture completeness.** Because SQL Server records information about a database update to the database's transaction log before it even writes it to the database, all the requested database modifications received by SQL Server leading up to the moment of an outage are copied over to the secondary server and written to that database.

- **Distribution and redundancy.** By requiring a secondary database instance to host your secondary database, log shipping makes your system more highly available by providing fallback options for your primary database server. The ability to ship database logs to multiple secondary database instances means that you can further limit your risk by increasing the number of fallback options you have available.

- **Geographic redundancy.** Log shipping does not face the distance limitations that come with database mirroring or failover clustering, allowing copies of your databases to be distributed to remote locations for true redundant protection of your data from large-scale disasters.

- **FILESTREAM compatibility.** SharePoint databases configured to use SQL Server's FILE-STREAM provider for Remote Binary Large Object (BLOB) Storage (RBS) can be log-shipped to a standby database instance for preservation. You can log-ship other third-party RBS providers if the provider supports it.

Log-Shipping Cons

As with most technology solutions, log shipping in SQL Server 2008 is not a perfect solution. Review the following list to see where it falls short and how that might affect your SharePoint environment.

- **Manual failover.** Out of the box, SQL Server does not automatically fail a system over to the log-shipped secondary database if the primary database goes down. Although it is true that log shipping does have a third server role—the monitor role—that role only tracks the status of log-shipping operations; it cannot make the log-shipping database instance a primary if something happens to the original primary instance. You can do additional configuration to automate this process, but by default you must manually switch over to the log-shipped databases. This can impact the time it takes to restore your system after an outage, depending on how quickly your IT staff is notified of the outage and what availability they have to restore the system to the log-shipped databases.

- **Latency.** Updates are not immediately copied to the secondary database when they are made in the primary database. Several factors can affect the time it takes for them to make it over to the secondary database, including these: the frequency with which your transaction logs are backed up, the size of those logs, and the bandwidth available between the primary and secondary databases. The data in your secondary database is not going to be up to date until the transaction logs are copied to it and restored, which can impact the content of a standby farm. Because log shipping does not update in real-time, you cannot use it to restore a database to the point in time immediately prior to a failure. If your organization's recovery point objective (RPO) and RTO requirements for SharePoint mandate instantaneous failover with no lost transactions or data, log shipping is not a viable HA solution for your SQL Server environment.

- **Poor status visibility.** Although the log-shipping process generates status reports for all its actions and allows for the configuration of a monitoring server, this information is not going to be easily available. You can access these reports only by logging on to the server where they are stored; the reports only raise alerts to operators of the associated SQL Server instances when they log into the instances. Additional custom measures or the use of a monitoring platform such as the Operations Manager platform from Microsoft is going to be required to make this information available to your SharePoint administrators or to automatically deliver the alerts as they occur without requiring administrators to log into a system.

- **Not a complete solution.** As previously mentioned, you are not able to log-ship all your SharePoint databases, requiring additional steps such as building a whole new farm or creating a standby farm to use the log-shipped databases in the case of a disaster.

- **Errors and data loss.** Any errors that are written to your primary databases are also transferred to your secondary databases via log shipping. Log shipping is not to prevent the loss of data due to accidental deletion; if it is deleted in the primary database, it is also deleted in the secondary database once the transaction is log-shipped over.

If the features and functionality of log shipping in SQL Server 2008 seem appealing but you still have concerns about some or all of the drawbacks to the process, have no fear. There are, however, other alternatives when it comes to HA for SQL Server, and the next one on the list, database mirroring, offers several enhancements to log-shipping's feature set while also improving on its weaknesses. (Keep in mind that database mirroring comes with its own set of weaknesses and drawbacks.) Although the two options are similar, there are definitely some differences between the two, especially when it comes to the increased cost of implementing database mirroring. In addition, you can implement both log shipping and database mirroring for your SharePoint environment, giving you the best of both worlds.

This isn't to say that log shipping is necessarily inferior to the other HA solutions available for SQL Server: database mirroring or failover clustering. Microsoft has designed these solutions to offer you a range of flexible and configurable options to meet your environment's specific needs, and log-shipping can play an important role in your disaster recovery design. Log shipping allows you to meet shorter RTOs than normal SQL Server backups, because you already have a copy of your databases up and running in a SQL Server environment, at a much lower cost than mirroring or clustering thanks to its less expensive infrastructure requirements. Log shipping also enables you to provide broader protection of your environment, because logs can be shipped to multiple locations and to diverse geographic locations. Finally, log shipping is attractive because you can use it with a much broader range of SQL Server functionality, such as RBS.

Database Mirroring

SQL Server's database mirroring functionality is similar to log shipping in the way it maintains a copy of the primary database for HA purposes; both approaches copy transaction log data from the primary to the secondary database. Although the similarities between the two HA solutions for SQL Server may be striking, the differences between them are even more so. Database mirroring differs from log shipping in several areas, the three most apparent being when the transaction log data is copied to the secondary server, how that data is transferred from one server to another, and how the databases behave when the primary server suffers an outage.

Database mirroring's most appealing advantage over log shipping is that transactions committed to the primary database are copied over to the secondary database instance at once after they are written to the database. This gives database mirroring a distinct advantage over log shipping by reducing latency and ensuring that the contents of the secondary database are completely current. When the transactions are sent to the secondary database, the individual transaction records are sent to the secondary database via TCP, not transaction log backups via a file system copy. But the most desirable aspect of database mirroring is that you can configure it to automatically fail over to the secondary server should the primary server suffer an outage. That's a big change from log-shipping's reliance on a manual failover.

Tip: If the network being used to send the transaction records is not secure, take precautions to secure and encrypt the database mirroring traffic as it is sent. For specific information on this subject, Microsoft has published an article on database mirroring transport security at http://msdn.microsoft.com/en-us/library/ms186360%28v=SQL.100%29.aspx.

The Server Components of Database Mirroring

Database mirroring requires at least two servers—a principal and a mirror—and allows the use of an optional third server, a witness, to automate failovers from the principal to the mirror in the case of an outage on the principal.

- **Principal.** This is the database you want to mirror to a SQL Server instance on a separate server. You must back up the principal database using the Full recovery model for the database to use database mirroring; mirroring is not available when using the Simple or Bulk-Logged recovery models. There can be only one principal server for a target database, and it can have only one mirror server as a partner in the mirroring session. You can implement this role on servers using the Enterprise or Standard licenses for SQL Server.

- **Mirror.** This is the database that functions as the mirroring partner for your principal database. You must initially restore the mirror database from a full backup of the principal database using the Restore with No Recovery option (and then any transaction log backups required to make the database up to date) before you can update it with transactions via database mirroring. See Figure 8.11 for an example of where this setting is selected. See the "How to Restore a SQL Server 2008 Database Backup" section of Chapter 7 for more information on how to restore a database in the SQL Server Management Studio. A single secondary server can host multiple databases acting as mirrors to principal databases on other servers. Databases hosted on the mirror instance not acting as a mirror can also be principal databases in database mirroring with other database instances. You can implement this role on servers using the Enterprise or Standard licenses for SQL Server.

- **Witness.** This server is optional and is needed only if you require SQL Server to automatically fail over to the mirror database if a failure or outage occurs on the principal database. The witness server does not perform resource-intensive activities or host content as part of the database mirroring process; its only role is to detect a failure in the principal database and enable automatic failover to the mirror. You can implement this role on servers using the Enterprise, Standard, Workgroup, or Express Edition licenses for SQL Server.

Caution: Microsoft does not support mirroring configurations where databases from the same principal database instance are copied to mirrors in separate database instances. Whenever possible, you should strive to mirror all the databases in a principal instance to a single mirror instance.

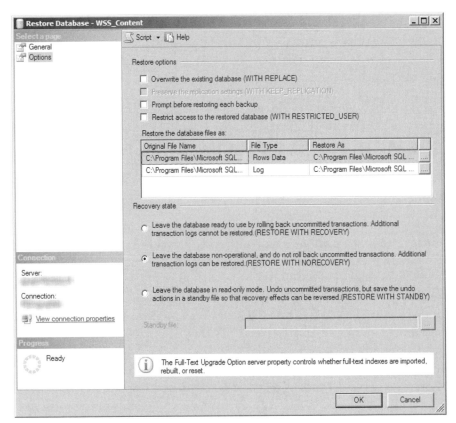

Figure 8.11   The Options page of the Restore Database dialog box with the Restore with No Recovery radio button highlighted.

How to Configure Database Mirroring

Your environment must meet the following requirements to enable database mirroring for one or more of your SQL Server databases:

- **Servers.** In addition to the server hosting your principal SQL Server database instance, you must have a second database instance hosting on a separate server to function as the mirror server. A witness server is optional but is required if you want to have automatic failover.

- **SQL Server license.** The principal and mirror servers must be running one of the following versions of SQL Server: SQL Server 2008 or 2008 R2 Standard Edition (synchronous mirroring only; the various modes of database mirroring available are discussed later in this section), or SQL Server 2008 or 2008 R2 Enterprise Edition. The witness server must be running one of the following versions of SQL Server: SQL Server Express Edition, SQL Server 2008 or 2008 R2 Standard Edition, SQL Server 2008 or 2008 R2 Workgroup Edition, or SQL Server 2008 or 2008 R2 Enterprise Edition. Database mirroring is not available with SQL Server Embedded Edition.

- **Permissions.** Your mirror database instance must provide the same permissions and roles that are granted to your principal database instance.

- **Recovery model.** The database targeted for database mirroring must be backed up using the Full recovery model.

The following steps provide an example of how to enable and configure SQL Server database mirroring with a principal, mirror, and witness server.

1. Open SQL Server Management Studio and right-click on the target database for database mirroring. Select the Properties item from the menu.

2. When the Database Properties dialog box opens (see Figure 8.1), click the Mirroring page link in the left pane.

3. This action opens the Mirroring page (see Figure 8.12) with most of its options disabled. Click the Configure Security button to configure the database mirroring security settings.

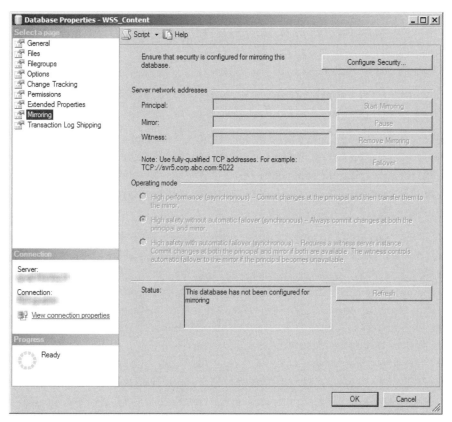

Figure 8.12 The Mirroring page of the Database Properties dialog box; most of its fields are disabled until database mirroring has been configured through the Configure Security button.

Figure 8.13   The opening screen of the Configure Database Mirroring Security Wizard.

4.   This opens the Configure Database Mirroring Security Wizard, as shown in Figure 8.13; click the Next button to continue.

5.   The wizard next prompts you for witness server configuration information (see Figure 8.14). If you want to set up a witness server and enable automatic failover for this database mirroring configuration, select the Yes option and click the Next button. If not, select the No button and click the Next button. In this example, select the Yes option button to configure a witness server.

6.   The wizard's Choose Servers to Configure screen opens (see Figure 8.15), displaying the three database mirroring server roles that can have the database mirroring security configuration saved on them, with check boxes to the left of them. The check boxes for the principal and mirror server instances are checked by default and disabled to prevent the selection from being modified. The witness server instance check box is checked by default but can be unchecked. Ensure that all three server instances are checked, and click the Next button to continue.

Note: If you choose not to configure a witness server, the third server role is not displayed in the screen.

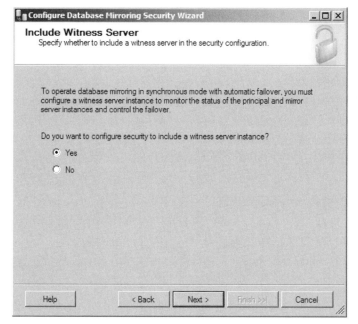

Figure 8.14   The Include Witness Server screen of the Configure Database Mirroring Security Wizard.

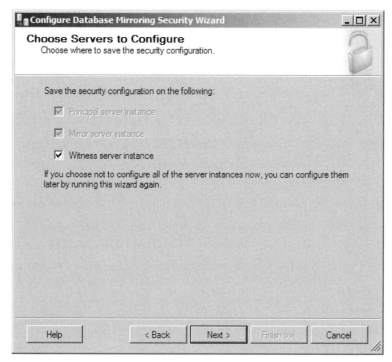

Figure 8.15   The Choose Servers to Configure screen in the Configure Database Mirroring Security Wizard.

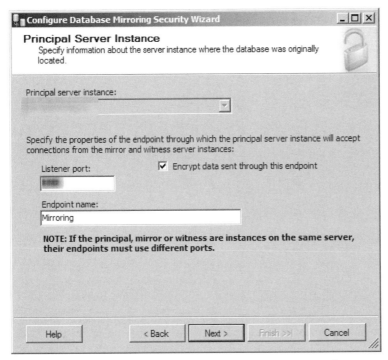

Figure 8.16   The Principal Server Instance screen in the Configure Database Mirroring Security Wizard.

7.   This opens the wizard's Principal Server Instance screen (see Figure 8.16). In this screen, you are shown the current database instance hosting the principal database for the mirroring process in a disabled drop-down menu. In this window, you can opt to have SQL Server encrypt each transaction as it is sent from the principal server by selecting the associated check box, specify the networking port that the principal server uses to communicate with the mirror and witness server, and rename the endpoint for transactions sent from the principal server. When you have entered the information and configuration data for your principal database instance, click the Next button to continue.

Tip: If you have previously established a database mirroring endpoint for the target database, the Encrypt Data check box, the Listener Port text field, and the Endpoint Name text field are disabled, preventing you from modifying the configured endpoint. To change the current mirroring endpoint, you must execute Transact-SQL commands to DROP or ALTER the mirroring endpoint.

---

8.   The wizard proceeds to the Mirror Server Instance screen (see Figure 8.17), which looks similar to the Principal Server Instance screen in Figure 8.16, except that the database

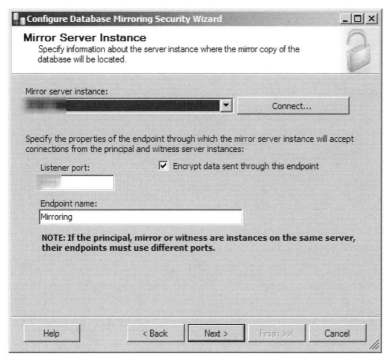

Figure 8.17   The Mirror Server Instance screen in the Configure Database Mirroring Security Wizard.

selection drop-down menu is now enabled. In this screen, you can select the database instance hosting the mirror database for the mirroring process from the drop-down menu. If the desired database instance is not available in the drop-down menu, click the Connect button to open a dialog box to log into the database instance or select the Browse for More option from the drop-down menu. After selecting the current database instance, you can opt to have SQL Server encrypt each transaction as it is sent from the mirror server by selecting the associated check box, specify the networking port that the principal server uses to communicate with the mirror and witness server, and rename the endpoint for transactions sent from the principal server. If you attempt to select the same database instance as the one you established as the principal server, SQL Server displays an error message instructing you to select another instance, and the Next button is disabled (see Figure 8.18). After you have entered valid information and configuration data for your mirror database instance, click the Next button to continue.

9. The wizard again opens a screen similar to the Principal Server Instance screen in Figure 8.16—the Witness Server Instance screen (see Figure 8.19)—and it has the database selection drop-down menu enabled. In this screen, you can select the database instance hosting the witness database for the mirroring process from the drop-down menu. If the desired database instance is not available in the drop-down menu, click the

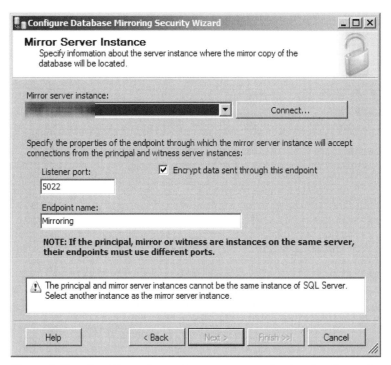

Figure 8.18 The Mirror Server Instance screen in the Configure Database Mirroring Security Wizard displaying an error when the principal database instance is also submitted as the mirror instance.

Connect button to open a dialog box to log into the database instance, or select the Browse for More option from the drop-down menu. After selecting the current database instance, you can opt to have SQL Server encrypt each transaction as it is sent from the witness server by selecting the associated check box, specify the networking port that the principal server uses to communicate with the mirror and witness server, and rename the endpoint for transactions sent from the principal server. Like the mirror server screen, if you attempt to select the same database instance as the one you established as the principal or mirror server, SQL Server displays an error message similar to Figure 8.18 instructing you to select another instance, and the Next button is disabled. After you have entered valid information and configuration data for your witness database instance, click the Next button to continue.

Note: If you opt not to include a witness server in step 5 or not configure its security in step 6, this screen is not displayed.

---

10.   The Service Accounts screen opens, allowing you to specify a service account in DOMAIN\ACCOUNT format for each of the servers in the database mirroring configuration. As Figure 8.20 shows, the screen provides instructions regarding when

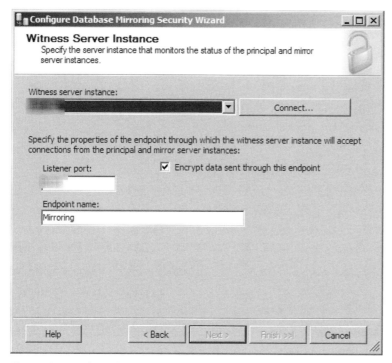

Figure 8.19   The Witness Server Instance screen in the Configure Database Mirroring Security Wizard.

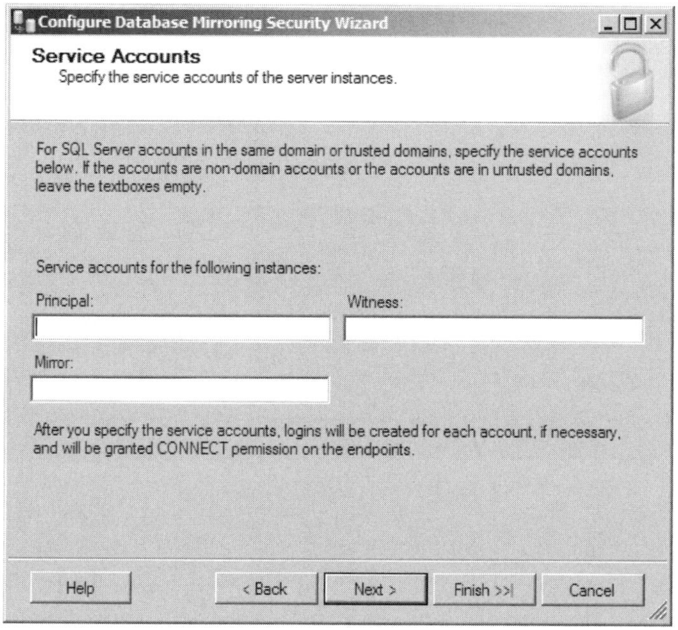

Figure 8.20   The Service Accounts screen in the Configure Database Mirroring Security Wizard.

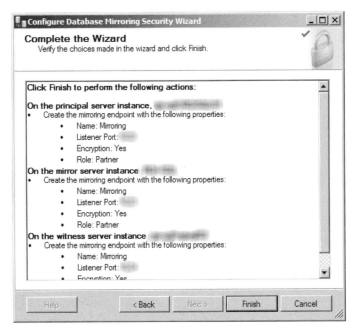

Figure 8.21   The Complete the Wizard screen in the Configure Database Mirroring Security Wizard.

accounts should and should not be specified, as well as what actions SQL Server takes if the accounts listed do not currently have SQL Server logins. Once you've configured the account information, click the Next button to continue.

Note: If you opt not to include a witness server in step 5, the text field for the Witness Service account is not displayed.

---

11.   The last screen of the wizard is now displayed (see Figure 8.21), allowing you to review what you have configured before clicking the Finish button to finalize the security configuration process. If you see any items that need to be modified, click the Back button to navigate to them and make your changes. When you are ready, click the Finish button to complete the wizard and have SQL Server begin to configure the database monitoring configuration's security.

12.   The Configuring Endpoints screen (see Figure 8.22) displays the progress of the security configuration as it executes. Once the tool is finished, ensure that all tasks have completed with a status of Success, review the status messages and reports as needed, and click the Close button to return to the Mirroring page of the database's Properties window.

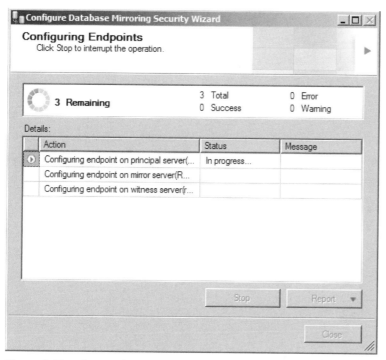

Figure 8.22   The Configuring Endpoints screen in the Configure Database Mirroring Security Wizard.

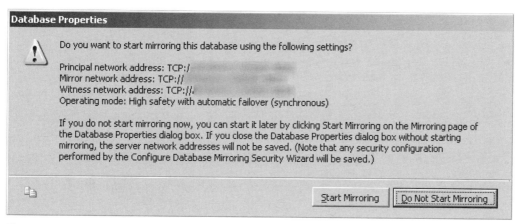

Figure 8.23   The Database Properties dialog box prompts the user to either start or not start database mirroring using the provided configuration.

13.   After SQL Server has completed the endpoint configuration process, the wizard closes and you are prompted with a window asking if you want to start database mirroring for the target database using the configuration that just completed, as shown in Figure 8.23. Click the Start Mirroring button if you are ready to enable the process, or click the Do

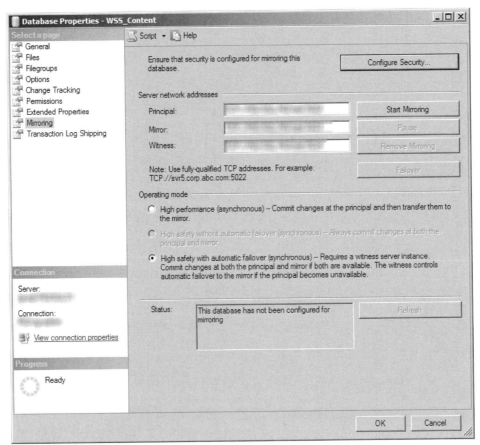

Figure 8.24 The Mirroring page of the Database Properties dialog box after the Configure Database Mirroring Security Wizard has completed without error.

Not Start Mirroring button if you are not. In this example, the Do Not Start Mirroring button was clicked.

14.   Regardless of whether you choose to start the mirroring process, when you return to the Mirroring page, it is apparent that many more fields are now enabled after security was configured, as shown by Figure 8.24. In the Server Network Address section, the text fields for the Principal, Mirror, and Witness servers are now enabled and populated with the network connection string used to contact each of these servers. If you did not start mirroring in step 13, only the Start Mirroring button is enabled. If you did start mirroring in step 13, the Pause, Remove Mirroring, and Failover buttons are enabled. In the Operating Mode section, the High Performance (Asynchronous) and High Safety with Automatic Failover (Synchronous) option buttons are enabled if you chose to include a witness server in step 5. If you did not include a witness server in step 5, the

High Performance (Asynchronous) and High Safety Without Automatic Failover (Synchronous) option buttons are enabled. In both cases, the latter radio button is selected by default. The Status section contains a text box displaying the database mirroring status for the database and a Refresh button, which is disabled if mirroring has not been started. If the Status field indicates that the database has not been configured for mirroring, click the Start Mirroring button to initiate the process.

15.   After mirroring has been started for the database, you can suspend the process by clicking the Pause button. A dialog box is displayed asking you to confirm your request, and you are then returned to the Mirroring page. The former Pause button is now marked as the Resume button and can be clicked to resume the mirroring process for the database.

Note: Pausing the mirroring process places the mirrored database in a suspended status and results in transactions not being transferred from the principal database to the mirrored database until mirroring is resumed. You can use the Pause option as a short-term solution to improve performance on the principal database instance, but you should not use it for extended periods. The transaction log of the principal database is not truncated while mirroring is paused so that all logged transactions can be sent to the mirrored database once the process is resumed. If mirroring is not resumed in a timely fashion, the transaction log can grow too large and use all of its available disk space, ultimately causing an outage of the principal database if it cannot write to its transaction logs.

---

16.   To completely stop the database from being mirrored, click the Remove Mirroring button. A dialog box is displayed asking you to confirm your request, and you are then returned to the Mirroring page. To restart mirroring for this database, you must manually re-create all the configured mirroring settings. This action permanently removes the mirroring associations and security settings between the principal, mirror, and witness servers, but the copy of the mirrored database is not deleted from the mirror database instance.

Note: If you chose to keep the mirrored database, you must perform a Restore with Recovery action against it to make it available, because it was originally created using Restore with No Recovery. You should consider renaming the mirrored database to avoid confusion between it and the principal database.

---

17.   To manually fail a database over from its principal to its mirror, click the Failover button. A dialog box is displayed asking you to confirm your request, and you are then returned to the Mirroring page. After completing the failover, the mirroring server roles of the two databases have been swapped, so the original principal now has the mirror role and the original mirror is now the principal database.

> **Note:** Keep in mind that this change of roles has only occurred in SQL Server from a mirroring perspective; it does not communicate this update to the applications or services that use the database and may influence their ability to access the database.

18.   If you want to change the operating mode of the mirroring process, simply select the button next to the option you want and click OK, closing the database's Properties window and saving your changes.

Step 14 briefly discussed a crucial component of SQL Server's database mirroring functionality: the operating mode. The option you select for this section directly impacts how SQL Server handles your mirrored database in the case of an outage. The three options available are described next:

- **High Performance (Asynchronous).** This operating mode commits changes to the principal database, sends them to the mirror, and then proceeds with normal processing without waiting for confirmation by the mirror server that the transfer was successful. High Performance mode offers improved performance because the principal server is not waiting on the mirror server to execute operations, but there is also an increased risk of error due to the lack of confirmation. This database mirroring mode is better suited when the operational performance of the database is more important to your organization and a zero-loss RPO isn't a strict requirement.

- **High Safety Without Automatic Failover (Synchronous).** This operating mode does not mark a transaction as completed until it has been written to the transaction log of both servers. Because it does not require a witness server, the database must be manually failed over to the mirror in the case of an outage. If your organization requires that a mirrored database meet a zero-loss RPO target, High Safety Without Automatic Failover is the best database mirroring choice available.

- **High Safety with Automatic Failover (Synchronous).** This operating mode does not mark a transaction as completed until it has been written to the transaction log of both servers, but it does provide automatic failover because it requires a witness server. High Safety with Automatic Failover mode is best suited if your organization places a high priority on real-time RTO targets for databases; the availability of automatic failover means that the database's downtime is limited to the time it takes to bring the mirror online.

As previously stated, one of the most attractive features for database mirroring is its ability to provide automatic failover capabilities for your SharePoint databases in the event of an outage on your principal database instances. It is also important to understand that this important feature is only available with one of database mirroring's three operational modes: High Safety with Automatic Failover. Neither High Performance nor High Safety Without Automatic

Failover allows for the mirroring configuration to be redirected from the principal to the mirror should an error occur on the principal. This fact, combined with some compatibility issues discussed in the following section, makes the operating modes without automatic failover much less compelling and useful. If you want to create a secondary copy of a database without automatic failover, consider using log shipping or database backups before using database mirroring. Both log shipping and backups require far less in terms of IT resources to implement and are much more flexible than database mirroring with the ability to create multiple redundant copies of a single database—something not possible with mirroring. In general, take some time to carefully consider the requirements and implications of your options prior to implementing database mirroring in your environment. The choice you make directly affects your database architecture, the performance of your system, and your disaster recovery and HA planning.

SharePoint and Database Mirroring

If you have had any experience using database mirroring as an HA solution for previous versions of SharePoint, you know that it wasn't a very good story. It wasn't as if the two solutions were incompatible, but there was a major piece of the puzzle that just wasn't there: true automatic failover. SQL Server's High Safety with Automatic Failover operating mode worked just fine and was definitely capable of failing over from the principal to the mirror when the situation called for it, but the problem was that SharePoint had no way of knowing that a failover had happened. And because it didn't know about failovers, it couldn't automatically update itself to point at the mirror instead of the principal, which meant that every server in a given SharePoint farm would have to be updated every time a failover occurred to point the farm at the correct database instance and database names.

The good news is that we have a much different story to tell about database mirroring with SharePoint 2010. It comes down to this: SharePoint 2010 is now "mirroring aware," which means it can recognize when SQL Server automatically fails databases from the principal to the mirror and update its configuration throughout the farm accordingly. Human intervention or custom scripting is no longer required to set up SharePoint to properly use database mirroring as a SQL Server HA solution.

SharePoint Database Mirroring Recommendations and Requirements

Microsoft has stated several recommendations and requirements you should understand, follow, or make your best effort to follow to achieve the best possible stability and consistency for your SharePoint database mirroring configuration. The following list outlines several of these items and describes their purpose:

- **Network latency less than one millisecond.** *Latency* is the time it takes for a data packet to travel from one point to another over a network. It can be measured for one-way trips or for round trips, although the latter is used much more commonly. The less latency your network has, the faster data moves between your servers. Database mirroring requires low latency to ensure that the mirror is kept as closely synchronized with the principal as possible. One major cause of network latency is physical distance, which means that principal and mirror servers often need to be located near each other and eliminates some of the true redundancy of the solution. Please note that this is a recommended value, not a requirement.

- **Network bandwidth one gigabyte per second (GB/s) or greater.** *Bandwidth* measures the amount of data that can be transferred over a network within a given period of time, usually one second. Microsoft recommends (not requires) that your network be capable of transferring at least 1GB of data per second between nodes in the network, due to the high amount of data that will be in the target databases' transaction logs as they are copied from the principal to the mirror.

- **Physical computing resources.** Microsoft recommends that both the physical and mirror SQL Server hosts be provisioned with sufficient processing, memory, storage, and networking resources to accomplish mirroring without impact on performance. Note the number of databases you are going to mirror in your environment; the more databases you mirror, the greater the strain on your servers. The good news is that, by default, database transaction logs are compressed by SQL Server 2008 as they are sent from the principal to the mirror. That does require more processing power to compress the files, but it ensures that the smallest possible file is sent over the network, which reduces network traffic and shortens the time it takes to deliver each file.

- **Database recovery model.** As noted earlier in this chapter, database mirroring requires that the target database is backed up using the Full recovery model. By default, SharePoint creates several databases that are configured to use the Simple recovery model; you are required to change that setting to configure them for mirroring and need to account for the additional overhead that accompanies change.

- **Database permissions.** The service accounts used by various components in your SharePoint environment must be configured to have the same rights in the SQL Server instance hosting the mirrored database as they do in the principal SQL Server instance. Pay attention to the rights granted the service account serving as the identity of all SharePoint's IIS application pools (especially the account for the Central Administration site), the database access service account, the default content access account, all accounts associated with Service Applications, and user accounts that have been added to the Farm Administrations SharePoint group.

- **Unique instance names.** If possible, do not configure the SQL Server instance hosting mirrored databases with the same server and instance names as the principal instance. This can add a great deal of unnecessary confusion and complexity to your environment and make it difficult to determine which instance is currently hosting which role in the configuration.

- **SQL aliases.** You can use SQL Server aliases to abstract the actual address of a SQL Server instance, allowing a client computer to be configured to target the alias rather than the SQL

Server instance directly. This abstraction is helpful for applications that have strong ties to their databases, such as SharePoint, because it adds more flexibility on the use of those database resources than is normally available. If the address for that SQL Server instance should change, or if a different server altogether is used, all that is required is a change to the SQL Server alias, rather than a major configuration change to the application. SQL Server aliases make database integration and management much easier for SharePoint in general and should be used whenever possible in your mirroring configuration. Should a mirroring target change, once the change is made in SQL Server's setup, you can update SharePoint via a small modification to the alias instead of a complex change to the farm's configuration.

- **Operational mode.** SharePoint can only be configured for awareness of database mirroring configurations that are using the High Safety with Automatic Failover operational mode. If either of the other two operational modes are used to configure the mirror and SQL Server fails over from the principal database to its mirror, administrator intervention or custom scripting is required to point SharePoint at the mirror database instead of the principal.

How to Configure SharePoint for Database Mirroring

The first thing you need to do if you want to set up database mirroring for your SharePoint farm's databases is to actually configure the mirroring in SQL Server, using the information and steps outlined earlier in this chapter. Make sure to take into account the items listed in the "SharePoint Database Mirroring Recommendations and Requirements" section, because they are crucial toward ensuring the best possible stability and integration for your mirroring configuration in conjunction with your SharePoint environment. Once mirroring is configured in SQL Server, you have two options available for making your SharePoint farm aware of your mirrored databases: the SharePoint Central Administration Site and PowerShell.

Tip: Please note that *you* are responsible for setting up the mirroring configuration in SQL Server for the databases that you want to mirror; SharePoint 2010 does not do that configuration for you. But the good news is that it *does* validate the mirroring configuration to ensure that it is properly set up and enabled once you notify SharePoint that a given database is mirrored.

If you are most comfortable administering SharePoint through its graphical user interface (GUI), the Central Administration site, you should be glad to hear that you can register SharePoint's content databases as mirrored in it. But, and this is a pretty big "but," keep in mind that we said "content databases" there. You can only use the Central Admin site to register mirroring for SharePoint content databases associated with a Web application, not Service Application databases or the farm's configuration database. These items can still be made mirroring aware within SharePoint; it's just that you must use PowerShell to do so.

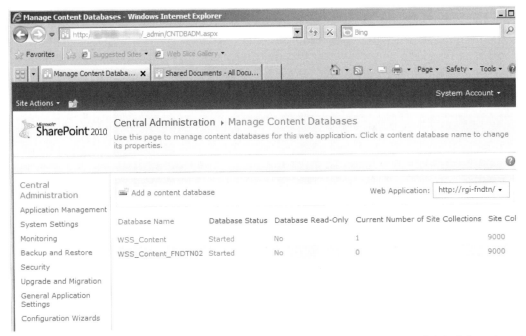

Figure 8.25 The Manage Content Databases page in the SharePoint Central Administration site.

Because of this limitation, registering a content database as mirrored in the Central Admin site is best used for one-off situations rather than a wholesale activity for every database within the farm. To set up a content database to make it aware of its mirroring configuration, see the instructions that follow:

1. Open the Manage Content Databases page. (It's found in the Databases section of the Application Management page.) See Figure 8.25 for an example of the Manage Content Databases page in the Central Administration site.

2. In the Manage Content Databases page, click the link for the content database you have mirrored in SQL Server to open the Manage Content Database Settings page (see Figure 8.26).

3. Once the Manage Content Databases page opens, locate the Failover Server section (circled in Figure 8.26). Enter the fully qualified domain name (FQDN) of the server (or the SQL alias pointing to it that you configured on the SharePoint server, which we highly recommend) hosting the mirror version of the database in the Failover Database Server field, and click the OK button at the bottom of the page to save your changes. If SharePoint is able to validate the mirroring configuration, you are returned to the Manage Content Databases page without error.

If you prefer doing your administration from the command line, or you want to configure mirroring awareness for SharePoint databases other than content databases, PowerShell is the way

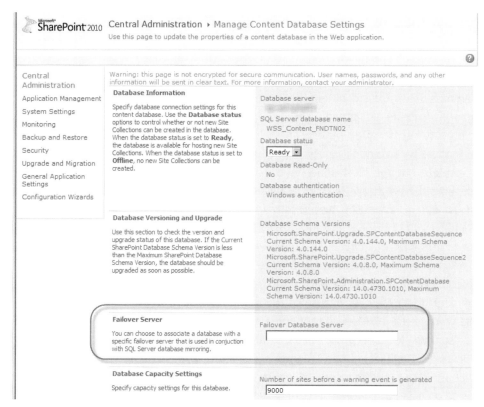

Figure 8.26   The Manage Content Databases Settings page in the SharePoint Central Administration site.

to go. Use the `Get-SPDatabase` cmdlet to obtain an object based on the name of the SharePoint database you are mirroring, and then update that object's `AddFailoverServiceInstance` property with the name of the SQL Server instance hosting the mirrored database. For more information on PowerShell and its vastly expanded role in SharePoint administration, see Chapter 10.

Although you have to make some tough decisions when configuring database mirroring for use with SharePoint's databases, a good portion of your configuration choices is driven by other factors—mainly, how your infrastructure is or can be implemented to meet your needs. For some enterprises, it may not be cost effective to implement multiple farms in geographically diverse locations, whereas for others it may be a business-critical requirement, and each option (plus all those in between) affects how you can use database mirroring and what can be mirrored.

For a single farm environment with components hosted in multiple datacenters, again you can use all three operating modes, but in this case you need to address sticking points as part of the architecture. In this type of environment, the mirrored database instance is hosted in a separate datacenter from the principal instance, providing geographical redundancy in the case of an outage. If you are using multiple datacenters to host your database mirroring configuration, pay special attention to the latency and bandwidth requirements listed previously in this section.

These constraints mean that the datacenters must be capable of providing large, fast connections to the servers they host and that, in most cases, these datacenters must be located closely to reduce latency (at the cost of increasing risk to localized catastrophes).

Additional Witness Server Considerations If a witness server is configured for automatic failover, Microsoft recommends placing it in a third datacenter to ensure that it can initiate the failover process in case of an outage on the principal server. Because this may not always be a feasible configuration, it is still possible to host the witness server in one of the two datacenters, but you must understand that it is exposed to the same risks as the other servers hosted with it, and a manual failover is required if the witness server is impacted by an outage. Microsoft also recommends hosting the witness server in the same datacenter as the mirrored instance so that a potential outage on the principal has a reduced chance of affecting the witness server as well, but this is not without its own drawbacks. When the witness is in the same datacenter as the mirror, a loss of the connection between it and your principal instance's datacenter can bring your entire database environment down. This is because of the way that database mirroring's quorum requirements work: if the principal cannot contact the witness or the mirror to establish a quorum, it also shuts down because it cannot maintain transactional stability. Regardless of where you place it within your environment, we strongly recommend including the witness server in any monitoring solutions you may establish, not only to track the status of the mirroring process but to confirm that the witness server is healthy and able to execute the failover when needed.

If you have multiple farms in separate datacenters, the synchronous operating modes for database mirroring really are not an option because of the time it would take for a transaction to be sent across the network and written to each database, and the results sent back across the network. These activities are directly influenced by network latency—something that is unavoidable over a wide area network (WAN) connection between datacenters that do not share large, fast connections. You can still use database mirroring with the asynchronous operating modes to provide mirrored copies of your crucial SharePoint data. The other drawback to using mirroring for multiple farms is that, like log shipping, you can use it only to mirror your content databases or Service Application databases as long as their associated Service Application is not hosting SharePoint's search functionality.

Tip: If using the High Performance (Asynchronous) or High Safety Without Automatic Failover operating modes for your mirroring configuration, there is no benefit to having a witness server. Witness servers are only required to provide automatic failover capabilities for a mirroring configuration using the High Safety with Automatic Failover operating mode; they are unnecessary when using the other two operating modes.

Database Mirroring Pros

Are you still unsure whether database mirroring is the best HA solution for your SQL Server 2008 instances and SharePoint databases? The following list describes the strong points of database mirroring and their benefits for SharePoint to help you with your decision:

- **Independent.** Like log shipping, database mirroring's functionality is not tied to SharePoint, nor is it affected by any other processes in the SQL Server database instance. This means that changes to your SharePoint configuration or its databases do not directly impact or harm your database mirroring procedures.

- **Highly configurable.** There are several options and configurations to be set to allow database mirroring to meet the needs of your environment.

- **Easily configurable.** Not only is database mirroring straightforward for an administrator to set up and configure, but the infrastructure to host it does not require specific hardware to implement it. Keep in mind that this does not necessarily mean it is easy to operate.

- **Immediate.** When a change is made to a principal database, it is also immediately sent to the mirror.

- **Automated.** If a witness server is configured along with the principal and mirror servers, when an outage occurs, a failover from the principal to the mirror can be automatically executed without administrator intervention, especially when combined with SharePoint 2010's awareness of mirroring configurations.

- **Responsive.** Failovers are executed quickly, regardless of whether they are manually or automatically requested.

- **Distributed and redundant.** As previously explained, you can use database mirroring in various ways to ensure the long-term stability of your SQL Server environment and the SharePoint farm that depends on it.

Database Mirroring Cons

Database mirroring also comes with its own set of drawbacks that you must consider before deciding to implement it, as described here:

- **One mirror per database.** A database cannot be mirrored more than once, creating a single point of failure for your HA solution. Regularly test and confirm your database mirroring configuration to ensure that it continues to function as expected.

- **No easy read-only option.** Mirrored databases cannot be made available for read-only querying without the creation of an additional snapshot based on the mirror.

- **Operational mode limitations.** Although you can use SharePoint with all three operational modes for SQL Server database mirroring, the only mode that it makes sense to use is High

Safety with Automatic Failover. SharePoint is not capable of automatically failing over to a mirrored database with the High Performance or High Safety Without Automatic Failover modes, and some SharePoint databases can *only* be mirrored with the High Safety with Automatic Failover mode or not at all. (See http://technet.microsoft.com/en-us/library/cc748824.aspx for more information on SharePoint Server 2010, its databases, and what can or cannot be mirrored.) Because the other operational modes do not offer the valuable feature of automatic failover, if you are not able to use the High Safety with Automatic Failover mode, or you do not want to use it, you may find that you are better served using log shipping to protect your SharePoint databases, rather than mirroring.

- **Performance impact.** Database mirroring requires multiple processing threads on its host servers, which can negatively affect the performance of your databases in general (specifically utilizing CPU and RAM), especially as more and more databases in the instance are mirrored. If you plan to highly utilize database mirroring, make sure you have the horsepower to account for it.

- **Dependence on networking.** Attempting to do synchronous database mirroring in a network with suboptimal bandwidth or latency leads to performance issues for your principal database and the SharePoint environment that uses it.

- **Geographical limitation.** Although database mirroring can be distributed across multiple datacenters, Microsoft has stated that these datacenters cannot be more than a few miles away from each other, which limits its ability to deliver true geographical redundancy.

- **Inability to configure failover criteria.** Administrators cannot configure or manage the criteria that SQL Server uses to determine when the configuration should be failed over from the principal to the mirror. Because SharePoint 2010 is now mirroring aware, this is less of a concern, but it is still problematic that you cannot configure its tolerances to allow for the specific state of your environment.

- **Incompatibility with RBS.** Databases configured to use RBS cannot be mirrored, regardless of whether they are using Microsoft's FILESTREAM provider or a third-party provider.

- **Complexity.** Database mirroring can be an order of magnitude more involved to implement than SQL Server backups or log shipping. It takes careful research and planning to develop a mirroring solution that is completely compatible with your infrastructure, SQL Server, and SharePoint configurations, due to mirroring's specific requirements. These requirements and several of the items listed can also make operation of a mirrored environment challenging.

Database mirroring is certainly a viable HA solution for SQL Server that's worth serious consideration. It lets you automatically fail over to a fallback database instance should your production database fail. It also gives you the confidence of knowing that the data in your fallback instance is an exact copy of your production database. It is flexible and can be used with various hardware and software configurations. But you may find that it is not a good fit for the needs of an organization and its HA requirements. What if you need your databases to always be online and cannot suffer an outage of even an hour while you update your SharePoint farm to point at your mirrored database instance? What if you need more than one fallback instance to add additional redundancy to your environment but the performance implications of log shipping rule it out as an option? These are just two examples of when configuring a cluster of servers running SQL Server may be the best solution to your problems.

Database Clustering

Clustering is not unique to SQL Server or even to database platforms in general. A server cluster consists of two or more servers, each configured identically, that are designed to consistently serve up an application or platform even if an error or outage occurs on one of the members of the cluster. Although this section focuses on how to use clustering with SQL Server, you can use it to provide HA capabilities for various platforms, such as Microsoft Exchange, Microsoft Hyper-V, and many more.

This section puts the spotlight on the failover clustering solution included in Windows Server 2008, but it is by no means the only clustering platform available to you for your SharePoint and SQL Server environment. Other clustering solutions are available in the marketplace to provide a viable HA solution for your database environment, each offering unique functionality, options, and challenges to give you some flexibility over how you cluster your SharePoint database. Although some products may be specific to the UNIX or Linux platforms, others, such as Symantec's Veritas Cluster Server, are completely compatible with SharePoint and SQL Server and have been successfully implemented as enterprise clustering solutions in the most demanding of situations.

Note: The decision to highlight Windows Server failover clustering in this section is not meant to endorse it as a clustering product or indict its competitors. The goal is to show you how to implement a widely used clustering product for your SharePoint and SQL Server environment, not laud one product over another. It is up to you to evaluate the products in this space and determine which one is the best solution for your enterprise, its infrastructure, and its requirements. Like so many other aspects of SharePoint, this is not a one-size-fits-all kind of situation.

The Server Components of Windows Server Failover Clustering

One advantage of clustering as the HA solution for your SQL Server environment is the flexibility it gives you in designing the architecture of your solution. To create a cluster, you need at least two servers; that way you can create two separate nodes within the cluster. Clustering's flexibility is that you can place more than one server in a node (failover clustering allows up to 16 servers in a node, depending on the edition of Windows Server 2008 being used), and you are not required to have the same number of servers in each node. So if you want to create a node with one server and a node with two servers, that option is available to you. You can also have up to 16 nodes in a cluster. Each node is expected to be able to serve as the primary provider of database services for the cluster, so that if a node is taken down or suffers an outage, you can bring another node in the cluster online to continue that service with no or little downtime.

Failover clustering is available as an included component of Windows Server 2008's Enterprise and Datacenter editions. Microsoft is careful to state that failover clustering is intended to be used as an HA solution but is not completely fault tolerant. *Fault tolerant* describes systems and solutions designed with an extremely high degree of redundancy and the ability to provide nearly instantaneous recovery times; the downside is that these systems often come with a prohibitively high price tag to match. Failover clustering was designed to enable systems to be highly available while using standardized, cost-effective hardware and software, rather than the specialized systems leveraged by a fault-tolerant solution. This is not to say that failover clustering is necessarily a low-cost solution, but it can implement an effective HA solution failover clustering at a much lower cost than a fully tricked-out solution designed to be fault tolerant.

Some aspects of clustering with failover clustering are inflexible—specifically the hardware required for the servers in the cluster and the way that hardware must be configured. The following list outlines the hardware and networking needs you are likely to encounter for failover clustering:

- **Servers.** As mentioned previously, at least two servers must be available to create a database cluster with failover clustering. Unlike log shipping and database mirroring, these servers cannot host databases that exist outside the cluster. Take special care to evaluate the needs of your database environment and confirm that the hardware configuration you select can meet those needs in a clustered configuration.

Note: In Windows Server 2003, Microsoft Clustering Services (MSCS) required the hardware used for a failover cluster to be on the Windows Hardware Compatibility List (HCL); that's changed in Windows Server 2008. Now, a failover cluster's hardware must be marked by its vendor as "Certified for Windows Server 2008," and the entire configuration must be validated with a new tool, the Validate a Configuration Wizard. (It is also known as the Cluster Validation Tool, or CVT.) This tool consists of a series of simulations and tests designed to confirm that the hardware planned for use in a failover cluster meets the specifications necessary to run it. The Validate a Configuration Wizard can also be run against a configured failover cluster as an additional test of its configuration to further ensure that it is ready for use, something we strongly encourage.

- **Identical configurations.** Each server within the cluster must have an identical configuration for its RAM, CPU, system disk, and so on.

- **Redundant network hardware.** Each server within the cluster must have at least two network interface cards (NICs): one for communication with the clients accessing the database server, and one to connect to its cluster node for heartbeat and status updates.

- **Advanced network hardware.** Each server within the cluster must be able to establish fast and reliable communications with the other members of the cluster, usually via specific hardware solutions such as a crossover cable (in the simplest case) or fiber optic cable.

- **Specialized storage.** Each server within the cluster must be able to access a centralized storage system, such as a storage area network (SAN), to access the data created, stored, and updated by a cluster, such as database files. Failover clustering follows the "shared-nothing" model in its use of storage within a cluster, meaning that all the servers in a cluster can access the cluster's storage repository, but it is updated and managed by only one server at a time: the primary server or node in the cluster.

Note: The maximum amount of shared storage space that a SQL Server database can use when hosted in a failover cluster is 2 terabytes (TB).

- **High-speed connection to shared storage.** Each server must have a high-speed connection to the cluster's central storage, such as Small Computer System Interface (SCSI), Fibre Channel (FC), or Internet SCSI (iSCSI).

- **Network resources.** At a minimum, you must provide a Network Basic Input/Output System (NetBIOS) name and a unique static Internet Protocol (IP) address for the cluster, as well as static IP addresses for all the NICs that servers within the cluster use.

Note: For more detailed information from Microsoft on the hardware requirements of Windows Server 2008 failover clustering, see http://technet.microsoft.com/en-us/library/dd197454%28WS.10%29.aspx.

Configuring Windows Server Failover Clustering

After you have procured, installed, and configured your hardware and network solution, you are ready to start configuring a database failover cluster using SQL Server 2008 and failover clustering. When you have built your servers and installed the Windows Server 2008 operating system on them, you must complete some prerequisite steps in the operating system of each server:

- **Enable the failover clustering feature.** You can enable this feature from the Initial Configuration Tasks window or the Server Manager in Windows Server 2008 Enterprise or Datacenter, as well as Windows Server 2008 R2 Enterprise or Datacenter.

- **Do not install antivirus.** Microsoft recommends *not* installing antivirus software on the server nodes in your cluster, because it can cause conflicts or problems with MSCS.

- **Do not compress hard drives.** You must uncompress the hard drive on each server node where SQL Server is to be installed.

- **Mount shared storage.** Windows Server allows additional drives or storage volumes to be mounted, including those presented via shared storage. It also requires a drive letter to be assigned to each drive when it is mounted, which limits a server to 25 mount points. You can avoid this latter limitation by mounting a local physical drive to a letter, such as D, and then mounting your shared volumes as directories under the D volume, a process known as a *mount-point folder path*.

Your system should now be ready for failover clustering to be configured and a cluster to be created with at least two servers functioning as nodes within the cluster. Unfortunately, this chapter cannot provide a walkthrough of how to configure a failover cluster; the shared storage required by the cluster is not a resource that you can easily acquire, and the available technical resources for creating the scenarios and walkthroughs in this book do not include shared storage. The following list highlights several issues to consider as part of planning and configuring your server cluster with failover clustering for it to host a SQL Server database instance:

- **Cluster service account.** Microsoft recommends the creation of a service account to be used as the identity of the failover clustering service running on each server node in the cluster. This account must be a domain account granted Local Administrator rights on every server in the cluster. This account must also be able to log into your clustered SQL Server database instance with public rights to monitor its status. By default, the server's Local Administrators group has this right, but in some cases database administrators remove that access as a security measure.

- **SQL Server service accounts.** The service accounts to be used as the identity of SQL Server's various services running on each server node in the cluster must be domain accounts, not local accounts on each server node.

- **Turning on and off server nodes and storage.** Review Microsoft's instructions for configuring failover clustering (http://technet.microsoft.com/en-us/library/dd197547%28WS.10%29.aspx), because they contain specific information regarding when to turn on and off the various server nodes and storage resources during a cluster's configuration.

- **Quorum mode.** With Windows Server 2008, Microsoft changed the way failover clustering tracked the status and health of the cluster. MSCS previously used a storage resource, called a *quorum disk*, to store the cluster's configuration data and log files on a dedicated volume, which was inevitably a single point of failure. Failover clustering's new approach for determining quorum requires that each node submit a "vote" for its status, and if a majority of votes are available, the cluster has achieved quorum. This removes the dependency on a single item, making failover clusters much more stable. You can actually use multiple quorum modes in a failover cluster; the Validate a Configuration Wizard recommends a quorum mode when it runs, and Microsoft's advice is to use that recommendation unless you have specific reasons to select another mode.

- **Failover Cluster Management application.** If your installed version of Windows Server 2008 includes the failover clustering feature, you can find this application in the Start menu's Administrative Tools directory. This is the tool you must use to create and manage your server clusters.

- **Cluster name.** The name of your cluster should follow Domain Name Services (DNS) naming rules. You can use upper- and lowercase letters, numbers, and dashes in the name, which must be between 1 and 63 characters. The name should also be unique within its parent domain.

- **Storage configuration options.** When running the New Server Cluster Wizard through the Cluster Administrator tool, in its Select Computer page, you are prompted to enter the name of the first computer to be added as a node in the new cluster. This page also includes an Advanced button that, when clicked, opens a dialog box where you can allow the wizard to automatically configure the cluster's shared storage (called the Typical configuration) or to manually do it yourself (Advanced configuration). With the Typical configuration, the wizard selects all the disks in the mounted shared source as disks available to the cluster and creates resources within the cluster for these disks. If you select the Advanced configuration, you must use the `Cluster.exe` executable to configure the cluster's shared storage.

- **Heartbeat.** After you've created the cluster and added additional server nodes to it, make sure to configure the heartbeats that the cluster uses to confirm that the network interfaces for each node are functioning properly. Without this configuration, the cluster has no way to know if a server node is available within a cluster.

- **Configuration review and testing.** Just because you have successfully created and configured your cluster does not mean your work is done. You should immediately test your cluster and confirm that it functions without error and is able to successfully fail over from one node to another when the primary node is unavailable. Review all server logs to confirm that no errors are being reported within the cluster. You should establish regular tests of this process, and any other cluster functions that you find mission critical, to verify that the cluster continues to function as designed.

Now that you have created your failover cluster, complete with at least two server nodes within it, you are ready to install SQL Server and create your database instance in the failover cluster. As with the creation of the server cluster, due to resource limitations, it's not possible to provide you with a detailed description of the steps necessary to create your database instance successfully. However, the following is a checklist of items that you should review and evaluate while completing the process:

- **Follow SQL Server security best practices.** Configure your new instance with the same security settings and measures as nonclustered instances, while taking into account the special requirements of the cluster service account and the fact that your SQL Server service accounts must be domain accounts.

- **Install SQL Server on a cluster.** To install SQL Server on each server node in the cluster, simply log on to the cluster at its shared IP address (rather than the address of the server acting as the active node in the cluster) and run the SQL Server installer. SQL Server is built to be aware of and work in a clustered environment. The installer can detect the cluster environment and install the software to each server node in the cluster you select through the wizard.

- **Validate the components to install.** If you are installing SQL Server via the GUI wizard, check the Create a SQL Server Failover Cluster check box in the Components to Install page. It appears as an indented item underneath the SQL Server Database Services check box and is not checked by default. You must check it for the installer to install SQL Server to all the nodes within the cluster.

- **Determine how to name your instances.** You can create failover clusters using either the default instance for the cluster or a named instance. The choice is up to you.

- **Review your failover configuration.** Installing a single database instance in the cluster is referred to as an Active/Passive failover configuration. You can also configure multiple instances to be hosted within a single cluster, referred to as an Active/Active failover configuration. In an Active/Active configuration, you must assign each instance a different primary server within the cluster. This configuration allows SharePoint's databases to be separated between the instances for scalability purposes.

Caution: If you are considering implementing an Active/Active failover configuration, remember that in a failover scenario, multiple active clusters can be hosted on a single node within the cluster. This means that each node in the cluster must be configured with sufficient hardware resources to host both clusters, or you must be willing to accept degraded performance for both clusters until an additional node can be brought online to accept one of the active clusters.

- **Correctly name the virtual server.** The value provided in the Virtual Server Name page of the installation wizard should be the name of the cluster, not the name of the current active node within the cluster.

- **Install SQL Server on every node in the cluster.** In the Cluster Node Configuration page, select every server node in the cluster so that SQL Server is installed to all of them.

- **Test your system.** When the installation wizard completes, completely test your system to confirm that the database instance is available to client connections, is not reporting errors, and can be successfully failed over from one node to another. Establish regular tests of this process, and any other cluster functions that you find mission critical, to verify that the cluster continues to function as designed.

SharePoint and Database Clustering

Now that you have successfully created a failover cluster for a SQL Server database instance, you can consider the implications of using that instance to host SharePoint databases. One major advantage to the use of a failover cluster for your SharePoint database instance(s) is that you can use it to host all types of SharePoint databases without a special configuration (beyond what it takes to create and configure the cluster). The only step requiring specific attention is how you identify the address of the database instance when creating the SharePoint farm; you must submit the name of the cluster, not the name of the active server node for the cluster.

> **Note:** SharePoint 2010 requires that SQL Server 2008 be patched at least to Service Pack 1 (SP1) and Cumulative Update 2 (CU2) if using it in a failover cluster.

SharePoint views the clustered instance as it does any other database instance. During installation of your farm, it creates all its needed databases without error. The configuration, Central Administration content, and Search databases can be hosted in the clustered instance because the name of the cluster is used and written to these databases instead of the name of the active server node in the cluster. So, in the case of an outage on the active server node, when the cluster fails over to another server node, you can still use these databases. The only outage that SharePoint experiences is during the failover itself; when the new active node comes online in the cluster, service is returned to normal without requiring updates to the SharePoint farm.

> **Note:** Keep in mind that you can use SQL aliases with a failover cluster, even though the address for the clustered instance that SharePoint uses does not change regardless of which node in the cluster is active. You should still consider using SQL aliases to further abstract the location of the clustered instance away from SharePoint to give yourself greater flexibility and scalability with your SQL Server back end.

Database Clustering Pros

Database clustering is a powerful, high-availability tool for SQL Server 2008 that offers several reasons for being a viable option for your SharePoint databases. The following list covers the most compelling reasons for its use:

- **True automatic failover.** When an active node within a cluster suffers an outage or failure, the cluster automatically fails over to another node within the cluster. Because SharePoint references the identity of the cluster and not a specific node within it, you do not need to update a farm's configuration data to recognize the change in database hosts.

- **Patching without outages.** You can complete Windows and SQL Server patching without making the cluster itself unavailable. Simply apply your patches to the inactive nodes in the cluster, then fail over the cluster manually to those update nodes, and patch the remaining nodes. You can do this without interrupting the services that the cluster provides by taking advantage of the cluster's failover functionality.

- **Rapid failover.** Clustering your database means that, in the case of an outage, your system has a drastically shorter time to return to normal service. It only takes the amount of time required for the cluster administration process to switch over to another server in the node; no manual intervention or configuration is required to implement the failover.

- **Scalable.** Because Windows Server 2008, failover clustering, and SQL Server 2008 support up to 16 server nodes within a cluster and use flexible shared technology for storage, you can configure your clustering solution in a variety of ways to meet the needs of your system and easily expand it to grow with your system.

- **Compatible with log shipping.** Like database mirroring, databases hosted with a cluster can be log shipping to another instance to provide even more redundancy for your data.

Note: Failover clustering is also compatible with database mirroring, but we wouldn't recommend it because of the complexity and high costs of implementing such a hybrid solution.

- **Choice of SQL Server backup model.** Unlike in database mirroring, you can back up databases in a cluster using any backup model. The only exception to this is if you are also using log shipping or database mirroring with your cluster, in which case the constraints of the associated technology also apply.

Database Clustering Cons

Unfortunately, database clustering also comes with some disadvantages that can prove to be stumbling blocks to its implementation. Following are those disadvantages:

- **Network requirements.** Although server nodes within a cluster can be located in separate datacenters, the bandwidth requirements for heartbeats and shared storage connectivity mean that nodes usually cannot be more than a few miles from one another.

- **SAN storage requirements.** The technology required to implement shared storage, from both a hardware and software perspective, requires special expertise to implement, operate, and maintain. This also adds a dependency on yet another system for your SharePoint environment's overall health and well-being.

- **Costs.** In addition to the effort required to implement shared storage, the hardware and software for the technology come at a high price. Various providers and configurations are available in the marketplace, but even the low end of the cost spectrum may prove prohibitive for your budget.

- **Fault tolerance.** Log shipping and database mirroring provide a certain level of fault tolerance because the redundant data they preserve is stored on a storage medium completely separate from that of its source. Because clustering uses shared storage to store the data files for your databases, an outage to that shared storage configuration affects your entire cluster and the applications that use it.

Conclusion

At least one blanket statement can be made when it comes to SQL Server and HA: no one ever wants a database to crash or become unavailable, especially not a SharePoint database. Unfortunately, even with the improvements that have been made in the quality, speed, and capacity of modern IT infrastructure and the software that runs on it, such events are inevitable. Hard drives fail, network connections are yanked, and lightning strikes, no matter what you do to try to prevent it. Your responsibility as an administrator is not to prevent the impossible; it is to design your system so that when disaster strikes, it has minimum impact on the least number of users possible. Microsoft recognizes this, and the solutions available to enable HA for SQL Server 2008 show the effort the company has put into helping you succeed in your role.

As a SharePoint administrator, you must be even more cognizant of your system's dependency on its database provider. An outage of your company's intranet, for even an hour, can result in a drastic loss of productivity and revenue. As SharePoint evolves as an application platform, organizations are finding more and more creative uses and ways to stretch it to its limits. You need your environment and its back-end databases to be as stable as possible, and SQL Server HA plays a large role in creating that stability.

Log shipping, database mirroring, and clustering offer attractive HA solutions for your database instances, but they also come with drawbacks that you need to carefully weigh and test. It is somewhat frustrating that there is no cut-and-dried solution to specific HA circumstances, but this is not an entirely bad thing. The range of approaches available to you and your database administrator gives you a great deal of flexibility when implementing SQL Server HA for your SharePoint environment, not only in how you configure a specific procedure but also because you have the ability to combine procedures to overcome their individual deficiencies.

Regardless of how you make your SQL Server databases highly available, you should seriously reflect on the possibility of implementing them in your environment. If the content in your SharePoint farm is business critical, irreplaceable, or unique, you should do everything you can to protect it. If your users depend on your SharePoint sites to always be available and cannot perform their work without SharePoint, you need to make sure it is online when they need it.

Now that you have SQL Server HA under your belt, see if you can confidently answer the following questions about SQL Server HA. You can find the answers to these questions in Appendix A, "Chapter Review Q&A," found on the Cengage Learning Web site at http://www.courseptr.com/downloads.

1. How many servers can receive a single database's transaction logs via log shipping?

2. What are the hardware requirements of database mirroring?

3. What resources must you configure to enable automatic failover of a mirrored database?

4. Can you name the editions of Windows Server 2008 that include failover clustering?

5. What SharePoint components can you include in a database instance hosted on a failover cluster?

9

SharePoint 2010 Central Administration Backup and Restore

In This Chapter

- Getting Started

- An Overview of Backup and Restore Capabilities

- Backup/Restore Prerequisites and Considerations

- Backing Up from Central Administration

- Restoring Within Central Administration

Administering an information technology (IT) platform is a difficult and sometimes thankless task. A common complaint of the IT professional is that no one notices when everything is working as it should; it is only when something breaks or shuts down that the professional receives attention. SharePoint is no different in that regard. When your SharePoint environment is up and running smoothly, it is the contents of the document libraries or the meeting workspaces that get all the attention—until something breaks and those document libraries and their precious contents become unavailable. At that point, you as an administrator are going to be noticed. Someone is going to want to know what you are doing to bring their collaboration site back online, and you need to be ready.

The good news is that every edition of the latest version of SharePoint is shipped with built-in administrative tools designed to back up and restore your SharePoint sites, databases, and even farms. This chapter covers the first of SharePoint's two built-in backup and restore toolsets specifically for administrators: the Central Administration site's Backup and Restore section. It demonstrates how to create backups with the Central Administration site's tool, reveals what the tool can back up, and discusses how to restore backups. After finishing this chapter, you should have a working understanding of the Central Administration site's tool's prerequisites, activities, outputs, and results.

Although Microsoft has done quite a bit for SharePoint administrators by including a number of useful backup and restore tools in SharePoint, we recognize that knowing how and when to use each tool and apply each concept can be a challenge. This chapter is designed to help you specifically with the Central Administration site's powerful backup and restore tools. In the bonus chapter found on the Cengage Learning Web site at http://www.courseptr.com/downloads, we also apply the concepts and information presented here with information from the other chapters in the form of disaster recovery case studies. The case studies offer an opportunity to see how you can use the Central Administration tools discussed here in conjunction with the other SharePoint disaster recovery tools you have at your disposal.

The visual examples provided in this chapter were generated in a testing environment using the following platforms and components. Depending on how your environment is configured, your experiences may vary slightly.

- **Operating system.** Microsoft Windows Server 2008 R2 Enterprise Edition (build 7600)

- **Database.** Microsoft SQL Server 2008 Standard Edition with Service Pack 1 (SP1, build 10.00.2714)

- **Web server.** Microsoft Internet Information Services (IIS) 7.5

- **Client Web browser.** Internet Explorer 8 (version 8.0.7600.16385)

- **SharePoint.** SharePoint Server 2010 Trial (Beta) with Enterprise Client Access License (build 4536)

This chapter also assumes that you possess access to your SharePoint farm's Central Administration site, an understanding of how to actually open and navigate to the site via browser, and access to the rights and resources necessary to use its backup and restore tools.

Getting Started

When it comes to administering a SharePoint farm using a Web browser, the Central Administration site is an administrator's one-stop shop. This holds true for working with SharePoint's backup and restore functions in a friendly and interactive way. In fact, all the backup and restore tools within SharePoint 2010's Central Administration site are conveniently organized and can be accessed through one page within the site.

Note: The examples that follow utilize a fictitious farm hosted on a server named SPDEV. The Central Administration site for the farm has a base URL of http://spdev:18080/. Simply substitute your farm's Central Administration site URL in place of http://spdev:18080 in the examples shown throughout the rest of the chapter to follow along where desired.

Figure 9.1 illustrates the primary point of entry to Backup and Restore functionality within the Central Administration site. For the sake of simplicity, we refer to this page simply as the Backup and Restore page for the remainder of the chapter. Take a moment to familiarize yourself with the appearance and links shown, because the Backup and Restore page is the point of entry for each setting and operation discussed throughout this chapter.

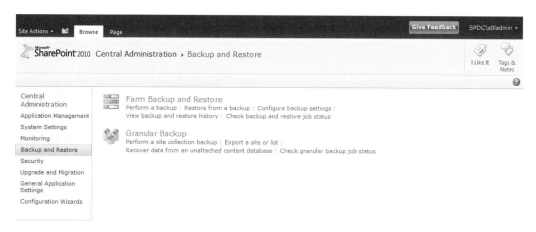

Figure 9.1 The Central Administration site Backup and Restore page.

You can access the Backup and Restore page through either or both of the following two routes:

- Through the Backup and Restore Quick Launch link along the left side of any Central Administration page

- By navigating directly to the `backups.aspx` page (http://spdev:18080/backups.aspx)

Before diving headlong into Central Administration, you need to know this: the bulk of your true disaster recovery planning efforts probably aren't going to revolve around Central Administration—at least for backup planning. One limitation that continues to exist with SharePoint's Central Administration site is its lack of fundamental scheduling and automation capabilities. Central Administration is a wonderful tool for interactively conducting backups and restores, but you cannot script it. For this reason, most disaster recovery plans employ automated scripts and job schedules for the SQL Server backup techniques discussed in Chapter 7 ("SQL Server 2008 Backup and Restore") and the PowerShell command line capabilities that are covered in Chapter 10 ("SharePoint 2010 Command Line Backup and Restore: PowerShell").

This doesn't mean that Central Administration is useless. As this chapter demonstrates, it's a fantastic tool for creating targeted, on-demand backups in an interactive fashion. Many administrators also prefer a visual interface when restoring data, adjusting backup settings, and more. Regardless of preferences, you can view the Central Administration site as simply another tool in your administrative toolbox.

An Overview of Backup and Restore Capabilities

The Central Administration site allows you to work with SharePoint in a visual and interactive way. When you cut past the Web pages and links, though, the Central Administration site is a wrapper around functionality that is exposed through the methods, properties, and events of key

SharePoint object model types. This is true of the PowerShell cmdlets described in the next chapter as well. The differences between Central Administration and the PowerShell cmdlets have less to do with function than they do with the form through which their common underlying functionality is exposed. Both Central Administration and PowerShell provide different mechanisms and options for carrying out disaster recovery operations, but they are both employing the same object model types for the actual grunt work behind the scenes.

When it comes to backing up and restoring your SharePoint environment, it helps to know a little bit about what is going on "under the hood," so to speak. Don't worry, though: this chapter isn't going to become a lesson on the SharePoint object model. Chapter 11, "SharePoint 2010 Disaster Recovery Development," spends more time looking at the object model sections that are relevant to disaster recovery. In this chapter, only a light sprinkling of the SharePoint internals are included to provide some context and facilitate understanding.

Generally speaking, the backup and restore capabilities of the Central Administration site fall into two broad categories, and these are presented to you on the Backup and Restore page as Farm Backup and Restore and Granular Backup. This chapter also looks at the special case of the Configuration-Only Backup, because its intent and usage patterns differ from what might be considered traditional backup and restore.

Farm Backup and Restore

"Full coverage" is a phrase that we all like to hear when shopping for insurance, and it is the best way to think about the capabilities that are supplied through the Farm Backup and Restore links on the Backup and Restore page. Backups of this type are commonly called *catastrophic backups*. That is the term that is employed throughout the rest of the chapter. These backups typically afford you the greatest coverage of any out-of-the-box SharePoint options.

What Catastrophic Backups Include

You'll often hear catastrophic backups in SharePoint referred to as "full farm" backups, but interestingly they really aren't. Before we get into what isn't included in them, let's talk about the objects that are available for catastrophic backup, using the SPDEV example farm.

As you can see in Figure 9.2, a catastrophic backup is capable of capturing and protecting a variety of the critical targets within a farm. In general, the targets that can be captured by a catastrophic backup fall into one of three categories, and these categories are organized hierarchically.

1. **Farm.** A SharePoint farm is a backup target, and it is normally the backup target at the top of the hierarchy. In addition to having its own content (the farm configuration database), the farm is a container for all other objects that can be targeted for backup within the environment.

2. **Services and Service Applications.** Many of the platform capabilities that SharePoint provides are driven by some form of service or Service Application. The Search Service,

Figure 9.2 Farm backup targets in catastrophic backup mode.

InfoPath Forms Services, and Managed Metadata Service are examples that fall into this category. The information that is captured in a backup of this type of object differs from Service Application to Service Application, but it commonly includes settings and any data that is stored in associated databases.

3. **Web applications.** In the hierarchical sense, Web applications are the children of SharePoint's Content Web Service. When targeted for backup, a Web application carries with it any content databases that are associated with the Web application. In addition, a backup includes IIS application pool and binding information, service accounts, alerts, managed paths, `web.config` changes (if made through the SharePoint object model or Central Administration), authentication settings, and sandboxed solutions that are associated with the Web application.

When a catastrophic backup is performed through the Central Administration site, selection of any target automatically includes all subordinate targets in the backup hierarchy. For example, selecting a Web application automatically includes all content databases and settings associated with that Web application. At the highest level in the hierarchy, selecting the top-level farm target captures all targets within the farm. You cannot alter this behavior.

Caution: Pay close attention to what is and is not in a catastrophic backup you perform. If you choose to perform something other than a full farm catastrophic backup of your environment, you may unintentionally exclude items that you need for a successful restore. For example, you cannot back up many Service Applications without performing a full farm catastrophic backup. Services and Service Applications that can be backed up individually often have a service proxy associated with them that does not get backed up when only the service or Service Application is selected. As another example, your farm's configuration database is backed up only when a full-farm catastrophic backup is executed. These are some of the reasons for executing full farm catastrophic backups unless you are constrained by storage space or have a specific selective component backup scenario you are attempting to address. The contents of a full farm catastrophic backup are flexible and can be used to restore not only the full farm, but individual subordinate elements such as specific Service Applications and content databases.

What It Doesn't Include

As is common with insurance, "full coverage" doesn't come without some fine print that you need to read and a variety of limitations you need to understand. In the case of catastrophic backups, "full coverage" is only complete in the sense that it covers all elements specifically within the boundaries of SharePoint.

The preceding chapters have discussed how SharePoint cannot exist in a vacuum. SharePoint relies heavily on the services and functionality of many systems, including SQL Server, Windows Server, IIS, and a host of additional systems. Many of these systems are service providers for SharePoint, but SharePoint itself isn't aware (nor should it be) of how these platforms implement or provide their services. This also means that a SharePoint catastrophic backup cannot capture settings and data needed to restore these external systems in the event of a disaster.

Even if you execute a full farm catastrophic backup, the following are some of the more common settings and data that backup does not capture:

- Application pool account passwords

- HTTP compression settings

- Time-out settings

- Custom Internet Server Application Programming Interface (ISAPI) filters

- Domain membership for the server

- IP security (IPsec) settings

- Network Load Balancing (NLB) settings

- Secure Socket Layer (SSL) certificates

- Dedicated IP address settings

- SharePoint integrated SQL Server reporting and analysis services databases

- Manual changes to any `web.config` file

- Decentralized customizations (see Chapter 5, "Windows Server 2008 Backup and Restore")

Just because a full farm catastrophic backup doesn't cover these items doesn't mean you cannot capture them with a backup. Many of these items and targets were discussed in Chapter 5, and techniques do exist to protect them. You simply cannot rely on a SharePoint full farm catastrophic backup to do the job for you.

When it comes to catastrophic backup limitations, a number of additional items are worth mentioning:

- **Service Application configuration data.** Just because a Service Application is selected for catastrophic backup doesn't mean that all of its configuration data is captured. In the case of the Secure Store Service Application, for instance, a passphrase is supplied at the time that the Service Application is configured. The passphrase is used to provide access to a Master Key that is used in the encryption of credential sets. Backing up the Secure Store Service Application does not backup the passphrase; you must save and protect the passphrase when you configure a Secure Store Service Application instance and have the information available if a restore must be performed. The Secure Store Service Application is probably the most common example of configuration information that isn't automatically captured, but others may exist. At some point in your backup planning, you should review each of the Service Applications you use in your farm and compile information like passphrases, credentials, and other information that must be tracked and made available for restore scenarios.

- **Remote Binary Large Object (BLOB) Storage, or RBS.** SharePoint's default action is to store images, documents, and other file types as BLOBs within SQL Server. When BLOBs are stored in content databases in this manner, they are captured when a catastrophic backup is run provided the content databases are selected for backup inclusion. If the SQL Server's BLOB storage behavior is altered through the use of an RBS provider other than the FILE-STREAM provider, a catastrophic backup does not capture BLOB contents when it is run. In such a situation, you must employ some other form of backup to ensure that all associated BLOB data is protected.

- **SQL Server Transparent Data Encryption (TDE).** SharePoint 2010 can perform catastrophic backups of SQL Server databases that leverage TDE, but SharePoint does not capture the database encryption key (DEK) and other encryption components during the process. It is your responsibility to manually back up and restore TDE components, such as the DEK, a signing certificate, and the private key associated with the signing certificate. Failure to capture these components may block your ability to make decrypted data available in restore scenarios.

- **Business Connectivity Services (BCS).** BCS is typically employed when SharePoint needs to interact with other line of business (LOB) data systems such as external relational databases, customer relationship management (CRM) systems, custom Web services, and virtually any other non-SharePoint system housing data of interest. Although a catastrophic backup can capture configuration information (such as external content type definitions) defining how SharePoint interacts with these external data systems, it cannot capture any of the actual business data housed within the systems. Protection of such data must be pursued separately and represents a different target or set of targets in the disaster recovery sense.

The preceding list of items describing what can and cannot be included in a catastrophic backup is far from the last word. Because you can extend the catastrophic backup system through custom code and third-party products, the list of targets that can be covered in your environment could be larger. If you've read all the previous chapters, you should recognize the need to test any backup and restore plan before ever having to rely on it. Such tests help you to identify the conclusive list of what actually can and cannot be covered by a catastrophic backup in your environment.

Examining the Catastrophic Backup Files

When you execute a catastrophic backup, you might be surprised to discover all the folders and files that are placed in the backup destination. In practice, a catastrophic backup is far from a straight file generation process. Understanding the files that constitute a catastrophic backup set can help you manage those files and aid in your understanding of the backup process.

During catastrophic backup execution, the backup set that is generated consists of several files and directories. See Figure 9.3 for an example of a backup storage directory containing the results of several catastrophic backup operations. Specifically at the root level of that location, you find two items related to that completed backup: a file called spbrtoc.xml and at least one directory named spbrNNNN. (NNNN designates a sequential four-digit hexadecimal number that

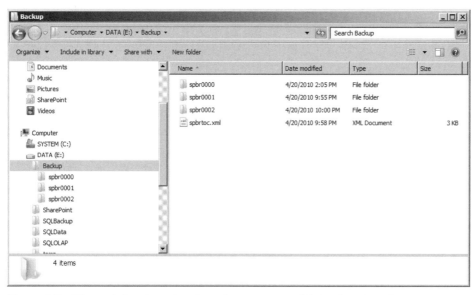

Figure 9.3 File and directory structure for a catastrophic backup location.

SharePoint uses as a unique numeric identifier for your backup files.) SharePoint automatically increments the NNNN number as you save additional backups to this directory, starting at 0000. If you change your target backup location to a new directory, SharePoint starts the numeric identifier back at 0000. spbrtoc.xml is an XML file storing the history information for the catastrophic backups stored in the target file location.

Note: spbrtoc.xml's file name is an acronym for SharePoint Backup Restore Table of Contents. If you change your target backup file storage location in the future, SharePoint creates a new spbrtoc.xml in that location as well.

Caution: Avoid manually updating or modifying the files in your catastrophic backup set. This action can potentially corrupt your backup files and lead to problems during a restoration. Microsoft does not support writing to, moving, deleting, or renaming any of the files in a SharePoint catastrophic backup set.

---

spbrtoc.xml (shown in Figure 9.4) contains SPHistoryObject children under the top-level SPBackupRestoreHistory element. One SPHistoryObject appears for each catastrophic backup set stored in the backup location, and the SPHistoryObject elements are ordered from most recent to oldest. The spbrtoc.xml file also contains entries for each restore operation run using the catastrophic backup sets that are stored in the backup location. Each SPHistoryObject contains the following child elements describing the backup set:

```xml
<?xml version="1.0" encoding="utf-8" ?>
- <SPBackupRestoreHistory>
  - <SPHistoryObject>
      <SPId>93604f5f-8dfb-4e6e-a31e-b0adad81439d</SPId>
      <SPParentID>b5e36666-5bc3-4418-80d5-6a078396cec9</SPParentID>
      <SPRequestedBy>SPDC\s0ladmin</SPRequestedBy>
      <SPBackupMethod>Differential</SPBackupMethod>
      <SPRestoreMethod>None</SPRestoreMethod>
      <SPStartTime>04/21/2010 01:58:48</SPStartTime>
      <SPFinishTime>04/21/2010 02:02:55</SPFinishTime>
      <SPIsBackup>True</SPIsBackup>
      <SPConfigurationOnly>False</SPConfigurationOnly>
      <SPBackupDirectory>\\BackupHost\Backups\spbr0002\</SPBackupDirectory>
      <SPDirectoryName>spbr0002</SPDirectoryName>
      <SPDirectoryNumber>2</SPDirectoryNumber>
      <SPTopComponent>Farm\Microsoft SharePoint Foundation Web Application</SPTopComponent>
      <SPTopComponentId>6e77eb94-5881-490a-ad62-cf415a4b3d13</SPTopComponentId>
      <SPWarningCount>0</SPWarningCount>
      <SPErrorCount>0</SPErrorCount>
    </SPHistoryObject>
+ <SPHistoryObject>
+ <SPHistoryObject>
  </SPBackupRestoreHistory>
```

Figure 9.4 An example of the contents of spbrtoc.xml.

- **SPId.** This is a globally unique identifier (GUID) that SharePoint generates automatically for the backup set.

- **SPParentId.** If the SPHistoryObject is the child of another SPHistoryObject, this element is present and populated with the SPId GUID of the parent. This element typically ties a differential backup to its parent full backup.

- **SPRequestedBy.** Displayed in DOMAIN\User format, this is the SharePoint administrator who submitted the backup request.

- **SPBackupMethod.** Options are Full or Differential.

- **SPRestoreMethod.** Options are None, Overwrite, or New. None indicates that the backup has not yet been restored. Overwrite indicates that the Same Configuration option was used to restore the backup, and New similarly maps to the New Configuration restore option.

- **SPStartTime.** This is the date and time that the backup process was initiated, displayed in MM/DD/YYYY HH:MM:SS format. The time is displayed in Coordinated Universal Time (UTC), not the local time zone of the server.

- **SPFinishTime.** This is the date and time that the backup process completed, displayed in MM/DD/YYYY HH:MM:SS format. The time is displayed in UTC, not the local time zone of the server.

- **SPIsBackup.** Options are True or False. If the entry in the file is for a backup, this value is True. If the entry is for a restore, this value is False.

- **SPConfigurationOnly.** Options are True or False. When both content and configuration settings are backed up, this value is False. If configuration settings are backed up without content, this value is True.

- **SPBackupDirectory.** This is the Universal Naming Convention (UNC) path to the folder containing the files that make up the backup set.

- **SPDirectoryName.** This is the name of the folder (relative to the spbrtoc.xml file) containing the files for the backup package.

- **SPDirectoryNumber.** This is the sequential number assigned to the backup package. The first package in the directory has a value of 0 (zero).

- **SPTopComponent.** This is the top-most component in the tree view hierarchy of the backup component selection page that was checked as a target for backup.

- **SPTopComponentId.** This is the GUID that internally identifies the SPTopComponent.

- **SPWarningCount.** This is the number of warnings generated during the backup process.

- **SPErrorCount.** This is the number of errors generated during the backup process.

Within each catastrophic backup set's specific `SPBackupDirectory` (see Figure 9.5 for an example), SharePoint creates numerous files that represent your selected backup targets.

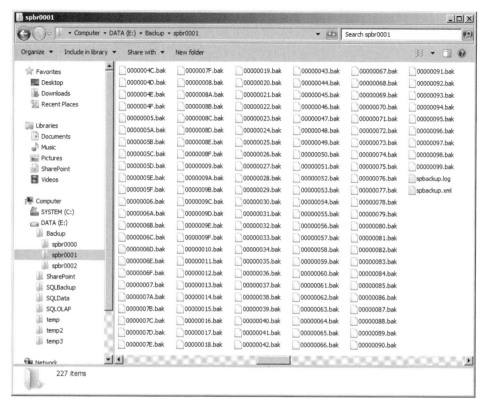

Figure 9.5 Some of the files that make up a catastrophic backup set.

Every directory contains the following elements:

- **One or more .bak files.** These files contain the contents of your selected backup components that come from a combination of the SharePoint farm and the SQL Server databases. Figure 9.6 shows an example of the more human-readable `.bak` files containing serialized SharePoint object data. The other type of `.bak` file that is written to the directory contains SQL database backup information. SQL Server backup files contain binary data that begins with a recognizable `TAPE` marker, as shown in Figure 9.7. Beyond the `TAPE` marker, though, the contents of the file aren't readable.

- **spbackup.log.** This text file contains the details of what occurred during the backup operation that generated the associated catastrophic backup set. Figure 9.8 shows an example of an `spbackup.log` file.

```
1   ⊟<object type="Microsoft.SharePoint.Taxonomy.MetadataWebServiceApplication, Microsoft.SharePoint.Taxonomy, Version=14.0.0.0,
      Culture=neutral, PublicKeyToken=71e9bce111e9429c">
2       <fld type="Microsoft.SharePoint.Taxonomy.MetadataWebServiceDatabase, Microsoft.SharePoint.Taxonomy, Version=14.0.0.0,
      Culture=neutral, PublicKeyToken=71e9bce111e9429c" name="database">ab9c7240-8451-4711-8a25-ca9e53cf2fb2</fld>
3       <fld name="m_DefaultEndpoint" type="null" />
4       <sFld type="Boolean" name="m_Shared">False</sFld>
5       <fld name="m_Comments" type="null" />
6       <fld name="m_TermsOfServiceUri" type="null" />
7       <fld name="m_SerializedAcl" type="null" />
8       <fld type="Microsoft.SharePoint.Administration.SPIisWebServiceApplicationPool, Microsoft.SharePoint, Version=14.0.0.0,
      Culture=neutral, PublicKeyToken=71e9bce111e9429c" name="m_ApplicationPool">8d0e68a7-19be-42f6-bf0c-d8a73f2d8fe2</fld>
9       <fld name="m_ServiceApplicationProxyGroup" type="null" />
10      <fld name="m_SerializedAdministrationAcl" type="null" />
11      <fld name="m_Versions" type="null" />
12      <fld name="m_UpgradeContext" type="null" />
13      <fld type="System.Collections.Hashtable, mscorlib, Version=2.0.0.0, Culture=neutral, PublicKeyToken=b77a5c561934e089" name=
      "m_UpgradedPersistedFields" />
14  ⊟   <fld type="System.Collections.Hashtable, mscorlib, Version=2.0.0.0, Culture=neutral, PublicKeyToken=b77a5c561934e089" name=
      "m_Properties">
15        <sFld type="String">Microsoft.Office.Server.Utilities.SPPartitionOptions</sFld>
16        <sFld type="Microsoft.Office.Server.Utilities.SPPartitionOptions, Microsoft.Office.Server, Version=14.0.0.0,
      Culture=neutral, PublicKeyToken=71e9bce111e9429c">UnPartitioned</fld>
17      </fld>
18      <sFld type="String" name="m_LastUpdatedUser">SPDC\svcSPFarm</sFld>
19      <sFld type="String" name="m_LastUpdatedProcess">"C:\Program Files\Common Files\Microsoft Shared\Web Server
      Extensions\14\BIN\OWSTIMER.EXE"</sFld>
20      <sFld type="String" name="m_LastUpdatedMachine">SPDEV</sFld>
21      <sFld type="DateTime" name="m_LastUpdatedTime">2010-01-20T17:44:36</sFld>
22  └</object>
```

Figure 9.6   Serialized SharePoint object data in a sample `.bak` file.

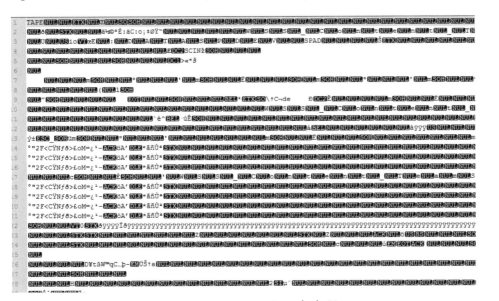

Figure 9.7   SQL Server database backup in another `.bak` file.

Note: All time stamps in this file are saved based on the local time zone of the server hosting the Central Administration site, not UTC.

■ **spbackup.xml**. This XML file contains all the metadata and settings information that was collected for each of the farm backup targets during execution of the catastrophic backup. Figure 9.9 shows an example. Each file contains a single SPGlobalInformation node that

```
 1  [4/20/2010 9:51:03 PM] Verbose: Using directory: \\BackupHost\Backups\spbr0001\.
 2  [4/20/2010 9:51:03 PM] Verbose: The backup/restore process included the following objects:
 3  [4/20/2010 9:51:03 PM]      Farm\
 4          [SharePoint_Config]\
 5          InfoPath Forms Services\
 6              Settings\
 7              Data Connections\
 8              Form Templates\
 9              Exempt User Agents\
10                  [crawler]\
11                  [googlebot]\
12                  [ms search]\
13                  [msnbot]\
14                  [msoffice]\
15                  [slurp]\
16          SharePoint Server State Service\
17              [State Service]\
18                  [StateService_293c4777011d441cafc1db8c03ef32f8]\
19          Microsoft SharePoint Foundation Web Application\
20              SharePoint - 80\
21                  WSS_Content\
22                  [job-workflow-failover]\
23                  [ExpirationProcessing]\
24                  [SchedulingUnpublish]\
25                  [job-solution-daily-resource-usage]\
26                  [SearchAndProcess]\
27                  [DocIdEnable]\
28                  [DocIdAssignment]\
29                  [job-audit-log-trimming]\
30                  [BulkWorkflow]\
31                  [HoldProcessing]\
32                  [VariationsPropagatePage]\
33                  [PolicyUpdateProcessing]\
34                  [VariationsCreatePage]\
35                  [job-change-log-expiration]\
36                  [job-dead-site-delete]\
37                  [RouterProcessingJob]\
38                  [job-upgrade-workitems]\
39                  [job-immediate-alerts]\
```

Figure 9.8 Contents of a sample `spbackup.log` file.

```
 1  <?xml version="1.0" encoding="utf-8"?>
 2  <SPBackup>
 3      <SPGlobalInformation>
 4          <SPId>b5e36666-5bc3-4418-80d5-6a078396cec9</SPId>
 5          <SPRequestedBy>SPDC\s0ladmin</SPRequestedBy>
 6          <SPCurrentPhase>Done</SPCurrentPhase>
 7          <SPNetworkServices>false</SPNetworkServices>
 8          <SPBackupMethod>Full</SPBackupMethod>
 9          <SPDirectoryNumber>1</SPDirectoryNumber>
10          <SPDirectoryName>spbr0001</SPDirectoryName>
11          <SPTopComponent>Farm\Microsoft SharePoint Foundation Web Application</SPTopComponent>
12          <SPTopComponentId>6e77eb94-5881-490a-ad62-cf415a4b3d13</SPTopComponentId>
13          <SPCurrentItem>97</SPCurrentItem>
14          <SPTotalItems>97</SPTotalItems>
15          <SPStartTime>04/21/2010 01:51:03</SPStartTime>
16          <SPFinishTime>04/21/2010 01:55:09</SPFinishTime>
17          <SPUpdateProgress>5</SPUpdateProgress>
18          <SPConfigurationOnly>false</SPConfigurationOnly>
19          <SPBuildVersion>14.0.4536.1000</SPBuildVersion>
20          <SPBackupThreads>3</SPBackupThreads>
21          <SPWarningCount>0</SPWarningCount>
22          <SPErrorCount>0</SPErrorCount>
23      </SPGlobalInformation>
24      <SPBackupNode>
25          <SPBackupObject Name="Farm">
26              <SPBackupRestoreClass>Microsoft.SharePoint.Administration.SPFarm, Microsoft.SharePoint, Version=14.0.0.0,
    Culture=neutral, PublicKeyToken=71e9bce111e9429c</SPBackupRestoreClass>
27              <SPBackupSelectable>True</SPBackupSelectable>
28              <SPRestoreSelectable>True</SPRestoreSelectable>
29              <SPName>SharePoint_Config</SPName>
30              <SPId>b43ef49f-fe81-4989-8f24-fa5f5ad21a9f</SPId>
31              <SPCanBackup>False</SPCanBackup>
32              <SPCanRestore>False</SPCanRestore>
33              <SPCurrentProgress>0</SPCurrentProgress>
34              <SPLastUpdate>04/21/2010 01:51:01</SPLastUpdate>
35              <SPCurrentPhase>NotSelected</SPCurrentPhase>
36              <SPParameters>
37                  <SPParameter Key="b43ef49f-fe81-4989-8f24-fa5f5ad21a9fSTATE.xml"><![CDATA[00000000.bak]]></SPParameter>
38                  <SPParameter Key="Id"><![CDATA[b43ef49f-fe81-4989-8f24-fa5f5ad21a9f]]></SPParameter>
```

Figure 9.9 Contents of a sample `spbackup.xml` file.

contains data on the overall backup, similar to the package's `SPHistoryObject` data in its associated `spbrtoc.xml` file. Below the `SPGlobalInformation` element appear many `SPBackupNode` elements for each of the farm components targetable by catastrophic backup operations—not just the ones that were selected for backup. Upon completion of the backup, `SPBackupNodes` that were actually selected for backup have a descendent `SPCurrentPhase` element value of `Done`. Those that were not included in the backup have an `SPCurrentPhase` element value of `NotSelected`. The `SPBackupNode` elements are hierarchically nested to reflect the relationships that exist between the components associated with each element.

In some situations, SharePoint may create additional files within the backup set's directory depending on the components selected for backup or subsequent actions that are taken with the backup set:

- **One or more folders with GUIDs for names.** Folders of this type appear if one or more Search Service Applications were targeted for backup. Within these folders exists a `Config` directory containing noise and thesaurus files and a `projects` directory containing the backed up Search indices for your environment.

- **sprestore.log.** SharePoint generates this text file if you have used the catastrophic backup set for restore operations. The log file contains the details of what occurred during the restore process using this backup package.

- **sprestore.xml.** This file is similar in content and purpose to `spbackup.xml`—the main difference being that it is associated with a restore operation and not a backup.

Note: All time stamps in these files are saved based on the local time zone of the server hosting the Central Administration site, not UTC.

When You Should and Shouldn't Use It

A full farm catastrophic backup offers the greatest degree of coverage for your farm of any out-of-the-box tools. This makes a full farm catastrophic backup the operation of choice anytime you plan to introduce significant changes into your SharePoint environment. The following operations are just a few examples of those that are more comfortably performed knowing that some catastrophic backups have been taken for insurance against unexpected problems or failures:

- Application of a service pack or hotfix

- Changes to farm topology or the farm environment, such as the addition of a new farm member or the relocation of a server

- The addition and deployment of a new solution package (WSP) within the farm

- Any operations that result in significant changes to content databases, such as site collection relocation using the `Export-SPWeb` and `Import-SPWeb` PowerShell cmdlets

In most cases, it is desirable to capture a catastrophic backup both before and after the operation being performed. Why two backups? Well, the backup that is captured before the change provides you with a catastrophic backup set that is stable and consistent. You can use it to roll back the farm or its elements in the event of failure following the change.

After you have made the change and verified that the farm is in a stable and consistent state, you should take another catastrophic backup. This backup set provides a new baseline for the farm going forward. This is not immediately useful within the context of the change you made, but it is important in that the backup becomes the first known stable and consistent point in the farm following the change. This is important because it gives you a fall-back point until you make the next major change to your environment. At that point, the backup/apply change/backup sequence just described is repeated.

There are certainly times when you should avoid a catastrophic backup. Executing a catastrophic backup, particularly a full farm catastrophic backup, can place a significant load on your SharePoint infrastructure. This load can adversely impact an end user's experience and other operations within your farm. As a responsible administrator, you should consider capturing performance metrics during catastrophic backups as they are being performed if you don't have a solid understanding of how such backups impact your farm. Observing SharePoint and SQL Servers to see how their memory, disk, and network utilization are affected can help you make informed decisions regarding when catastrophic backups can or should be run. As a general rule of thumb, run catastrophic backups during off hours or times of low SharePoint use whenever possible.

SharePoint's catastrophic backups can also consume a lot of disk space, and the platform includes no built-in mechanism to prune or manage backup storage. If your disk space is constrained or you spend less time managing your storage space than you would like, you should probably think twice about frequent use of catastrophic backups.

Granular Backup

The bulk of the Granular Backup functionality that is included with SharePoint 2010 was included in some form in SharePoint 2007, but it was not available from within the Central Administration site. You could perform a site collection backup easily with SharePoint 2007, for example, but you had to go to a command line and type `STSADM -o backup -url <YourSite'sUrl> -filename <SiteCollectionBackupFilename>`. With SharePoint 2010, this functionality is exposed within Central Administration along with some brand new capabilities.

How Granular Backup Is Different from Farm Backup and Restore

Although the Granular Backup functions are exposed in the same area of Central Administration as the Farm Backup and Restore functions, they are not the same. Under the hood, the catastrophic Farm Backup and Restore functionality that has been discussed thus far leverages a number of types that are contained within the `Microsoft.SharePoint.Administration.` `Backup` namespace of the SharePoint object model. The functions that are exposed by Granular Backup, on the other hand, are tied to a collection of other types that reside in a variety of namespaces. For example, the Export a Site or List option exposes functionality that resides in the `Microsoft.SharePoint.Deployment` namespace—an area of the application programming interface (API) that is associated with content deployment, not backup and restore.

This distinction is important because you shouldn't mistakenly think that the Granular Backup functions operate and behave the same way that the catastrophic backup and restore operations do. This is especially true for export operations that use the content deployment types. Content deployment operations are not intended to be full fidelity, meaning that only a subset of content and property values can be exported or imported. Backup and restore operations, on the other hand, *are* full fidelity. This may seem like a minor point, but it carries implications for the scenarios in which you can utilize backups and exports.

Tip: For additional discussion and detail regarding the differences between backup/restore and export/import, see Chapter 11.

Site Collection Backup

As its name implies, the Site Collection Backup allows you to back up a single site collection within a Web application residing within your SharePoint environment. To perform this type of backup, SharePoint executes a combination of database queries and export calls to yield a single backup file. The backup file is commonly assigned a `.bak` extension, but you can actually assign any extension you would like. This file can then be used to restore the targeted site collection in-place or in one or more other Web applications.

This is the same site collection backup that could be performed with SharePoint 2007 through STSADM.exe using the command line syntax STSADM `-o backup -url` `<YourSite'sUrl>` `-filename` `<SiteCollectionBackupFilename>`. Central Administration in SharePoint 2010 simply wraps the site collection selection and file name specification within a graphical user interface (GUI) for more visually oriented administrators.

Note: You can still perform site collection backups using the command line approach in SharePoint 2010, but PowerShell is recommended instead of STSADM. See Chapter 10 for more information.

Prior to starting, the backup operation temporarily sets the lock state for the site collection to read-only if the site collection's lock state is either Not Locked or Adding Content Prevented. In such a situation, the site collection's original lock state is restored upon completion of the backup. This lock state change is made to reduce the likelihood of content changes during the backup process because such changes could result in an inconsistent backup.

Microsoft doesn't recommend the use of site collection backups with site collections that are larger than 85GB, but this is not a hard limit. As your site collections approach and exceed 85GB, though, you would be wise to investigate the use of SQL Server content database backups or SharePoint's native catastrophic backup functionality as a more appropriate alternative to site collection backups.

Note: At the time when this book was written, Microsoft's TechNet site included a specific note stating that site collection backups did not include workflow information. This note is incorrect. Backups that are performed with the site collection backup approach are full-fidelity and contain all workflow information, including workflow history and workflow state. The note was originally intended as a warning for exports that are performed with granular export operations through types within the Content Deployment API, not site collection backups.

Content Export

"Microsoft giveth, and Microsoft taketh away" is a good way to summarize the arrival of the Export a Site or List function in Central Administration. Although the GUI-based manifestation of this functionality is new to Central Administration with SharePoint 2010, the capabilities existed in the previous version of SharePoint Designer for SharePoint 2007. With the redesign of SharePoint Designer 2010 to make the application more task oriented, however, GUI-based content backup and export functionality was removed.

Much like the Site Collection Backup function just discussed, the Export a Site or List function does exactly what its name suggests. Through a series of drop-down selection controls, you can select an entire site collection, a specific site, or a specific list within a site for export to a content migration package file set. The file set is commonly given a `.cmp` extension, but that isn't required. If no extension is specified for the file, `.cmp` is assigned. You have the option of exporting security information with the package, and you are given the option to decide whether all or some versions of files and lists are exported.

As with the site collection backup capability, administrators still maintain the ability to execute export operations from the command line using both PowerShell and STSADM.exe.

When You Should Use It

The Granular Backup options overlap with the catastrophic backup and restore operations in some places, but they are generally intended to complement them. Catastrophic backup and restore operations focus on the objects that exist at the macro scale above the content database level—objects such as the farm, services, and Web applications. It is best to think of the Granular Backup functions as addressing those objects that exist within or below the content database level, such as site collections, Webs, and lists.

Granular Backup operations are well suited to migrating and moving content around, and they are generally preferable to catastrophic backup and restore operations for this purpose. Granular Backup operations generate a limited file set (oftentimes only one file of interest), and their output is intended for use in content duplication efforts. Copying content from one site to another is a much easier affair with Granular Backup than it is with Farm Backup and Restore options.

This flexibility comes with some constraints, though. The practical size limitation for site collection backups was already discussed. Granular operations, on the other hand, target only one object at a time, be it a site collection, site, list, or document library. Granular Backup operations are also harder on SharePoint's infrastructure resources due to their read-intensive and processing-intensive nature.

One of the biggest limitations for visually oriented administrators, though, is the complete lack of restore options for Granular Backups and exports within Central Administration. Central Administration provides a wonderful interface for site collection backups and content exports, but it provides no complementary functionality for restores and imports of the items that result from these actions. Administrators must instead turn to command line operations and Power-Shell for such activities.

Configuration-Only Backup

The concept of a configuration-only backup is new to SharePoint 2010, and it is a direct response to one of the heaviest criticisms levied against full farm backup and restore in previous SharePoint versions; namely, it isn't possible to perform an out-of-place restore on a backed-up farm to create a clone of it. Farm configuration databases are tightly coupled to a SharePoint farm at both the logical and physical levels due to the way server names and database connection strings are used, and practical use cases involving the restoration of a farm configuration database through any means are so narrow and uncommon that they are nearly nonexistent.

Despite this fact, the desire to find some way to make farm configuration settings portable under SharePoint is common. Many administrators, for example, require a way to create copies of their production environments for use in disaster recovery, testing, development, content authoring, and other scenarios. Unfortunately, platform support for this type of operation didn't exist in SharePoint 2007. In most cases, administrators had no practical choice but to build a new farm each time and reapply configuration settings through a carefully assembled script (at best) or in an ad-hoc fashion (at worst).

To ease the administrative burden associated with these types of scenarios, Microsoft introduced configuration-only backup and restore with SharePoint 2010. Although it isn't a complete solution itself, it does improve the situation in this area relative to SharePoint 2007.

When a catastrophic backup is being set up, you have the option of backing up content and configuration settings or configuration settings only, as shown in Figure 9.10.

Figure 9.10 Configuration-only backup settings.

For the purposes of a configuration-only restore, both of these backup types include the configuration information that is needed if a configuration-only restore is to be performed later. Put another way: you can perform a configuration-only restore using either a configuration-only backup or a catastrophic backup. The information that is restored includes the following type of portable configuration data:

- Antivirus settings

- Information rights management (IRM) settings

- Outbound e-mail settings

- Customizations and solution packages

- Diagnostic logging settings

When you perform a configuration-only restore, these portable configuration items are written to the configuration database of the target farm. The target farm can be the farm where the configuration settings were backed up using a catastrophic backup or configuration-only backup, thus providing a mechanism for configuration rollback. The target farm can also be another farm altogether, allowing the cloning of settings from one farm to another.

Unfortunately, configuration-only backup and restore is not a complete solution for configuration documentation and replication. It fails to capture configuration data associated with a number of critical components, including Web application and Service Application settings. For this reason, configuration-only backup and restore won't remove the need for complete farm documentation anytime soon. It does, however, bring administrators one step closer to a future that is free of manual configuration tracking.

Tip: Microsoft recognizes that completely documenting a SharePoint farm's configuration is challenging. In an attempt to provide administrators with some assistance in this area, Microsoft has created a PowerShell script that does a solid job of documenting the overwhelming majority of configuration items and settings in the typical SharePoint farm. See http://technet.microsoft.com/en-us/library/ff645391.aspx for additional details and the script.

Backup/Restore Prerequisites and Considerations

The basic concepts associated with backup and restore operations are easy to understand. Back-ups capture data, and restore operations put that data back. The devil is always in the details, though, and this is especially true with SharePoint's backup and restore capabilities. Before attempting any form of backup or restore with SharePoint, you need to check a number of line items in a rather lengthy checklist.

The good news is that once you have configured your environment properly for backup operations, there is little else that you must configure to successfully conduct restore operations.

Backup Settings

Only a handful of high-level settings exist for configuration of catastrophic backup and restore operations within Central Administration, and you access these through the Configure Backup Settings link on the Backup and Restore page. Clicking this link takes you to the BackupSettings.aspx page, as shown in Figure 9.11.

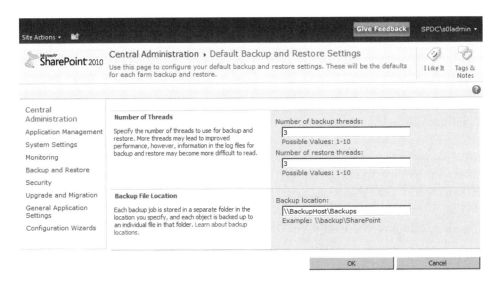

Figure 9.11   The default Backup and Restore Settings page.

Number of Threads

SharePoint 2010 gives you control over the number of threads that are spun-up to carry out both catastrophic backup and catastrophic restore operations. By default, each of these operations is configured to utilize three threads during execution.

If you aren't familiar with threading, it is easiest in this scenario to equate a thread with an object that is being backed up or restored. Specifying three backup threads, for example, roughly translates into three objects being backed up in parallel during the execution of the backup operation. Three restore threads, on the other hand, means that three objects at a time can be restored simultaneously. The greater the number of threads of execution, the greater the degree of parallelism and the faster you can potentially process your objects for catastrophic backup or restore.

So, what is to stop you from dialing your backup and restore threads up to their maximum value of 10? First of all, there is the obvious warning on the `BackupSettings.aspx` page indicating that it could become difficult to interpret the log files that are generated during the backup and restore operations. With 10 concurrent writers to a single file, the contents are bound to appear jumbled.

More important than jumbled log files, though, is the potential impact that 10 threads of parallel execution carries with regard to server resources. Processing 10 objects at once puts a significantly greater strain on the memory, CPU, and disk resources of your SharePoint servers than processing only 3 objects at a time. In addition, streaming backup or restore data for 10 objects at once across a network places a greater load on your infrastructure if it is involved in the equation. At the extreme, this extra load could simply cause thrashing at one or more bottleneck points on your servers and infrastructure, leading to poorer overall performance instead of better.

As with most dials, some amount of experimentation is required to find the sweet spot that allows you to maximize your catastrophic backup and restore performance without unintended side effects. Consider running multiple backup and restore operations as a test, and vary only the number of threads in use for each one. While conducting these tests, pay attention to the memory, CPU, and disk load being placed on each server and infrastructure component that is involved in the backup or restore operation. Once you have found settings that offer the desired balance of performance and system load, lock them in and document them. Remember, too, that settings are specific and relevant only to the environment in which they were tested and measured.

Backup File Location

Your choice of catastrophic backup location is an important one. Microsoft recommends that you use local disks whenever possible for maximum performance, and this recommendation is easily observed when all elements of the SharePoint farm, including SQL Server, are installed on a single physical or virtual server. In the case of an all-in-one server, local drive references for both SharePoint and SQL Server point to the same location on the drive-mapped storage medium.

For most practical purposes, multiserver SharePoint farms that intend to leverage SharePoint's catastrophic backup and restore capabilities must be able to reach a network share that is accessible through a UNC path specification. Microsoft also suggests that network shares with 1 millisecond or less of latency between themselves and the SQL Server(s) housing SharePoint content should perform well.

When you select a backup file location on the `BackupSettings.aspx` page, SharePoint doesn't help you with any of the latency-related issues described thus far. SharePoint does, however, notify you of problems and potential remedies if you try to specify an invalid location, as shown in Figure 9.12.

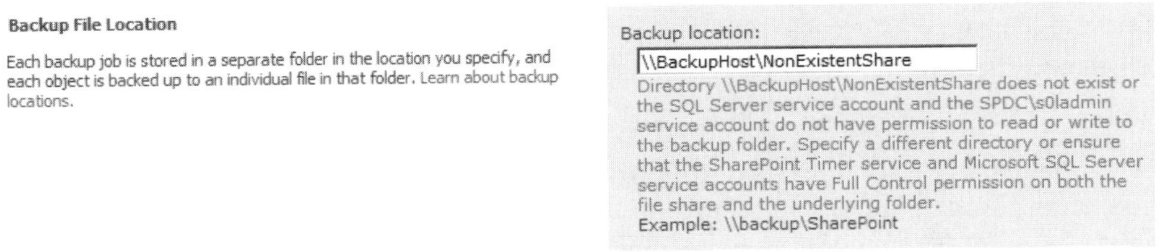

Backup File Location

Each backup job is stored in a separate folder in the location you specify, and each object is backed up to an individual file in that folder. Learn about backup locations.

Backup location:

\\BackupHost\NonExistentShare

Directory \\BackupHost\NonExistentShare does not exist or the SQL Server service account and the SPDC\s0ladmin service account do not have permission to read or write to the backup folder. Specify a different directory or ensure that the SharePoint Timer service and Microsoft SQL Server service accounts have Full Control permission on both the file share and the underlying folder.
Example: \\backup\SharePoint

Figure 9.12   Selecting an invalid backup file location.

You can only accept changes by clicking the OK button after valid settings have been supplied. If valid settings cannot be supplied, the only option is to click Cancel.

Services, Accounts, and Permissions

The execution of backup and restore operations through Central Administration engages quite a few moving parts. Each time one of these operations is attempted, a number of different services, file locations, and security contexts end up in the mix. Understanding the interactions of these elements is essential to proper backup configuration and troubleshooting.

Understanding the Security Context

The key to understanding backup and restore operations that are initiated through Central Administration is realizing that little actually happens within the security context of the currently logged-on administrator. Instead, administrators configure and prepare operations, such as a backup, that are then handed off to other services for execution. The following list of actions roughly represents the steps that are carried out when a full farm catastrophic backup is run:

1.   You, the administrator, specify the parameters of the backup operation.

2.   A SharePoint Timer service backup job is created and scheduled for one-time execution using the settings you specified.

3.   During a sweep, the Timer service begins execution of the backup job and engages SQL Server for some of the required backup operations.

4.   Both the Timer service and SQL Server write directly to the designated backup area to carry out the backup.

5.   Upon completion, SQL Server is disengaged and the Timer service backup job completes.

6.   The backup is finished.

In the execution of the previous steps, the only step that actually occurs within your administrative account context is step 1. Each step after the first one occurs within the context of a service account. Timer service actions are carried out in the context of the SharePoint farm database access account—the same account that is used as the Central Administration site's IIS application pool identity. SQL Server actions are carried out in the context of the account under which the SQL Server database engine is running. This differs significantly from the backup and restore operations that are carried out through PowerShell, where your administrative account context is the one that is primarily utilized for SharePoint operations.

Services and Their Accounts

Ensuring that the appropriate services are enabled and possess the necessary privileges to carry out backup and restore tasks can be tricky. Thankfully, Central Administration provides some useful guidance to ease the burden of configuration in this area. At the top of each backup and restore application page within Central Administration is a Readiness area. For each backup and restore operation exposed, Central Administration alerts you to the services that need to be running and their current state of readiness for the desired operation. Figure 9.13 illustrates the Readiness area when a catastrophic backup operation is selected and you are directed to the Backup.aspx page.

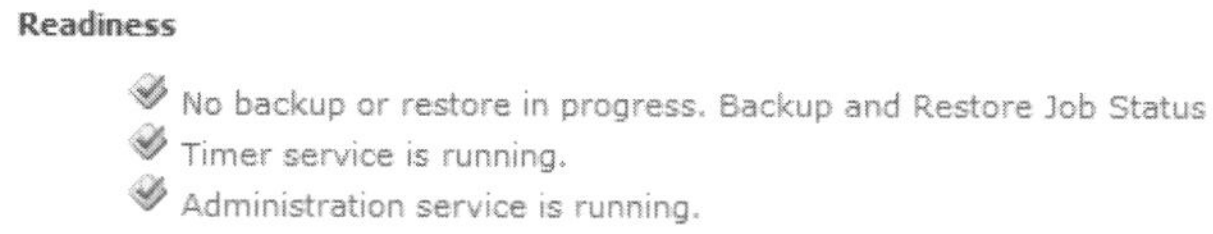

Readiness

✔ No backup or restore in progress. Backup and Restore Job Status
✔ Timer service is running.
✔ Administration service is running.

Figure 9.13   The Readiness area for Perform a Backup.

If either the Timer service or the Administration service isn't started when you navigate to the Backup.aspx page, you receive a warning and a red exclamation mark instead of the check mark for the affected service(s). You can continue your configuration of the backup operation, but attempts to start a backup without addressing the Readiness warnings result in an error and failure.

Note: Readiness warnings identify the Timer service as the Microsoft SharePoint Foundation Timer 2010 service and the Administration service as the Microsoft SharePoint Foundation Administration 2010 service. If you attempt to locate services with these names in the Microsoft Management Console (MMC) Services snap-in, you won't find them. In reality, these services appear in the Services snap-in as the SharePoint 2010 Timer service and the SharePoint 2010 Administration service, respectively.

In addition to the aforementioned services running, you need to address a couple of permission issues before carrying out a catastrophic backup or restore operation. As mentioned in the full farm catastrophic backup example earlier, both the SharePoint Timer service and the SQL Server service read from and write to the backup file location you specify. For these services to carry out their duties, the accounts that the SharePoint Timer service and SQL Server service run under must have Full Control permissions on the backup file location for catastrophic backup and restore operations. If one or both of the accounts that are associated with the services lack the permissions they require on the backup file location, your requested operation will fail.

Note: If your SQL Server service is configured to use one of the built-in accounts such as Network Service, be aware that SQL Server presents itself to network resources using the machine's computer account—not a separate domain user account.

The access requirements are slightly different in the case of Granular Backup and Restore operations. Each of these operations is carried out by the SharePoint Timer service alone. SQL Server is not involved, so the rights of the SQL Server service account aren't a factor. For Granular Backup and Restore operations, only the SharePoint Timer service must have Full Control permissions on the backup file location.

User Accounts

Even though Central Administration hands off the actual execution of backup and restore jobs to service accounts, there are still some rights that you, the administrator, require to access and carry out the necessary configuration steps.

- **Granular Backup.** To access Granular Backup functions, you require nothing more than membership in the Farm Administrators group. If you aren't a member of the Farm Administrators group, it is generally pretty obvious because you can't access Central Administration.

- **Farm Backup and Restore.** The catastrophic backup and restore functions that are available within Farm Backup and Restore require that you are a member of the local Administrators group on the server housing Central Administration. If you are not a member of the server's Administrators group but are a member of the Farm Administrators group, a couple of the Farm Backup and Restore functions are still available. As Figure 9.14 illustrates, though, the critical links to access backup, restore, and settings configuration pages are removed via security trimming. For comparison, see the full list of links available to a Farm Administrator who is also a local Administrator depicted in Figure 9.1.

Figure 9.14   Security trimming of backup and restore links.

Full Backups Versus Differential Backups

One of the options that is available to you when you are preparing a catastrophic backup is whether to perform a full backup or a differential backup. A full backup performs a complete backup of all objects you select, whereas a differential backup only performs a backup of the selected objects that have changed since the last full backup. By extension, this means that differential backups tend to be smaller than full backups—an attractive consideration if you are trying to make the most of your investment in disk storage.

As stated, differential backups only capture changes that have been made to the selected objects since the last full backup. For differential backups to work, a full backup of the selected objects must exist as a point of comparison to identify what has changed. Without a full backup as a point of comparison, you cannot perform differential backups. If you attempt to create a differential backup without first having taken a full backup, SharePoint simply throws up an informative error and aborts the operation.

Caution: When mixing and matching full and differential backup types, we have a simple recommendation: the first backup created in the file backup location should be a full farm catastrophic backup. If you begin with a full farm catastrophic backup, you can subsequently execute a differential backup of any farm object (including the full farm) without fear of potential problems or loss. You can run into trouble if you try the opposite scenario, such as executing a full backup of only a Web application followed by a differential backup of your entire farm. SharePoint allows you to execute this sequence of backup operations without error, but subsequent catastrophic backups, whether full or differential, never capture more data than just the original Web application until you perform a full backup of greater scope. This scenario can be confusing and result in unintentional data loss if you mistakenly expected the second full farm differential backup to contain data for more than just the Web application that was originally captured.

Using Unattached Content Databases

Another interesting addition to the toolbox of Central Administration capabilities in SharePoint 2010 is the ability to browse and recover data from SharePoint content databases that are not attached to the farm, as shown in Figure 9.15.

The `UnattachedDbSelect.aspx` page shown in Figure 9.15 is the entry point to working with unattached content databases, and you can access it easily from the Backup and Restore page through the Recover Data from an Unattached Content Database link. From this area, it is possible to browse a content database, back up a site collection within the content database, or export content directly from the database.

To understand why this feature is so powerful, you must first understand some of the constraints of content databases and how recovery operations from them were handled in the past.

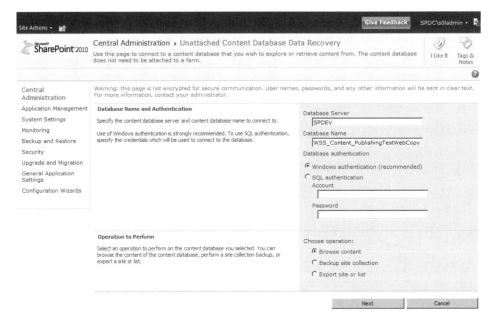

Figure 9.15 Unattached Content Database Data Recovery page.

Content Recovery Prior to SharePoint 2010

This chapter spends a great deal of time discussing how to handle catastrophic backup and restore scenarios, but in reality catastrophic farm failures occur infrequently. On a day-to-day basis, administrators more commonly find themselves faced with the problem of content loss in some limited form. Whether through error, unintended or accidental site deletion, or some other set of circumstances, users lose content from within their SharePoint sites. This type of loss doesn't constitute a catastrophic failure; nonetheless, there is a real need for some type of recovery from a catastrophic backup of the content database that housed the content prior to its deletion or loss.

With SharePoint 2007, this type of recovery scenario presented some specific challenges. In most of these content recovery scenarios, the desire wasn't to replace the entire content database from backup. The goal was to simply recover a specific item, list, site, and so on that had been deleted. These object-level recovery scenarios were possible, but they were difficult with SharePoint's native backup/recovery and export/import tools. Without additional tools, you commonly executed such a recovery according to the following series of steps:

1. You, the administrator, were notified of the lost content and asked to recover it from backup.

2. You needed to locate a backup of the content database that contained the lost content. The backup could take the form of a SharePoint catastrophic backup, a SQL Server database backup, or something else entirely.

3.   You restored the content database to a separate recovery farm environment—or at least a farm that was not the current production farm.

4.   After attaching the content database to a Web application in the recovery farm, you located the object to be recovered and exported it. Such an export was typically conducted through an `STSADM.exe -o export` operation.

5.   The export package that was generated from step 4 was copied to the production farm environment.

6.   In the production farm environment, the export package was imported to the appropriate site or other container using an `STSADM.exe -o import` operation.

7.   The recovered content was available for users once the import operation completed.

The greatest pain in this sequence of steps typically centered on the recovery farm requirement described in step 3. Why was an entirely separate SharePoint farm needed just to recover some content? The answer, quite simply, is because two copies of the same content database cannot be attached to the same SharePoint farm at once. Every content database in SharePoint possesses a GUID that differentiates it from all other content databases. If you attempt to attach a content database possessing a specific identifier to a farm where a database with that same identifier is already attached, the operation fails.

In the case of a content database that was restored from backup under SharePoint 2007, it wasn't possible to leverage the SharePoint object model (including the functionality within the Content Deployment API that is needed for the `STSADM -o export` operation) to recover objects from the database without first attaching that database to a farm. The option to first detach the existing content database from the production farm was always a possibility, but it involved taking down all site collections housed in the target content database—not just the site collection that was tied to the content recovery operation. In most cases, the practical response to these constraints was the use of a separate farm for recovery purposes.

Content Recovery Improvements in 2010

SharePoint 2010 simplifies content recovery efforts tremendously by allowing you to work with content databases and perform object model operations against those databases without requiring that the databases are attached to a SharePoint farm. This means that a recovery farm is no longer needed, because SharePoint 2010 can continue to work with a production content database that is attached to the farm at the same time it is exporting content from an unattached copy of the same content database that was restored from backup. In short, two copies of the database are present in SQL Server, but only one of them is actually attached to the SharePoint farm.

Note: For the record, there isn't anything stopping you from using the unattached database recovery capability to back up or export data from a normal production database that is actually still attached to the farm. This capability is redundant with the site collection backup and content export functions that are built into Central Administration, though, so an actual usage scenario involving unattached recovery from an attached database is left up to your imagination.

Removing the need for a recovery farm obviously saves you the cost and overhead associated with the maintenance of an additional SharePoint environment. It depends on your specific needs and SharePoint environment, but the unattached content database recovery capabilities of SharePoint 2010 may also allow you to meet more aggressive recovery time objectives (RTOs) for content restore operations. With SharePoint 2007, recovery farms were commonly built as virtualized environments that lacked the processing power and resources of their associated production environments. A fair amount of time during content recovery operations was spent locating backups, moving them between environments, patching the recovery environment to an equivalent or greater version than production, and other "busy work" tied to the second farm environment. With the ability to execute a database restore and content recovery in one farm environment, much of that extra time and overhead goes away or is at least reduced.

Backing Up from Central Administration

After a discussion of all the background and technological underpinnings, it's time for you to kick the tires on Central Administration's backup and restore capabilities with some operational walk-throughs.

Full Farm Catastrophic Backup

There is absolutely no doubt that the most important backup and restore operation you should know how to perform within Central Administration is a full farm catastrophic backup. Executing a full farm catastrophic backup provides you with the greatest variety of options for recovery in the event of a catastrophic failure, content loss, or some other unfortunate event.

The example that follows demonstrates how to use Central Administration to perform a full farm catastrophic backup and save the resultant backup set to a network share located at \\BackupHost\Backups.

Before you begin, ensure that you are a member of both the SharePoint Farm Administrators group and the local Administrators group on the server housing the Central Administration site. Both the SQL Server service and SharePoint Timer service accounts require Full Control permissions to your backup location. In addition, ensure that you are logged into a computer that can access the SharePoint Central Administration site. This is often your own workstation, but in some highly secure environments, access to the Central Administration site may be restricted to only a select group of servers and workstations:

1. Open a browser and navigate to the Central Administration site. In the case of the fictitious farm described at the beginning of the chapter, the default URL of the Central Administration site is http://spdev:18080.

2. Depending on the configuration of both the SharePoint farm and your client browser, you may be prompted to log into the Central Administration site. If you are so prompted, supply both your username and password. In most cases, your username and password are your domain login credentials.

3. When the Central Administration site loads, navigate to the Backup and Restore page. You can do this by clicking the Backup and Restore link in the Quick Launch menu along the left side of the page. Alternatively, you can click the Backup and Restore link in the main zone near the middle of the page to reach the Backup and Restore page, as shown earlier in Figure 9.1.

4. Click the Perform a Backup link. It is the first link under the Farm Backup and Restore section in the main zone of the page, and it takes you to the component selection page for backup operations.

Tip: If you don't like all the clicking around, you can navigate directly to the component selection page if you have the correct URL. For the fictitious farm being used in this example, the URL is http://spdev:18080/_admin/Backup.aspx. Combine your Central Administration site's protocol and host name information with the /_admin/Backup.aspx path to construct the appropriate endpoint URL for your farm.

---

5. The Backup.aspx selection page allows you to select the components of your farm for catastrophic backup. Each selectable component in the farm has a selection check box next to it; placing a check mark in the box selects any given component and those components below it in the backup hierarchy. In addition to displaying a check in their check box, components that are selected for backup are highlighted in blue. Because a full farm catastrophic backup is being performed, place a check mark in the first check box, as shown in Figure 9.16.

6. Ensure that each of the items under the Readiness header displays a check mark to signal that it is in a state that is conducive to backup. Both the SharePoint timer and SharePoint administration services on the server hosting the Central Administration site must be started to actually carry out a backup operation. If another backup or restore operation is in-process, it must complete before you can create a new job.

7. Click the Next button at the bottom of the page to move to the backup options page shown in Figure 9.17.

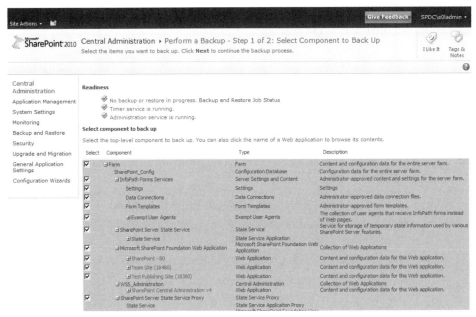

Figure 9.16   All farm components selected for catastrophic backup.

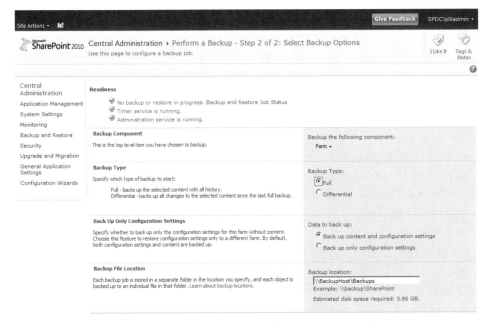

Figure 9.17   Selecting options for the catastrophic backup operation.

8.   Select the type of backup you want to perform, either full or differential. If no other backup operation has been performed to the destination location, your only real option is to perform a full backup. If you attempt to perform a differential backup without having already performed a full backup to the backup file location, your backup operation fails immediately and an error page is displayed when the backup is launched. For this example, a full backup is selected.

9.   Indicate whether you want to perform a configuration-only backup with the Back Up Only Configuration Settings options. The Back Up Content and Configuration Settings button, which is selected by default, captures both the content and configuration settings of your farm and is the most versatile of the two backup options. You can use this option to restore both content and configuration settings at a later time. The Backup Up Only Configuration Settings option, on the other hand, does not capture content and supports only the restoration of configuration settings. Unless you want to specifically back up only the configuration settings for the farm, stick with the default selection. In this example, both content and configuration settings are backed up.

10.   The Backup File Location is prepopulated with the location that is set through the Default Backup and Restore Settings page shown in Figure 9.11, but you are free to change the location to suit your needs. In most enterprise scenarios, the location is specified using a UNC share name. In single-server scenarios where SQL Server and SharePoint coexist on the same server, you can use a local drive path specification. Regardless of how the location is specified, ensure that the location is correctly accessible for all the necessary accounts and ready for backup operations. In the case of this example, the path \\BackupHost\Backups is specified.

11.   An estimate of the amount of disk space required for the backup operation appears below the Backup Location text box. Ensure that the location selected contains enough free space to accommodate the backup. As a rule of thumb, it is safest to add some padding to the estimates that the Central Administration site provides. The last thing you want is to go through minutes or hours of a backup, only to have it fail near the end of the operation due to lack of free space. The actual amount of that padding varies widely based on a large number of factors; this is another one of those cases where it really pays to know how your environment behaves. You are best served by testing your backups multiple times to establish a baseline around how much storage space an average backup requires.

12.   When you are satisfied with all the backup options, scroll down the page shown in Figure 9.17 and click the Start Backup button at the bottom of the page to launch the backup operation. When you click the button, SharePoint creates and configures a timer job instance with the backup options you specified. The timer job instance is then scheduled to execute once. When this process is complete, you are redirected to the Backup and Restore Job Status page shown in Figure 9.18.

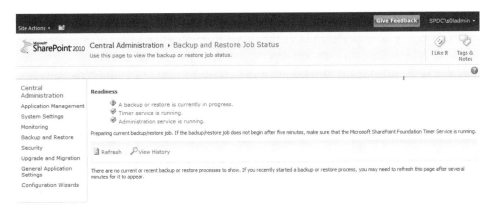

Figure 9.18   The Backup and Restore Job Status page.

13.   Initially, the status page shown in Figure 9.18 is blank. The page refreshes every 30 seconds, though, and the page begins displaying usable status information once the timer job carrying out the backup operation is started.

14.   You can track the overall state of the catastrophic backup using the block of information that appears just under the blue Backup band once the timer job gets underway. The backup status of each farm component appears below the general information block. Each component being backed up begins with empty Progress, Last Update, and Failure message details. As the backup progresses and each component is addressed, these fields update. Eventually, all selected components are backed up, and the operation completes as shown in Figure 9.19.

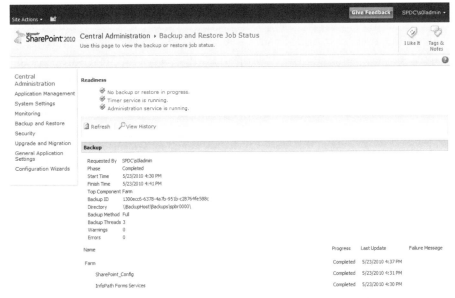

Figure 9.19   The status of a completed full farm catastrophic backup.

15. The catastrophic backup operation may take minutes or hours to complete. The amount of time it takes to fully complete depends on many factors, including the size of your farm, your network speed, the latency between your SharePoint server and the backup location, and more.

16. When the backup is complete, you can review the status of each component that was backed up. No "go back" or cancel button exists on the Backup and Restore Job Status page. To navigate back to the other functions of Central Administration, simply use one of the links that appears in the Quick Launch menu on the left side of the page.

17. If you would like to review additional detail regarding the backup operation that completed, you can review the `spbackup.log` file that is generated in the backup set folder (in the backup file location).

It's worth noting that because the SharePoint Timer service carries out backup and restore jobs, you are not required to stay on the Backup and Restore Job Status page while the backup job executes. You are free to navigate away from the page and carry out other operations within Central Administration. SharePoint dutifully continues the execution of your specified operation in the background. If you later decide that you want to check up on the status of your operation, simply navigate to the Backup and Restore page and click the Check Backup and Restore Job Status link under the Farm Backup and Restore header.

Note: During or just after the backup operation, remember to make a note of any additional configuration information you might need to track and associate with the catastrophic backup set. This includes the Secure Store Service Application passphrase if the Secure Store is in use, credentials that are supplied for accounts and services, and so on. You typically need information captured in this fashion if you must perform a restore operation using the backup set generated.

Site Collection Backup

The site collection backup operation is one that administrators use on a daily basis. In practice, it tends to see more use for site collection copying and migration than it does for actual site protection. Regardless of how you intend to use it, though, the site collection backup operation is a good one to have in your administrative toolbox.

The example that follows demonstrates how to use Central Administration to perform a site collection backup for a SharePoint team site that resides within the fictitious farm at http://spdev:18480/sites/ts1. This backup operation results in the generation of a single file called `TS1.bak` in the `E:\Backups` directory of the server hosting the Central Administration site.

Ensure that you are a member of the SharePoint Farm Administrators group and that the SharePoint Timer service account has Full Control permissions to your backup location before beginning. In addition, ensure that you are logged into a computer that can access the SharePoint Central Administration site. This is oftentimes your own workstation, but in some highly secure environments, access to the Central Administration site may be restricted to only a select group of servers and workstations.

1. Open a browser and navigate to the Central Administration site. In the case of the fictitious farm described at the beginning of the chapter, the default URL of the Central Administration site is http://spdev:18080.

2. Depending on the configuration of both the SharePoint farm and your client browser, you may be prompted to log into the Central Administration site. If you are so prompted, supply both your user name and password. In most cases, your user name and password are your domain login credentials.

3. When the Central Administration site loads, navigate to the Backup and Restore page. You accomplish this by clicking the Backup and Restore link in the Quick Launch menu along the left side of the page. Alternatively, you can click the Backup and Restore link in the main zone near the middle of the page to reach the Backup and Restore page, as shown earlier in Figure 9.1.

4. Click the Perform a Site Collection Backup link. It is the first link under the Granular Backup section in the main zone of the page, and it takes you to the Site Collection Backup page.

Tip: If you don't like all the clicking around, you can navigate directly to the Site Collection Backup page if you have the correct URL. For the fictitious farm being used in this example, the URL is http://spdev:18080/_admin/SiteCollectionBackup.aspx. Combine your Central Administration site's protocol and host name information with the /_admin/ SiteCollectionBackup.aspx path to construct the appropriate endpoint URL for your farm.

---

5. The SiteCollectionBackup.aspx page appears as shown in Figure 9.20. Site collection backups are less complex to configure than catastrophic backups, which is reflected by the fact that only the target site collection and backup path are available to you for specification.

6. Select the site collection you want to back up using the Site Collection drop-down selection box. The drop-down contains only one item, Change Site Collection, and selecting it opens the Select Site Collection dialog box seen in Figure 9.21.

7. Specifying a site collection for backup requires that you specify two pieces of information: the Web application that houses the site collection, and the site collection itself. You must select the Web application first with the drop-down selection box that

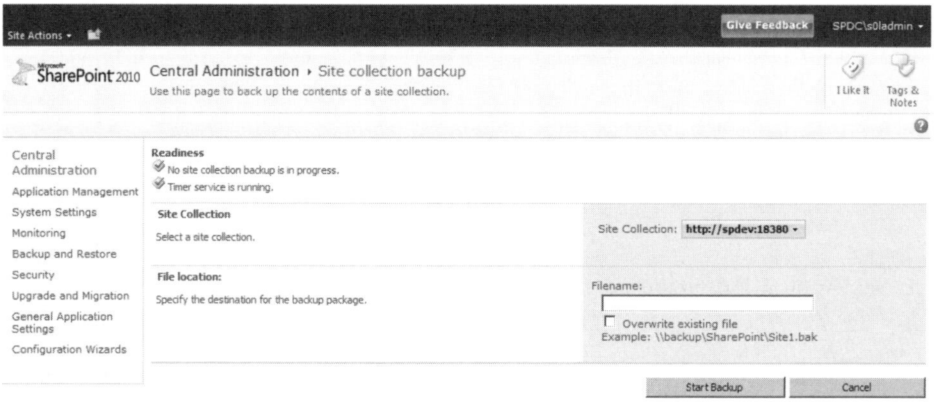

Figure 9.20   Specifying the parameters for a site collection backup.

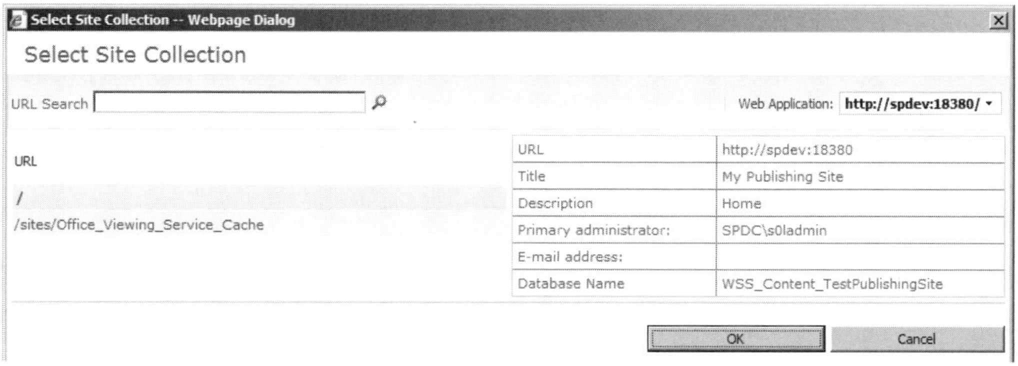

Figure 9.21   Select Site Collection dialog box.

appears near the top right of the dialog box. The drop-down selection box contains only one item, Change Web Application, and selecting it opens the Select Web Application dialog box seen in Figure 9.22.

8.   When the Select Web Application dialog box opens, the currently selected Web application is highlighted and bold. The site collection that is going to be backed up in this example is in the Team Site (18480) Web application, so you must select that Web application. The name of each Web application is actually a link, so clicking the Team Site (18480) name link selects the Web application and closes the Select Web Application dialog box.

9.   Once the Select Web Application dialog closes, the Select Site Collection dialog box updates to reflect the site collections that are available for backup within the selected Web application. In this example, the team site with a URL of /Sites/Ts1 is the desired site collection for backup. Much like the previous dialog box's name links, each

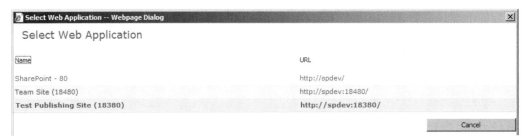

Figure 9.22   Select Web Application dialog box.

of the URLs is a link in the Select Site Collection dialog box. Clicking the /Sites/Ts1 link selects the desired team site and updates the Title, Description, and other related information, as shown in Figure 9.23. Clicking the OK button closes the Select Site Collection dialog box and returns you to the Site Collection Backup page.

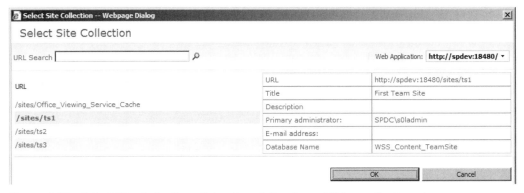

Figure 9.23   Select Site Collection dialog box following a Web application change.

10.   The Site Collection drop-down selection box on the Site Collection Backup page updates to reflect your choice in the previous step. In the case of the current example, the site collection targeted for backup is http://spdev:18480/sites/ts1.

11.   Specify the path for the site collection backup file using the Filename text box. Because SQL Server doesn't require access to the backup location in the same way that it does for catastrophic backups, you have a bit more flexibility in where you can place the file that is created. You can specify the backup location and file name through either a UNC path, such as \\BackupHost\SiteCollections\TS1.bak, or a local path such as E:\Backups\TS1.bak. The choice of UNC path or local path is not dependent on the number of servers in the SharePoint farm, and you can use a local path in a multiserver farm. In this example, the latter specification is supplied.

12.   Each site collection backup generates a single file. If a backup file matching the one you intend to create already exists, you must select the Overwrite Existing File check box

before proceeding. If you do not, you receive an error indicating that you must select the check box to overwrite the file.

Tip: The Site Collection Backup page doesn't provide an estimate of the backup file size the same way that the catastrophic backup options page does. Before moving forward with a backup, ensure that the selected location has ample storage for the file that is created. If you have access to the Web analytics reports under the Site Settings menu for the site collection in question, you can use the Total Storage Used (MB) metric as a starting point for estimation.

---

13. When you are satisfied with the parameters, click the Start Backup button to begin the site collection backup process. When you click the button, SharePoint creates, configures, and schedules a one-time Timer service job to carry out the backup operation. You are then taken to the Granular Backup Job Status page, as shown in Figure 9.24.

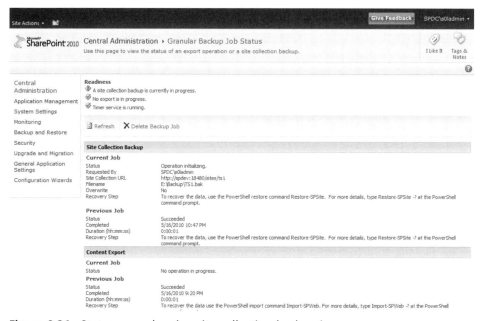

Figure 9.24   Status page showing site collection backup in-process.

14. The Granular Backup Job Status page contains two sections. The top section of the main page area contains the status of the current and previous site collection backup operations and is the area of interest here. The bottom section contains the status for the content export operations that are discussed next in "Exporting Content." The status page refreshes every 30 seconds, and the Current Job area of the Site Collection Backup section updates as the site collection backup proceeds.

Note: While the backup is executing, Central Administration ensures that the site collection is placed under a Read-Only lock to prevent content changes during the operation. Users of the site can continue to read and browse content, but additions and modifications to the content and site collection itself are not permitted. If you do not want SharePoint to lock the site collection during backup, you must use a tool other than Central Administration for the operation.

---

15.   When the site collection backup is complete, the appropriate Current Job status area changes to No Operation in Progress. No "go back" or cancel button exists on the status page. To navigate to the other functions of Central Administration, simply use one of the links that appears in the Quick Launch menu on the left side of the page.

As with catastrophic backups, you aren't required to stay on the Granular Backup Job Status page until the backup completes. The SharePoint Timer service carries out the actual backup operation, so you are free to conduct other operations both inside and outside of SharePoint Central Administration while the backup runs. If you navigate away from the Granular Backup Job Status page, you can easily return to it using the Check Granular Backup Job Status link on the Backup and Restore page.

Remember that Microsoft doesn't recommend site collection backups for use with site collections larger than 85GB. As your site collection approaches and exceeds 85GB, it's in your best interest to find some other way to back up, copy, or migrate your site collections.

Exporting Content

Sometimes you need to recover data that has been accidentally deleted through unintended system action or user error. Other times, you simply need to export a list so that you can include it in a different site or site collection. In both of these cases, possessing a solid understanding of Central Administration's export capabilities is going to make your job quite a bit easier than it would be otherwise.

In the example that follows, a specific list titled `Images` and located at http://spdev:18380/PressReleases/TestSubSite/PublishingImages within a fictitious site is exported to a file called `ImagesExport.cmp`. The export file is placed on a network share that is accessible at `\\BackupHost\Backups` during the export operation.

Before you attempt to perform an export, ensure that you are a member of the SharePoint Farm Administrators group and that the SharePoint Timer service account has Full Control permissions to your backup location. Also, make sure that you are logged into a computer that can access the SharePoint Central Administration site. This is often your own workstation, but in some highly secure environments, access to the Central Administration site may be restricted to only a select group of servers and workstations.

1. Open a browser and navigate to the Central Administration site. In the case of the fictitious farm described at the beginning of the chapter, the default URL of the Central Administration site is http://spdev:18080.

2. Depending on the configuration of both the SharePoint farm and your client browser, you may be prompted to log into the Central Administration site. If you are so prompted, supply both your user name and password. In most cases, your user name and password are your domain login credentials.

3. When the Central Administration site loads, navigate to the Backup and Restore page. You do this by clicking the Backup and Restore link in the Quick Launch menu along the left side of the page. Alternatively, you can click the Backup and Restore link in the main zone near the middle of the page to reach the Backup and Restore page, as shown earlier in Figure 9.1.

4. Click the Export a Site or List link. It is the second link under the Granular Backup section in the main zone of the page, and it takes you to the Site or List Export page, as shown in Figure 9.25.

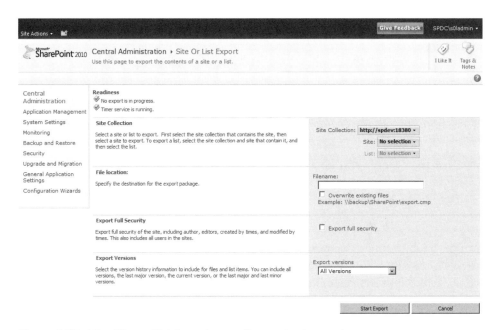

Figure 9.25   The Site or List Export page for content exports.

Tip: If you don't like all the clicking around, you can navigate directly to the Site or List Export page if you have the correct URL. For the fictitious farm being used in this example, the URL is http://spdev:18080/_admin/SiteAndListExport.aspx. Combine your Central Administration site's protocol and host name information with the /_admin/SiteAndListExport. aspx path to construct the appropriate endpoint URL for your farm.

5. To begin the process of configuring an export, you need to identify the site collection, subsite, or SharePoint list that is going to be exported through the Site Collection, Site, and List drop-down selection boxes. The Site Collection drop-down selection box is identical to the one that is used for site collection backups, and the Site and List drop-down selection boxes permit further refining of the object that will be selected for export.

    You can combine the contents of the three drop-down selection boxes in four ways to select content and objects at different levels within a site collection. Figure 9.26 demonstrates the four possible combinations applicable to the current example.

	Site Collection	Site	List
Export entire site collection including all subsites	http://spdev:18380	No Selection	No Selection
Export only the root web of site collection; no subsites	http://spdev:18380	/	No Selection
Export a single subsite	http://spdev:18380	/PressReleases/TestSubSite	No Selection
Export a list within a site	http://spdev:18380	/PressReleases/TestSubSite	Images

Figure 9.26 Site Collection, Site, and List combinations for export.

    The Images list that is going to be exported is located within the publishing site collection located at http://spdev:18380, so the first step toward identifying the list for export is to select the appropriate site collection using the Site Collection drop-down selection box.

Note: The use and operation of the Site Collection drop-down selection box is described in steps 6 through 10 of the previous Site Collection Backup walk-through.

6. Once the http://spdev:18380 Site Collection is chosen, the next step is to select the subsite that houses the target Images library. In this case, the relevant subsite is located at /PressReleases/TestSubSite. Selecting this subsite is simply a matter of using the Site

drop-down selection box in much the same way that you used the Site Collection drop-down selection box in step 5. Rather than selecting a site collection, though, the object that is selected from within the Select Site dialog box is the /PressReleases/ TestSubSite subsite URL. Once you select the subsite, click the OK button to lock in the choice and return to the Site or List Export page.

7. When the Site drop-down selection box is populated, the List drop-down selection box becomes selectable. This makes sense when you consider that it isn't possible to enumerate the lists within a site or subsite until you choose the site or subsite. In the case of the current example, you need to select the Images list using the List drop-down selection box. With only some slight variations, you carry out this action in the same way that you chose the subsite in step 6. Instead of a subsite URL, you select the Images list title. Click the OK button to close the Select List dialog box and return to the Site or List Export page.

8. After you specify the list, identify the full path for the export package you'll create. You create export packages as content migration packages, commonly with a .cmp extension. For the current example, the Filename text box is populated to reflect the desire to save the package to a network share: \\BackupHost\Backups\ImagesExport.cmp. If an export package with the same file name already exists at that location, check the Overwrite Existing Files check box to overwrite the existing file and avoid an error.

9. Determine whether you want to include security related information with your export package. When the Export Full Security check box is checked, the export package that is created contains security information such as SharePoint user and group information along with the actual export content.

10. The final option you have available to you, Export Versions, allows you to specify the quantity of data that is exported from lists and libraries that support versioning. All Versions is the default and highest-fidelity option, and it instructs SharePoint to select all major and minor versions for each item in a list or library that is targeted for export. The remaining options allow you to indicate that only a subset of the data available should be exported. Choosing a subset of the versions available can result in a substantially smaller export package and quicker export times, but the ability to review and roll back to previous major and minor version items at the destination once the content is exported may be impacted. For the current example, choose the All Versions option to avoid the loss of previous versions.

11. With all configuration parameters specified, the Site or List Export page appears, as shown in Figure 9.27. To begin the export process, click the Start Export button. SharePoint proceeds to create, configure, and schedule an export timer job instance according to the parameters supplied. You are then redirected to the Granular Backup Job Status.

Figure 9.27 Parameters specified for an export operation.

12. The Granular Backup Job Status page is the same one that is monitored for site collection backup operations. You can see the export job that is executing under the Content Export section in the lower half of the main page area. The page refreshes every 30 seconds; once the export is complete, the Current Job status changes to No Operation in Progress, as shown in Figure 9.28.

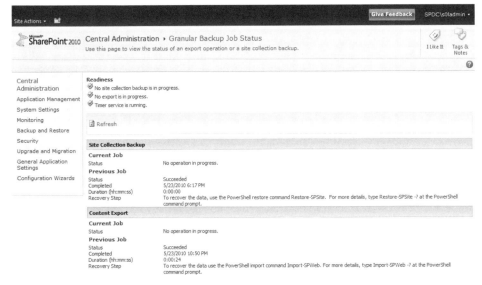

Figure 9.28 A completed content export operation.

13. No "go back" or cancel button exists on the Granular Backup Job Status page. To navigate to the other functions of Central Administration, simply use one of the links that appears in the Quick Launch menu on the left side of the page.

14. If you need additional detail on the export operation, a log file is generated where the content migration package is placed. The log file carries the same base name as the content migration package, but it has an added extension of .export.log. In the case of this example, the name of the log file that is generated is ImagesExport.cmp.export.log.

Unattached Content Database Data Recovery

Aside from browsing a content database's hierarchy of objects, the options afforded by the unattached database recovery feature are identical to the site collection backup and content export functions that have already been covered. The difference with the unattached database recovery feature is that the database on which backup or export operations are to be performed must be specified first.

To use an unattached content database for site collection backup or content export purposes, follow these steps:

1. Open a browser and navigate to the Central Administration site. In the case of the fictitious farm described at the beginning of the chapter, the default URL of the Central Administration site is http://spdev:18080.

2. Depending on the configuration of both the SharePoint farm and your client browser, you may be prompted to log into the Central Administration site. If you are so prompted, supply both your user name and password. In most cases, your user name and password are your domain login credentials.

3. When the Central Administration site loads, navigate to the Backup and Restore page by clicking the Backup and Restore link in the Quick Launch menu along the left side of the page. Alternatively, you can click the Backup and Restore link in the main zone near the middle of the page to reach the Backup and Restore page as shown earlier in Figure 9.1.

4. Click the Recover Data from an Unattached Content Database link. It is the third link under the Granular Backup section in the main zone of the page, and it takes you to the Unattached Content Database Data Recovery page, as shown in Figure 9.29.

Tip: If you don't like all the clicking around, you can navigate directly to the Unattached Content Database Data Recovery page if you have the correct URL. For the fictitious farm being used in this example, the URL is http://spdev:18080/_admin/UnattachedDbSelect. aspx. Combine your Central Administration site's protocol and host name information with the /_admin/UnattachedDbSelect.aspx path to construct the appropriate endpoint URL for your farm.

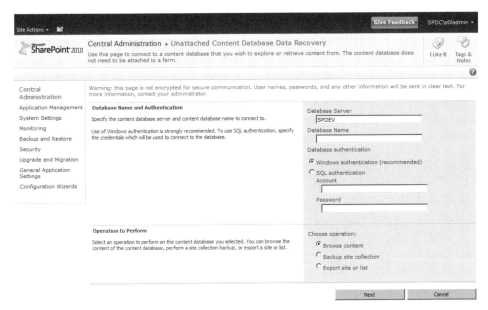

Figure 9.29 The Unattached Content Database Data Recovery page.

5. The Database Server text box is initially populated with the name of the default content database for the SharePoint farm. Verify that this is the SQL Server database instance where your unattached content database resides. If it isn't, change the text box contents to reflect the desired database instance. If the Database Server text box doesn't contain a valid entry, an error is generated when SharePoint attempts to contact the invalid database. Note that such an error comes after a delay because the error is thrown at the end of a timeout period.

6. The Database Name text box must be populated with the name of the content database you want to attach to. Being able to enter a valid database name into this text box means that you have some knowledge of how the content databases are named in SQL Server. If you aren't sure of the name of the database you want to attach to and have the rights to connect to SQL Server, you can open a SQL Server Management Studio session to browse the list of available databases. System-generated SharePoint content databases commonly begin with WSS_Content_. This may help you narrow your search.

7. You need to specify the SQL Server authentication mechanism. The default, Windows Authentication, is the best selection in the majority of cases. When Windows Authentication is selected, SharePoint attempts to connect to the specified database using the SharePoint Timer service account. This generally proceeds without issue. If your SQL Server is running with mixed-mode authentication and you have specifically configured your SharePoint farm to use SQL Server authentication, you need to select the SQL Authentication option and specify the appropriate SQL Server user ID and password to connect to the database.

8. Indicate whether you want to browse the content in the database, execute a site collection backup, or export content from the content database using the appropriate radio buttons.

9. Click the Next button. Assuming all database and authentication parameters are correct, you are taken to a page that reflects the operation you want to perform.

In most cases, you are going to eventually end up executing a site collection backup or content export from the unattached content database. Even if you begin by browsing the content database, performing some action while browsing requires that you eventually select a site collection backup or content export operation.

The good news is that the site collection backup and content export operations proceed according to the walk-throughs that have already been provided. In fact, unattached database operations use the same administration pages cited earlier for these operations. The only indication that an unattached content database is involved during a backup or export comes in the form of a ?IsUnattached=1 query string parameter at the end of each page URL.

Restoring Within Central Administration

The flipside of backup is restore, and carrying out restore operations is one of those things that tends to peg the average administrator's stress meter. In many cases, restore operations are being carried out under duress and on a tight timeline; given these facts, it makes sense that you should practice them when you have the opportunity. As you repeatedly execute restore operations, you get better, more efficient, and ultimately more comfortable with them.

Many administrators prefer Central Administration for restore operations simply because it tends to offer a better end user experience compared to command line operations. Selection of restore targets tends to be much easier, quicker, and less error prone when done through a GUI. Central Administration also provides quite a bit of feedback at each step of a restore; this feedback can reassure and help in troubleshooting measures if something does go awry.

Restoring a Full Farm

Full farm restoration is usually associated with the disaster scenario you never want to find yourself in. If you have to restore a complete SharePoint farm from a catastrophic backup, something has gone very, very wrong.

Note: In SharePoint 2010, you still cannot use a full farm restore to clone an entire farm. A configuration-only restore can address this need to a large extent, but it doesn't cover all the configuration settings, properties, and items of interest.

What a Full Farm Restore Really Is

First, you need to be aware of one important fact: SharePoint's full farm restore capabilities do not support bare-metal recovery scenarios. In addition, there is one prerequisite you must address before you can consider a full farm recovery; specifically, the servers that are the target of the farm recovery operation need to already be set up as a functional SharePoint farm. The farm also needs to be running a version of SharePoint that matches the version of the full farm catastrophic backup that you are going to restore.

Did you catch that part about needing a functional SharePoint farm? This may seem highly contradictory; after all, why would you need to create a farm to restore a farm? Doesn't that defeat the purpose of a full farm restore in the first place?

If you think about it for a moment, you probably realize that the answer is "no." Executing any sort of restore operation from the Central Administration site requires a functional farm. After all, Central Administration doesn't run as a stand-alone site. In addition, the SharePoint catastrophic backup and restore APIs require some form of functional SharePoint instance to execute against. Like Central Administration, the SharePoint APIs don't run in a vacuum.

Note: When you understand and accept these facts and prerequisites, you quickly realize that a full farm restore using SharePoint's built-in tools comes with some rather hefty limitations from a disaster recovery standpoint. These limitations, and the times when SharePoint's catastrophic restore capabilities may be realistically employed, are discussed a bit more in the bonus chapter found on the Cengage Learning Web site at http://www.courseptr.com/downloads.

In reality, a full farm restore is more appropriately thought of as a "restore as much farm as possible" operation. A full farm restore is intended to restore Service Applications, content, and as much portable configuration as possible while leaving the target restore farm intact. Full farm restores are not intended to completely overwrite every aspect of the farm they target.

This may also help you understand why a full farm restore doesn't restore the SharePoint farm configuration or Central Administration content databases. Overwriting the configuration database wholesale effectively destroys the target farm, whereas overwriting the Central Administration content database disrupts SharePoint because the Central Administration site is hosting the restore operation.

Executing the Full Farm Restore

To perform a catastrophic farm restore from a full farm catastrophic backup that you have, ensure that you are logged into Central Administration with an account that is a member of the Central Administration server's local Administrators group, and execute the following series of steps:

1.   Open a browser and navigate to the Central Administration site. In the case of the fictitious farm described at the beginning of the chapter, the default URL of the Central Administration site is http://spdev:18080.

2. Depending on the configuration of both the SharePoint farm and your client browser, you may be prompted to log into the Central Administration site. If you are so prompted, supply both your user name and password. In most cases, your user name and password are your domain login credentials.

3. When the Central Administration site loads, navigate to the Backup and Restore page by clicking the Backup and Restore link in the Quick Launch menu along the left side of the page. Alternatively, you can click the Backup and Restore link in the main zone near the middle of the page to reach the Backup and Restore page shown earlier in Figure 9.1.

4. Click the Restore from a Backup link. It is the second link under the Farm Backup and Restore section in the main zone of the page, and it takes you to the backup selection page for restore operations.

5. The Backup and Restore History page appears as seen in Figure 9.30. The Backup Directory Location text box initially contains the farm's default backup file location, and the backup sets that are stored at the location specified are shown below the text box in order from the most recent backup set to the oldest backup set.

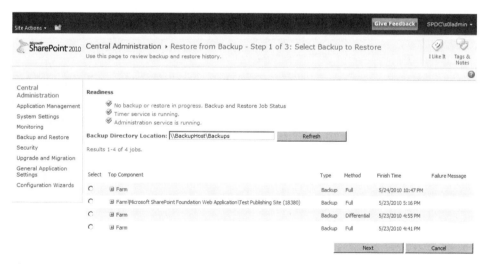

Figure 9.30   The Backup and Restore History page.

Tip: If you don't like all the clicking around, you can navigate directly to the backup selection page if you have the correct URL. For the fictitious farm being used in this example, the URL is http://spdev:18080/_admin/BackupHistory.aspx?restore=1&filter=1. Combine your Central Administration site's protocol and host name information with the /_admin/Backup.aspx?restore=1&filter=1 path to construct the appropriate endpoint URL for your farm. Omitting the `?restore=1&filter=1` query string changes the look of the page slightly, but you are still able to perform a restore operation, albeit in a slightly different fashion. Leaving off the query string is also equivalent to simply clicking the View Backup and Restore History link from the Backup and Restore page.

6. Ensure that the Backup Directory Location points to the location containing the catastrophic backup set you want to use for the restoration. If you change the location in the text box, click the Refresh button to populate the page with a list of the backup sets present at the new location.

7. Locate the catastrophic backup set you want to use for the farm restoration in the list that appears below the Backup Directory Location text box. If you have a large number of backup sets in the location selected, you may find it easier to locate the desired backup set by reviewing some of the details for each set. Figure 9.31 shows a full farm catastrophic backup with expanded details that has been selected for restore.

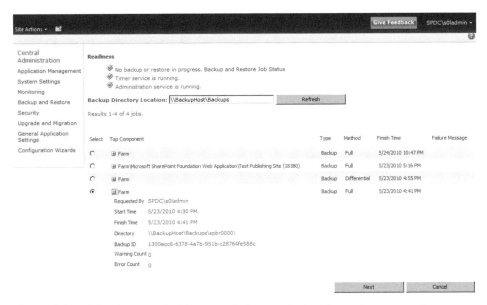

Figure 9.31 A backup set that is expanded and selected for restore operations.

8. Once you have selected the desired catastrophic backup set, click the Next button to advance to the Select Component to Restore page.

9. The Select Component to Restore page appears, and it looks similar to the backup component selection page shown earlier in Figure 9.16. The page displays the hierarchy of components that were available for backup in your farm when the catastrophic backup set was created. Components that you can select for the restore operation you are

conducting have check boxes next to them. Assuming that the backup set you selected on the previous page was from a full farm catastrophic backup, all components starting at the farm level and proceeding down the hierarchy should be available for selection. If the backup set that you selected wasn't a full farm catastrophic backup, only the subset of farm components that were captured in the backup are selectable for restore.

10. Select the check box next to the Farm node in the component hierarchy to select the entire farm for restore. All objects that are selected for restore are shaded, as shown in Figure 9.32. When you have reviewed the selected components and determined that you are ready to continue, click the Next button at the bottom of the page.

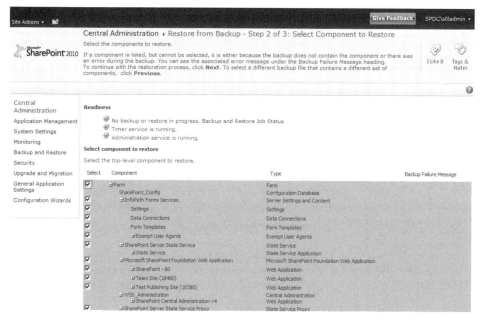

Figure 9.32   All farm components selected for restore.

11. The Select Restore Options page appears, as shown in Figure 9.33. Don't be alarmed if you begin scrolling down the page and find it to be long and intimidating. If you are performing a full farm restore and want to bring your farm back to the state it was in at the time the backup set was created, most of the settings on the page can be left as is. The first thing you need to do, though, is change the Type of Restore selection from New Configuration to Same Configuration. Making this change displays a dialog box warning you about component overwrites that occur during Same Configuration restores. Click the OK button to accept the warning and move on.

12. The second task you must perform on the Select Restore Options page is to verify each of the application pool login names in the Login Names and Passwords section. You

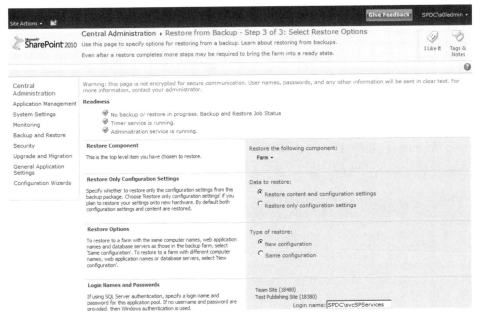

Figure 9.33   The Select Restore Options page.

must also supply the password for each of the accounts associated with an application pool before proceeding. The number of accounts you must verify and supply passwords for varies according to the number of application pools that were established for your content Web applications and SharePoint's own Service Applications.

13. If you wanted to perform a configuration-only restore, the Data to Restore option could be changed from Restore Content and Configuration Settings to Restore Only Configuration Settings. Since the restore in this example is a full farm recovery, leave the Restore Content and Configuration Settings option selected.

14. The text boxes in the New Names section are associated with the farm components that are being restored; frankly, there tend to be a lot of them with a full farm restore. For a Same Configuration restore, these text boxes are disabled. If you needed to change properties for one or more of the backup components during the restore operation, a New Configuration Type of Restore (specified in step 11) could be selected. Specifying a New Configuration restore allows you to do things like change the SQL Server to which databases are restored, change database names, alter service names, and more. Because this example is a full farm restore using the Same Configuration, though, the text boxes remain disabled.

15. When you have verified your settings on the Select Restore Options page and ensured that no red exclamation marks appear in the Readiness area of the page, click the Start Restore button at the bottom of the page. SharePoint proceeds to create a timer job

instance, configure it with the restoration parameters you specified, and schedule the job for one-time execution. It then redirects your browser to the Backup and Restore Job Status page. Figure 9.34 shows the status page after the restore operation has gotten underway.

Figure 9.34   A full farm restore in-process.

16.   The Backup and Restore Job Status page refreshes every 30 seconds so that you can track the execution of the restore operation. When the restore operation has completed, you can review the status of each component that was restored on the status page. If additional detail is desired, you can review the log file that is generated in the specific folder of the catastrophic backup set that was used for the restore operation. The file containing additional restore detail is named `sprestore.log`.

17.   Review your farm's services and Service Applications following the restore to determine if you need to start one or more of them. To do this, click on the Application Management link in the Quick Launch on the left side of the page. When the Application Management page appears, click on the Manage Services on Server link under the Service Applications section in the main page area. This opens the Services on Server page, as shown in Figure 9.35. If any of the listed services or Service Applications should be running but aren't, click on their associated Start links under the Action column to start them. At the same time, be aware that a limited subset of the services and Service Applications may require some manual reconfiguration for properties and settings that could not be restored from the catastrophic backup set. Probably the most common

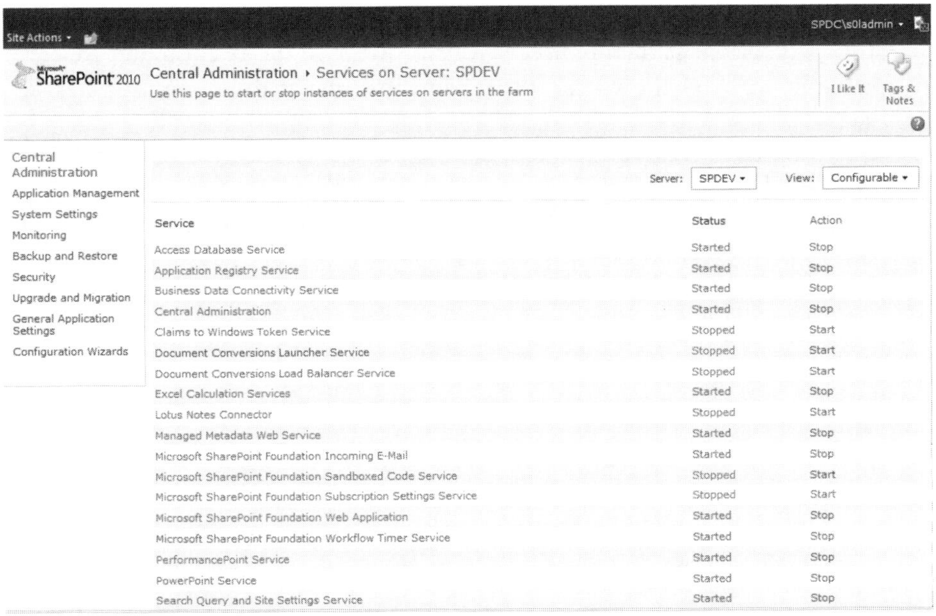

Figure 9.35   The Services on Server page.

example of such is the Secure Store Service Application. Before it functions following a restore, you must supply to the Secure Store Service Application the passphrase that was active (and manually captured) when the backup set was created. Without the passphrase, you cannot decrypt and use credentials stored by the Service Application.

Note: The Services on Server page in Figure 9.35 displays services for only one server at a time. If your farm has multiple SharePoint servers, you need to review and restart services and Service Applications on potentially each server in the farm. You can use the Server drop-down box just above the Status column to ascertain and select the active server.

---

18.   Finally, reestablish any trust relationships you need if your farm is publishing services for other SharePoint 2010 farms to consume or is consuming services from another farm. Note that establishing trusts is beyond the scope of the farm restore operation being conducted. For guidance on farm trust establishment and certificate exchanges, see http://technet.microsoft.com/en-us/library/ee806868.aspx.

The process of restoring a farm from backup can take substantial time, and much of that time is spent in step 16. Although you don't need to wait on the status page because the restore operation is being conducted in the background, you are somewhat limited in other activities that you can conduct across the farm. After all, the farm is in the process of changing quite a bit while the restore is being performed. As a rule of thumb, it's best to avoid making changes and conducting operations throughout the farm until the restore has finished to avoid potential restore collisions and issues.

Restoring a Content Database for Subsequent Unattached Recovery Operations

You can restore individual content components from a catastrophic backup set using the same basic steps that were outlined for a full farm restore. The key for such restores is to select a specific component or group of components rather than the entire farm in step 9 of the walkthrough.

A slight variation on the component restore theme is created when you want to restore a content database to leverage SharePoint 2010's unattached content database recovery capabilities. In this scenario, the only component to restore is an individual content database. The twist, though, is that you cannot use the Same Configuration option during the restore. Doing so would overwrite the existing production database. Instead, you need to restore the content database using the New Configuration option to change the name of the database.

In the example that follows, a content database for the Test Publishing Site (18380) Web application is restored using a different database name. Before continuing, ensure that you are logged into Central Administration with an account that is a member of the local Administrators group on the server that houses the Central Administration site:

1. Execute steps 1 through 7 of the full farm restore walk-through. Execution of these steps leaves you in a position to select the backup set that is used for the restore operation.

2. Select the catastrophic backup set that contains the desired version of the publishing site's content database. In the case of the backup sets displayed in Figure 9.31, the backup set with a top component of Farm\Microsoft SharePoint Foundation Web Application\Test Publishing Site (18380) is selected.

3. Click the Next button, and the Select Component to Restore page appears. Then select for restore the content database for the Test Publishing Site (18380) Web application, as shown in Figure 9.36. One detail worth noting in this example is that only the Test Publishing Site (18380) component and its subcomponents are available for selection. This is because the Test Publishing Site (18380) Web application was the only component selected for catastrophic backup when the backup set was generated. Even though the entire farm component hierarchy is displayed, you cannot restore components if they weren't actually backed up and part of the backup set.

4. Click the Next button at the bottom of the page to advance to the Select Restore Options page. Compared to the Select Restore Options page that appeared in the case of the previous full farm restore walk-through, the current page is relatively

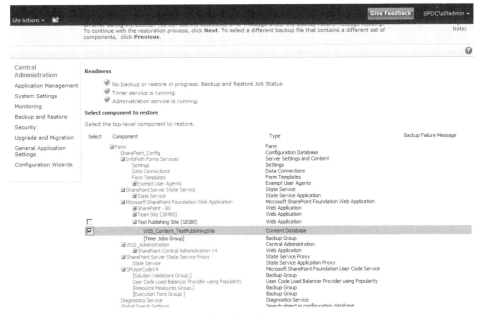

Figure 9.36   Specifying the content database for restore.

uncluttered. Because only a single content database has been selected for restore, only that database's limited set of configuration items is available for modification.

5.   The intention of this example is to restore the content database as a copy of the current production database, so ensure that the New Configuration option is selected as the Type of Restore.

6.   The New Names section gives you the option of changing the directory name, database name, and database server for the content database during restoration. In this example, only the name of the content database is changed to `WSS_Restore_TestPublishing-Site`, as shown in Figure 9.37. Both the target SQL Server and the local directory on the SQL Server where the database is going to be created remain the same.

7.   Click the Start Restore button at the bottom of the page. This results in the creation, configuration, and scheduling of a one-time restore job instance to carry out the selected restore operation. You are then taken to the Backup and Restore Job Status screen.

8.   The execution of the restore job may take minutes or longer to execute, and the Backup and Restore Job Status screen refreshes every 30 seconds to keep you apprised of the progress being made.

9.   Somewhat counterintuitively, the job completes but indicates failure, as shown in Figure 9.38. If you scroll down the page to locate the actual Failure message, you see that the failure was caused by SharePoint's inability to attach the restored content

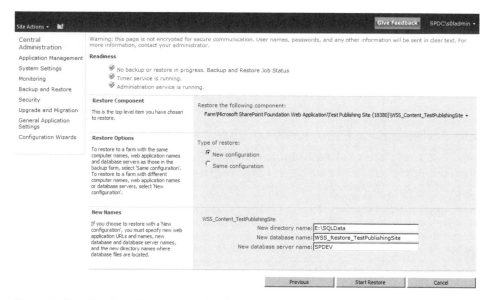

Figure 9.37 Altering the content database configuration on restore.

Figure 9.38 Content database restore complete (but with an error).

database to the farm. This is expected behavior; after all, the restored content database has the same identifier as an existing production database. Two content databases with the same identifier cannot be attached to one SharePoint farm—that's why SharePoint 2010 comes with unattached content database recovery capabilities.

10. Even though you can't attach the content database to the SharePoint farm, it exists within SQL Server and is available for use as `WSS_Restore_TestPublishingSite`. To continue with an export of content from the database, use the new database name with the Unattached Content Database Data Recovery and Exporting Content walk-throughs described earlier.

Restoring a Site Collection or Exported Content

Unfortunately, no mechanism exists within Central Administration to restore a site collection from a backup file (commonly with a `.bak extension`) or import a content migration package (typically one or more files with a `.cmp extension`) that was generated through a content export operation. For these operations, you need to see Chapter 10.

Conclusion

Taking the limitations of the Central Administration site's backup and restore tools into account, it sometimes makes a lot of sense to use them to back up and restore your SharePoint environment. As mentioned earlier, the tool is useful for backing up your farm or components within it prior to a planned change or update to your environment. For example, it is a best practice to back up SharePoint both before and after you apply patches or hotfixes to your installed SharePoint environment. The biggest reason for this is that the majority of Microsoft updates to SharePoint do not provide a mechanism to undo changes in the case of an error or conflict caused by the update. This is caused by SharePoint's heavy reliance on its back-end databases to store content and configuration data. If an update modifies the tables or schemas of SharePoint's databases, you cannot revert those changes without the loss of the data in those databases. So the only way to recover from an error caused by an update or patch is to rebuild your SharePoint installation and restore a backup of your content. The backup and restore tools of the Central Administration site can be a valuable component of your change management process, allowing you to easily preserve your business-critical SharePoint content prior to an upgrade and restore it in case complications arise.

Another advantage to using the Central Administration backup and restore tools is the flexibility and feedback they give administrators while using them. The tool automatically enumerates the SharePoint components in your environment that are available for backup and allows you to make your selection through a graphical interface rather than the command line. Similarly, the tool shows the backup packages in your storage location and important historical data about those packages to assist you in selecting the proper target for restoration. Finally, along every step of the way, the Central Administration site's backup and restore tools give you the opportunity to review and confirm your selections before initiating an operation, an important feature to take advantage of given the impact your actions can have on your environment.

Upon completing this chapter, you should feel comfortable answering the following questions about the Central Administration site's backup and restore tools. You can find the answers to these questions in Appendix A, "Chapter Review Q&A," found on the Cengage Learning Web site at http://www.courseptr.com/downloads.

1. Which accounts require Full Control rights to your backup location to perform a full farm catastrophic backup?

2. Site collection backups should be limited to site collections of what size and smaller?

3. Which must come first: a full or a differential backup? Why?

4. What is a recovery farm, and why is it no longer needed with SharePoint 2010?

5. What are the major drawbacks to relying on the Central Administration site as the only tool for backing up your SharePoint environment?

10 SharePoint 2010 Command Line Backup and Restore: PowerShell

In This Chapter

- Assumptions

- Setting the Stage

- Using SharePoint 2010's Catastrophic Backup Cmdlets

- Using SharePoint 2010's Catastrophic Restore Cmdlets

- Reviewing Your Backup and Restore History

- Documenting Your Configuration

- Granular Backup and Restore via PowerShell

Since the initial release of SharePoint Team Services in 2001, the primary command line tool available to administrators for configuring SharePoint's servers, sites, and databases had been STSADM.exe. However, that situation changed drastically with SharePoint 2010. Yes, STSADM.exe is still available for use in the command line, but the SharePoint product team has fully embraced Microsoft's new command line shell, PowerShell, as SharePoint 2010's command line administrative tool. STSADM.exe's operations still work with SharePoint 2010, but a few new operations have been added to it in the 2010 release from the more than 200 operations that were available in SharePoint 2007. Contrast that with the well over 500 SharePoint-specific cmdlets that now ship with SharePoint 2010, and it's apparent where the command line emphasis is being placed for SharePoint. Not only that, but Microsoft has made it clear that PowerShell is its administrative command line tool of the future, which means that any new functionality that it releases for SharePoint 2010 is going to be in the form of PowerShell cmdlets, not updates to STSADM.exe.

Note: The content in this chapter assumes that you have a certain knowledge of Power-Shell and understand its proper usage. You'll need to be familiar with concepts such as *cmdlets* (the basic commands in PowerShell that carry out specific tasks), the pipeline, and its scripting language. If you are not yet comfortable with PowerShell, we highly recommend making it a priority, given its usefulness and importance to SharePoint 2010 administration. For more information on PowerShell from Microsoft, as well as several lists of excellent content outside of Microsoft on PowerShell, see http://technet.microsoft. com/en-us/scriptcenter/powershell.aspx.

SharePoint 2010's PowerShell cmdlets offer many of the same features and limitations as the Central Administration site's graphical user interface (GUI) backup and restore tool. These include the requirement for a Universal Naming Convention (UNC) path for backup files, allowance for the backup of search indices, full or differential backups, no option to include Microsoft Internet Information Services (IIS) configurations and files in backups, and the inability to clean up old or expired backup files. PowerShell's cmdlets can create backups with the same granularity as the Central Administration site's backup and restore tool, and its backups can be restored in the same usage scenarios as the Central Administration site's GUI tool.

But there are differences between SharePoint 2010's cmdlets and the Central Administration site, as well as distinct advantages to using the former over the latter. One difference between the backup and restore cmdlets and the Central Administration site's backup and restore tool is that PowerShell does not rely on the SPTimer service to execute its functions; it runs independently of that service on the target server. The Central Administration site's tool actually uses the same functionality as PowerShell to run a backup or restore, but as mentioned in Chapter 9, "SharePoint 2010 Central Administration Backup and Restore," the Central Administration site's backup and restore operations run as timer jobs executed via the SharePoint farm's database access service account. This means that directly using PowerShell's cmdlets reduces the chance of affecting the performance of other timer jobs, because it runs in its own process on the server and does not immediately impact the other SharePoint processes running on the server.

Caution: Although backup and restore operations requested via the Central Administration site are run using the identity of the farm database access account, PowerShell's backup and restore cmdlets are run using the security credentials of the user running the PowerShell session used to run the cmdlets. This means that the account used to run PowerShell must be assigned the rights necessary in the SQL Server database instance hosting the farm's databases as well as in the SharePoint farm itself to properly execute, and dbo rights in the SharePoint databases targeted by the STSADM.exe operation. The process for properly distributing these rights to users running the cmdlets is discussed later in this chapter.

There are several interesting features available with SharePoint 2010's backup and restore cmdlets that do not have an equivalent capability in the Central Administration Web site. Several of the new backup cmdlets discussed in this chapter can back up against SQL snapshots of live SharePoint databases, not just the databases. There's also greater flexibility and control over the output of the backup files that the cmdlets create, such as setting their allowed sizes and their compression. This level of control just isn't possible through the Central Administration site; you can only accomplish it via the PowerShell cmdlets.

The biggest advantage to using SharePoint 2010's PowerShell cmdlets is that they are executed via a command line, which means they can be configured as scheduled tasks in Windows on their own or as part of a batch script and run with the Task Scheduler. You can set them up to run as automatic tasks that do not require manual intervention to run. This is an important component of properly protecting your environment in a disaster, and one not directly offered by SharePoint out of the box without some additional development and configuration by an administrator.

Tip: To run PowerShell scripts using the SharePoint 2010 backup or restore cmdlets, you must configure the server for your scheduled tasks to properly allow those scripts to be executed. PowerShell uses something called an execution policy to determine how, or if, scripts can be run on a computer; you can configure this policy dynamically to meet the needs of your environment. By default, PowerShell's execution policy is set as "Restricted," which means that no custom scripts can be run on the server. You can use the `Get-ExecutionPolicy` cmdlet to see what it is currently set at on your server, and the `Set-ExecutionPolicy` cmdlet to update it to a value that allows your scripts to run. For more information on those cmdlets, check out their PowerShell help documentation.

Obviously, the introduction of PowerShell cmdlets specifically for SharePoint 2010 has drastically changed the command line administration picture compared to previous releases of the platform. In general, PowerShell is much more flexible, comprehensive, and potent (see how we stayed away from the obvious "powerful" cliché there and used a synonym instead?) than what was previously possible with the Windows Command Shell, even before taking into account the benefit of SharePoint-specific cmdlets over STSADM.exe. One appealing side effect to this change is that there is no longer a single application with hundreds of obscure operations and inputs. With SharePoint 2010, the use of cmdlets allows administrative tasks to be completed with a much more readable and comprehendible cmdlet instead of the generalized STSADM. This makes understanding which cmdlet to use in a given situation much more straightforward than it was in previous releases of SharePoint.

Although the introduction of specific PowerShell cmdlets for specific operations is a good thing, there's still a lot more goodness to talk about when it comes to SharePoint 2010's cmdlets. Microsoft has included in these cmdlets the entire set of backup and restore functionality previously available in STSADM.exe, but it has added a great deal of new functionality in those areas as well. Some of this functionality you learned about in Chapter 9, such as configuration-only backups. However, some of it is available only through PowerShell, such as the ability to back up the configuration database not connected to any active SharePoint 2010 farm.

Finally, the ability to leverage some of PowerShell's core capabilities alongside SharePoint 2010's disaster recovery-oriented cmdlets creates some excellent opportunities for you to script out deep automated coverage for your SharePoint environment. The new `Backup-SPFarm` cmdlet allows you to back up your entire farm and can be combined with PowerShell's access to the file system of the server storing your backup files to archive or delete old backups, improving your ability to manage your storage effectively. You can now use the `Get-SPSite` cmdlet to generate a collection of SharePoint site collections, which you can send directly to the `Backup-SPSite` cmdlet via PowerShell's pipeline functionality. These are but two limited examples of what is now possible with PowerShell and SharePoint 2010. You now have a vast range of opportunities and capabilities to protect your SharePoint 2010 farm according to your specific needs and constraints.

Assumptions

The visual examples provided in this chapter were generated in a testing environment using the platforms and components listed next. Depending on how your environment is configured, your experiences may vary slightly. Unless a specific item indicates that it is unique to SharePoint Server 2010, the features and functionality covered in this chapter apply to both SharePoint Foundation 2010 and SharePoint Server 2010 in the same fashion.

- **Operating system.** Microsoft Windows Server 2008 R2 Enterprise Edition (build 7600)

- **Database.** Microsoft SQL Server 2008 Developer Edition with Service Pack 1 (SP1, build 10.0.2740)

- **Web server.** Microsoft Internet Information Services (IIS) 7.5

- **SharePoint.** SharePoint Foundation 2010 Release Candidate 1 (build 4730)

Setting the Stage

Before we can get into the nuts and bolts of using SharePoint 2010's new PowerShell backup and restore cmdlets, it's important to look at the things you need to have in place and understand to properly use PowerShell, SharePoint 2010, and its cmdlets in your environment. Accessing the SharePoint 2010 cmdlets is not something you can do by simply opening a PowerShell command prompt, and there are certain prerequisites that must be met to have the rights and resources necessary to use them properly. You also need to be mindful of several important points about how to properly use and integrate these cmdlets in your own custom scripts. So let's examine what you'll need to do to avoid these issues and others like them before getting to the meat of this chapter: the cmdlets themselves.

Accessing the SharePoint 2010 Management Shell

On a Windows Server 2008 server with SharePoint 2010 installed, SharePoint 2010's PowerShell cmdlets can be accessed two ways: via the SharePoint 2010 Management Shell shortcut in the Start Menu's Microsoft SharePoint 2010 Products directory, or by loading the SharePoint 2010 snap-in (`Microsoft.SharePoint.PowerShell`) for PowerShell via the `Add-PSSnapin` cmdlet. Both approaches load the same set of SharePoint 2010 cmdlets into the current PowerShell session, so you can use them to configure and administer your SharePoint environment.

Note: SharePoint 2010 requires PowerShell 2.0 to be installed on the server for the product to be installed, ensuring that the features and functionality necessary to use the solutions discussed in this chapter are available by default on your SharePoint servers.

In previous releases of the SharePoint platform, it was at best a challenge to determine what rights a user needed to have to run administrative commands from the command line. It was often more of a blindfolded fishing expedition through a minefield of incomplete information and half-truths. (Unless you read the *SharePoint 2007 Disaster Recovery Guide*—we never steered you wrong!) Well, as if the addition of PowerShell itself wasn't good enough, SharePoint 2010's command line administration story is so much better this time around thanks to one specific cmdlet designed to make the process of permission and rights assignment much simpler: `Add-SPShellAdmin`.

Every cmdlet we'll be discussing in this chapter requires that the account used to run it be granted rights within the targeted SharePoint farm via `Add-SPShellAdmin`, so you need to be ready to use it for any account you may use to run these cmdlets. But what does `Add-SPShellAdmin` do? As you can probably infer from the name (naming conventions for PowerShell cmdlets are discussed later in this chapter), it grants a named user's account administrative rights in SharePoint via PowerShell. Now, there are some specific things that the `Add-SPShellAdmin` cmdlet does to grant those SharePoint administrative rights, and it is important to understand what it does behind the scenes within your SharePoint environment before you just go blindly running it for all your administrative users. `Add-SPShellAdmin` grants targeted accounts the following rights:

- **SharePoint_Shell_Access database role membership.** The user's login is added to the `SharePoint_Shell_Access` role. (If this role does not exist in the target database, the cmdlet creates it.) This is important to note, because the user's login gains SQL Server's `db_owner` and `securityadmin` rights in the database targeted by the cmdlet by associating it with that SQL Server role, something you should not take lightly.

- **Database-specific rights.** `Add-SPShellAdmin` can target specific databases within your farm via the `-Database` input parameter. If you specify a database, the user is added to a role that has those rights in the farm's configuration database, the Central Admin site's content database, and the targeted database. If you do not specify a database, the cmdlet grants the user rights for the farm's configuration database by default.

■ **WSS_ADMIN_WPG security group membership.** The user is also added to the WSS_ADMIN_WPG local security group on all servers in the farm with the SharePoint Foundation 2010 Web Application role, which grants certain administrative rights in IIS and the file system of those affected servers.

As you can see, these are certainly nontrivial rights within your farm, and only administrators who you trust to use those powers properly should be added to the SharePoint_Shell_Access role. A single misstep with these rights can drastically impact your environment, and that's something we would encourage you to impress upon any administrator you place within the role.

Before covering the various cmdlets that can protect your SharePoint 2010 farm, it's important to briefly examine the structure of PowerShell cmdlets and how they are used. First and foremost, cmdlets follow a strict naming convention, starting with a verb describing the action the cmdlet performs followed by a noun that describes the target of the action. Directly following the name of the cmdlet is its input parameter(s), which defines the specific conditions that the cmdlet should use when run. For a complete listing of the PowerShell cmdlets available with SharePoint Foundation 2010, see http://technet.microsoft.com/en-us/library/ff686791.aspx, and for a similar listing for SharePoint Server 2010, see http://technet.microsoft.com/en-us/library/ff678226.aspx.

Note: PowerShell is not case sensitive; you can execute its cmdlets using all caps, all lowercase, or a combination of the two. It does not behave differently depending on the casing used.

Tip: One incredibly useful feature of PowerShell is its built-in Get-Help cmdlet. A call to Get-Help followed by the name of the target cmdlet displays a great deal of information on the cmdlet, as well as a display of all the input parameters you can use when running the target operation. It's also invaluable to add -Examples to the end of the call, because it provides actual examples of how to use the cmdlet.

PowerShell Backup and Restore Prerequisites

In addition to the rights granted via Add-SPShellAdmin, the account you are using to execute SharePoint 2010's backup and restore cmdlets, as well as the account serving as the identity of the SQL Server service on the SQL Instance (or instances) hosting your farm's SharePoint database, must have the right to read from the directory used as the target storage location for the backup files that will be created. It must also be able to write and update files in the directory. The configuration of that target storage location is somewhat flexible, depending on your SharePoint farm's configuration. If the SharePoint server you're using to run the cmdlets is also the server hosting the farm's SQL Server database instance, you can map the directory you use as the target storage location via a file system path such as `C:\backups`. In all other cases, a file share mapped via a UNC path, such as `\\server\backups`, is the only way you can reference the location when using the cmdlets. Shared UNC paths are the type of location most commonly used; separating the farm's database instance to its own server is a highly recommended configuration, especially for larger environments.

Caution: As with the Central Administration site's backup and restore tool, the amount of storage space available in your target storage location is important to consider before backing up your SharePoint farm with SharePoint 2010's PowerShell cmdlets. The cmdlets do not automatically compress files or archive older files to free up additional space as needed, so the onus is on your organization to ensure that the selected storage location is large enough to hold your backup files. For more information, see the "Backup/Restore Prerequisites and Considerations" section in Chapter 9.

Scripting SharePoint 2010's Backup and Restore Cmdlets

The majority of this chapter is geared toward explaining what you can and can't do with Share-Point 2010's backup and restore cmdlets, but before we get to that, we want to get you thinking about something else: how you can and should use them. The most important use of these cmdlets you need to be thinking about is how you can create PowerShell scripts that include and extend them, so you can protect your farm completely, manage your farm's resources effectively, and be confident that your farm is being protected the same way each time a script is run. As we cover each of the cmdlets to follow, we'll provide you with basic examples for how to use them, as well as (when it makes sense) more advanced descriptions of how to integrate each into an effective script for protecting your SharePoint 2010 farm.

Note: Keep in mind as you're reading this chapter that many of the tangible scripting examples focus on the cmdlets that back up SharePoint 2010, not those that restore it. The fact of the matter is this: backing up is a repeatable exercise that you have control over when and how it executes. On the other hand, restoring a backup is usually something you don't know you have to do until a need is at hand and the circumstances and conditions surrounding that restore operation are impossible to predict. Now, don't let that dissuade you from scripting a restore operation; there are times it may make sense to do so, such as an automated process to replicate a production farm's configuration into a testing or development environment. But in our context of SharePoint 2010 disaster recovery, there just isn't a lot of need for scripting restore operations, so we haven't spent much time covering that topic in depth.

You need to understand some things about creating successful scripts that use and take advantage of these new SharePoint 2010 backup and restore cmdlets. Keep in mind that, although these cmdlets offer a range of functionality, there are still things they cannot do. Don't forget: these cmdlets are written to work in both manual and scripted situations, so they have to be able to handle one-off uses just as much as they do repeated uses. This means that your script may have to include some logic or processing that varies the way a given cmdlet is called based on variable circumstances, because these cmdlets are not capable of such behavior.

The best example of this shortcoming is in the area of storage management. With a one-off use of a backup cmdlet, all you need is a storage location with enough space to hold your backups. But if you're scripting a backup process, it's a different story. Continually using the same backup location to store a backup, especially a full backup of a complete SharePoint 2010 farm, requires an astronomical amount of storage. It is far more likely that your script is going to have to help you manage your storage, say by taking actions like deleting backup files older than a certain date, running differential backups on a much more regular basis than full backups, or a combination of the two.

Note: SharePoint backup cmdlets do help in this area somewhat by automatically saving backups into unique directories, which can make it easier to identify and classify backup files over time but still does not directly address the issue of storage consumption.

The type of backups you take is important from another perspective: the amount of time it takes to restore your backups. Although differential backups are great for their lower use of storage, it can take longer to restore large groups of differential backups because you must apply each in succession to fully include updates to the targeted item since its last full backup. Having a high number of differential backups can affect your ability to meet recovery time objectives (RTOs). Your script should allow for some flexibility in the scheduling and type selection of your backups so that you can achieve the best possible balance between reducing the storage impact of your backups and reducing the time it takes to restore those backups.

Take some time to consider whether there are items within your farm that need to be protected uniquely, say by backing them up on a different schedule than the rest of the farm, having them stored in a different location, or using a different set of parameter inputs. If you have a series of high-profile site collections within your farm, they may have a more stringent set of recovery point objectives (RPOs) and RTOs than the rest of the farm. You may find that your users' My Sites do not need to be backed up as frequently. Perhaps you need more granular status reporting for a complex Web application that often has failing backups. Regardless of the reason, make sure to take requirements like these into account when creating your scripts.

Just because you may be an IT professional writing an administrative script, don't overlook the opportunity to incorporate key software development best practices into your script, such as error reporting, logging, and testing. Your SharePoint backup and restore scripts need to be rock solid. You need to have complete faith in a resource you're creating to protect your SharePoint environment day in and day out, so make sure to write a script that inspires that kind of faith. First and foremost, always test your scripts to make sure they do exactly what they're supposed to do; it is far better to take some extra time to identify a potential issue up front than to have it identified for you in a production environment during a catastrophic failure. Integrate logging and reporting into your script, so that if there is an error, you can be notified as soon as possible and work to correct it. PowerShell offers the ability to communicate in a lot of different ways (the Windows Event Log, e-mail, text messages via Short Message Services [SMS], and so on), so take advantage of that.

Finally, PowerShell's scripting language offers you unbelievable access to a huge range of functionality, code, and tools to really enhance your scripts. Its intrinsic pipeline capability allows you to send the output of one cmdlet directly to another for further processing, a robust feature that simplifies a script's logic and helps you to better manage data within the script. It has direct access to Microsoft's .NET Framework, as well as the SharePoint Object Model, allowing you to access code and functionality that may not be exposed by SharePoint 2010's other PowerShell cmdlets. You can also access more traditional Windows resources such as Windows Management Instrumentation (WMI) objects, the Windows Registry itself, and the file systems of your servers. Don't overlook any potential available resources that these items, and many others, may offer you when writing your backup scripts; they can make your scripts more useful and perform better when put to good use.

Using SharePoint 2010's Catastrophic Backup Cmdlets

Now that we've set the stage with some of the key information you need to keep in mind when using PowerShell with SharePoint 2010, let's take a closer look at the SharePoint 2010's cmdlets used for or related to backing up some or all of your SharePoint farm.

Backup-SPFarm

Backup-SPFarm has a broad-reaching scope and can be put to use in a number of versatile ways. As its name implies, the primary use of this cmdlet is to create a backup of an entire SharePoint farm. You can also use it to identify individual content components within a farm that can be backed up, back up those individual components, or create a backup of a farm's configuration settings. Let's look at an example of how Backup-SPFarm can make a full backup of a Share-Point 2010 farm:

```
Backup-SPFarm -Directory \\foo\backups -BackupMethod Full
```

Now, this example is pretty straightforward; in it we passed the Backup-SPFarm cmdlet two input parameters—one indicating the directory that the backup files should be stored in, and one indicating what type of backup should be created. The parameters you choose to provide with your call to Backup-SPFarm directly affect what kind of output it generates when run. There are two distinct sets of parameters you can use to call `Backup-SPFarm`: one to generate backups and one to identify components within a farm to back up. The following lists highlight the available parameters for each set, as well as what data you should be supplying for those parameters.

The first parameter set we'll examine is the bread and butter of `Backup-SPFarm`. It is used to create a backup of your farm or an individual component within it. The items in the list that follow describe the various parameters to call `Backup-SPFarm` to create that desired backup:

- **`Directory`.** When you're performing a backup with `Backup-SPFarm`, this parameter is required (unless the `-ShowTree` parameter is provided; see the next list for further information). The target directory can be on the file system if SharePoint is installed on the same server as its back-end database; otherwise, it must be a UNC shared directory. You can use this directory to store multiple backups for your farm. SharePoint automatically creates child folders within the directory to store each backup's files.

- **`BackupMethod`.** When you're performing a backup with `Backup-SPFarm`, this parameter is required (unless the `-ShowTree` parameter is provided). Acceptable input parameter values are "Full" or "Differential" and determine what type of backup is made for the target SharePoint component. For more information on the differences between full and differential backups, see the "Full Backups Versus Differential Backups" section in Chapter 9. Remember, to complete a differential backup with this cmdlet, you must have already run at least one full backup of the item you are targeting. Interestingly, some service applications always require a full backup; if you use the Differential option when backing up one of these service applications, SharePoint still performs a full backup.

- **`AssignmentCollection`.** This is an optional parameter, intended to allow for the proper disposal of objects. This parameter allows those objects to be assigned to a variable with an object of type `SPAssignmentCollection`, which the cmdlet disposes of when it is done with them. For more information on this important parameter, see the "SharePoint Object Disposal" sidebar following this list.

- **`BackupThreads`.** This parameter is not required. It determines the number of threads SharePoint uses to complete the backup operation and must be an integer from 1 to 10. If no `BackupThreads` value is provided, SharePoint defaults to three threads.

Note: The more threads that are used, the more components that can be backed up at the same time, which has the potential to reduce the time necessary to complete the backup operation. The trade-off with this is that the use of additional threads adds more data to your backup logs and makes them more difficult to read, because entries are entered in the order they occur with no correlation to which thread they are related to. If you are troubleshooting issues with your backups, reducing this value to one thread makes the log files much more readable.

- **ConfigurationOnly.** This is an optional parameter that does not actually require that an input value be provided for it. If this switch is used, the cmdlet only backs up the configuration data for the item targeted, whether that is the full farm or an individual component of that farm. For more information on configuration-only backups, see Chapter 9. It is also important to note that you can only use this parameter against the configuration data for the farm that the server hosting the session for the SharePoint Management Shell belongs to. There is another SharePoint 2010 backup cmdlet that provides similar functionality to `Backup-SPFarm` when this parameter is used but is not constrained by this restriction to the current farm, `Backup-SPConfigurationDatabase`, which we'll cover later in this chapter.

- **Confirm.** This is an optional parameter. If this parameter is used with an input value of True, the cmdlet prompts the user to confirm that he wants to proceed with the action. If a value of False is provided, the cmdlet proceeds without prompting for permission once executed. The default value for this parameter is False.

- **Force.** This is an optional parameter that does not actually require an input value to be provided for it. If this switch is not used, the cmdlet does not proceed with the backup operation if it estimates that there is not enough disk space available to store the backup. If it is used, that check is overridden, and the backup is executed regardless of how much storage is available.

- **Item.** This parameter is not required. By default, if no item is specified, the entire farm is backed up. If an `Item` input parameter is provided to specify the SharePoint component to be backed up, it must be a valid item in the farm. If the item has spaces in its name, the entire item must be enclosed within quotation marks (" "). If the exact name or path for the desired component is not known, you can use the `ShowTree` switch to list the components available within the farm. (See the following list for more information on the `ShowTree` switch.) This parameter allows the cmdlet to be used to protect Web applications, service applications, content databases, and much more within your SharePoint farm.

- **Percentage.** This input parameter is not required. If a value is specified for the `Percentage` input parameter, it must be an integer between 1 and 100 and is used to determine the frequency with which `Backup-SPFarm` reports progress of the backup operation. For example, specifying a value of 20 displays the progress of the backup operation for every 20 percent of the operation that is completed. If no `Percentage` parameter is specified, STSADM.exe defaults to reporting progress every 5 percent of the operation. This input parameter has no impact on the outcome of the backup operation; it only affects the amount of information that the cmdlet reports about its activities during the operation. SharePoint is not able to calculate the percent completed of the backup operation with 100 percent accuracy. You may find that your actual progress updates do not appear with exactly the requested frequency.

Tip: For large SharePoint components, Microsoft recommends that a `Percentage` input of 1 be used to provide the best status data about your backup operation.

- **WhatIf.** This is an optional parameter. If this parameter is used, PowerShell displays a message stating what the outcome of running the cmdlet will be, but the cmdlet itself is not executed. This can be helpful when testing scripts, allowing you to verify that you can provide the correct set of inputs and parameters to the cmdlet.

SharePoint Object Disposal One thing SharePoint administrators must come to terms with when using PowerShell to work with SharePoint, regardless of whether it is for backing up, restoring, or another action, is overcoming an issue that SharePoint developers have been dealing with already: object disposal. Some objects within SharePoint's object model, such as `SPWeb` and `SPSite`, can require, and more importantly, hold on to a great deal of memory when used. You must properly dispose of them when an application is done using them to free up that memory.

This is a challenge that developers have had to tackle in SharePoint for quite some time, dating back at least to SharePoint's 2003 releases. In the past, Microsoft has made tools like the SharePoint Dispose Checker to help developers and administrators identify issues with object disposal in custom applications. Furthermore, Microsoft has included the `AssignmentCollection` parameter in all of its SharePoint 2010 cmdlets as a way to reduce their potential for risk in SharePoint 2010 PowerShell scripts. Carefully consider using this parameter if your call of `Backup-SPFarm` also involves using SharePoint's `SPWeb`, `SPSite`, or `SPSiteAdministration` objects; otherwise, it may not be necessary, but it is still something you need to be mindful of and consider.

In general, SharePoint 2010's PowerShell cmdlets expose so much more of SharePoint's inner workings and functionality that developers normally accessed, not just with its cmdlets but via its object model and Web services. Because of the power of this new access, you need to constantly evaluate your SharePoint 2010 PowerShell scripts to avoid memory leaks and performance issues. This can be a major risk to your SharePoint environment, and one that we highly recommend you invest time in learning more about. One great place to start that process is an outstanding blog post by SharePoint MVP Gary Lapointe on SharePoint 2010's cmdlets. The second half of the post is devoted to the subject and two key cmdlets you need to know more about. The first cmdlet is `Start-SP-Assignment`. Calling it creates an object with a type of `SPAssignmentCollection`, which you can pass to other SharePoint 2010 cmdlets using the `AssignmentCollection` parameter. The second cmdlet is `Stop-SPAssignment`.

Calling it disposes of the SPAssignmentCollection object when your script is done. You can find Lapointe's post at http://stsadm.blogspot.com/2009/10/sharepoint-2010-stsadm-and-powershell.html.

The second parameter set for Backup-SPFarm is best used to obtain valuable information about your farm for backing it up, rather than backing it up itself. The key parameter in this set is the -ShowTree parameter. Its presence indicates that the second parameter set is being used instead of the first.

- **ShowTree.** This is an optional parameter. If the ShowTree parameter is included with the call of Backup-SPFarm for a backup, the cmdlet does not complete a backup of any SharePoint components. Instead, it displays the components in the farm so that you can use their names to request a backup. If a value is specified via the Item parameter, any components that are not children of that input are excluded and marked with an asterisk (*). Any components that cannot be backed up are enclosed within square brackets ([ ]). See Figure 10.1 for an example of the output produced when you use this parameter with Backup-SPFarm.

- **AssignmentCollection.** This is an optional parameter. It is used with this parameter set in the same way that it is in the first parameter set.

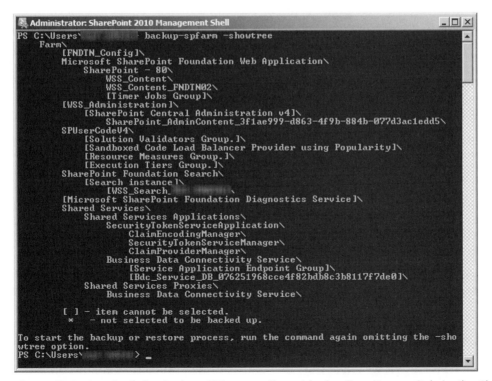

Figure 10.1 A call of the Backup-SPFarm cmdlet with the ShowTree switch in the SharePoint 2010 Management Shell window, and the output of the operation.

- **ConfigurationOnly**. This is an optional parameter. It is used with this parameter set in the same way that it is the first parameter set.

- **Item**. This is an optional parameter. It is used with this parameter set in the same way that it is the first parameter set.

- **WhatIf**. This is an optional parameter. It is used with this parameter set in the same way that it is the first parameter set.

The beautiful thing about PowerShell is that most cmdlets (when they're well designed and written), do exactly what their names say they do, and that's certainly the case with `Backup-SPFarm`. It definitely backs up a SharePoint farm. Using the first parameter set and the minimal set of inputs for it, you can easily back up your entire farm: its configuration, its contents, and its service applications. When we start to talk about the new PowerShell cmdlets for restoring content into SharePoint 2010, this becomes even more important, because we can restore each of these components in a SharePoint 2010 farm, something that was not necessarily possible in previous versions of SharePoint.

Another important aspect of the `Backup-SPFarm` cmdlet is its ability to back up individual components with the `Item` parameter. By specifying a section of your farm with the `Item` parameter, you can back up and protect it separately from the rest of your farm. If you want to make a copy of a Web application's content database to transfer down to a farm in your testing environment or take an exact copy of the configuration of your farm's Search service application for use in another production farm, you can do it with the `Backup-SPFarm` cmdlet and its `Item` parameter. The `Item` parameter also becomes much more potent when you combine it with PowerShell's pipelining and looping capabilities; with some clever use of the PowerShell language and the `Backup-SPFarm` cmdlet and its `ShowTree` and `Item` parameters, you can individually protect multiple components within your farm without a great deal of effort. The possibilities for how you can use this cmdlet and its valuable options within your environment to meet its specific needs are quite impressive and give you diverse and creative options for protecting your SharePoint farm.

Don't overlook the ability to back up the data about the configuration of your farm with `Backup-SPFarm`'s `ConfigurationOnly` parameter. This parameter highlights a new aspect of SharePoint 2010 that wasn't possible in previous versions of SharePoint: backing up the configuration data and settings for your SharePoint 2010 farm, not just its contents. This means you can capture the overall setup of your farm and use it to re-create a farm with most of the same settings in another environment, such as a development farm or a disaster recovery environment for failover, both which are cases where having an environment identical to the production one can be valuable. Interestingly, this feature is so important in SharePoint 2010 that it's also available via a separate cmdlet, which we'll look at in a bit.

Please take note, however, that we did not say that the `ConfigurationOnly` parameter makes a "complete" backup of your farm's configuration data. That's because it doesn't. SharePoint 2010's configuration backups don't make an exact copy of a farm's settings; they only capture *some* of its portable settings and configurations. As we mentioned in Chapter 9, this parameter does not have the ability to include configuration data for most of SharePoint's service applications or the SharePoint Web applications currently existing in the farm.

Now that you're familiar with `Backup-SPFarm`, let's look at an example of a comprehensive approach to using that cmdlet to effectively and flexibly back up your SharePoint 2010 farm. The PowerShell function listed next, `Backup-Farm`, is designed to not only back up a SharePoint farm, but check its output log files for errors and then use another function (`Record-Event`) to report its findings. The function can be used to execute both full and differential backups via the `$backupMethod` input parameter and is set to target the entire farm regardless of the method provided. You can also specify the storage location of the backups via an input to allow for customization; the final two inputs are solely for error reporting.

```
Function Backup-Farm ($backupMethod, $backupDir, $errorFlag, $entryType)
{
 # Run a farm backup with the SP2010 CMDLET using the parameters passed in
 Backup-SPFarm -directory $backupDir -backupmethod $backupMethod

 # Get the most recently modified backup folder
 $newestFolder = (Get-ChildItem -path $backupDir | Sort -property LastWriteTime '
                 | Select-Object -last 1 -property FullName | format-table '
                 -hidetableheaders | out-string| foreach { $_.trim() } )

 # Build the file path for the most recently created backup log file
 $newestLog = Join-Path -path $newestFolder -childpath "spbackup.log"

 # Getting the number of errors in the backups log file
 # (subtracting 1 for the reporting line at the end of the document)
 $errorLog = Get-Content $newestLog | Out-String
 $errorCount = [regex]::matches($errorLog,"error").count - 1

 # If there is an error, report it
 If ($errorCount -gt 0)
 {
 # Create Error Message
 $eventMsg = $eventMsg + "At least one error was found while making a " '
     + $backupMethod + "backup, stored in the " + $newestFolder + "directory. " '
     + "Please review the spbackup.log file in that directory carefully to " '
     + "diagnose and resolve the issue before running another backup."

 # Report an error
 Record-Event -eventMsg $eventMsg -entryType "Error"
```

```
# Set the Error flag to "On"
$errorFlag = 1
}
Else #Report the successful Farm backup
{
 # Report the Deletion Event
 $eventMsg = "A " + $backupMethod + " backup of the farm was successfully " '
             + "backed up to " + $newestFolder + ". See " + $newestLog '
             + " for more information."
 Record-Event -eventMsg $eventMsg -entryType "Information"
 }
}
```

Backup-SPConfigurationDatabase

As we've already mentioned, the `Backup-SPConfigurationDatabase` cmdlet is another option you have available to back up a SharePoint 2010 farm's configuration, without including any of its contents. It works much like the `Backup-SPFarm` cmdlet when used with the `ConfigurationOnly` parameter, but there are some differences between that and the `Backup-SPConfigurationDatabase` cmdlet. The intent of each of these two options is similar, and the functionality that they use behind the scenes is pretty much the same, but those differences are crucial to understand.

When we were talking about the `Backup-SPFarm` cmdlet, you may not have noticed it, but we were careful to say that `Backup-SPFarm` is for use with your farm—the current farm that the server you're running the cmdlet on is part of. That's the way it works; `Backup-SPFarm` is for use with the current farm only; you cannot run it against other SharePoint 2010 farms if the server executing the cmdlet is not attached to them. But the constraint does not bind `Backup-SPConfigurationDatabase`; you can run the cmdlet against any farm's configuration database, as long as the server hosting the cmdlet can connect to the database over the network and you as the cmdlet's operator can provide the proper credentials to access the database. But the most important thing to take in about this cmdlet is that configuration databases targeted by `Backup-SPConfigurationDatabase` don't even have to be used by an active farm. You can use the cmdlet to create a backup of any SharePoint 2010 configuration database as long as that database is attached to a SQL Server instance and running. Here's an example of how to call `Backup-SPConfigurationDatabase` to back up a configuration database in a remote Share-Point server farm:

```
Backup-SPConfigurationDatabase -Directory \\foo\backups -DatabaseServer
RemoteSQLInstance -DatabaseName RemoteSPConfigDB
```

This capability may seem a little strange at first, but in reality, this is a powerful feature. It allows you to back up any configuration database, whether it's from a running farm, a farm you shut down a few weeks ago, or even a SQL Server backup of a configuration database that you've brought back online for the express purpose of capturing its farm's configuration and settings. Once you have that backup, there's quite a bit you can do with it. This is another of those situations in which SharePoint 2010 gives you a great deal more flexibility and functionality than its previous versions. Now you can back up a farm's configuration and have a template you can use to deploy as many times as you want, the same way every time. Now you can capture the exact settings of your farm, even if it's encountered an error and offline, so you can recover not just your content, but the specific setup of the farm that was hosting it. Now you have a lot more ways to protect yourself from errors, corruption, and disaster and recover from them more effectively.

It may seem nice from a backup coverage perspective, but `Backup-SPConfigurationDatabase`'s ability to directly address configuration databases for other farms really starts to make the most difference when you think about it from the restore side of the equation. It's not so much about targeting other active farms, because you can always just run the cmdlet directly in that farm. Creating a backup straight from a configuration database in SQL Server that isn't associated with a live farm really allows you to protect your farm in a way that few, if any, of the other tools discussed in this book can. This becomes even more impressive when you consider the limitations of those other tools.

Microsoft does not support directly restoring a SQL backup of a configuration database to an existing or new SharePoint 2010 farm. The Central Administration site can back up a farm's configuration, but you can't schedule those backups. Even Windows Server's Volume Shadow Copy Service (VSS), a backup technology discussed in greater detail later in Chapter 11, "SharePoint 2010 Disaster Recovery Development," is incapable of restoring a farm's configuration data or its Central Administration Web site.

But with `Backup-SPConfigurationDatabase`, you can restore a farm's configuration data with little more than SQL Server backups of the database. This means that it makes a lot more sense to do regular backups of your farm's configuration database with SQL Server; the backups can now play into a restore scenario, in much the same way that you can use the configuration database to protect your farm's content databases. In the event of a disaster where you've lost your entire farm, you can restore a SQL Server backup of your configuration database into a SQL Server instance and with `Backup-SPConfigurationDatabase` create a SharePoint configuration-only backup of it. Then you can restore that configuration data into a new farm with the `Restore-SPFarm` cmdlet. It isn't going to bring back everything, but it does restore important data about a farm and enables you to get that data restored much more quickly than other alternatives.

There are many similarities between the `Backup-SPConfigurationDatabase` and `Backup-SPFarm`, such as the `Item` and `ShowTree` parameters. They both create backup files in the same manner; they both write to the `spbackup.log` file; they're both Pisces (just kidding). Really, most of the other difference between `Backup-SPFarm` and `Backup-SPConfigurationDatabase` are mechanical: they do have slightly different input parameters you can use to call them. Out of those differences, the only one worth noting is that there are no differential backups with `Backup-SPConfiguration-Database`; it only takes a full backup of a configuration database. Because the best use case for `Backup-SPConfigurationDatabase` is in a restore scenario in which you're only running it once anyway, this isn't a big deal (not to mention that the files generated by the cmdlet stay pretty small).

Before we dive into the specifics of the `Backup-SPConfigurationDatabase`, we want to mention one other difference about the two cmdlets. When run with its default settings, `Backup-SPFarm` uses three threads to back up a SharePoint 2010 farm; with the default settings, `Backup-SPConfigurationDatabase` only uses two. This is a pretty minor point (especially because you can't control the number of threads that `Backup-SPConfigurationDatabase` uses), but if you ever get into fine-tuning the performance of your backups, you may want to take that difference into consideration so you know that they're going to behave differently unless you specify the number of threads. If you're concerned about performance, `Backup-SPFarm` is the only one of the two cmdlets that allows you to set the number of threads used; `Backup-SPConfigurationDatabase` doesn't offer a `BackupThread` parameter.

To paraphrase B. A. Baracus, enough with all the jibber jabber; let's talk about the details of `Backup-SPConfigurationDatabase`. The items in the list that follow describe the various parameters used to call `Backup-SPConfigurationDatabase` to create a backup of a SharePoint 2010 configuration database:

- **Directory.** When you're performing a backup with `Backup-SPConfigurationDatabase`, this parameter is required (unless the `-ShowTree` parameter is provided; see the next list for further information). The target directory can be on the file system if SharePoint is installed on the same server as its back-end database; otherwise, it must be a UNC shared directory. This directory can store multiple backups for your farm. SharePoint automatically creates child folders within the directory to store individual backup files.

- **AssignmentCollection.** This is an optional parameter, intended to allow for the proper disposal of objects. Carefully consider using this parameter if your call of `Backup-SPConfigurationDatabase` also involves using SharePoint's SPWeb, SPSite, or SPSiteAdministration objects; otherwise, it is not likely to be necessary.

- **DatabaseCredentials.** This parameter is not required; you should use it only if the account that executes the `Backup-SPConfigurationDatabase` cmdlet is not a member of the db_backupoperator role in the SQL Server instance hosting the targeted configuration database or SQL Authentication is used to connect to a database. The credentials provided should have administrator rights in SQL Server. If this parameter is not provided and required, the cmdlet prompts the user for the username and password values.

- **DatabaseName.** This is an optional parameter that does not actually require that an input value be provided for it. If this parameter is used, the cmdlet backs up the configuration database specified. If no value is supplied for this parameter, the cmdlet defaults to selecting the configuration database for the farm that the SharePoint 2010 server hosting the cmdlet is a member of.

- **DatabaseServer**. This is an optional parameter that does not actually require that an input value be provided for it. If this parameter is used, the cmdlet uses the SQL Server instance name to target the configuration database specified via the DatabaseName parameter, which should be hosted in that database instance. If no value is supplied for this parameter, the cmdlet defaults to selecting the database instance hosting the configuration database for the farm that the SharePoint 2010 server hosting the cmdlet is a member of.

- **Item**. This parameter is not required. By default, if no item is specified, the entire farm is backed up. If an Item input parameter is provided to specify the SharePoint component to be backed up, it must be a valid item in the farm. If the item has spaces in its name, you must enclose the entire item within quotation marks (" "). If the exact name or path for the desired component is not known, you can use the ShowTree switch to list the components available within the farm. (See the following list for more information on the ShowTree switch.) This parameter allows the cmdlet to be used to protect Web applications, service applications, content databases, and much more within your SharePoint farm.

- **ShowTree**. This is an optional parameter. If the ShowTree parameter is included with the call of Backup-SPFarm for a backup, the cmdlet does not complete a backup of SharePoint components. Instead, it displays the components in the farm so that their names can be used to request a backup. If a value is specified via the Item parameter, any components that are not children of that input are excluded and marked with an asterisk (*). Any components that you cannot back up are enclosed within square brackets ([ ]).

The syntax to use Backup-SPConfigurationDatabase in a script is really not that different from what you use with Backup-SPFarm. In fact, you may find that in most scripted situations, Backup-SPFarm with the ConfigurationOnly parameter works well enough to keep you from introducing another cmdlet into the script. Backup-SPConfigurationDatabase works just fine in scripted scenarios to protect your farm's configuration data, but its primary use case is really more of a one-off, ad hoc type of situation in which you execute it when a specific need and situation arises.

Backup-SPSite

With the larger, farm-wide aspects of backing up SharePoint via PowerShell out of the way, let's look at the more granular backup operations you can perform with SharePoint 2010's PowerShell cmdlets. Well, "operations" is a bit of a misnomer—there's really only one additional cmdlet that we haven't talked about for nongranular backup activities with PowerShell in SharePoint 2010: the Backup-SPSite cmdlet.

Before we dive into the nitty-gritty of that cmdlet, remember that the `Backup-SPFarm` cmdlet can granularly protect a SharePoint environment. You can use `Backup-SPFarm`'s `Item` input parameter to back up service applications, Web applications, content databases, search databases, and other content components down to the database level. If you need to protect an item higher up in SharePoint 2010's logical hierarchy, you're going to need to use `Backup-SPFarm`. But if you want to completely back up individual site collections in a farm, your only option is `Backup-SPSite`, because the smallest item that `Backup-SPFarm` can back up is a SharePoint content database.

Keep the specifics of that distinct level of granularity in mind when preparing to use `Backup-SPSite`; you can use it only to create backups of SharePoint 2010 site collections. You cannot individually target subsites (also known as *webs* within SharePoint 2010's Object Model) beneath a site collection with the cmdlet, nor can you target individual items, lists, or libraries within a site collection or subsite. Administrators can back up site collections with the cmdlet by calling the `Backup-SPSite` cmdlet. In that call, they must specify at least two parameters: the `-Identity` parameter with a uniform resource locator (URL) or globally unique identifier (GUID) of the target site collection as an input parameter, and the `-Path` parameter with the details of where to create and store the backup file (either in the local file system of the server or a remote server via UNC path).

```
Backup-SPSite -Identity http://foo/bar -Path \\backups\foo.bak
```

> **Caution:** Another limitation of the `Backup-SPSite` cmdlet is that it can only complete full backups of a site collection; unlike `Backup-SPFarm`, it cannot execute differential backups of a site collection once a full backup has been made. This should affect only the largest of site collections, but keep it in mind when considering the tool.

The `Backup-SPSite` cmdlet is also a great example of why the use of PowerShell to administer SharePoint 2010 is such an important development. PowerShell's core features, such as pipelining, object orientation, and looping, make it much, much easier to individually back up multiple site collections in a single process; something that would take quite a bit of VBScript and calls with STSADM.exe in previous versions of SharePoint can now be accomplished in a single line of PowerShell scripting. For example, let's say that you need to back up all the site collections within a Web application owned by your company's chief operating officer (COO), a Mr. John Doe, on a much more frequent schedule than the rest of your SharePoint farm, because Mr. Doe is kind of a big deal. An excerpt of the PowerShell script necessary to do that should look something like this:

```
$webApp = Get-SPWebApplication -identity http://foo
$sites = Get-SPSite $webApp -filter {$_.Owner = "BAR\JDOE"}
Backup-SPSite -identity $sites -path \\foo\backups
```

Now, you may notice that there's no looping logic in the preceding script, and there's a reason for that. Every PowerShell cmdlet returns its results as an object, and cmdlets that return multiple objects actually return those results as an array of objects. So the $sites variable is populated with all the site collections that Mr. Doe owns, not just one. That array is then passed to Backup-SPSite, which iterates through each site collection within the array and backs up each one individually.

Another great thing about PowerShell is that you can continue to improve these three lines of script in a couple of ways. First, there's no need to hardcode the URL of the targeted Web application, the account ID for Mr. Doe's account, or the location of the backup files created by the process. Instead, you can configure those items as parameters, which can be passed into a function containing the script, or as parameters for an entire script that the code would reside in. This allows you to reuse the script as needed to cover multiple Web applications, users, and storage locations.

The other thing you can do is rewrite the script as shown next to reduce the number of lines needed to execute the desired backups:

```
Get-SPWebApplication -identity $URL | Get-SPSite -filter {$_.Owner = $siteOwner} | Backup-
SPSite -path $backupStorage
```

This version of the script has done away with the local variables and is sending the result of one cmdlet directly to the next one listed in the line. PowerShell uses a feature called *pipelining* to enhance that transfer process; it allows multiple cmdlets to be strung together, passing the output of one cmdlet directly into another. The pipe characters (|) between cmdlets in the preceding example represent the pipelining activity.

This is just one example of some of the exciting and useful things that administrators can do with PowerShell thanks to its advanced features and functionality. Because of that, it is important to not just zero in on what a single cmdlet like Backup-SPSite can do, but to consider how to combine with other SharePoint 2010 cmdlets like Get-SPWebApplication as well as other cmdlets, objects, application programming interfaces (APIs), and Web services that PowerShell makes available to you and your scripts. But before you can really get into the creation of those scripts, you need to have a good understanding of what is needed to effectively use this key cmdlet to properly back up a SharePoint 2010 site collection. The list that follows details each switch that you can use with Backup-SPSite and its purpose:

- **Identity**. When you back up a site collection, this parameter is required and must be a valid URL or GUID for the target site collection.

- **Path**. When you back up a site collection, this parameter is required and must be a valid UNC or Windows directory path to a file that the backup is saved in. The account logged into the SharePoint 2010 Management Shell must have permission to write to the directory specified for this input.

Tip: Although you must specify a file name for the backup with this input parameter, there is no required extension to use when specifying the file name for your backup. Use something easily identifiable as a backup file, such as `.bak`. Regardless of the extension you specify, SharePoint creates your backup at the selected path.

- **AssignmentCollection**. This is an optional parameter, intended to allow for the proper disposal of objects. Carefully consider using this parameter if your call of `Backup-SPSite` also involves using SharePoint's `SPWeb`, `SPSite`, or `SPSiteAdministration` objects; otherwise, it is not likely to be necessary.

- **Confirm**. This parameter is optional. When used in a call of `Backup-SPSite`, it forces the cmdlet to prompt the user for confirmation prior to executing the backup.

- **Force**. This parameter is optional; using it forces `Backup-SPSite` to overwrite any existing backup file matching the value of the `-Identity` parameter should one already exist.

- **NoSiteLock**. This parameter is optional; its use keeps `Backup-SPSite` from locking a site during the execution of the site collection backup. If this parameter is not used, the target site collection is only available for users to read content from. They are not able to add, modify, or delete content in it until the backup is done and the site is unlocked. If you expect your users to write to a target site collection while it is being backed up, do not use this parameter unless you absolutely have to. Allowing write access to a SharePoint site while it is being backed up can lead to inconsistencies or corruption in your site's content. Keeping the target site collection locked during the backup process ensures the highest-quality backup and provides the best possible long-term experience for your users.

- **UseSqlSnapshot**. This parameter is optional. When you use it, `Backup-SPSite` creates a SQL Server database snapshot of the content database containing the site collection, and the backup of the site collection is created by referencing the snapshot rather than the database. Once the backup is completed, the cmdlet deletes the database snapshot. This parameter can be used only if your SQL Server instance supports the creation of database snapshots, so it is important to review your SQL Server edition prior to using it. If your instance does support snapshots, this parameter is recommended because it makes your site collection fully available to users during the backup. Because the cmdlet is reading from the snapshot and not the database, there is a drastically reduced chance of resource contention between it and the activities of your users.

- **WhatIf**. This is an optional parameter. If this parameter is used, PowerShell displays a message stating what the outcome of running the cmdlet will be, but the cmdlet itself is not executed. This can be helpful when testing scripts, allowing you to verify that you can provide the correct set of inputs and parameters to the cmdlet.

Using SharePoint 2010's Catastrophic Restore Cmdlets

Restoring a backup created with SharePoint 2010's backup cmdlets is completed in much the same manner as the process you followed to create the backup in the first place. The restore cmdlets use many of the same switches and parameters that the backup cmdlets do, with some distinctions. There are some distinct permissions required to restore SharePoint backups: the service account for the farm's SQL Server instance, the farm's Timer service account, and the identity of the farm's Central Administration site's application pool must have read access to the storage location for your backup files. But the main difference is that now the names of these cmdlets start with `Restore` as their verb instead of `Backup`. As with SharePoint 2010's backup cmdlets, there are two restore cmdlets: `Restore-SPFarm` and `Restore-SPSite`.

Tip: You can only restore a SharePoint 2010 backup into a farm patched to the same or more recent version as the farm that the backup was made in. SharePoint 2010's restore cmdlets do not allow you to restore a backup to a farm with an older version than the farm that the backup originated from. You also cannot restore a backup created with a previous release of SharePoint, such as SharePoint 2007, into a SharePoint 2010 farm.

Restore-SPFarm

The `Restore-SPFarm` cmdlet is the yang to `Backup-SPFarm`'s yin, the white to its black, the 1 to its 0. You get the idea, right? `Backup-SPFarm` makes the backups, and `Restore-SPFarm` restores them. Neat, huh? Now, there is one other interesting thing about `Restore-SPFarm` worth noting: there is no `Restore-SPConfigurationDatabase`, so if you've made a configuration backup with `Backup-SPConfigurationDatabase`, you need to restore it with `Restore-SPFarm` just like you would a SharePoint 2010 backup that includes both content and configuration data. Whether you're restoring content or configuration data, the options for `Restore-SPFarm` are the same; you'll find that you can use its two parameter sets for either situation. Following is an example of `Restore-SPFarm` in action to perform a restore of the most recent backup file in the target directory:

```
Restore-SPFarm -Directory \\foo\backups\ -RestoreMethod New
```

Note: You can also use `Restore-SPFarm` to restore catastrophic backups that were created through the Central Administration site.

The list that follows outlines the details of the first parameter set for `Restore-SPFarm`, which actually restores a backup file.

- **Directory.** When you're performing a restore with `Restore-SPFarm`, this parameter is required (unless the `-ShowTree` parameter is provided; see the next list for further information). This parameter indicates the location of the backup to be restored. The target directory can be on the file system if SharePoint is installed on the same server as its back-end database; otherwise, it must be a UNC shared directory. This directory can store multiple backups for your farm. The most recent backup is used unless a `BackupID` parameter is also provided.

- **RestoreMethod.** When you're performing a restore with `Restore-SPFarm`, this parameter is required (unless the `-ShowTree` parameter is provided). Acceptable input parameter values are New or Overwrite, and they determine whether you are restoring the backup to a different farm (the New option) or to the current farm (the Overwrite option). You should use the Overwrite option when you are restoring the backup to the same farm that the backup was created with; if you are restoring the backup to a different farm, use the New option.

- **NewDatabaseServer.** This input parameter is not required and can be used only with the `RestoreMethod` parameter. When used, it is set as the default database instance for the restored farm.

- **AssignmentCollection.** This is an optional parameter, intended to allow for the proper disposal of objects. Carefully consider using this parameter if your call of `Restore-SPFarm` also involves using SharePoint's `SPWeb`, `SPSite`, or `SPSiteAdministration` objects; otherwise, it is not likely to be necessary.

- **RestoreThreads.** This parameter, which must be an integer from 1 to 10, is not required. It determines the number of threads SharePoint uses to complete the restore operation. If no `RestoreThreads` value is provided, SharePoint defaults to three threads.

Note: You need to take the same considerations for performance and resources mentioned for the `BackupThreads` parameter in the `Backup-SPFarm` cmdlet into account with the `RestoreThreads` parameter of `Restore-SPFarm`.

- **ConfigurationOnly.** This is an optional parameter that does not actually require an input value to be provided for it. If you use this switch, the cmdlet only restores the configuration data for the item targeted, whether that is the full farm or an individual component of that farm. If you are restoring a backup created with the `Backup-SPConfigurationDatabase` cmdlet, you must use this switch to properly restore the configuration backup. Remember: restoring a farm's configuration data does not include its service applications or Web applications. You must re-create these items or restore them via content backups after the configuration backup is complete to return them to your farm.

- **Confirm.** This is an optional parameter. If this parameter is used with an input value of True, the cmdlet prompts the user to confirm that he wants to proceed with the action. If a value of False is provided, the cmdlet proceeds without prompting for permission once executed. The default value for this parameter is False.

- **Force**. This is an optional parameter that does not actually require an input value to be provided for it. If this switch is not used, the cmdlet does not proceed with the restore operation if it is going to overwrite an existing SharePoint 2010 farm. If it is used, that check is overridden, and the restore is executed no matter what.

- **Item**. This parameter is not required. By default, if no item is specified, the entire farm is restored. If an Item input parameter is provided to specify the SharePoint component to be restored, it must be a valid item in the farm. If the item has spaces in its name, the entire item must be enclosed within quotation marks (" "). If the exact name or path for the desired component is unknown, you can use the ShowTree switch to list the components available within the farm.

Tip: If you are using the Item parameter to restore a farm's Secure Store Service, you must refresh the store's passphrase with the Update-SPSecureStoreApplicationServerKey cmdlet after you have successfully restored it.

- **Percentage**. This input parameter is not required. If a value is specified for the Percentage input parameter, it must be an integer between 1 and 100 and is used to determine the frequency with which Restore-SPFarm reports progress of the restore operation. For example, specifying a value of 20 displays the progress of the restore operation for every 20 percent of the operation that is completed. If no Percentage parameter is specified, STSADM.exe defaults to reporting progress every 5 percent of the operation. This input parameter has no affect on the outcome of the restore operation; it only affects the amount of information that the cmdlet reports about its activities during the operation. SharePoint is not able to calculate the completed percent of the restore operation with 100 percent accuracy. You may find that your actual progress updates do not appear with exactly the requested frequency.

Tip: For large SharePoint components, Microsoft recommends that a Percentage input of 1 be used to provide the best status data about your restore operation.

- **BackupID**. This input parameter is not required. If you use it, it must be a valid GUID for a backup package in the storage directory indicated by the Directory parameter. You can find the GUIDs for the backup packages in the target directory via the Get-SPBackupHistory cmdlet, discussed later in this chapter. If no BackupID parameter is used, the cmdlet selects the most recent backup in the target directory.

- **FarmCredentials**. This input parameter is not required. If you use it, this parameter indicates the credentials that the farm employs once it is restored, such as application pools for restored SharePoint Web applications. If a Web application's application pool already exists, this data is ignored, and the farm uses the existing credentials.

- **WhatIf.** This is an optional parameter. If this parameter is used, PowerShell displays a message stating what the outcome of running the cmdlet will be, but the cmdlet itself is not executed. This can be helpful when testing scripts, allowing you to verify that you can provide the correct set of inputs and parameters to the cmdlet.

The second parameter set for Restore-SPFarm is best used to obtain valuable information about your farm for restoring it, rather than an actual restore operation. The key parameter in this set is the -ShowTree parameter; its presence indicates that the second parameter set is being used instead of the first.

- **Directory.** When you're performing a restore with Restore-SPFarm, this parameter is required (unless the -ShowTree parameter is provided; see the next bullet for further information). This parameter indicates the location of the backup to be restored. The target directory can be on the file system if SharePoint is installed on the same server as its back-end database; otherwise, it must be a UNC shared directory. This directory can store multiple backups for your farm, the most recent backup is used unless a BackupID parameter is also provided.

- **ShowTree.** This is an optional parameter. If the ShowTree parameter is included with the call of Restore-SPFarm for a restore, the cmdlet does not complete a restore of any SharePoint components. Instead, it displays the components in the target backup package so that you can use their names to request a restore. If a value is specified via the Item parameter, any components that are not children of that input are excluded and marked with an asterisk (*). Any components that cannot be restored are enclosed within square brackets ([<item that can't be restored>]).

- **AssignmentCollection.** This is an optional parameter. It is used with this parameter set in the same way that it is in the first parameter set.

- **ConfigurationOnly.** This is an optional parameter. It is used with this parameter set in the same way that it is in the first parameter set.

- **Item.** This is an optional parameter. It is used with this parameter set in the same way that it is in the first parameter set.

- **WhatIf.** This is an optional parameter. It is used with this parameter set in the same way that it is in the first parameter set.

Restore-SPSite

If you think of the Restore-SPFarm cmdlet as peanut butter is to the Backup-SPFarm cmdlet's jelly, the Restore-SPSite cmdlet is the bacon to the Backup-SPSite cmdlet's eggs—two great tastes that are great together. When you need to restore a site collection backup created with `Backup-SPSite`, you're going to use `Restore-SPSite`. Makes sense, right? In fact, `Restore-SPSite` is the only way to restore a site collection backup created with SharePoint's out-of-the-box tools; you can't restore that backup through the Central Administration site or with SQL Server's management tools. Here's a quick example of `Restore-SPSite` in action:

```
Restore-SPSite -Identity http://bar/sites/foo -Path \\foo\backups\bar.bak
```

The list that follows outlines each parameter available to be used with the `Restore-SPFarm` cmdlet and the possible options you can use for each parameter:

- **Identity**. When you're restoring a site collection backup, this parameter is required and is the URL that you want users to enter when accessing your restored site collection. You can restore `Backup-SPSite`'s site collection backups to a new URL and attempt to update all the paths within the backup package to reflect the new URL for the site collection, as long as SharePoint is able to create a site collection at that path. Make sure to fully test the restored site collection's resources that depend on this information, such as links, navigation controls, and search results, to confirm that all the collection's data was correctly updated to the new path. You can also use a URL for an existing site collection, which completely overwrites the existing site collection, but you must use the `Force` parameter to enable this action.

- **Path**. When you're restoring a site collection, this parameter is required and must be a valid UNC or Windows file path to a backup package created via `Backup-SPFarm`.

- **AssignmentCollection**. This is an optional parameter, intended to allow for the proper disposal of objects. Carefully consider using this parameter if your call of `Restore-SPSite` also involves using SharePoint's `SPWeb`, `SPSite`, or `SPSiteAdministration` objects; otherwise, it is not likely to be necessary.

- **HostHeaderWebApplicationURL**. When you're restoring a site collection backup, this parameter is not required. You use it if you want to restore your site collection to a Web application with a different URL than the value specified for the `URL` input parameter. This parameter is explained in more detail later.

- **Confirm**. This is an optional parameter. If it is used with an input value of True, the cmdlet prompts the user to confirm that he wants to proceed with the action. If a value of False is provided, the cmdlet proceeds without prompting for permission once executed. The default value for this parameter is False.

- **ContentDatabase**. This is an optional parameter. If this parameter is used, the site collection is provisioned within the content database matching the value provided. If the parameter is not used, the site collection is automatically placed in the content database with the least number of site collections in it and a status of Ready.

- **Force.** When you're restoring a site collection backup, this switch is not required. Using it instructs `Restore-SPSite` to overwrite any existing site collection matching the value of the `URL` parameter.

- **GradualDelete.** This optional parameter alters the mechanics of the restore operation when you also employ the `Force` parameter. When you execute a site collection restore that overwrites an existing site collection, two sets of operations take place at the database level. The first set of operations entails the deletion of all existing items within the target content database that are tied to the site collection being overwritten. Once the existing site collection data is deleted, the second set of operations that take place involve the actual restoration of the site collection and the insertion of new rows into the content database. Without the use of the `GradualDelete` parameter, the delete and insert operations execute in serial fashion. Because the deletion of existing content throughout the content database can take a significant amount of time, poor performance on restore may result. When you employ the `GradualDelete` parameter, however, the deletion of existing site collection data from the content database is effectively deferred until after the restore operation has taken place. Deferred deletions are handled by a Gradual Site Delete timer job that is established and defaults to running daily for each Web application in the farm. Deferring deletion of site collection content can result in significant performance increases, particularly when a substantial amount of existing site collection content resides in the content database. Using this parameter when overwriting an existing site collection can reduce the performance impact of the operation on the SharePoint servers in your farm, as well as on SQL Server. Microsoft recommends using this parameter when restoring large site collections; we recommend that you test this parameter whenever possible to assess its impact and implications on the usability of a target site collection before using it in a production environment.

- **WhatIf.** This is an optional parameter. It is used with this parameter set in the same way as it is in the first parameter set.

You can use the `HostHeaderWebApplicationURL` parameter to restore a site collection to a URL different from the URL of its parent Web application. If you pass a value of http://bar for the `HostHeaderWebApplicationURL` parameter as an addition to the previous example, the restore operation creates a site collection for the foo address under the bar Web application even though they have different URLs. When it runs the restore operation, `Restore-SPSite` generates a host header for the target Web application in IIS so that requests submitted to the server for http://foo are mapped to the restored site collection even though it is within a Web application with a different URL (http://bar).

SharePoint site collections created using a host header in this fashion are called *host-named site collections*. Unlike normal site collections, host-named site collections use IIS host headers to direct traffic to the correct site collection instead of managed paths. This allows multiple site collections within a single Web application to have a unique URL that can be used to access its content independent of the other site collections in the Web application. Keep in mind that there are some drawbacks to host-named site collections; they are not compatible with alternate access mappings (AAMs) or the use of any zone other than the Default zone, so each site collection can only respond to traffic on a single URL. For more information on host-named site collections and their impact on the architecture and administration of your SharePoint farm, review this article from the Microsoft Knowledge Base: http://technet.microsoft.com/en-us/library/cc424952.aspx.

`Restore-SPSite` also has a second parameter set available for use, although it includes most of the same parameters and options as the first set. This second set allows for more control over what SharePoint content database the site collection is stored in when the cmdlet restores it. The only parameter from the first set not used by the second set is `ContentDatabase`. It is replaced by the two parameters listed next. (All the other parameters from the preceding list above can be used in conjunction with these two parameters as desired.)

- **DatabaseName.** This is an optional parameter. If you use this parameter, the site collection is provisioned within the content database matching the value provided, as long as it is a valid database name. If the parameter is not used, the site collection is automatically placed in the content database with the lowest number of site collections and a status of Ready.

- **DatabaseServer.** This is an optional parameter. It is used to specify the SQL Server instance that contains the database provided by the `DatabaseName` parameter. The value provided for this parameter must be a valid SQL Server instance that the farm can access. Furthermore, a valid value must be provided for the `DatabaseName` parameter for the cmdlet to successfully use this parameter.

Reviewing Your Backup and Restore History

The purpose of the `Get-SPBackupHistory` cmdlet is pretty self-explanatory. It outputs a listing of the `Backup-SPFarm` and `Restore-SPFarm` operations that have been conducted using the files in the specified directory. The `Get-SPBackupHistory` cmdlet uses the `spbrtoc.xml` file stored within the target backup storage directory to determine and display information.

Caution: The `Get-SPBackupHistory` cmdlet can only be used to display information on backups created via the `Backup-SPFarm` cmdlet, restores conducted via the `Restore-SPFarm` cmdlet, or catastrophic operations run using the Central Administration site's backup or restore tools. It does not work for other types of backups, such as site collection backups via `Backup-SPSite`.

A sample `Get-SPBackupHistory` request is listed next:

```
Get-SPBackupHistory -Directory \\backups
```

You can use the following switches and input parameters with the `Get-SPBackupHistory` operation:

- **`Directory`.** This input parameter is required when running `Get-SPBackupHistory`. The same rules apply to this parameter as the `Directory` input parameters for the restore and backup cmdlets discussed earlier.

- **`AssignmentCollection`.** This is an optional parameter, intended to allow for the proper disposal of objects. Consider using this parameter if your call of `Get-SPBackupHistory` also involves using SharePoint's `SPWeb`, `SPSite`, or `SPSiteAdministration` objects; otherwise, it is not likely to be necessary.

- **`ShowBackup`.** This input switch is not required when running `Get-SPBackupHistory`. When used, it filters the output of the operation so that the cmdlet returns only backup operation history data.

- **`ShowRestore`.** This input switch is not required when running `Get-SPBackupHistory`. When used, it filters the output of the operation so that the cmdlet displays only restore operation history data.

Note: If you omit the `Backup` and `Restore` switches from the `Get-SPBackupHistory` request, the cmdlet returns the history data for all backup and restore operations. If you use the `Backup` and `Restore` switches with the `Get-SPBackupHistory` request, the cmdlet returns the history data for all backup and restore operations.

Now that you have successfully run the `Get-SPBackupHistory` cmdlet, let's talk about its output and what you can do with it. A review of its output demonstrates why PowerShell makes command line administration in SharePoint 2010 so much better. Because `Get-SPBackupHistory` returns an array of all backup and restore operations run in the target directory, it provides much more useful and manageable data than what was available with similar commands in previous versions of SharePoint. This means you don't have to transform the cmdlet's output into a useable format first if you want to extract pertinent data from it with a scripted process; it's already in such a format. And thanks to PowerShell's pipelining capabilities, you can do things like pass its output right into a query to select the most recent successful backup, and then pass the `BackupID` for that instance directly to `Restore-SPFarm`. The result: in one line of PowerShell script, you can use `Get-SPBackupHistory` to automatically restore your most recent backup.

Documenting Your Configuration

As hard as it may be to consider such a possibility (especially with the new functionality that has been added to SharePoint 2010 that we've been talking about for the past several pages), there is still a chance that you may not be able to completely and successfully restore your SharePoint 2010 farm to its original state before disaster struck. You could have a backup that failed the night before, a backup set that has become corrupted, or backup files that were deleted or lost altogether. Regardless of what may cause such a situation, it is a good idea to have an idea of how you need to go about reconstructing your SharePoint 2010 environment if you don't have the luxury of restoring its content and configuration from backups. Not to mention, there are items in your SharePoint 2010 farm, such as its service applications, that you may not be able to back up and therefore cannot restore from a backup file.

But the problem is that in most IT systems, the only constant in the environment is change. Because your farm's configuration and setup can be constantly changing and is often being modified by more than one user at once, it becomes important to have an effective change control process in place for your organization to better track, manage, and approve changes to your farm. Not to mention the human factor: it can be all too easy for an administrator to put off documentation or omit key data in documentation. That's understandable; the level of detail that these functions require to properly execute can be daunting at best and insurmountable at worst.

The question becomes this: what do you do to capture that configuration data? We've already covered tools like `Backup-SPFarm` with the `ConfigurationOnly` parameter and SQL Server backups of your configuration database combined with `Backup-SPConfigurationDatabase`. And don't forget to consider other options for preserving your SharePoint farm's configuration information, like querying the Windows Event logs, IIS logs, SharePoint logs, and scripting queries against Windows Management Instrumentation (WMI) objects within your farm's servers. Microsoft also has configuration management tools in the System Center suite, such as Configuration Manager and Service Manager, that you can use to control and track changes you make in your farm.

Another one of those things we love about PowerShell is that its 2.0 version also offers a cmdlet designed to help you mitigate the risk of change, which offers an additional approach for recording details about how your farm is configured: `Export-Clixml`. `Export-Clixml` converts any objects (such as PowerShell objects) into XML and stores that XML data in a file. The cmdlet also provides several options for use, such as the ability to identify how deeply into the object the conversion process should go. (The default is two; deciding how many levels of data from within another object can be time-consuming.)

The ability of the `Export-Clixml` cmdlet to transform objects into XML documents means that you can take the output of any SharePoint 2010 cmdlet and convert it into a static text document that lists the current state and configuration of many important facets of your SharePoint 2010 farm. For example, you can pipe the results of `Get-SPWebApplication` to `Export-Clixml` to create a complete list of your farm's Web applications, or you can convert the output of `Get-SPFarm` and `Get-SPFarmConfig` to obtain detailed data about your entire SharePoint 2010 farm and its configuration.

The major drawback to this solution is that it is all documentation; you cannot restore its output to another SharePoint 2010 farm in the event of a disaster. Instead, you must use the data created by these cmdlets as a point of reference, with the intention of manually re-creating your farm's setup and configuration in a new SharePoint 2010 farm. Keep in mind, though, that any effort you make to gather more point-in-time data about the configuration and setup of your farm can greatly improve your ability to not just get SharePoint back up and running after a disaster but return it to a state as close to its condition prior to the disaster as possible. For more information on `Export-Clixml` and an effective example of how to use it in a script to completely document the configuration of your farm, take a look at http://technet.microsoft.com/en-us/library/ff645391.aspx.

Granular Backup and Restore via PowerShell

In Chapter 9, we introduced the concept of granular backup and restore: export and import functionality that you can use to protect individual subsites (also known as *webs* in the Share-Point object model) and lists (such as document libraries, form libraries, announcements lists, or custom lists) through the SharePoint Central Administration site. Similar functionality is also available through the SharePoint 2010 Management Console's PowerShell cmdlets, allowing those items to be protected via scripted or manual use of those cmdlets. Keep in mind that, like the Central Administration site's granular backup and restore tools, these cmdlets do not protect their targeted SharePoint components as completely as the backup and restore cmdlets we have discussed in this chapter. The information we've already provided in Chapter 9 covers these differences nicely and goes into excellent detail about the uses of and purposes for these cmdlets. We recommend reviewing that chapter if you need a refresher on the matter. The following sections contain specific information and instructions for using each of these export and import cmdlets.

Export-SPWeb

The `Export-SPWeb` cmdlet exports the contents of a web or list within a web to one or more files, as shown in the example that follows:

```
Export-SPWeb –Identity http://foo/sites/bar/site1 -Path c:\backups\site1.cmp
```

If you want to script a call of `Export-SPWeb`, especially if you want to protect multiple webs at once, the approach you'll be most likely to take is going to be similar to what we've outlined previously in the section on `Backup-SPSite`. The difference is that you're not quite done once you've arrived at one or more target site collections; you still need to select the desired webs within those site collections with the `Get-SPWeb` cmdlet. Once you've selected the correct webs with `Get-SPWeb`, you can pass that array of webs to `Export-SPWeb` for a granular backup. Following is an example of how to accomplish this:

```
Get-SPWebApplication -identity $URL | Get-SPSite -filter {$_.Owner = $siteOwner} | Get-SPWeb | Export-SPWeb -path $backupStorage
```

The items in the list that follow describe the various parameters that can be used to call `Export-SPWeb` to export or create a granular backup of a SharePoint site, one or all of its subsites, or a list within a site:

- **Identity.** When you export a web or a list within a web, this parameter is required and must be a valid URL or GUID for the target item.

- **Path.** When you export a web or a list within a web, this parameter is required and must be a valid UNC or Windows directory path to a file that the backup is saved in. The account logged into the SharePoint 2010 Management Shell must have permission to write to the directory specified for this input.

- **AssignmentCollection.** This is an optional parameter, intended to allow for the proper disposal of objects. Carefully consider using this parameter if your call of `Export-SPWeb` also involves using SharePoint's `SPWeb`, `SPSite`, or `SPSiteAdministration` objects; otherwise, it is not likely to be necessary.

- **CompressionSize.** This parameter is not required. If used, it indicates the maximum size that the compressed export files are allowed to be created to and allows you to set a preferred target size for the CAB files (typically saved as files with a `.cmp` extension) created by the operation. If the total size of the export is greater than that amount, it is automatically broken into multiple files.

- **Confirm.** This is an optional parameter. If this parameter is used with an input value of True, the cmdlet prompts the user to confirm that he wants to proceed with the action. If a value of False is provided, the cmdlet proceeds without prompting for permission once executed. The default value for this parameter is False.

- **Force.** This is an optional parameter that does not actually require an input value to be provided for it. If this switch is not used, the cmdlet does not proceed with the backup operation if it estimates that there is not enough disk space available to store the backup. If it is used, that check is overridden, and the backup is executed regardless of how much storage is available.

- **Item.** This parameter is not required. It sets the URL of the Web application, GUID, or object to be exported and must be a valid SharePoint URL within the farm. When using this parameter, the full address of the target item is not required. For example, if you are targeting the subsite bar within the http://foo site collection, you would provide /bar for this parameter. Targeting the Calendar list within that bar subsite would be /bar/Lists/Calendar. Of course, you could also use the GUID for each of these items to specify them.

- **HaltOnError.** This input parameter is not required; if it is included, the export process is stopped and not completed if errors are encountered.

- **HaltOnWarning.** This input parameter is not required; if it is included, the export process is stopped and not completed if warnings are encountered.

- **IncludeUserSecurity.** This input parameter is not required; if it is included, the export process includes the user security settings of the targeted item in the export files.

- **IncludeVersions.** This input parameter is not required; if it is included, the export process includes the versioning data of the targeted item in the export files based on the type of file or list item history provided as a parameter. If no value is provided for this parameter, a default value of 1 is used to export the target's last major version, which can also be targeted with a value of LastMajor. You can use this parameter to target the most current version (major or minor) using a value of CurrentVersion or 2, both the last major and minor versions for the item with a value of LastMajorandMinor or 3, or all versions for the targeted item with a value of All or 4.

- **NoFileCompression.** This input parameter is not required; if it is included, the export process does not compress the export files it creates. Using this parameter does create a simple problem if you do not direct the export to its own directory. Because the files are not compressed, they are not contained in a CAB file. For performance reasons, Microsoft recommends compressing the export files; their research shows that compression reduces the completion time for export processes by up to 30 percent. If this parameter is used during an export operation, it must also be used during an import operation using the export files it creates.

- **NoLogFile.** This input parameter is not required; if it is included, the export process does not create a log file for the export process. It should only be used to improve performance of the export process in extreme conditions; in most circumstances, a log file is desired for export operations.

- **UseSQLSnapshot.** This input parameter is not required; when you use it, Export-SPWeb creates a SQL Server database snapshot of the content database containing the targeted item. The export is created by referencing the snapshot rather than the database. Once the export is completed, the cmdlet deletes the database snapshot. You can only use this parameter if your SQL Server instance supports the creation of database snapshots. That's why it is important to review your SQL Server edition prior to using it. If your instance does support snapshots, this parameter is recommended because, unlike Backup-SPSite, the targeted site collection is not automatically locked during the operation. Unless you manually take action to set the target to read only, your users can modify it during the export process. Because the cmdlet is reading from the snapshot and not the database, there is a drastically reduced chance of resource contention between it and the activities of your users.

- **WhatIf.** This is an optional parameter. If you use this parameter, PowerShell displays a message stating what the outcome of running the cmdlet will be, but the cmdlet itself is not executed. This can be helpful when testing scripts, allowing you to verify that you can provide the correct set of inputs and parameters to the cmdlet.

Tip: There are several other SharePoint 2010 cmdlets designed to export data out of a specific area of aspect of a farm that you may want to evaluate and test for use within your farm. Many of these cmdlets are intended to protect specific service applications or functionality that is available only in SharePoint Server 2010, which can limit their scope and usefulness depending on what version of SharePoint 2010 you're using and what you've chosen to implement and enable within your farm. These cmdlets include, but are not limited to, `Export-SPBusinessDataCatalogModel`, `Export-SPBusinessDataCatalogPartitionData`, `Export-SPEnterpriseSearchTopology`, `Export-SPInfoPathAdministration-Files`, `Export-SPMetadataWebServicePartitionData`, `Export-SPProfileService-ApplicationTenant`, and `Export-SPSiteSubscriptionSettings`.

Import-SPWeb

`Import-SPWeb` is the flip side of the `Export-SPWeb`'s coin; it imports the contents of exports created with `Export-SPWeb` back into a SharePoint 2010 environment. The example that follows shows an import operation that imports both the content and the version data contained in the export file and overwrites any SharePoint content already existing in the target location:

```
Import-SPWeb –Identity http://foo/sites/bar/site1 -Path c:\backups\site1.cmp
-UpdateVersions -Overwrite
```

The items in the following list describe the various parameters that can be used to call `Import-SPWeb` to import or restore a granular backup of a SharePoint subsite or list:

- **`Identity`**. When you import a web or a list within a web, this parameter is required and must be a valid URL or GUID for the target item that the export is imported into.

- **`Path`**. When you import a web or a list within a web, this parameter is required and must be a valid UNC or Windows directory path to the file or files to be imported. The account logged into the SharePoint 2010 Management Shell must have permission to read to the directory specified for this input.

- **`AssignmentCollection`**. This is an optional parameter, intended to allow for the proper disposal of objects. Carefully consider using this parameter if your call of `Import-SPWeb` also involves using SharePoint's `SPWeb`, `SPSite`, or `SPSiteAdministration` objects; otherwise, it is not likely to be necessary.

- **`ActivateSolutions`**. This parameter is not required. If used, it indicates that any user solutions should be activated as part of the import process.

- **Confirm.** This is an optional parameter. If this parameter is used with an input value of True, the cmdlet prompts the user to confirm that he wants to proceed with the action. If a value of False is provided, the cmdlet proceeds without prompting for permission once executed. The default value for this parameter is False.

- **Force.** This is an optional parameter that does not actually require an input value to be provided for it. Using it instructs `Import-SPWeb` to overwrite any existing item matching the value of the `Identity` parameter.

- **HaltOnError.** This input parameter is not required; if it is included, the import process is stopped and not completed if errors are encountered.

- **HaltOnWarning.** This input parameter is not required; if it is included, the import process is stopped and not completed if warnings are encountered.

- **IncludeUserCustomAction.** This input parameter is not required; if it is included, the import process includes the user custom actions of the targeted item in the import files.

- **IncludeUserSecurity.** This input parameter is not required; if it is included, the import process includes the user security settings of the targeted item in the import files.

- **UpdateVersions.** This input parameter is not required; if it is included, the import process uses it to determine how version data in the imported file is integrated into existing versions in the target item. If no value is provided for this parameter, a default value of 1 is used to import the version data as a new version, which can also be accomplished with a value of Append. You can also use this parameter to overwrite the target item with a value of Overwrite and all its existing versions with the newly imported item, or you can ignore any existing files in the targeted location with a value of Ignore.

- **NoFileCompression.** This input parameter is not required; if it is included, the import process does not compress the import files it creates. For performance reasons, Microsoft recommends compressing the import files. Their research shows that it reduces the completion time for import processes by up to 30 percent. If you use this parameter during an export operation, you must also use it during any import operation using the export files it creates.

- **NoLogFile.** This input parameter is not required; if it is included, the import process does not create a log file for the import process. It should only be used to improve performance of the import process in extreme conditions; in most circumstances, a log file is desired for import operations.

- **WhatIf.** This is an optional parameter. If you use this parameter, PowerShell displays a message stating what the outcome of running the cmdlet will be, but the cmdlet is not executed. This can be helpful when testing scripts, allowing you to verify that you can provide the correct set of inputs and parameters to the cmdlet.

Tip: Just like `Export-SPWeb`, there are several other SharePoint 2010 cmdlets that can import previously exported data into a specific area of aspect of a farm that you may want to evaluate and test for use within your farm. These cmdlets include, but are not limited to, `Import-SPBusinessDataCatalogModel`, `Import-SPBusinessDataCatalogPartitionData`, `Import-SPEnterpriseSearchTopology`, `Import-SPInfoPathAdministrationFiles`, `Import-SPMetadataWebServicePartitionData`, `Import-SPProfileServiceApplicationTenant`, and `Import-SPSiteSubscriptionSettings`.

Conclusion

SharePoint 2010's backup and restore PowerShell cmdlets are versatile tools. They can cover your entire farm down to units as small as the contents of a list and most of the configuration data for that list, and they can tailor your requests to meet your specific requirements. If you are an administrator who prefers using the command line and scripting to manage SharePoint over graphical tools, these cmdlets should certainly appeal to you. But they are not the only tools you need to preserve and recover from your SharePoint environment in the case of a disaster.

On its own, SharePoint 2010's backup and restore cmdlets, like the Central Administration site backup and restore tools, provide you the most benefits when used before you modify your SharePoint environment. The tool allows you to submit just a single administrative operation at a time and runs it immediately, so you have to know when you are going to need it before you run it, and you cannot schedule a backup or restore to run in the future. By itself, PowerShell does not provide options to schedule a regularly repeated operation, such as a nightly run of the backup operation, but that does not mean such an activity is not possible.

Because PowerShell is a command line shell, you can create a Windows scheduled task on your server that submits a request to run a scripted PowerShell backup operation on a defined regular basis, allowing you to incorporate programming logic and additional operations into your request. SharePoint 2010's backup and restore cmdlets share some other common drawbacks with the Central Administration's tool. As previously mentioned in this chapter, you cannot completely back up components smaller than a site collection. The export and import operations allow you to migrate the contents of subsites and lists as needed, but they do not constitute a full-fledged backup option. The backup and restore cmdlets covered in this chapter do not allow you to manage the backup files they create. Therefore, if you are not careful about monitoring and managing the disk space that your storage location uses, you could run out of room to store your crucial files or end up retaining backups that have gone stale and are no longer relevant.

Now that you have seen SharePoint 2010's PowerShell cmdlets related to backing up and restoring your SharePoint environment, you should be able to answer the following questions about their capabilities. You can find the answers to these questions in Appendix A, "Chapter Review Q&A," found on the Cengage Learning Web site at http://www.courseptr.com/downloads.

1. What are the two ways to back up a farm's configuration data independent of its content?

2. What cmdlet should you use to back up the configuration data of a farm that the server hosting the cmdlet is not attached to, and what parameters should you use to target that remote farm?

3. What aspects of a SharePoint 2010 farm are not included in a configuration-only backup?

4. What SharePoint 2010 cmdlet can you use to view the history of all backup and restore operations that have been executed using the files in a targeted directory?

5. What are the benefits of using the `UseSQLSnapshot` parameter for the `Export-SPWeb` cmdlet?

SharePoint 2010 Disaster Recovery Development

In This Chapter

- Hey Administrator—I'm Talkin' to You!

- The SharePoint Object Model

- Volume Shadow Copy Service

- Rolling Your Own Backup and Restore Approach

- Designing Applications for Disaster Recovery Readiness

In a book that approaches SharePoint disaster recovery with a strong eye toward infrastructure administration and operations, it may seem surprising to find this chapter nestled among discussions on topics such as SQL Server high availability, SharePoint server farm architectures, and the most appropriate backup mechanism to support a given disaster recovery strategy. Furthermore, many are of the opinion that custom development and infrastructure activities mix about as well as oil and water. This book adopts a more holistic view.

As far as Web-based platforms go, SharePoint is a behemoth. Much like the Roman Empire in 117 A.D., SharePoint reaches to all corners of the technological landscape. To leverage SharePoint to greatest effect, you must figuratively wear many hats and have a multidisciplinary understanding of the platform. Cultivating a healthy respect and some degree of skill in a variety of disciplines such as networking, server management, database technologies, and custom development is essential. Custom development is the primary focus of this chapter.

Hey Administrator—I'm Talkin' to You!

This probably doesn't surprise you, but we assume that you are more likely an administrator or a disaster recovery architect than a developer. We expect some developers to pick up this book and take an interest in this chapter, but they are probably in the minority.

Based on that rough demographic breakdown, you might be one of the many thinking, "Okay, so I'm a SharePoint administrator. I'm not a developer. Why should I even bother with this chapter?" If that's what you are thinking, then pull out a ruler, rap yourself across the knuckles, and re-read Chapter 10, "SharePoint 2010 Command Line Backup and Restore: PowerShell."

PowerShell is here, and it is a game changer. With the proliferation of PowerShell throughout SharePoint and many of Microsoft's other server platforms, the once clear line of separation between administrators and developers has become exceptionally blurry. For most practical purposes, it can even be said that the line is gone altogether.

The Dark Days Before PowerShell

Before PowerShell, there were a significant number of administrative tasks that could only be accomplished through custom code. Many of the tasks weren't particularly difficult or involved; they just couldn't be performed without the help of a developer. If STSADM.exe didn't include support for the task to be accomplished, you were out of luck. SharePoint veteran administrators may remember the days of seeking a developer's help to write small console applications to make seemingly simple changes to site collections, Web applications, the SharePoint farm, and other aspects of their SharePoint environments.

For example, SharePoint 2007 provided a mechanism (which is still present in SharePoint 2010) that allowed a Web application to return a custom HTML page when a user received an HTTP 404 error for requesting a page that couldn't be found. Configuring a Web application to use a custom 404 page was as straightforward as setting the `FileNotFoundPage` property on a target Web application. Unfortunately, there was no simple way for an administrator to do this. In fact, Microsoft wrote a support article (http://support.microsoft.com/kb/941329) that described the creation of a command line application just to make the change. The application that resulted from carrying out the steps in the support article worked as advertised, but it forced administrators to enlist a developer to make what should have been a basic administrative change.

Administrative Capabilities with PowerShell

With the arrival of PowerShell on the scene, the single-use command line applications just described have become largely a thing of the past. For example, suppose you want to specify a single custom 404 page called `Custom404.htm` for all Web applications in your farm where an error page hadn't yet been assigned. Instead of creating a command line application as described in the Microsoft support article, you could simply open the SharePoint 2010 Management Shell and execute the following sequence of PowerShell commands:

```
Get-SPWebApplication | Where-Object {$_.FileNotFoundPage -eq $NULL} | ForEach-Object
{$_.FileNotFoundPage = "Custom404.htm"; $_.Update()}
```

That's it. Executing one continuous sequence of PowerShell commands assigns `Custom404.htm` for use by all Web applications that don't have a custom "file not found" error page assigned to them.

Observant readers may recognize the new `Get-SPWebApplication` PowerShell cmdlet from Chapter 10. The `FileNotFoundPage` property, though, isn't one you can easily find in Share-Point's PowerShell cmdlet documentation. The property is one of many that are readily available for use, though, provided you understand a bit about the SharePoint object model.

Although the SharePoint application programming interface (API) is where developers spend quite a bit of their time, administrators can still leverage the API as needed. With PowerShell, you have complete access to all the methods and properties that are exposed by each of the types in the SharePoint object model and the .NET Framework. The new SharePoint 2010 PowerShell cmdlets expose some of the more useful types, methods, and properties for you to use, but they don't cover everything. There is far more for you to exploit if you're willing to spend some time getting your hands dirty in the SharePoint object model.

The tasks that you can tackle with PowerShell are expansive provided you understand a little bit about development, object models, and how all the associated pieces fit together. This chapter provides you with the overview you need for employing disaster recovery–related types and operations in your custom scripts or applications for SharePoint.

To quote Lenny Nero from the movie *Strange Days*: "Are you beginning to see the possibilities here?"

The Disclaimer

As the cover states, this is a book about SharePoint disaster recovery. It is not a book that is dedicated to covering all the many facets of SharePoint development. Much as other books cover the topic of disaster recovery in a section or chapter, so too does this book cover custom development and associated concerns.

There is a limit to the amount of information and guidance that can be presented in one chapter, so a conscious decision was made to steer clear of general development topics and instead stay focused on those aspects of the SharePoint object model that are most applicable to the topic of disaster recovery. In addition, patterns and technologies that can be leveraged directly for disaster recovery purposes are covered where appropriate. Some topics are also discussed in a restricted fashion to simply provide an awareness of options available to you. These topics, although relevant to disaster recovery application design, are simply too complex or deep to cover in depth given chapter size and time constraints.

Source code and scripts are provided only insofar as is expedient and needed to illustrate a concept or point. General best practices for SharePoint development, such as the use of Features to deploy code, the packaging of components into SharePoint Solution Packages (also known by their file extension as `.wsp` files), and which objects should and should not be explicitly disposed of, are absent from this chapter. These practices still apply; they simply aren't discussed. Many good books cover these topics in detail. If you're serious about SharePoint development, buy one of them.

The Price of Admission

The screenshots, examples, and code samples in this chapter were put together in a testing environment with the following software and configuration. Depending on how your environment is configured, your experiences may vary slightly.

- **Operating system.** Microsoft Windows Server 2008 R2 Enterprise Edition (build 7600)

- **Database.** Microsoft SQL Server 2008 R2 Enterprise Edition (build 10.50.1600.1)

- **Web server.** Microsoft Internet Information Services (IIS) 7.5

- **Client Web browser.** Internet Explorer 8 (version 8.0.7600.16385)

- **Development environment.** Visual Studio 2010 Ultimate (version 10.0.30319.1 RTMRel)

- **SharePoint.** SharePoint Server 2010 RTM with Enterprise Client Access License (build 4763)

In addition to an environment that can be used for development and testing, we recommend that you equip yourself with a reference to the SharePoint 2010 API. Microsoft maintains an online version of the SharePoint software development kit (SDK) that is appropriate for this purpose, and it publishes a downloadable version of the SDK that is periodically updated. You can access both the online and downloadable versions of the SDK through Microsoft's SharePoint Developer Center at http://msdn.microsoft.com/en-us/sharepoint/default.aspx.

The SharePoint Object Model

Despite SharePoint's wealth of tools and functionality, there is still more that you can do to enhance and extend its feature set. Luckily, SharePoint 2010 is nothing if not extensible. Although both SharePoint Foundation 2010 and SharePoint Server 2010 offer ample features and capabilities, it's fairly common to work with the platform and after a while wish that it did "just this one thing" differently or that it took certain capabilities a bit further than it does. If your disaster recovery needs are not met by SharePoint's out-of-the-box feature set and you're in the realm of thinking about how a particular feature could be made better, custom development options are probably worth exploring.

This section explores some of the more logical disaster recovery extension points for the SharePoint object model and how you might utilize them. This chapter employs numerous domain-specific concepts and a significant degree of development terminology, so some fluency with .NET development, object model hierarchies, and object-oriented programming is a definite plus. Even without this knowledge, though, there is content in each section that can boost your understanding of how SharePoint carries out its backup/recovery and export/import operations.

Extending Catastrophic Backup and Restore Through the SharePoint API

When you are interested in working with farm-level backup and recovery operations, the most logical place to focus your attention is on SharePoint's catastrophic backup and restore types. Catastrophic backup and restore operations focus on the components of a SharePoint farm that reside at the content database level and higher in SharePoint's logical hierarchy. This includes the farm itself, Service Applications, Web applications, and additional objects that are either associated with or the direct children of these components.

The Central Administration site exposes an interface to these types through its Farm Backup and Restore functions. SharePoint 2010 also exposes these types through a variety of cmdlets such as `Backup-SPFarm`, `Restore-SPFarm`, `Get-SPBackupHistory`, `Backup-SPConfigurationDatabase`, and several others.

SPBackupRestoreConsole and Related Types

When SharePoint backups are configured and executed, whether through PowerShell or the Central Administration site, they leverage the `SPBackupRestoreConsole` class within the SharePoint object model and the types with which it is associated. Custom applications seeking to orchestrate backup and restore operations for SharePoint direct most of their calls through the `SPBackupRestoreConsole` class in some fashion.

Although not a true static class, `SPBackupRestoreConsole` largely behaves like one. Only one instance of the class exists at any given time within the scope of the SharePoint farm, and the bulk of its members and properties are static. Backup and restore operations, job history operations, and informational requests such as the amount of disk space a particular backup operation may consume all begin with calls to the `SPBackupRestoreConsole`.

You can find the `SPBackupRestoreConsole` and primary related types in the `Microsoft.SharePoint.Admininstration.Backup` namespace within the `Microsoft.SharePoint.dll` assembly. The relationship of key types within the namespace to one another is represented by the Unified Modeling Language (UML) diagram shown in Figure 11.1.

The circled numbers within the diagram represent several types, patterns, and interactions worthy of mention:

1. As mentioned, the `SPBackupRestoreConsole` type is the entry point into catastrophic backup and restore operations originating at the SharePoint farm level. With methods such as `CreateBackupRestore`, `DiskSizeRequired`, `GetHistory`, and `Run`, `SPBackupRestoreConsole` is capable of queuing, monitoring, and directing all farm and component-level catastrophic backup and restore activities.

2. One or more `SPBackupRestoreHistoryObject` instances can be retrieved via call to the `GetHistory` method on the `SPBackupRestoreConsole`. Objects of this type provide all

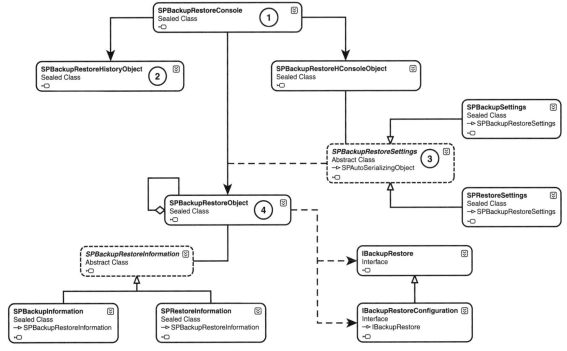

Figure 11.1   Relationships between the SPBackupRestoreConsole and associated types.

the information needed to determine if a backup succeeded or failed, when it was attempted, who initiated it, and more.

3.   The preparation for actual backup or restore operations typically employs a derived type from the SPBackupRestoreSettings abstract class (SPBackupSettings and SPRestoreSettings for a backup or restore, respectively) and an SPBackupRestore-ConsoleObject instance. Generally speaking, you prepare an instance of the appropriate SPBackupRestoreSettings subclass to identify the location and type of backup or restore to be performed. Execution of the CreateBackupRestore method on the SPBackupRestoreConsole returns a globally unique identifier (GUID) that can be used for the bulk of the remaining backup, restore, querying, and related operations. Since the SPBackupRestoreConsole only processes one backup or restore at a time, the GUID serves as the identifier needed to direct the SPBackupRestoreConsole to act on the associated SPBackupRestoreConsoleObject instance.

4.   Instances of SPBackupRestoreObject are composite objects that identify a particular item for backup or restore (such as a Service Application or a content database) and possibly reference children (also SPBackupRestoreObject types) that are below them within the backup/restore hierarchy. One root SPBackupRestoreObject exists

representing the entire farm, and a number of subordinate SPBackupRestoreObject instances represent the child components that are selectable for backup or restore, such as Web applications, services, and so on. The hierarchy represented by the collection of composite SPBackupRestoreObject instances reflects the farm's catastrophic component backup and restore hierarchy.

An example demonstrating the basics of how to orchestrate a full-farm catastrophic backup using the types and techniques described appears in Listing 11.1. Although functional, the example is just a starting point and omits a number of steps such as backup location free space checking, subfarm component selection, and other items that are important in a production implementation.

Note: The code shown in Listing 11.1 assumes that the Microsoft.SharePoint.dll assembly is referenced and that the Microsoft.SharePoint.Administration. Backup namespace has been imported for use by the ExecuteFarmBackup method. In addition, the Visual Studio project containing the ExecuteFarmBackup method should be configured to target the .NET Framework 3.5 on an x64 platform.

Listing 11.1

```
public static void ExecuteFarmBackup()
{
    // They are set through code in this example, but normally you should give
    // users the option to specify the backup location and method (whether full
    // or differential).
    String BACKUP_LOCATION = @"\\BackupHost\SPFarmBackups\";
    String BACKUP_METHOD = SPBackupMethodType.Full.ToString();

    // This creates a usable set of backup settings needed to get a backup operation
    // going. The resultant settings object is a combination of the assigned
    // values for location and method plus default values for backup thread
    // count, content + configuration backup, and so on.
    SPBackupSettings backupSettings = SPBackupRestoreSettings.GetBackupSettings
        (BACKUP_LOCATION, BACKUP_METHOD);

    // Actually create (but don't start) the backup job. This registers the job with
    // the SPBackupRestoreConsole. Future references to the job are done using the
    // GUID that is returned.
    Guid backupGuid = SPBackupRestoreConsole.CreateBackupRestore(backupSettings);
```

```
try
{
    // The SPBackupRestoreConsole can execute only one job at a time, so
    // this call is a way of bringing the SPBackupRestoreConsole to focus
    // on the new backup job. If another job is running, the call fails
    // and an exception is thrown.
    if (!SPBackupRestoreConsole.SetActive(backupGuid))
    {
        throw new Exception("Backup or restore already in progress.");
    }

    // Actually execute a full-farm backup synchronously. The call won't
    // return until the backup is complete.
    if (!SPBackupRestoreConsole.Run(backupGuid, null))
    {
        throw new Exception("Full farm backup failed. Check spbackup.log.");
    }
}

finally
{
    // The backup job completed in some form, so the associated job GUID should
    // be removed for "good SharePoint hygiene."
    SPBackupRestoreConsole.Remove(backupGuid);
}
}
```

It's worth explicitly stating that the full-farm catastrophic backup set that is the output of this backup code sample is completely interoperable with both Central Administration's farm-level restore capabilities and SharePoint's Restore-SPFarm PowerShell cmdlet.

One potential application that might leverage this portion of the SharePoint object model jumps out immediately: a new user interface (UI) for SharePoint's catastrophic backup and restore operations. Although the Central Administration site and PowerShell cmdlets provide mechanisms for full farm backups and restores, they are limited in both their UI and reporting. You could develop an application that delivers a rich user experience and does significantly more monitoring and reporting than the built-in tools. Such an application could also offer greater control and access to reports regarding previous backup and restore attempts. In addition, the hypothetical application could interface with scheduling systems such as Windows Task Scheduler to manage scheduled farm backups that operate outside the realm of SharePoint. In essence, you could create a more robust, more interactive experience for farm-level SharePoint backups and restores.

Content Components and Implementing IBackupRestore

By default, SharePoint is capable of backing up and restoring a variety of component types: entire farms, Service Applications, Web applications, and more. Each of these objects that can be backed up and restored is known as a *content component* and is represented by an `SPBackupRestoreObject` instance, as shown in Figure 11.1.

As shown in Figure 11.1, an `SPBackupRestoreObject` content component references additional types that drive its backup and restore behavior. One required type in all cases is an object that derives from the abstract `SPBackupRestoreInformation` class—either an `SPBackupInformation` instance or an `SPRestoreInformation` instance. Both of these types convey information about the backup or restore that is being conducted, such as the backup location that is in use, the parent of the current content component (an `SPBackupRestoreObject` instance itself), and other relevant properties. The information in these `SPBackupRestoreInformation`-derived objects provides the content component with the data it needs to understand and properly carry out the requested backup or restore operation.

The second object that an `SPBackupRestoreObject` references is another object that implements the `IBackupRestore` interface. This `IBackupRestore` implementer contains the custom code that is executed during the various stages of both the backup and restore life cycles for the content component. In the case of a backup, for instance, the object must provide implementation logic for methods such as `OnPrepareBackup`, `AddBackupObjects`, and `OnBackup`.

Under normal operations, a one-to-one mapping exists between a derived type of the `SPBackupRestoreInformation` class and an associated `IBackupRestore` implementation for any given `SPBackupRestoreObject`. Because both `SPBackupInformation` and `SPRestoreInformation` are sealed types, and the `SPBackupRestoreObject` itself is a sealed type, your ability to customize and extend the backup and restore capabilities of SharePoint to include custom objects lies with the `IBackupRestore` interface and types that implement it.

To understand how this could be useful, consider a couple of examples:

- **`Web.config` files.** As discussed in Chapter 5, "Windows Server 2008 Backup and Restore," you must implement a strategy for the backup and restore of critical system files alongside SharePoint's own backup and restore mechanisms to ensure complete coverage of all critical and dependent SharePoint farm targets. `Web.config` files are so closely tied to SharePoint Web applications that many would prefer a mechanism that couples `web.config` files to their Web applications when SharePoint backup and restore operations are performed.

- **Associated databases.** In some environments, it is not uncommon to find additional SQL Server databases that are both used by SharePoint and housed in the SQL Server instances supporting SharePoint. Such databases could be critical to some facet of farm operations, but custom databases (that is, those that are not SharePoint content databases) are not included within SharePoint's backup and restore operations by default.

In both of the examples just cited, creation of a content component that implements `IBackup-Restore` can be an avenue to the inclusion of the desired items (`web.config` files and custom databases) in SharePoint's catastrophic backup and restore operations.

Creation of types that implement `IBackupRestore` is an involved process that goes significantly deeper than this chapter is able to cover in a step-by-step fashion. Microsoft provides an informative walk-through on the creation of these types in the SharePoint Foundation 2010 SDK, though. Look for the "How to: Create a Content Class That Can Be Backed Up and Restored" section in either the online or downloadable version of the SDK for more information.

Configuration-Only Backup and Restore

New to SharePoint 2010 is the concept of configuration-only backup and restore. In essence, this process allows you to capture the portable configuration and settings that are present in one farm and apply them in another farm as a sort of template. Technically, a configuration-only restore can also be performed to the same farm from which the backup was performed to roll back affected settings to an earlier point in time.

From a development standpoint, the creation of types that support configuration-only backup and restore is similar to the creation of custom content components for backup and restore. Much like the creation of a custom content component, an `SPBackupRestoreObject` and an `SPBackupRestoreInformation`-derived type are in play when a custom configuration component is backed up and restored. As you might guess from looking at Figure 11.1, the major difference rests with the `IBackupRestoreConfiguration` interface.

Custom configuration components implement the `IBackupRestoreConfiguration` interface instead of the `IBackupRestore` interface, and it is through the `CanBackupRestoreAsConfiguration` property on the interface that they signal their ability to participate in configuration-only backup and restore operations.

Classes that implement `IBackupRestoreConfiguration` must represent truly portable configuration data and other information that is not specific to a particular server, farm topology, or other similar aspect of a SharePoint environment. In addition, even though `IBackupRestoreConfiguration` implementers participate in both configuration-only and standard configuration-with-content backups and restores, they themselves must not contain anything that represents farm content, such as site collections, lists, list items, supplemental databases, nonconfiguration files, and so on.

The Special Case of Web Service Applications

Web Service Applications (derived from `SPIisWebServiceApplication`) and Web Service Application proxies (derived from `SPIisWebServiceApplicationProxy`) are new to SharePoint

2010 and represent a special case when it comes to catastrophic backup and restore. Support for backup and restore operations isn't supplied by the standard catastrophic types that reside in the `Microsoft.SharePoint.Administration.Backup` namespace, but rather through a few specific types in the `Microsoft.SharePoint.Administration` namespace that are part of the Service Application Framework.

Note: The Service Application Framework does not participate in configuration-only backups and restores—only content-plus-configuration backup and restore operations.

If you create your own Web Service Applications and proxies and want to include them in backup and restore operations, know that the creators of the Service Application Framework have already done most of the heavy lifting for you. Unlike the process of implementing the `IBackupRestore` interface for custom content components, Web Service Applications and their proxies can be included in backup and restore operations with the assignment of one of the following attributes at the application class level:

- `IisWebServiceApplicationBackupBehaviorAttribute` for Web Service Applications
- `IisWebServiceApplicationProxyBackupBehaviorAttribute` for Web Service Application proxies

When you use these attributes, the Service Application Framework automatically takes care of backing up and restoring the following resource types that are tied to your Web Service Applications and proxies:

- Persisted objects
- Platform-level access control lists
- Service endpoints
- Associated application pools
- Topology service-based load balancers
- Databases and round-robin load balancers referenced through `SPDatabase`-derived classes

If your Web Service Applications or proxies maintain custom resources that should be backed up and restored, such as load balancers that don't derive from the `SPDatabase` type, you need to do some custom coding. Neither the `IisWebServiceApplicationBackupBehaviorAttribute` nor the `IisWebServiceApplicationProxyBackupBehaviorAttribute` type is sealed, and you can extend them to support the inclusion of custom resources in the backup and restore process.

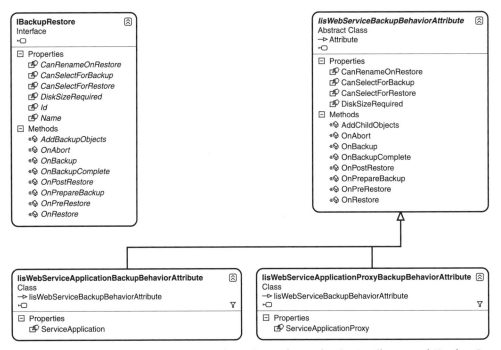

Figure 11.2   Similarities between IisWebServiceBackupBehaviorAttribute and IBackupRestore.

Both of these attributes derive from the IisWebServiceBackupBehaviorAttribute abstract type. As shown in Figure 11.2, the IisWebServiceBackupBehaviorAttribute includes many of the methods and properties that the IBackupRestore interface uses for custom content component protection. When you execute backups and restores, interactions with protected Web Service Applications and proxies occur in much the same way that custom content components are engaged through the IBackupRestore interface.

It is worth noting that backups for Web Service Applications and proxies are supported by Microsoft only when they're done through the use of the IisWebServiceApplicationBackup-BehaviorAttribute and IisWebServiceApplicationProxyBackupBehaviorAttribute attributes. It is only through the use of these attributes that certain elements, such as service-related application pools, can be properly backed up and restored.

Export, Import, and Associated Types

Catastrophic backup and restore types aren't the only options available to you when you're trying to capture SharePoint data programmatically. Export and import types are also available, but they operate in a significantly different fashion.

The Content Deployment API

SharePoint's Content Deployment API, also known as the PRIME API (internally at Microsoft), offers another set of tools and approaches for preserving and migrating SharePoint content and

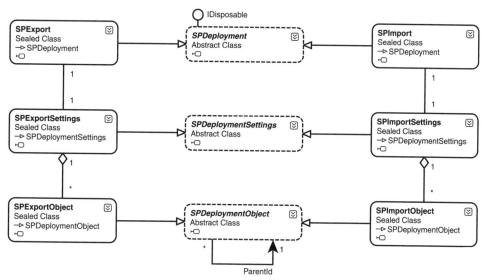

Figure 11.3 Relationships between key Content Deployment types.

structure. The bulk of the Content Deployment API types live in the `Microsoft.SharePoint.Deployment` namespace. The UML shown in Figure 11.3 represents the key types within the namespace:

Out of the box, the SharePoint platform leverages the Content Deployment API in different ways and areas. Here are just a few:

- **PowerShell.** Both the `Export-SPWeb` and `Import-SPWeb` cmdlets leverage the Content Deployment API to carry out their export and import operations.

- **SharePoint Server Content Deployment.** Available as a feature within SharePoint Server (not SharePoint Foundation), Content Deployment permits administrators to define deployment paths (sources and destinations) and jobs (scheduled executions) for the movement of site content from one site collection to another. This is commonly used in publishing scenarios to push content from an authoring farm to a production farm.

- **Central Administration Granular Backup.** The ability to export site collections, sites, and lists from within the Central Administration site relies on the Content Deployment API.

As implied by the descriptions thus far, the Content Deployment API does not operate from the classic perspective of backup and restore; rather, the content deployment classes approach site persistence with the goal of copying from one site and importing into (or merging with) another. It is easier to think of backup and restore as a cloning process: that which is restored matches that which was backed up. That isn't the case with the Content Deployment API. Depending on how an export and import are run, how associated dependencies are handled, whether or not content already exists in the destination site, and so on, the results on the import side of an export/import operation set may differ significantly from the export source. This tends to make the Content Deployment API less suited to full-fidelity backups and more useful for exporting portions of a site, merging content on import, and more.

For basic export and import functionality, though, the Content Deployment API is relatively easy to use. An example demonstrating the export of a single SharePoint site (that is, an SPWeb) is shown in Listing 11.2.

Note: The code shown in Listing 11.2 assumes that the `Microsoft.SharePoint.dll` assembly is referenced and that the `Microsoft.SharePoint.Deployment` namespace has been imported for use by the `ExecuteSiteExport` method. In addition, the Visual Studio project containing the `ExecuteSiteExport` method should be configured to target the .NET Framework 3.5 on an x64 platform.

Listing 11.2

```
public static void ExecuteSiteExport()
{
    // Establish values to cover the basics of the export operation that is going
    // to be performed. The site and location variables are fairly self-explanatory.
    // Because content exports can result in the creation of more than one file, the
    // current variable value (below) may yield FreshNewsExport.cmp, FreshNewsEmport2.cmp,
    // FreshNewsExport3.cmp, etc., series depending on how much content exists for export.
    Uri siteToExport = new Uri("http://spdev:18380/freshnews");
    String exportLocation = @"\\BackupHost\SPSiteExports\";
    String exportFilenameBase = @"FreshNewsExport";

    // The SPExportSettings object defines the export operation to perform. You can exercise
    // a great deal of control over the export operation with the SPExportSettings'
    // collection of properties.
    SPExportSettings baseSettings = new SPExportSettings(siteToExport, exportLocation,
exportFilenameBase);
    baseSettings.ExportMethod = SPExportMethodType.ExportAll;
    baseSettings.FileCompression = true;
    baseSettings.FileMaxSize = 256;
    baseSettings.IncludeSecurity = SPIncludeSecurity.All;
    baseSettings.IncludeVersions = SPIncludeVersions.All;
```

```
// SPExport actually carries out the export operation. The type raises a number of
// events that can be tapped, if desired, to respond to export changes and progress
// notifications. Because SPExport implements IDisposable, it needs to be disposed of
// properly with either a using block (as seen below) or with an explicit Dispose call.
using (SPExport exporter = new SPExport(baseSettings))
{
    exporter.Run();
}
}
```

The result of running the code shown in Listing 11.2 is a single `FreshNewsExport.cmp` file at the selected export location provided the content in the `http://spdev:18380/freshnews` site is less than roughly 256MB following compression. The `FileMaxSize` property defines how big each `.cmp` file is allowed to get before the file is closed and a new one is opened for export. If the `FileMaxSize` property were assigned a value of 32 and a total of 100MB of content (post-compression) existed in the site to be exported, approximately three files would be created at the export location: `FreshNewsExport.cmp`, `FreshNewsExport2.cmp`, and `FreshNewsExport3.cmp`. "Approximately" is specified because SharePoint's ability to break an export into chunks of the desired size depends on the content that's actually going into the files. The total number of files and their size can vary from export to export.

You can leverage the Content Deployment API in other ways as well. You can use it to execute incremental exports, support path updating on imports, export with compression to produce loose file sets, and more. In specific situations, it may be of greater use and application than the catastrophic backup and restore types of the `Microsoft.SharePoint.Administration.Backup` namespace.

The SharePoint PowerShell cmdlets described in Chapter 10 that execute exports and imports leverage the Content Deployment API; you can generate and use export packages interchangeably between the two. You can use exports that are created using the types in the `Microsoft.SharePoint.Deployment` namespace with the `Import-SPWeb` PowerShell cmdlet without issue. You can import the site collection, site, and list exports that you generate using Central Administrations granular backup capabilities into a site using types that reside within the `Microsoft.SharePoint.Deployment` namespace. This also holds true for imports that are generated using the `Export-SPWeb` PowerShell cmdlet.

Site Collection Backup and Restore

Thus far you have been introduced to two different approaches that the SharePoint object model offers for data capture and protection. At one end of the spectrum sits the catastrophic backup and restore capabilities that are provided by types that reside primarily within the `Microsoft.SharePoint.Administration.Backup` namespace. At the other end of the spectrum are the content duplication and migration functions that are exposed by the types in the `Microsoft.`

SharePoint.Deployment namespace. Sitting somewhere in between both of these is the SPSiteCollection type.

The Somewhat Unusual Case of the SPSiteCollection Type

The Backup and Restore methods of the SPSiteCollection type are responsible for carrying out the site collection backup and restore operations you might expect them to. Microsoft considers these operations part of the SharePoint granular backup and export architecture, but they don't quite fit the modus operandi of the other export and import types in the Deployment namespace. In fact, the SPSiteCollection type resides within the Microsoft. SharePoint.Administration namespace and doesn't interact at all with the Content Deployment API.

At the same time, the SPSiteCollection type doesn't interact with the catastrophic backup and restore types in the Microsoft.SharePoint.Administration.Backup namespace. This lack of coupling to catastrophic backup and restore is further evidenced by the fact that the SPSite-Collection type doesn't implement the IBackupRestore interface, which is the hallmark of a content component.

Note: At first glance you might think that the SPSiteCollection type represents a single site collection. In actuality, it represents a collection of SPSite objects—that is, a collection of site collections. It is an administration object that is typically used to manipulate the site collections that are associated with a particular Web application (SPWebApplication).

If you dig deep enough into the SharePoint object model, you find that the SPSiteCollection Backup and Restore methods drill through to the BackupSite and RestoreSite methods on SharePoint's core SPRequest type. The BackupSite and RestoreSite methods are basically nothing but thin wrappers around external calls to SharePoint's legacy component object model (COM) infrastructure, meaning the actual site collection backup and restore operations are handled in opaque (and basically untouchable) unmanaged code.

Leveraging Site Collection Backup and Restore

Although the underpinnings of the site collection backup and restore operations are based in COM, you can still employ these operations through the SPSiteCollection type. In fact, site collection backups and restores are the easiest of all backup and restore operations to run. Each only involves a single method call and no dependent objects, as demonstrated in Listing 11.3.

Note: The code shown in Listing 11.3 assumes that the Microsoft.SharePoint.dll assembly is referenced and that the Microsoft.SharePoint.Administration name-space has been imported for use by the ExecuteSiteCollectionBackup method. In addition, the Visual Studio project containing the `ExecuteSiteCollectionBackup` method should be configured to target the .NET Framework 3.5 on an x64 platform.

Listing 11.3

```
public static void ExecuteSiteCollectionBackup()
{
    // Establish the variables that are used to drive the backup operation. The
    // variables are assigned directly here, but a more practical application of
    // the Backup method involves values being passed into the method.
    String backupFilename = @"\\BackupHost\SPSiteBackups\SampleSiteBackup.bak";
    String siteCollectionUrl = @"http://spdev:18380";
    Boolean overwriteIfExisting = true;

    // The Web application that hosts the site collection of interest isn't known
    // directly, so it is looked up. The code then uses that Web application's
    // SPSiteCollection (from the Sites property) for the Backup operation.
    SPWebApplication hostingWebApp = SPWebApplication.Lookup(new Uri(siteCollectionUrl));
    SPSiteCollection associatedSPSites = hostingWebApp.Sites;

    // Execute the actual backup operation to generate the backup file.
    associatedSPSites.Backup(siteCollectionUrl, backupFilename, overwriteIfExisting);
}
```

Restoring a site collection backed up in this fashion is as simple as changing the `Backup` method call to a `Restore` method call. Even the method parameters and their ordering remain the same between calls.

Backups created in this fashion are written out as a single file, which further drives home the differences between backups performed in this fashion and those that are performed through the `Microsoft.SharePoint.Administration.Backup` namespace; specifically, no backup and restore history is maintained for operations carried out through the `SPSiteCollection` type. Logging of backup and restore operations is not performed, either, making use of the `SPSite-Collection` type more of a lightweight approach to backup and restore operations.

Use of the `SPSiteCollection.Backup` generates the same type of file output as that which is generated when running a site collection backup from Central Administration or a site collection backup using the SharePoint `Backup-SPSite` PowerShell cmdlet. You can restore site collections generated using the code in Listing 11.3 with the `Restore-SPSite` cmdlet. By the same token, you can restore site collection backups that are created using Central Administration's site collection backup operation or the `Backup-SPSite` PowerShell cmdlet with the `SPSiteCollection.Restore` method.

As an example of where you could leverage the SPSiteCollection type particularly effectively, consider the following scenario. Out of the box, only farm administrators or those who possess administrative-level access to the servers that SharePoint runs on can execute SharePoint backups. Because you can easily execute site collection backups from within a SharePoint site through custom code leveraging the SPSiteCollection type, you can develop a solution to give site administrators the capability to execute on-demand backups for site collections for which they have some responsibility. Such a solution might take the form of a custom administrative action, user control, or Web Part, and you can enable or disable it for specific groups and individuals as governance policies demand.

Programmatically Using SQL Snapshots

As described in Chapter 7, "SQL Server 2008 Backup and Restore," SQL Server Developer and Enterprise editions include support for database snapshots. Although this support has been present in the SQL Server product since SQL Server 2005, it is only with the 2010 platform that an awareness of snapshots extends to SharePoint. Now that SharePoint is aware of SQL Server's database snapshot functionality, you can leverage that functionality in code that you write.

The SPDatabase type in the Microsoft.SharePoint.Administration namespace represents a SQL Server database, and SharePoint uses SPDatabase and its derived types to read, write, and manipulate the contents of databases that are used by the farm. Particularly noteworthy among the SPDatabase-derived types is the SPContentDatabase type, which represents a content database housing site collections.

In SharePoint 2010, the SPDatabase type has been extended with a Snapshots property. As shown in Figure 11.4, the Snapshots property exposes a collection of type SPDatabaseSnapshotCollection. Through the Snapshots collection and each of its SPDatabaseSnapshot items, it is possible to create, delete, and manage SQL Server snapshots for the database in the underlying SQL Server instance.

When a snapshot is created, either programmatically through the SharePoint object model or directly through SQL Server, that snapshot is treated as if it were a completely different read-only database on SQL Server. Although snapshots are commonly created from live SharePoint content databases, they are not attached to the SharePoint farm. Because the snapshots aren't affiliated with a SharePoint farm, you need to use the new unattached content database model (through the SPContentDatabase.CreateUnattachedContentDatabase method) to interact with them.

Listing 11.4 demonstrates the same site collection backup operation that was shown in Listing 11.3, but it shows how you can use a database snapshot to enhance the overall backup process. By executing the SPSiteCollection.Backup operation against a database snapshot instead of the live content database, there is no need to lock the live database while the backup is being

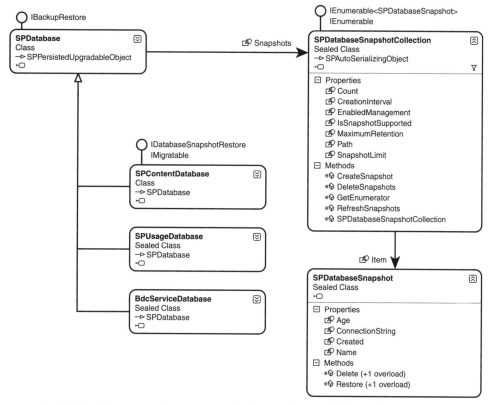

Figure 11.4   Database snapshot support for SPDatabase and derived types.

performed. Users can continue to conduct read and write operations as they normally would, and the backup operation can proceed against the snapshot without worries of corruption or inconsistencies. When the backup operation is complete, the snapshot is deleted to free any resources it held on SQL Server.

Note: The code shown in Listing 11.4 assumes that the `Microsoft.SharePoint.dll` assembly is referenced and that the `Microsoft.SharePoint`, `Microsoft.Share-Point.Administration`, and `Microsoft.SharePoint.Administration.Backup` namespaces have been imported for use by the `ExecuteSiteCollectionBackup-WithSnapshot` method. In addition, you should configure the Visual Studio project containing the `ExecuteSiteCollectionBackupWithSnapshot` method to target the .NET Framework 3.5 on an x64 platform.

Listing 11.4

```
public static void ExecuteSiteCollectionBackupWithSnapshot()
{
    // As with the ExecuteSiteCollectionBackup method, these variable values
    // would normally be supplied to the method rather than set here.
    String backupFilename = @"E:\Backup\SampleSiteBackup.bak";
    String siteCollectionUrl = @"http://spdev:18380";
    Boolean overwriteIfExisting = true;

    // These two variables are set with properties from the SPSite object that
    // is created.  To minimize the size of the using block that follows, the
    // variables are scoped here.
    SPContentDatabase housingDb;
    String rootRelativeUrl;

    // Obtain the critical property values that are needed from the SPSite.
    using (SPSite siteToBackup = new SPSite(siteCollectionUrl))
    {
        // The content database that houses the site collection is needed to
        // generate a snapshot. The relative site collection URL
        // is needed for the eventual unattached DB backup operation.
        housingDb = siteToBackup.ContentDatabase;
        rootRelativeUrl = siteToBackup.ServerRelativeUrl;
    }

    // Only Developer and Enterprise versions of SQL Server support snapshots. If
    // snapshots aren't supported, the process can't continue.
    if (!housingDb.Snapshots.IsSnapshotSupported)
    {
        throw new NotSupportedException("Snapshots not supported.");
    }

    // Each SPDatabase-derived type (including SPContentDatabase) has a Snapshots
    // collection that serves as the gateway to working with snapshots. Refresh
    // the collection and then use it to create a new snapshot.
    SPDatabaseSnapshotCollection allSnapshots = housingDb.Snapshots;
    allSnapshots.RefreshSnapshots();
    SPDatabaseSnapshot hostingDbSnapshot = housingDb.Snapshots.CreateSnapshot();

    // Once SQL Server creates the snapshot, it's just like any other database.
    // SharePoint's unattached content database functionality is used to attach to
    // the snapshot as if it were a read-only content database.
```

```
    SPContentDatabase snapshotDb = SPContentDatabase.CreateUnattachedContentDatabase
(hostingDbSnapshot.ConnectionString);

    // With a valid SPContentDatabase reference, the collection of site collections
    // in the snapshot can be referenced and used to perform the site collection backup.
    SPSiteCollection sitesInSnapshot = snapshotDb.Sites;
    sitesInSnapshot.Backup(rootRelativeUrl, backupFilename, overwriteIfExisting);

    // When the backup operation is over, delete the snapshot to instruct SQL Server
    // to release the resources associated with it.
    hostingDbSnapshot.Delete();
}
```

A parting word of caution regarding the use of snapshots is warranted. Listing 11.4 includes a call to the `RefreshSnapshots` method to ensure that the collection of `SPDatabaseSnaphot` objects is current prior to any collection manipulation activities. This is done because there are regular processes within SharePoint Foundation, such as the Microsoft SharePoint Foundation Snapshot Management timer job, that can create and delete database snapshots. Any `SPDatabaseSnapshotCollection` that has an `EnabledManagement` property value of true is subject to regular snapshot maintenance by SharePoint, and this maintenance can lead to the addition and deletion of snapshots during the execution of your code. For this reason, it is prudent to refresh the contents of the collection through the `RefreshSnapshots` method before attempting any manipulation of the collection within your code.

Volume Shadow Copy Service

Discussion of custom development for the purpose of catastrophic protection has thus far focused on the SharePoint object model and types it exposes for your use in backup and restore operations. Although these types provide a variety of ways to leverage and extend SharePoint's built-in capabilities, they suffer from a significant number of constraints. The following are just a few:

- The approach that the SharePoint object model employs for backup and restore isn't particularly scalable. As a SharePoint farm grows, use of the types in the `Microsoft.SharePoint.Administration.Backup` namespace have a growing impact on normal farm operations. With extremely large farms containing terabytes of content, execution of a built-in catastrophic backup can literally bring a farm to its knees.

- All of SharePoint's catastrophic backup operations are based on writing backup data to a file share through standard file operations. This is less than desirable in many circumstances, because the file operations can't be altered to incorporate encryption, compression, backup location grooming, and many other expected functions.

- Data that you might consider important for backup purposes that isn't tied directly to the farm and recognized within SharePoint's content component hierarchy is difficult to protect.

Although it is true that SharePoint's catastrophic backup and recovery system can be extended using the `IBackupRestore` interface, the `IBackupRestoreConfiguration` interface, and attributes offered by the Service Application Framework, the implementation tasks are far from trivial. Even if significant time and effort are invested to create new content components to integrate with the built-in catastrophic backup system, the other limitations already discussed still apply.

In light of these and other limitations, most enterprise-scale backup systems that are designed to protect SharePoint stay clear of the types in the `Microsoft.SharePoint.Administration.Backup` namespace and opt for a different approach. In many cases, these systems leverage VSS.

What Is VSS?

The Volume Shadow Copy Service, or VSS, is a somewhat mysterious-sounding set of extensible backup-related APIs that Microsoft has been developing and evolving since they first appeared in Windows XP. VSS was designed from the ground up to provide applications, including the Windows operating system, with a mechanism for creating consistent point-in-time snapshots of file system data—even if some or all of the files captured in the snapshot are in use when the snapshot is taken. You can then use these volume snapshots as the source for backup operations and subsequently dispose of them if you no longer need them.

The heart of VSS is the VSS itself. This service is implemented as a Windows service that runs in the Local System context and is started and stopped on demand to create volume snapshots as directed.

Types of Snapshots

VSS is aware of the underlying file system at the block level, and the built-in system provider is capable of creating volume snapshots in either full copy or differential copy modes. A full copy of a file system volume is exactly what its name implies: a clone of the data on the volume that is targeted for a shadow copy snapshot. When the full copy operation is complete, the result is a shadow copy volume that exists independently of the source volume and can be used for read-only backup operations.

Differential copies are similar to full copies in that they result in the creation of a read-only shadow copy snapshot that is suitable for backup operations, but the underlying execution of the snapshot process is significantly different and typically much faster. Differential copies leverage a differencing area and a copy-on-write system that tracks only those blocks of data that have changed in the original volume since the snapshot was taken.

Differencing areas start out empty because the source volume and the snapshot volume are identical at the time of snapshot creation. As changes are made to the source volume during normal activities, the original file system blocks (which are about to be overwritten by the new data) are copied from the source volume to the snapshot's differencing area. As changes continue, the differencing area continues to grow to hold all the original source volume blocks that have been overwritten since the snapshot was taken.

For backup consumers, the snapshot volume that is exposed ends up being a combination of the current source volume plus the blocks of the differencing area overlaid on top. The result is a read-only volume that appears exactly as it did when the differential copy snapshot was taken.

VSS Components

The options you have available to you when working with VSS depend on how you intend to leverage it. To understand the architecture of VSS, it helps to understand the different component types that are involved in the creation of a shadow copy:

- **VSS.** As described earlier, the VSS is integrated into the Windows operating system and is responsible for exposing, orchestrating, and coordinating the actions of most of the other component types related to the creation and management of volume shadow copies.

- **Writer.** A *writer* is a component that serves as a bridge between VSS and an application or service that possesses data that can be included in a VSS operation. Writers integrate knowledge of their application or service and work with the VSS to ensure that applications and services are quiesced—their pending operations are settled and operational activities suspended. This ensures that application and service data is consistent prior to VSS executing a snapshot. Writers also commonly provide some form of post-restore synchronization support for their applications or services. Writers are available for SQL Server, Hyper-V, SharePoint, Windows Management Instrumentation (WMI), the Registry, and a multitude of other services and applications.

- **Provider.** A *provider* is a component that actually carries out the shadow copy process and manages the storage volumes that are associated with VSS operations. Providers can either be software based, like the built-in system provider that is supplied with the operating system, or they can be hardware based and tied to their associated storage arrays. Regardless of the actual implementation, providers do the "grunt work" of point-in-time volume snapshot generation, management of the underlying volumes to store the critical pieces of a snapshot (such as differencing areas), and more.

- **Requestor.** A *requestor* is an application that consumes VSS for the purposes of backing up or restoring data. A good example of a VSS requestor is the Windows Server Backup application that is built into Windows Server 2008 and described at length in Chapter 5. When Windows Server Backup needs to create a backup, it engages the VSS to generate a snapshot of the data to be backed up. Once VSS generates the snapshot, Windows Server Backup creates a backup from the snapshot and then releases it.

Each of these component types is a critical piece in the overall architecture of VSS. Leveraging VSS for SharePoint backup operations focuses primarily on two of the four component types mentioned, though: writers and requestors.

The Role of the SharePoint Foundation VSS Writer

After reading the component description of a VSS writer and how writers are associated with applications and services, you may be wondering if SharePoint has its own writer. If so, the answer is "yes." In fact, it technically has two.

The SharePoint Foundation VSS writer (or SPF-VSS writer) is installed when either SharePoint Foundation 2010 or SharePoint Server 2010 is installed on a server. Once registered, the writer integrates with the VSS infrastructure to provide the application the intelligence and capabilities it needs to generate consistent and usable shadow copies of each of the components that make up a SharePoint farm. This includes content databases, Service Application databases, registered third-party databases, and more. The SPF-VSS writer also works with a secondary search index writer that is installed at the same time as the SPF-VSS writer to provide snapshot and restore support for SharePoint's file-based search indexes.

An important point to note is that the SPF-VSS writer itself doesn't create backups or execute restores. The VSS (in conjunction with one or more VSS providers) is still responsible for creating shadow copies of the volumes housing SharePoint data, and actual backup and restore operations are orchestrated by a VSS requestor. The key advantages that the SPF-VSS writer offers are based on its application knowledge of SharePoint:

1. **Consistent snapshot state.** Prior to VSS snapshot creation, the SPF-VSS writer transitions the SharePoint farm into a consistent state on disk. Databases are quiesced, pending transactions may be flushed, search index file operations are completed, and the entire farm is effectively paused for a brief period to allow the VSS to generate its snapshot. This is a critical step. If a snapshot were taken of the farm in an inconsistent state, there's a reasonable chance that a restore operation that is conducted using data in the snapshot could fail.

2. **Post-restore activities.** When a requestor or its parent application restores SharePoint farm data that was backed up from a VSS snapshot, there are typically some post-restore synchronization steps that must be carried out to get the SharePoint farm back to a fully functional state. When the SPF-VSS writer is notified by a requestor that a restore operation is taking place, the SPF-VSS writer takes care of the farm synchronization steps once the restore is completed.

These qualities make the SPF-VSS writer an integral part of any backup and restore solution that intends to leverage VSS for SharePoint farm protection.

Developing Solutions with VSS

Without a doubt, VSS brings a lot to the table if you are seeking to develop an enterprise-ready, scalable, robust backup and restore store system for SharePoint. The primary component type of interest for custom backup and restore application development is the VSS requestor. Requestors are the ultimate users and orchestrators of VSS services, and a custom backup and restore application falls squarely into the requestor component type category.

Now that you're probably excited about leveraging the power of VSS, we need to share some potentially bad news: Microsoft doesn't supply any form of managed libraries or extensions that would allow you to use VSS in your .NET applications. Microsoft's support for application development against VSS is provided through a set of COM and C++ types that are packaged into the Windows SDK. This leaves you with a couple of options:

- Develop your requestor in a language such as unmanaged C++.

- Write or leverage a wrapper library around the VSS types of interest and generate a runtime callable wrapper (RCW) that a .NET application can consume. This approach still requires that you do some C++ or equivalent development—just less of it.

Neither of these approaches is trivial for the average .NET developer. In addition, the orchestration of VSS operations is tricky and fraught with pitfalls. Creating a snapshot isn't as simple as making a single call such as `vss.GenerateSnapshot()`. Writer metadata has to be gathered and processed, writers must be enlisted for snapshot operations, dependencies across writers must be established, the snapshots have to be taken and released, and more. The tasks and processes are documented in the Windows SDK, but there is a significant amount of material to learn and incorporate.

Tip: If you are a .NET developer and still have your heart set on working with VSS after all that's been said, know that there are at least a couple of resources available to you. At a minimum, you need to download the Windows SDK and become familiar with its contents. The quickest path to productivity lies with the AlphaVSS project on CodePlex (http://alphavss.codeplex.com), though. AlphaVSS is a managed library around the interfaces you need to work with VSS. It is well documented and highly instructive. It won't make you instantly productive with VSS, but it dramatically reduces the learning curve and work you have to do.

Given the described requirements and complexity, a working example of VSS in action for SharePoint backup is well beyond the scope of this book.

Rolling Your Own Backup and Restore Approach

Each of the custom approaches discussed thus far has its own unique set of advantages and disadvantages. The types within the `Microsoft.SharePoint.Administration`, `Microsoft.SharePoint.Administration.Backup`, and `Microsoft.SharePoint.Deployment` namespaces offer a variety of built-in capabilities for preserving and recovering content and other important

SharePoint data within your farm. VSS is a proven technology that gives you a way to generate consistent point-in-time snapshots for the overwhelming majority of the SharePoint configuration and content data in your farm. In many cases, some combination of these technologies and code approaches will prove adequate for your needs.

We clearly recognize that the approaches discussed thus far may only get you part of the way toward achieving your ultimate goal. Just as there is no one-size-fits-all approach to SharePoint disaster recovery, so too is there no master set of custom code that can solve every backup and restore need.

The two sections that follow offer a couple of additional techniques you may use to tackle aspects of your custom disaster recovery development needs. Neither of the techniques is specific to disaster recovery development, but both can be leveraged in a variety of custom development scenarios tied to SharePoint disaster recovery.

Object Model Walking

If your custom development scenario is focused on capturing a variable set of content within the SharePoint environment, particularly at the site collection or subsite collection level, the idea of object model walking may be of interest to you.

At a basic level, *object model walking* is a general term for traversing hierarchically organized groups of objects (an object graph) to conduct some operation on them or extract information of interest from them. For purposes of capturing and protecting data in SharePoint, you might apply this concept to save or restore data of interest within a site collection and some subset of its subordinate objects. In essence, this is how SharePoint's own Content Deployment API is built. Figure 11.5 demonstrates a selective hierarchy of types that span from the site collection level (SPSite) down to the SharePoint list level (SPList).

Although the Content Deployment API provides you with mechanisms for exporting from and importing to a SharePoint site collection, you are bound by the API's constraints and modes of operation. These are adequate in most cases, but they may fall short in others. Consider the case of workflows, for example. Data that is acted on by workflows is relatively straightforward to capture, but the state of the workflows is not. The Content Deployment API doesn't allow you to capture or export workflow state.

If the Content Deployment API proves to be more of a barrier than a building point, you may decide to avoid it altogether and come up with a custom mechanism for protecting all the data of interest. If you elect to protect site collections and their data, you would likely start by examining the site collection (SPSite) of interest to read and capture all the data of interest that is represented by it—workflows, work items, users, permissions, recycle bin information, activated features, and more. The list is extensive. Some objects and properties can be read directly, whereas others require the use of helper objects or predefined access sequences.

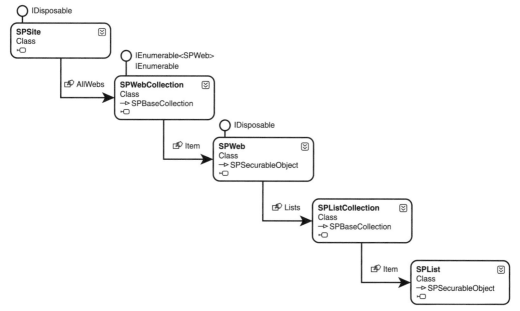

Figure 11.5 Object hierarchy from SPSite to SPList.

Of course, the SPSite is just the tip of the iceberg. Each SPSite contains at least one SPWeb object in the form of the RootWeb, and in all likelihood the SPSite instance contains many more SPWeb objects that are organized below it in a hierarchy. These SPWeb objects also have their own properties and collections of objects that require processing. Some of the data can be cleanly extracted and reconstituted into object form later, but many of SharePoint's objects can't be created or manipulated outright; they possess constraints, dependencies, and logic that require careful orchestration to arrive at a point where a reconstituted object matches the state that existed at the time its original object was persisted.

Ultimately, the amount of data and the fidelity with which it is captured is a decision that is left completely up to you. Also left up to you is the manner in which you read, persist, load, and reapply the content you are protecting. There is no predefined way to translate SPSite, SPWeb, and dependent objects for storage with the call of a single method. At the same time, re-creating those objects in a usable form from your storage is going to prove challenging.

If you're thinking that this approach to content protection sounds like it could be an awful lot of work, you're absolutely right. The amount of work is tied to the fidelity with which you intend to capture and restore data. A full-fidelity backup codebase that is based on object model walking is certainly possible, but it would be a complex undertaking. Object model walking in your own code is most appropriate when you are trying to capture either a limited subset of SharePoint data or data that isn't captured through the catastrophic and deployment types.

Employing Serialization Surrogates

Serialization surrogates aren't specific to SharePoint, nor are they a new concept to .NET development. They come in handy, though, when you want to serialize class instances that you don't control the source for. To understand why this is applicable in the case of protecting SharePoint data, you need to have some familiarity with SharePoint's history and how it works under the hood.

Under the Hood with SPRequest

Although SharePoint 2010 comes with a rich object model you can employ to address all manner of custom development challenges, it has a dirty little secret—underneath its managed library hood, SharePoint runs on an engine that has a significant chunk of COM in it. Digging into the `Microsoft.SharePoint.dll` and the `Microsoft.SharePoint.Library` namespace reveals the `SPRequest` type. The `SPRequest` type is the managed wrapper around a wealth of methods that are exposed by the `OWSSvrLib.dll` dynamic link library. The majority of the functionality that is exposed to .NET callers in the `SPRequest` type gets mapped directly through to unmanaged methods in the `OWSSvrLib.dll` COM library.

You might be wondering why the `SPRequest` type is so special and merits the mention that it's gotten so far. It would be a fair question, and the answer is pretty straightforward. Two of the most common types you use when working with SharePoint content are backed by the `SPRequest` type. Those two types are `SPSite` and `SPWeb`. Without `SPSite` and `SPWeb`, the options for working with content in SharePoint grow slim pretty quickly.

Serialization Challenges

You might recall from the "Object Model Walking" section that data protection schemes based on object model walking are often challenging due to issues of persistence. Protection of SharePoint content revolves around the `SPSite` and `SPWeb` types, and both of these types contain a dizzying array of properties, methods, and associated collections. The object model graphs that begin with these types are typically deep, complicated, and span the boundary between managed and unmanaged code.

In most areas of .NET development, deep and complicated object graphs like the ones described are routinely dealt with using serialization types and techniques. *Serialization* is the process of converting an object graph into a form that can be stored or transmitted, and *deserialization* is the complementary process of converting the stored or transmitted form back into a usable object graph. Binary serialization of objects in .NET is typically handled by the types residing in the `System.Runtime.Serialization` namespace, but binary serialization isn't the only type available to .NET developers. XML serialization is common, as well, and is typically used in areas such as Web service communications.

Because serialization is commonly used to persist object graphs, you might be wondering why it wasn't mentioned in the "Object Model Walking" section. Unfortunately for SharePoint developers, SPSite, SPWeb, and many of the other types that are tied to site collection content aren't good candidates for straight serialization.

- The easiest way to grant a class serialization support via .NET's built-in serialization types is to adorn it with the [Serializable] attribute. This won't work for the SharePoint types, though, because you don't control the source code for those types.

- SPWeb and SPSite aren't sealed objects, so technically you could subclass them to create your own derived types and control the serialization behavior through the subclasses. This approach is less than desirable, though, because at their core the SPWeb and SPSite types simply weren't designed to be serialized given their COM origins. In addition, integrating your custom derived types with other (native) SharePoint types, methods, and properties would prove problematic at best—if possible at all.

Although direct serialization support for SharePoint types is likely a dead end, there is an alternative.

Serialization of SharePoint Types via Surrogate

The .NET Framework supports the use of serialization surrogates when you want to serialize and deserialize objects that weren't originally designed to support these activities. A *serialization surrogate* is a separate class that understands a specific nonserializable type (like the SPSite type) and can act as a stand-in when serialization requests are made to serialize or deserialize instances of the nonserializable type.

To better illustrate this concept, examine the activity diagram shown in Figure 11.6 for the series of steps that are carried out when .NET is called upon to serialize an object.

The branch of the diagram marked by a circled number one shows the path that is followed when objects that have a surrogate are serialized. The path marked by a circled number two shows serialization under nonsurrogate conditions.

The primary benefit of serialization surrogates when working with SharePoint objects is the fact that the SharePoint objects themselves are really only passed as data for the surrogates to operate upon. The actual data that is written out for serialization is left up to the surrogate. Although this is conceptually similar to the straight object model walking scenario presented earlier, you should bear in mind that there isn't a need to create all the custom persistence plumbing and infrastructure in the same way that you would have to in the object model walking case. In addition, surrogates support a number of advanced scenarios, such as surrogate selector chains and type remapping during deserialization, that make them worthy of consideration in custom persistence scenarios.

Implementing a functional serialization surrogate example is beyond the scope of this chapter. For additional information, examine the types in the System.Runtime.Serialization namespace and the ISerializationSurrogate interface in particular. For good walk-throughs and

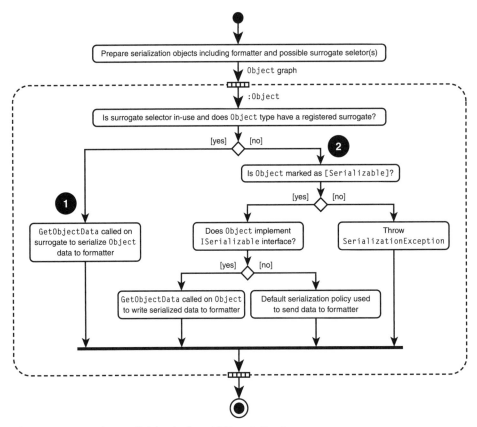

Figure 11.6 Paths available during .NET serialization.

examples on using serialization surrogates, see the "Run-Time Serialization, Part 3" article in the September 2002 issue of *MSDN Magazine* at http://msdn.microsoft.com/en-us/magazine/cc188950.aspx.

Designing Applications for Disaster Recovery Readiness

Thus far, this chapter has discussed ways to develop against the SharePoint object model and similar APIs to provide functionality that is not present within the out-of-the-box platform. This information is highly relevant to the topic of disaster recovery, but there is another area that is often overlooked in a discussion of disaster recovery and custom application development. That area can best be summarized with the following question: how do you engineer an application for maximum supportability in a disaster recovery situation or scenario?

Although conventional best practices relating to .NET programming call for the implementation of certain code patterns, some of these patterns can actually run counter to the "bigger picture" (which includes disaster recovery) if it is taken into account. What's best for performance, for instance, can actually operate counter to a strategy that maintains maximum supportability and location portability at its core.

This section approaches SharePoint development (and .NET code development in general) from a disaster recovery mindset and makes a handful of suggestions that are consistent with maximum recoverability, redundancy, and supportability for most custom applications in the event of a disaster.

Storage of Application Configuration Data

Nearly all applications, regardless of origin or intent, depend on some form of configuration data for proper operation. *Configuration data*, in this case, is defined as data that (a) is required for proper application operation, and (b) can vary based on the environment in which the application is installed and executed. This data can take many forms and be stored in many locations, including the following:

- Paths to file system–based configuration data

- Database sources and their associated connection strings

- Resources describing internal error codes and their associated descriptions

- Application credentials (encrypted or not) to access local and remote resources

- Locale-specific settings and assemblies

- References to assemblies that contain shared components

- Logging settings and associated reporting information

- If capable of unattended execution, schedules for noninteractive processing

- E-mail recipients, templates, and conditions under which e-mail should be sent

- Product IDs, registrations, and other codes

- Version information

When it comes to disaster recovery, the rule of thumb regarding the storage of configuration data is this: if the data can be externalized, every reasonable attempt should be made to do so. Configuration and operational data should also be separated from actual application logic whenever possible. Practices such as embedding string literals within application code are not recommended. Under these guidelines, rethink custom code that demonstrates a reddish-brown color within the Visual Studio environment (indicative of the use of string literals) and declarative programming patterns.

Development within the .NET environment is made substantially easier (from a disaster recovery perspective) with the use of `web.config` files for Web-based applications and `app.config` files for Windows forms applications. These files, which are tied to an application, can abstract the storage of application-specific settings, database connections strings, external type registrations, and more in a way that readily supports disaster recovery. If you're leveraging these configuration files, though, you must realize that the configuration files are typically tied to the installation location of their associated application. If the application is not installed to a directory or drive that backup operations support, the configuration data present in the externalized file or files is typically lost with the application in the event of a disaster.

In addition to the use of `web.config` and `app.config` files, storage of application configuration data can be externalized through the use of a database, a separate custom settings file (such as an XML configuration file), Web services, or a host of other options. Each option offers a different set of strengths and weaknesses, so the decision regarding which to use depends on the acceptable trade-offs. Storage of configuration data in a database is attractive from a supportability and abstraction standpoint because the database itself is likely stand-alone and backed up, but use of a database in this fashion can result in a poorly performing solution. The use of an XML file tends to be better performing, but it also tends to encourage a custom storage scheme that is less supportable across an enterprise unless schemas are standardized.

When you're storing application configuration data for custom SharePoint solutions, both `web.config` storage and SharePoint database storage are highly feasible options and should be considered for use based on application needs and governance requirements. Because a SharePoint site is an ASP.NET site, it's easy to store and retrieve settings data from `web.config` files. The SharePoint object model also includes some specialized types (such as the `SPWebConfigModification` type) that make it easy to integrate configuration data changes during installation or activation of custom code. At the same time, many SharePoint object types representing easily recognized entities (such as `SPFarm`, `SPService`, and `SPWeb`) have a `Properties` collection that can be used to persist custom data to the associated SharePoint databases. This means that use of the `Properties` collection to store configuration data for the aforementioned types results in that data being included in any backup approach that covers the SharePoint databases.

The only proscribed options for configuration storage have been mentioned. Placing string literals in-line with application code greatly reduces supportability and location portability. One notable addition to the list is the Windows Registry. In the days of COM, storage of settings in the Windows Registry was considered a step forward; from a disaster recovery perspective, storage of application settings in such a fashion is not recommended if you can avoid it. Although current backup mechanisms often capture the Registry and its settings, accessing and modifying the settings contained within the Registry is much more involved and less friendly than working with external settings files or Web services positioned for configuration storage. It would be a challenge to identify circumstances under which the storage of SharePoint settings in the Registry would be preferable to the use of the `SPFarm.Properties` collection.

Storage of Transient and Persistent Application Business Data

Configuration data may be responsible for getting an application running and identifying how it should interact within its runtime environment, but it is an application's business data that is tied to the real value that the application brings to an organization. Business data takes many forms; the list that follows contains just a few of the multitude of file and data types that fall into this category:

- Spreadsheets

- Written documents, including e-mail messages

- Presentations, multimedia files, and other audio/visual assets

Whereas configuration data is required for an application to simply execute, business data can generally be thought of as the data that is produced or consumed in the day-to-day operations of an application. Business data can be persistent and live beyond the scope of execution of the application; it can also be transient or temporary data that an application uses during computations, auto-saves, and so on.

The question of where an application should store business data is not a new one. The following are some recommendations and points for consideration:

- **Clearly separate business data from other data.** On both servers and client workstations, a best practice is to format at least two separate logical disks for local storage requirements. One logical drive typically contains the Windows system and program files (typically C:\), whereas another (oftentimes E:\) contains application and business data. The use of at least two separate logical drives in this fashion makes the creation, maintenance, and targeting of backup operations much easier.

- **Leverage environment variables.** Environmental portability and disaster recovery are aided significantly when you avoid assumptions regarding the structure of the file system hosting an application. This is particularly true when it comes to the storage of transient application data. Many applications need to use the hosting system's file system for activities such as compression/decompression, encryption/decryption, and other stream-related operations. In these instances, you can use environment variables that the hosting operating system supplies to ensure that proper file system locations are employed. In the case of temporary or working files, for instance, the %TEMP% environment variable defines the default temporary files location for users who are currently logged onto the operating system.

- **Make business data storage locations configurable.** This is an extension to the point that was made with the previous item. When the storage of persistent data is a requirement, you must provide some mechanism to permit the configuration of the storage location. This could be something as common as the Save As dialog box seen throughout the Windows world, or it could be an application configuration file setting that drives all data to a known location.

Regardless of the mechanism selected, avoid assumptions about the hosting system's file system structure at all costs.

■ **Employ network-available services when possible.** Disaster recovery operations are significantly aided when you can centralize critical business data for backup and restore purposes. Traditional file shares represent one example of how such centralization can be achieved, but they are by no means the only mechanism. Databases, custom business services, and even SharePoint (through WebDAV and the WebClient service) can be utilized for this purpose.

■ **Consider the cloud.** Microsoft, Amazon, Google, and many other vendors have been steadily increasing the capability and reliability of their cloud-based storage offerings. At the same time, the tools and APIs needed to interact with cloud-based storage have been getting easier for developers to learn and use. When it comes to offsite storage that is itself redundant and ready for disaster recovery tasks, it is well worth the time invested to see if you can integrate cloud-based storage into your design.

With SharePoint custom solutions, the storage of transient data should obey the points just described. The storage of persistent business data, however, tends not to be a large issue. Simply storing business data in SharePoint lists and document libraries ensures that the business data is covered in the event of a disaster provided you have a well-conceived, implemented, and tested SharePoint disaster recovery strategy.

Accessing Network Resources

In today's highly interconnected computing environments, network resources are a common reality and storage location for much of the data leveraged by applications. The following are common examples of network resources:

■ File shares (that is, file system storage locations not resident on local disks)

■ E-mail stores (POP3, IMAP) for e-mail-enabled applications

■ Databases

■ FTP sites

■ Any HTTP/HTTPS-enabled sites and services (overlaid file shares, Web services, and so on)

The best support for disaster recovery scenarios for network resources comes when those resources are accessed through indirection or some form of abstraction layer. Although the abstraction of such resources can be an application-specific exercise, several mechanisms are built into common operating systems and network stacks to decouple the naming of such resources and services from their actual implementations:

■ **Domain Name Services (DNS).** DNS is perhaps the most common approach to separating uniform resource locators (URLs) and namespaces from actual resource implementations.

DNS is the standard for Internet naming. If a user supplies a common English name (such as www.amazon.com) to a DNS server, the DNS server resolves the host name to an IP address (72.21.203.1). DNS decouples names from IP addresses, but it comes with a cost in the form of DNS servers, increased management overhead, and some need to update names and their associated IP addresses.

- **Distributed File System (DFS).** Practically speaking, DFS can be regarded as a "file system switchboard" service. Enterprise wide, DFS supports the practice of specifying, mapping, and redirecting network file paths. This approach decouples file path references from their underlying implementations, but it carries with it the need for additional maintenance and administration.

- **SQL Server aliases.** Use of a SQL Server alias creates a machine-local abstraction layer between a SQL Server instance and applications that want to interact with databases on a SQL server. When an alias is defined on a machine, you must specify a minimum of two parameters: a server name and an alias name. Once you have established such an alias, connection strings that would normally use the server name can instead use the alias name. If the server name needs to be changed or updated, updating the alias is all that is required. The use of aliases affords a great deal of flexibility and portability for SharePoint farms and applications that leverage them.

- **Mapped network drives.** Mapped network drives are a common approach to identifying network resources using local path specifications. Nearly all applications and platforms support the notion of mapped drives in some sense, making them a solid backward-compatible approach to separating identifier from implementation. Unfortunately, mapped drives tend to be established on a per-user or per-session basis. This limits their potential usefulness in many cases, particularly regarding activities that are carried out within the context of a noninteractive account.

The only methods that should be avoided wholesale when accessing network resources are those involving direct IP address access and the use of NetBIOS or straight machine names. Both of these methods fail to leverage an abstraction layer of some sort, so their viable use within a functional disaster recovery environment is questionable. After all, most "live" data centers (or failover targets) have servers and naming schemes that differ from those being used in the standard production environments that are being protected by the disaster recovery implementation.

When it comes to custom SharePoint applications, developers are advised to simply use DNS whenever possible if calls to other sites or network resources are required. SharePoint's alternate access mapping (AAM) capability simplifies the process of extending any SharePoint site that may have an IP address in its URL to make it addressable by DNS name, so SharePoint is exceptionally DNS friendly for applications attempting to access its sites and Web services. Because SharePoint's AAM capabilities and zone mappings are also accessible through the SharePoint object model (using the `SPWebApplication.AlternateUrls` property, for instance), it's easy to ensure that custom SharePoint applications can cope with environmental changes and gracefully fall back to alternate access points to a site if needed.

Application Logging and Monitoring

The previous design readiness suggestions focused primarily on ways to decouple addressing and usage of application resources and data. The final recommendations offered in this section focus on providing insight and understanding into how an application is operating.

Logging and monitoring are fairly common application requirements, but these areas are often inadequately addressed or supported when development is undertaken. Many times, they are seen as a "nice to have," rather than a critical facet of a fully functional and well-architected application.

In a disaster recovery scenario, logging and monitoring take on additional importance. This is especially true when a custom application may have a recovery time objective (RTO) that is measured in hours or maybe even minutes. You simply don't have the luxury of taking any measurable amount of time in such circumstances to focus on troubleshooting a problematic application. If an application has issues coming online when recovered, the reasons for those issues need to be clearly spelled out.

At a minimum, applications should communicate not only errors, but critical informational items regarding where data is being accessed and utilized, security checks that pass and fail, anytime an application is falling back to a default value, and so on. A common mechanism for the communication of this information is the Windows Event Log, but items that are more "informational" in nature are often better supported and controlled through the use of trace switches and flags.

Being built upon ASP.NET, SharePoint has access to ASP.NET's full array of event tracing and notification capabilities. Errors, warnings, and other informational items can be written to the ASP.NET trace logs and event sinks. Critical application errors can be added to the `AllErrors` collection of the `SPHttpContext` for further processing and analysis downstream in the ASP. NET pipeline. In addition to these capabilities, SharePoint has its own unified logging service (ULS) to which developers can write messages of any sort. SharePoint 2010 also introduces correlation IDs for troubleshooting and the logging database for aggregating information from across a farm. These capabilities greatly simplify the problem of pinpointing issues that arise with custom SharePoint code and applications.

Including Windows performance counters is another step forward that can promote greater supportability and troubleshooting with mission-critical applications. This is particularly true for applications that operate as services or lack any form of interface. Thoughtfully chosen and implemented counters can mean the difference between befuddled head scratching and insight when attempting to identify the source of a problem during recovery.

Both SharePoint and ASP.NET come with a variety of performance counters that you can leverage out of the box to troubleshoot application and performance problems. In addition, developers have the standard abilities offered by .NET to create performance counters of their own for their SharePoint applications.

Conclusion

Although SharePoint disaster recovery operations are typically the province of farm administrators and operations personnel, knowledge of the ways in which you might customize, extend, and automate the SharePoint platform can prove useful. Possession of some custom development and PowerShell knowledge can help you avoid repetitive tasks that commonly lead to errors, permit the development of tailored solutions that solve novel or business-specific technology problems, and generally save countless hours and many headaches in the long run.

When the SharePoint platform lacks the facilities to adequately address disaster recovery needs, custom development using the SharePoint API can be used in situations and scenarios that are either inappropriate or simply too complex for PowerShell scripting alone. SharePoint makes a number of options available for custom backup and restore operations, including the catastrophic backup and restore types of the `Microsoft.SharePoint.Administration.Backup` namespace and the relatively self-contained `SPSiteCollection` type. SharePoint also offers a Content Deployment API that is exposed through the `Microsoft.SharePoint.Deployment` namespace. You can leverage the types found within to extend export and import operations.

In addition to the built-in types mentioned, you are free to craft your own solutions for content protection, backup, and restoration. Managed code implementations may center on object model walking with some type of custom persistence or serialization scheme. Enterprise-ready industrial solutions, on the other hand, often involve the use of VSS in conjunction with the SharePoint Foundation VSS Writer to achieve backup consistency and scalability.

Finally, you should factor a number of techniques and considerations into the design of any application that is a candidate for location and operation in multiple environments, because this often happens in a disaster recovery scenario when multiple data centers and workstation environments are in play. Certain practices such as indirect access to network resources, clear segregation between applications and their associated configuration data and business data, and the centralization of business data can significantly aid in the recoverability of an application and greatly reduce downtime in the event of a disaster. Architecting applications to adequately support logging and performance monitoring can also greatly improve troubleshooting efforts when an application does encounter problems in both disaster and nondisaster scenarios.

Having completed this chapter, you should now be able to answer the following questions. As with the other chapters, answers to the following questions appear in Appendix A, "Chapter

Review Q&A," found on the Cengage Learning Web site at http://www.courseptr.com/downloads.

1. Through what object are all operations involving farm-level catastrophic backup and restore operations conducted?

2. If you intend to tap into the catastrophic backup and restore object model, what two interfaces do you need to be aware of? How do they differ?

3. How do backups performed through the `SPSiteCollection` type differ from standard farm-level backups?

4. True or false: The Content Deployment API is leveraged by both the `Backup-SPFarm` and `Export-SPWeb` PowerShell cmdlets?

5. What is the difference between a VSS writer and a VSS requestor?

12 SharePoint 2010 Disaster Recovery for End Users

In This Chapter

- What Has Changed in SharePoint 2010

- Recycle Bins

- Versioning

- Templates

- WebDAV and Explorer View

- SharePoint Workspace 2010

Amidst the discussions surrounding SharePoint disaster recovery, server redundancy, data backups, and related areas, it is easy to overlook the majority stakeholders in your activities: the end users. End users typically create the data you want to protect. They often don't have any real familiarity with the technical aspects of disaster recovery, and they typically rely on you for recovery of their data and restoration of system functionality in the event of a disaster.

The dependence that end users have on information technology (IT) personnel like you can be a source of anxiety for them, and it isn't hard to understand why. No one likes to feel as if they possess little or no control over their own fate—or the fate of their data. To many administrators, an end user's data is just an abstract entity that has to be protected by a disaster recovery plan. An end user's relationship with his data is typically much more personal. To an end user, his data can be the result of countless hours' worth of research, pictures that can never be replaced, or documents that he is legally bound to store and produce on-demand for years.

End users don't forfeit all rights to their data when they place it in SharePoint, nor do they require blind faith in an administrator's ability to bring things back when even minor outages limit SharePoint access. SharePoint includes features that give some control back to content authors and owners. This chapter discusses disaster recovery–related options that average end users can leverage to safeguard their data and recover from minor losses. It also covers the aspects of those options that you, the administrator, need to be familiar with.

What Has Changed in SharePoint 2010

If you are familiar with the data protection and recovery options that were available to end users in SharePoint 2007, you already know most of the options that SharePoint 2010 brings to the table. The form and presentation of some features have changed a bit, but items like Recycle Bins and the creation of site templates are still very much a part of SharePoint 2010.

Not everything remains the same, however. Microsoft decided to change the playing field in 2010 by altering the operation of two important applications:

- **Microsoft SharePoint Workspace 2010.** When moving from Office 2007 to Office 2010, Microsoft chose to overhaul and rebrand Microsoft Office Groove 2007 as Microsoft SharePoint Workspace 2010 (also known simply as SharePoint Workspace). SharePoint Workspace is a rich client application that builds on capabilities that existed in Groove 2007 and provides end users with a variety of options for working with SharePoint data in offline and multiuser concurrent editing scenarios. Because SharePoint sites and data contained within them can be taken offline and synchronized between client systems and the SharePoint server environment, a number of data replication and protection options have arisen that were previously difficult or impossible to achieve.

- **Microsoft SharePoint Designer 2010.** SharePoint Designer also received an overhaul in the move from 2007 to 2010, but it became significantly less functional with regard to SharePoint data protection. Although SharePoint Designer 2010 retains its ability to link to a SharePoint site for the purpose of creating site and list templates, it loses both its Web site backup and its personal Web package export capabilities. The loss of these two capabilities means that SharePoint Designer no longer offers any additional form of data protection to end users beyond what is offered by the browser-based user interface (UI) itself.

A Word on End Users and Disaster Recovery

Let's cut to the chase: when the chips are down and you are formulating a disaster recovery strategy for your SharePoint environment, the tools and techniques that are discussed in this chapter aren't going to play a significant part in the plan you assemble. At best, they may play a small role in some of your outage mitigation plans, but they simply aren't enterprise-ready or designed for use in true disaster recovery scenarios.

That doesn't make the contents of this chapter irrelevant to the overall disaster recovery picture, however. As was mentioned earlier, the SharePoint end user population is commonly overlooked when administrators assemble their plans to keep servers running and recover from enterprise-level outages. End users can independently employ many of the tools and techniques that are described in this chapter to continue operating during minor outages and recover data in limited scenarios.

Although this chapter discusses concepts and capabilities that are ultimately of interest primarily to end users, there is an administrative perspective on these concepts and capabilities that is of interest to you. We structured this chapter to give you a basic explanation of each tool or technique that end users may employ; that explanation is then followed with the points that you, the administrator, need to understand and integrate to effectively manage and support the associated tool or technique in your environment. We placed emphasis on exposing control points and settings that you can employ to safeguard your SharePoint environment against inappropriate storage consumption, slowdown of the user experience, and other adverse operational effects that might be brought on by excessive use or misuse of the end user capabilities described within.

So even if the contents of this chapter don't help you directly in all cases, a solid understanding and careful application of the concepts within may allow your end users to continue working when they otherwise might not be able to. An end user who is still working is an end user who isn't calling you, the administrator, for data recovery or support help.

Trying It Out

The screenshots and examples in this chapter were put together in a virtual environment with the following software and configuration. Depending on how your environment is configured, your experiences may vary slightly.

- **Operating system.** Microsoft Windows Server 2008 R2 Enterprise Edition (build 7600)

- **Database.** Microsoft SQL Server 2008 R2 Enterprise Edition (build 10.50.1600.1)

- **Web server.** Microsoft Internet Information Services (IIS) 7.5

- **Client Web browser.** Internet Explorer 8 (version 8.0.7600.16385)

- **SharePoint.** SharePoint Server 2010 RTM with Enterprise Client Access License (build 4763)

Recycle Bins

SharePoint 2007 brought integrated Recycle Bins to the platform, and they remain in SharePoint 2010 as a cornerstone of the end user self-service recovery landscape.

How They Work

If you have worked with any version of the Windows operating system since Windows 95, you are probably well acquainted with the concept of a Recycle Bin and its operation. When content is deleted from the file system in Windows, it isn't immediately deleted from the hard drive or local media where it is located if a Recycle Bin is active for that location. Instead, the deleted content is moved from where it resides to a special system folder.

Recycle bins address the end user problem of unintentionally and accidentally deleted content. If content is accidentally deleted from the Windows file system, you can recover it from the Recycle Bin and put it back into general availability within the file system. Deleted content sits in the Recycle Bin until it is either recovered or deleted (emptied) from the Recycle Bin.

Content that is emptied from the Recycle Bin is permanently deleted. Third-party tools exist that can help with the recovery of content that is permanently deleted from the Windows file system, but no mechanism is built into the operating system to assist in this regard.

Recycling in SharePoint

SharePoint's Recycle Bin system is conceptually similar to the Recycle Bin that the Windows operating system employs, but there are a handful of noteworthy differences and points worth discussing:

■ **SharePoint Recycle Bins are configured at the Web application level.** You can configure Recycle Bin settings for each Web application in your SharePoint farm through the Web Application General Settings dialog box in the Central Administration site, as shown in Figure 12.1. By default, each newly created Web application is provisioned with the settings shown in Figure 12.1, and these settings apply to all site collections that are created within the Web application.

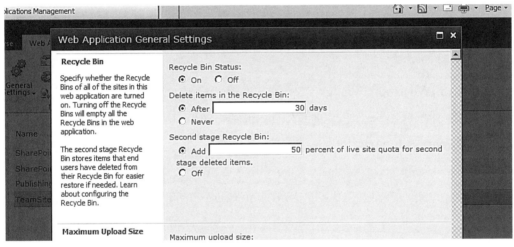

Figure 12.1 Recycle Bin settings for a Web application.

■ **The SharePoint Recycle Bin has two configurable stages.** As shown in Figure 12.1, SharePoint's Recycle Bin system actually has two separate stages. When a user deletes an item, a document, or some other content from a site collection, the deleted item is moved into the first stage Recycle Bin. The first stage Recycle Bin is an area from which end users can recover their own documents; it is basically the equivalent of their own personal Recycle Bin. If a user then deletes an item from the first stage Recycle Bin, the item is actually moved from the first stage Recycle Bin to the second stage Recycle Bin. Only site collection administrators can recover items from the second stage Recycle Bin. When items have been deleted from the second stage Recycle Bin, they are permanently deleted. By default, both the first and second stage Recycle Bins are enabled in a Web application, so site collections created in the Web application have first and second stage Recycle Bins available to them.

■ **Recycle Bin contents can be auto-expired.** Items in the first and second stage Recycle Bin areas have a lifetime of 30 days by default. After 30 days, these items are permanently deleted regardless of their Recycle Bin stage. This means that items in the first stage of the Bin are permanently deleted, as well; there is no promotion or movement of items from the first to the second stage of the Recycle Bin after the expiration period has elapsed, for example. You can adjust the auto-deletion period for items or turn it off entirely for site collections in a Web application using the Web Application General Settings dialog box.

■ **The size of the Recycle Bin is configurable.** To be more specific, the amount of storage available to the second stage Recycle Bin is configurable. There is no separate storage set aside for items in the first stage Recycle Bin; items count against any maximum storage quota that has been established for a site collection. The second stage Recycle Bin, on the other hand, is allotted an additional amount of storage that is equal to 50 percent of the amount allotted to the site collection by the quota template that is in effect. You can adjust this percentage from 1 percent all the way up to 500 percent. There are no size restrictions on a site collection's first and second stage Recycle Bins if no quota template is in effect for the site collection.

Configuring Recycle Bins

By default, both Recycle Bin stages are enabled for new site collections that are created in a Web application that utilizes the default Recycle Bin settings. This means that end users automatically gain Recycle Bin protection for their site collections, but the Web application defaults don't include safeguards to prevent uncontrolled site collection growth. Applying reasonable limits for Recycle Bin usage and site collection growth is relatively easy to do if you have Farm Administrator access within the Central Administration site.

First, you must create a quota template for assignment to the target Web application. The quota template then becomes the basis for the limits that are placed on the size of the first and second stage Recycle Bins on newly created site collections within the Web application.

Second, you must configure the target Web application to use the quota template by default for new site collections when they are created. While the quota template is being assigned, the Web application settings are also adjusted to set desirable Recycle Bin limits for site collections created within the Web application based on values that are specified in the quota template.

Creating a Web Application Quota Template

The example that follows demonstrates how to use Central Administration to create a new quota template called 500MB Maximum Template that restricts site collections that use the template to no more than 500MB, as suggested by its name. You can then use the quota template in the next walk-through titled "Configuring a Web Application's Recycle Bin Settings."

Before attempting this walk-through, ensure that you are a member of the SharePoint Farm Administrators group. In addition, make sure that you are logged into a computer that can access the SharePoint Central Administration site. This is often your own workstation, but in some highly secure environments, access to the Central Administration site may be restricted to only a select group of servers and workstations.

1. Open a browser and navigate to the Central Administration site. This example uses a fictitious SharePoint 2010 Server farm with a Central Administration site URL of http://spdev:18080. If you intend to follow along in your own environment, simply substitute your farm's Central Administration site URL where appropriate.

2. Depending on the configuration of both the SharePoint farm and your client browser, you may be prompted to log into the Central Administration site. If you are so prompted, supply both your username and password. In most cases, your username and password are your domain login credentials.

3. When the Central Administration site loads, navigate to the Application Management page, as shown in Figure 12.2. You do this by clicking the Application Management link in the Quick Launch menu along the left side of the page. Alternatively, you can click the Application Management link in the top-left region of the main zone on the page.

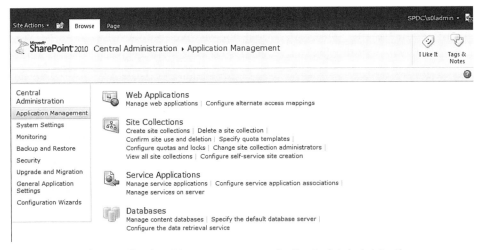

Figure 12.2 The Application Management page in Central Administration.

4. Click the Specify Quota Templates link. It is the fourth link under the Site Collections section in the main zone of the page, and it takes you to the Quota Templates page.

5. Select the option button to Create a New Quota Template, and leave the starting template default value intact so the quota template isn't based on another quota template. In the New Template Name text box, enter 500MB Maximum Template.

6. In the Limit Site Storage to a Maximum Of text box, supply a value of 500. This prevents new site collections that are created in a Web application using the quota template from growing beyond 500MB. Ensure that the check box associated with the text box remains checked.

7. In the Send Warning E-Mail When Site Collection Storage Reaches text box, supply a value of 450 and ensure that the associated check box remains checked. If the site collection grows to 450MB or greater, an e-mail is sent to the primary and secondary (if specified) site collection administrators for the site collection warning that the storage threshold has been crossed.

8. Leave the Sandboxed Solutions with Code Limits controls intact with their default values.

Note: If you intend to execute sandboxed solutions in one or more of the site collections associated with the Web application that a quota template will be applied to, you must specify usage limit point values that are greater than the defaults of zero; however, the use and configuration of sandboxed solutions is beyond the scope of this book.

---

9. When you have executed these steps, the settings for the new quota template to be created should appear as in Figure 12.3. To actually create the quota template, scroll to the bottom of the page and click the OK button.

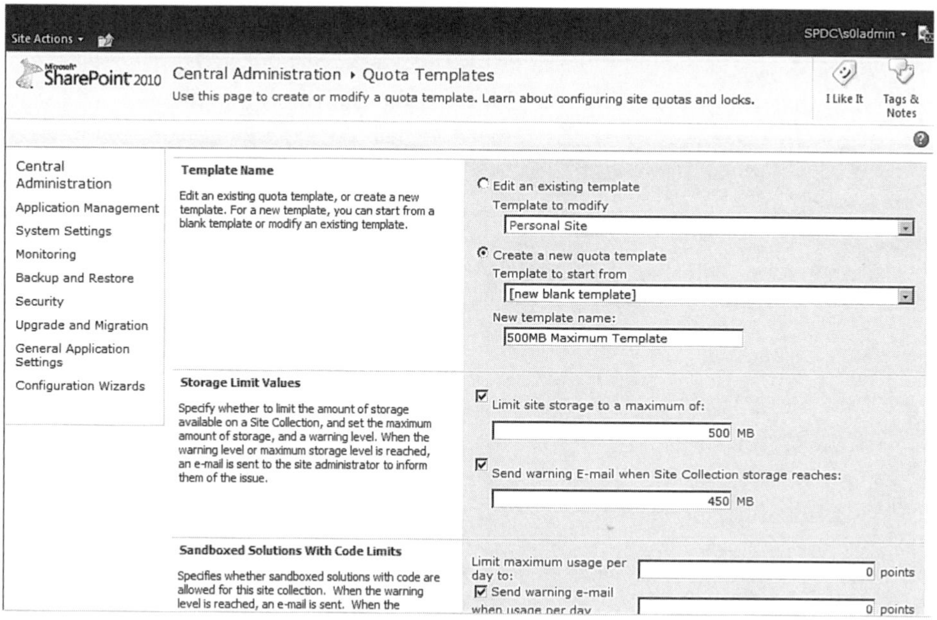

Figure 12.3   The new 500MB Maximum Template quota template.

Configuring a Web Application's Recycle Bin Settings

With a quota template in hand, you are ready to configure the Web application of your choice. In this example, a fictitious Web application with a URL of http://spdev:18380/ is configured to use the 500MB Maximum Template quota as the default quota template for new site collections that are created within it. The assignment of the quota template permits limits to be set on the amount of storage consumed by new site collections that are created within the Web application. A reduction in the size of the second stage Recycle Bin to a limit of 100MB per new site collection is also carried out in this example.

Before attempting this walk-through, ensure that you are a member of the SharePoint Farm Administrators group. In addition, make sure that you are logged into a computer that can access the SharePoint Central Administration site. This is often your own workstation, but in some highly secure environments, access to the Central Administration site may be restricted to only a select group of servers and workstations.

1. Repeat steps 1 through 3 in the previous walk-through to arrive at the Application Management page in the Central Administration site.

2. Click the Manage Web Applications link. It is the first link under the Web Applications section in the main zone of the page, and it takes you to the Web Applications Management page.

3. If you are new to the Fluent UI, also known as "the ribbon," Figure 12.4 may not be familiar to you. Many of the functions that are performed on Web applications are performed through the ribbon once a Web application has been selected. The first step in working with the ribbon is ensuring that it is visible. If you don't see the ribbon as shown in Figure 12.4, you probably have the Browse tab selected. Click the Web Applications tab that is circled in Figure 12.4 to make the ribbon visible.

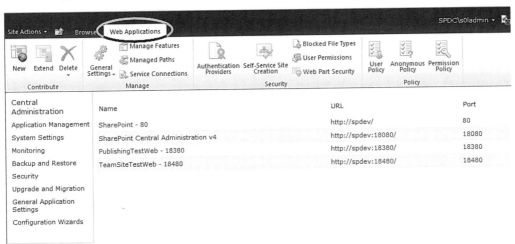

Figure 12.4   Clicking the Web Applications tab to make the ribbon visible.

4.   The Web application of interest in this example is the PublishingTestWeb – 18380 Web application with a URL of http://spdev:18380/. To select the Web application, click on the Web application link shown in Figure 12.5. Once you have selected the Web application, the links and menus in the ribbon shift from grayed-out and inactive to live and available.

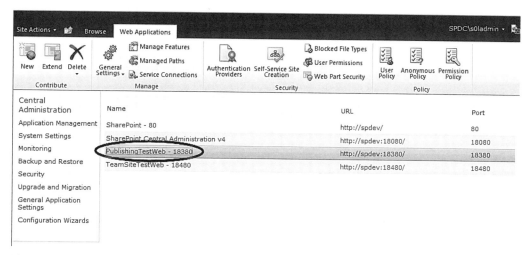

Figure 12.5   Selecting the target Web application.

5.   Expand the General Settings drop-down menu in the ribbon, as shown in Figure 12.6, and select the General Settings menu item. Doing so opens the Web Application General Settings dialog box pictured in Figure 12.7.

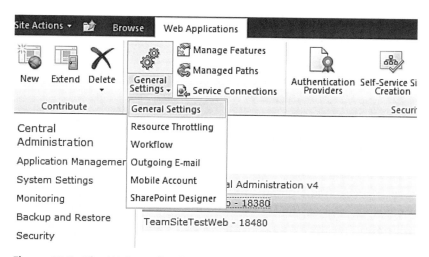

Figure 12.6   The Web application General Settings drop-down menu.

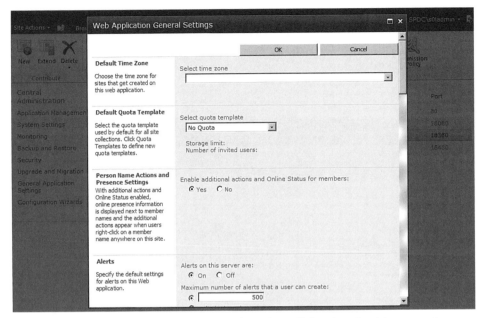

Figure 12.7   The Web Application General Settings dialog box freshly opened.

6. The Select Quota Template drop-down selection box appears in the Default Quota Template section, and by default it is set to No Quota. If the last walk-through was completed successfully, the 500MB Maximum Template should appear in the list of available quota templates, as shown in Figure 12.8. Select it so that new site collections that are created within the Web application are constrained to no more than 500MB by default.

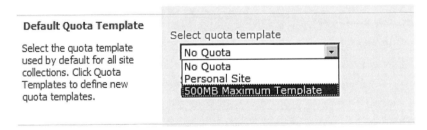

Figure 12.8   Selecting the 500MB Maximum Template.

7. Scroll down to the Recycle Bin section, as shown earlier in Figure 12.1. Items that are placed in the first stage Recycle Bin count against the maximum storage of 500MB per site collection, but this is not true of the second stage Recycle Bin. The 50 percent additional storage allocation means that deleted items that end up in the second stage (site collection) Recycle Bin could consume up to an additional 250MB of storage. To tighten up the amount of extra space that might be consumed, change the Percent of

Live Site Quota for Second Stage Deleted Items value from 50 to 20. Once you make this change, items in the second stage Recycle Bin are then only able to consume up to an additional 100MB of storage (that is, 20 percent of 500MB) on top of the 500MB already allocated per new site collection in the Web application.

8. Scroll down to the bottom of the Web Application General Settings dialog box and click the OK button to apply the changes made.

Note: If you have been reading carefully, you have probably noticed that quota-related changes to a Web application affect only new site collections that are created within the Web application after a quota template has been assigned. At the same time, it is possible to override the default quota template specified for a Web application during the site collection creation process. This means that individual site collections within a Web application may possess a variety of different quota settings. If you later want to change the quota settings that are applied to an existing site collection, you need to use the Configure Quotas and Locks link on the Application Management page or the Set-SPSite PowerShell cmdlet with its QuotaTemplate parameter. The Site Collection Quotas and Locks page that appears provides the mechanism you need to alter the quota and alert settings on existing site collections. With PowerShell and Set-SPSite, you can script out a process to update the quota template for multiple site collections in one fell swoop.

Versioning

Versioning is another SharePoint feature that is relatively easy to grasp. Simply put, *versioning* is a feature that allows you to store multiple revisions or copies of a particular item within a document library or list. An example can illustrate how exceptionally useful this is for end users.

Consider the fictitious example of several authors working to assemble a book. Those authors decide to use a SharePoint document library as a repository for the storage of the chapters they are writing. The book is a collaborative effort, so each of the authors is expected to contribute something to each chapter. In this type of editing scenario, it's important to track the state and contents of the chapters as they are edited by each author in turn. At the same time, it's occasionally desirable to go back to a previous revision of the chapter to see how it existed before some changes were made. Versioning can satisfy these needs and more.

Types of Versioning

Versioning is a central feature of the SharePoint platform that you can use with any document library or list. Versioning is enabled for some of the out-of-the-box document libraries, such as the Pages library that is created in the top-level site where the SharePoint Server Publishing Infrastructure is active. With most document libraries and lists, though, you must explicitly enable versioning.

Although "versioning" has been used as a singular term thus far, versioning actually exists in two different forms within SharePoint:

- **Major versioning.** This type of versioning is available for use on both document libraries and lists. Each time an item in a list or document library is edited, updated, or changed in some way, a new version of that item is created when it is put back into the list or document library. Version numbers begin at 1 and increment by 1 for each new version that is stored in the list or document library. The initial version of an item is version 1, the second is version 2, the third is version 3, and so on.

- **Major and minor (draft) versioning.** This type of versioning is available only on document libraries and other libraries based on them, such as Picture Libraries. It is not available on lists. This type of versioning extends the major versioning approach just described with the addition of draft versions that are denoted by a "point" version number. For example, a document may be initially uploaded into a document library as version 1.0. As changes are made to the document, drafts of the document may accumulate as minor versions: 1.1, 1.2, 1.3, and so on. Once the revision process is complete and another version is ready for general viewing or usage, the version number is incremented to 2.0. Major version numbers (1.0, 2.0, and so on) denote published versions, whereas minor versions (1.1, 1.2, 2.1, and so on) denote minor or draft versions.

Versioning Benefits

Figure 12.9 illustrates a document library for which major and minor versioning is active. In the figure, the menu selections for Chapter 11, "SharePoint 2010 Disaster Recovery Development," are displayed. Selecting the Version History menu item from the drop-down selection menu opens the Version History dialog box shown in Figure 12.10.

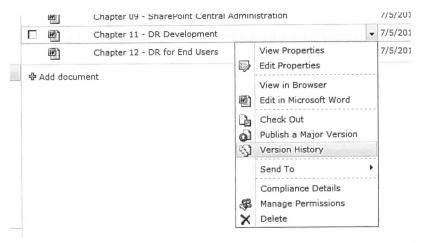

Figure 12.9 An item's drop-down menu in a document library where versioning is enabled.

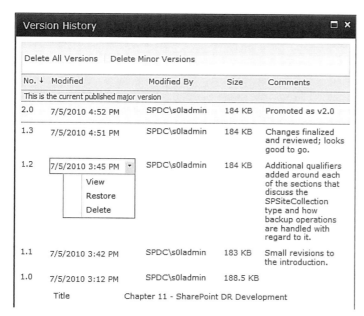

Figure 12.10 The Version History dialog box for a selected document library item.

Several benefits are afforded by versioning regardless of the type of versioning that is in use or whether versioning is enabled on a list or library:

- **Version history.** The Version History dialog box is the primary point of interaction when viewing and working with item versions. Each time an item is changed, a new version is created. As demonstrated in Figure 12.10, each of the versions that are available for a given document or list item is clearly shown.

- **Auditing and change tracking.** Along with the version numbers, the Version History dialog box makes it clear when an item was modified and by whom. The size of the item is also noted, along with any comments that were supplied by the individual creating the version. As long as good comments were supplied when the version was created, it can be a snap to locate a version or revision of interest.

- **Management of versions.** The Version History dialog box also affords you the means to manage the current item version and those that are historical, either individually or as a group. As shown in the open drop-down menu for version 1.2 in Figure 12.10, you can view the item as it existed in version 1.2 or delete that version of the item altogether. You can also replace the current version (2.0, in this case) with a historical version, although the term "replace" is a bit inaccurate. If you elected to replace version 2.0 with the selected version (1.2) shown in Figure 12.10, a version 2.1 would be created with the contents of version 1.2. Version 2.0 would not actually be replaced or overwritten. Figure 12.11 illustrates the results of such a replacement operation.

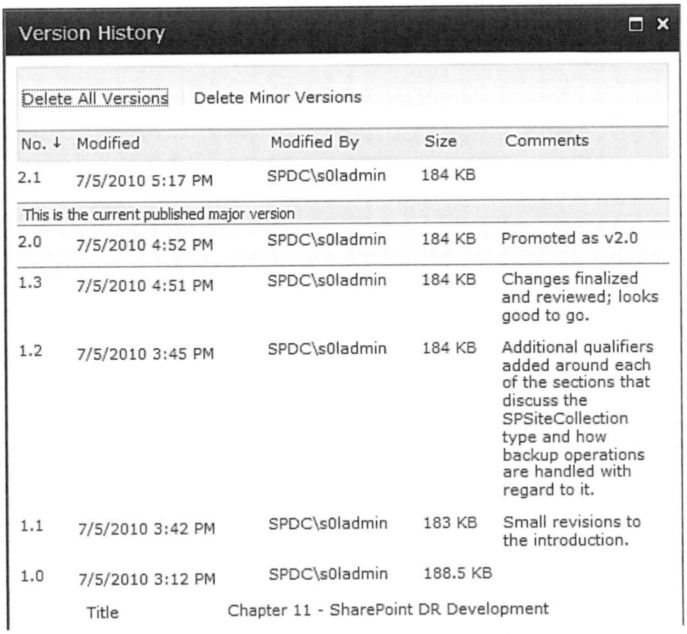

Figure 12.11   Replacement of the current item version with a previous version.

From an end user disaster recovery perspective, the biggest benefit that versioning gives users is the ability to "roll back" to a previous version of a document if the current version includes changes or differences that aren't desired. When a user can roll back to a previous document or item version, it is one less call that he's placing to you for an item-level recovery.

Administrative Concerns

Versioning is controlled on a per-list/library basis. Because lists and libraries are managed within the confines of a site collection, there isn't a whole lot that you, as a SharePoint administrator, need to worry about in terms of farm-wide impact as long as you employ site collection quotas to limit the consumption of content database storage.

As you might imagine, though, the use of versioning does increase storage consumption. Each time a new major or minor item version is added to a list or library, another copy of that item is created. Take the Version History for the Chapter 11 – SharePoint DR Development list item shown earlier in Figure 12.11. A total of six versions for the document exist: 1.0, 1.1, 1.2, 1.3, 2.0, and 2.1. Each of the versions consumes roughly 185KB, so even though the active 2.1 version is only 184KB in size, the total storage space consumed by all versions is more than 1MB.

For lists and libraries in which collaboration activities are used heavily, the overhead of multiple versions can quickly add up, consume storage, and push a site collection size toward its allocation limit on storage space as defined by its quota. Fortunately, SharePoint provides a "maximum number of versions retained" mechanism that provides some degree of control over the extent to which item and document versions may impact your overall site collection storage profile.

Configuring Versioning

The example that follows demonstrates how to enable versioning on a document library called Book Chapters at the root of a fictitious SharePoint team site with a URL of http://spdev:18480/. In addition to enabling versioning, the maximum number of versions that can be stored for each document in the library are specified.

If you attempt this walk-through on a SharePoint site of your own, ensure that your account possesses a minimum permission level of Contribute within the site housing the document library.

1. Open a browser and navigate to the site's URL of http://spdev:18480/. If you intend to follow along in your own environment, substitute this URL with the URL of a team site in your environment.

2. Depending on the configuration of your client browser and the Web application housing the site, you may be prompted to log in. If you are so prompted, supply both your username and password. In most cases, your username and password are your domain login credentials.

3. When the team site loads, you are greeted with the default page. Under the Libraries heading in the quick launch menu along the left side of the screen is a Book Chapters link. Click the link to take you to the Book Chapters document library shown in Figure 12.12.

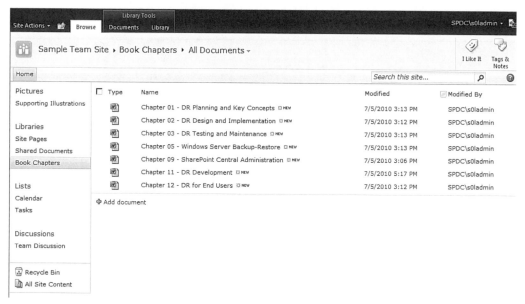

Figure 12.12 The Book Chapters document library in a sample team site.

4. By default, the Browse tab is selected near the top of the document library. Before you can begin configuration, click the Library tab under the Library Tools grouping. This displays the Documents Library Settings ribbon shown in Figure 12.13.

Figure 12.13   The ribbon for Documents Library Settings.

5. The actual contents of the ribbon and how they are presented depend on the width of your browser window. The link of interest on the ribbon is near the right side, though, and it is called Library Settings. When you have located it, click the link to bring up the Document Library Settings page for the library.

6. Under the General Settings category along the left side of the main area is a link titled Versioning Settings. Click the link to display the Versioning Settings page shown in Figure 12.14.

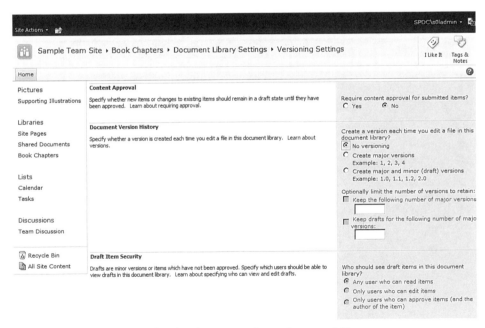

Figure 12.14   The Versioning Settings page for a document library.

7. By default, the Document Version History indicates that No Versioning is in use. To begin using versioning within the document library, select either Create Major Versions or Create Major and Minor (Draft) Versions. The latter tends to be the more useful form of versioning when tracking documents, so select it.

8. Once you select the Create Major and Minor (Draft) Versions option button, the version retention check boxes and text boxes just below it become active. The check boxes and text boxes provide a way to control the total number of retained versions. Set the first check box and text box for major version retention to appear, as shown in Figure 12.15. With these values in effect, ten major versions (1.0, 2.0, and so on) are available at any given time. Once version 11.0 is placed into the document library, version 1.0 is dropped from the available version history. When version 12.0 is placed into the document library, version 2.0 is dropped. This pattern repeats to ensure that only ten major versions are available at any given time.

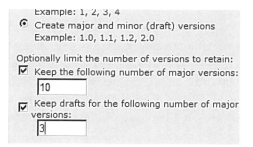

Figure 12.15   Specifying major version and draft retention settings.

9. Set the second check box and text box, as shown in Figure 12.15. Specifying that three major versions' worth of drafts are retained results in all drafts other than those belonging to the current major version and the two previous ones being discarded. If the most recent major version is 8.0, for example, only the draft (point) versions for versions 6.0, 7.0, and 8.0 are available. Any drafts that existed for previous versions (such as 5.1 and 5.2) are discarded. When version 9.0 is made available, all existing drafts for version 6.0 are dropped with these settings. When version 10.0 is made available, drafts for version 7.0 are dropped. You get the idea.

10. Scroll to the bottom of the Versioning Settings page and click the OK button to place your changes into effect.

As an administrator, you should be happy to hear that Recycle Bins and versioning work together and complement one another quite well. When a list item is deleted from a document library or list, the version history for the item goes with it to the Recycle Bin. By the same token, recovering an item from either the first or second stage Recycle Bins also restores that list item's version history.

Templates

Customization of SharePoint sites through the UI is a labor of love for some. For others, it's simply work. Regardless of how or why it is done, customization is something that end users can spend countless hours doing in SharePoint. Customization activities include altering the look and feel of a site, creating custom views for lists, modifying the usage and settings for Web parts, and much more.

Note: In the context of this section, the term *customization* is being used to describe changes that end users make to a SharePoint site or its constituent parts through the browser-based UI or SharePoint Designer. Customization does not refer to farm-deployed solutions, sandboxed solutions, or any other form of code-based solution unless explicitly indicated.

One way that end users can capture and save such customizations within the SharePoint environment is through the use of templates. For example, a template can be used to bundle up the changes that are made to a list, modifications that have been made to the columns it contains, views that have been added or changed, and more. In addition to capturing these structural changes, templates can be used to save data and content. In the case of the list example, end users have the option of choosing to include the data that is in a list at the same time the structural information is captured in a template.

Once you have created a template, it is available for re-use within the site collection it was created within. End users can also download templates that have been created for use in other site collections and SharePoint environments; this use is most attractive to the average end user from a content protection and disaster recovery perspective.

With the removal of personal Web package export and backup creation capabilities from SharePoint Designer 2010, templates remain one of the few mechanisms that end users have at their disposal to package and move content out of SharePoint sites in a structured form. Templates that can be created, exported, and imported by users come in two varieties: list templates and site templates.

List Templates

The first type of template that end users can generate through the SharePoint browser-based UI is a list template. The overwhelming majority of data and content within SharePoint is stored in list form, so the ability to create a reusable template from virtually any list in SharePoint is quite powerful.

As described earlier, a list template allows end users to capture the structure and customizations that are tied to a specific list or document library in SharePoint. At the same time, end users can choose to include all the list item content that the list or document library possesses at the time of template creation.

The process of list template creation can be distilled into the following sequence of steps:

1. Customize a list or document library and optionally load it with content in the form of list items.

2. Select the Save … as Template link from within the settings page for the list or document library in the browser-based UI.

3. On the Save As Template Web page that is displayed, provide a file name, template name, and description. Optionally, you can specify that list or document library content be included with the template.

4. SharePoint adds a new list item to the List Template Gallery for the site collection containing the list or document library that was used to generate the template.

Templates that are present in the List Template Gallery as a result of the steps just described are available for end users to select when they go to create a new list or document library in the site collection. You can also download templates in the List Template Gallery with the Save Target As option that is available when you right-click a template name, as shown in Figure 12.16.

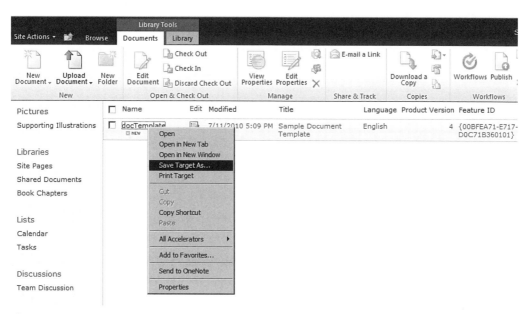

Figure 12.16   Saving a template from the List Template Gallery.

Templates that you download can be imported into another site collection using the Upload Document option on the ribbon of the List Template Gallery. Once you have uploaded a list template to the List Template Gallery, it becomes available for use in the creation of new lists in the destination site collection just as it had been in the source site collection.

Site Templates

The second type of template that can be generated from within the browser-based UI is a site template. Whereas you use a list template to capture the structure and content of a single list or document library, you use a site template to capture the equivalent information for an entire SharePoint site or subsite. The template process doesn't recursively capture subsites below the site targeted, though—only the site itself.

In most regards, the process of creating and using a site template is the same as the process that was described for list templates. There are a few differences worth noting, though.

- The link to create a template is located under the Site Actions menu of the Site Settings page.

- Templates that you create are stored (somewhat nonintuitively) in the Solutions Gallery for the site collection. You can download existing templates from the Solutions Gallery, and you can upload templates that you want to import to the Solutions Gallery.

- Templates in the Solutions Gallery are available for selection when end users want to create a new site or subsite, such as through the New Site options on the Site Actions menu.

SharePoint Designer and Templates

If you have used SharePoint Designer 2010 and examined the application's ribbon while working with either a site or list, you have probably seen the Save As Template button that is shown circled in Figure 12.17.

Figure 12.17 SharePoint Designer's Save As Template ribbon button.

As was the case with SharePoint Designer 2007, this button doesn't launch application-specific functionality within SharePoint Designer 2010. Instead, it opens a browser window and directs the browser to the `savetmpl.aspx` application page in SharePoint's `_layouts` virtual directory. From the `savetmpl.aspx` page, you have the ability to create both site and list templates. That's the extent to which SharePoint Designer assists with site and list template creation.

Interestingly enough, the `savetmpl.aspx` page is the same page from which site and list templates are created when using the browser-based UI for these tasks. In reality, SharePoint Designer doesn't really provide template creation capabilities—it simply hands control over to a SharePoint application page and removes itself from the operation.

An Administrative Perspective on Templates

Much like versioning, the creation and use of both site and list templates are tasks that end users can carry out on their own without having to trouble you, the administrator. There are a few template-related points of note, though, that you should be aware of.

Templates and Publishing Sites

When your users begin working with templates, they may report that the links to create site and list templates don't always appear within the Site Settings and List Settings pages. In addition, your users may report that the Template Creation button on the ribbon in SharePoint Designer is sometimes grayed out.

In most cases, this behavior is by design and is tied to site collections that are based on publishing templates such as the Publishing Portal and Enterprise Wiki. Due to some of the unique relationships that exist within publishing sites, such as the relationship between layout pages and content types, Microsoft does not support the creation of templates from publishing sites and lists within them. This lack of support is reinforced through the disablement of template creation links in publishing sites.

Strictly speaking, it is still possible to create templates for publishing sites and lists by navigating directly to the savetmpl.aspx application page within the _layouts virtual directory of a publishing site, but it is obviously not recommended and supported for reasons already mentioned.

Setting Limits on Templates That Can Be Generated

Another common barrier that users encounter with templates is the maximum size of the template they can create. By default, the maximum size of a list or site template that can be created is roughly 50MB in SharePoint 2010. Attempts to create a template that is larger than 50MB are met with an error dialog box similar to the one shown in Figure 12.18.

Figure 12.18   Error that results from attempting to create a template that is too large.

Storage of 50MB is typically ample for templates that include structural elements without site content and list items, but templates that include content from large lists and sites can easily exceed this limit.

As an administrator, you have the ability to increase or decrease the maximum size limit for list and site templates that end users can generate from within SharePoint sites. However, before making changes to the limit, there are a few points worth mentioning:

- Any changes that you make to the maximum size limit apply to all site collections within the SharePoint farm.

- The creation of large templates can place a significant load on the Web server where the template is generated. This can adversely affect the performance of your SharePoint environment.

- Attempts to create templates that are too large may lead to erratic behavior and browser timeouts. The actual point at which undesirable behavior manifests varies from environment to environment, so you should understand how your farm behaves under load before setting the maximum template creation size to too large of a value.

If changing the maximum template creation size is something you conclude that you want to do, there are two ways to accomplish it. The recommended approach involves a few simple lines of PowerShell script to change the MaxTemplateDocumentSize property value on the content Web service for the SharePoint farm:

```
$cws = [Microsoft.SharePoint.Administration.SPWebService]::ContentService
$cws.MaxTemplateDocumentSize = <new maximum>
$cws.Update()
```

Alternatively, you can fall back to using STSADM.exe to make the same change:

```
STSADM -o setproperty -pn max-template-document-size -pv <new maximum>
```

In both the PowerShell and STSADM.exe examples, the <new maximum> value specified is the new template size creation limit in bytes. A value of 150000000, for example, changes the maximum template creation size to approximately 150,000,000 bytes, or 150MB, for all site collections within the farm.

Templates and Security

As an administrator, there is an additional point you must consider when determining how templates are or are not going to be used within your organization: security. Although the creation of templates that contain only structural information don't pose much of a concern, a user's ability to include list item content within a template does. If sites or lists contain sensitive content, that content can be written out in a template by default. Once the content is written to a template and subsequently downloaded, anyone who can access the downloaded template has access to a copy of the content data that was exported.

There are a couple of simple options available to you if you want to restrict how templates can be created and downloaded.

- You can tune and reduce the maximum size of a template that can be created. Because list item content can quickly "bulk-up" a list, some experimentation may allow you to set a maximum template creation size that is adequate to allow the creation of structural templates without permitting the creation of templates that include list item content.

- By controlling the permissions on the List Template Gallery and Solution Gallery for a site collection, you can control who can create templates, who can access templates, whether or not templates can be deleted, and more.

Additional options exist, particularly if you or your organization is willing to employ custom code solutions or develop special information rights management (IRM) policies that can be applied to templates. Such discussions are beyond the scope of this chapter, however.

WebDAV and Explorer View

One interesting, yet often overlooked, method to access the contents of a SharePoint site and its lists is through Windows Explorer, using either the Explorer View option available on Share-Point lists and libraries or a protocol known as WebDAV (for Web-based Distributed Authoring and Versioning). SharePoint's Explorer View functionality opens a SharePoint library or list in Windows Explorer so that you can manage files in a SharePoint list in the same way you manage files in a folder in a Windows operating system. WebDAV provides most of the plumbing needed by users to access those contents within the familiar folder structure of Windows Explorer via a Universal Naming Convention (UNC) path.

The ability to access a SharePoint site, document library, or other type of list via Windows Explorer is pretty powerful, because it allows end users to easily manage the files and items in those repositories like they would any other folders in their Windows workstation's operating system, rather than using the limited tools that are available through a browser. With the Windows Explorer interface, a user can drag a document into a SharePoint list to add it, rather than clicking through multiple Web pages, and do the same to copy that file back down to his workstation. Even more importantly, this can be easily done with multiple files, which can save time.

How WebDAV and Explorer View Are Used

To access a SharePoint resource, such as a document library, in Explorer View, navigate to the target resource in a Web browser and click the library's Open with Explorer button that is present on the Library tab of the document library's ribbon, as shown in Figure 12.19.

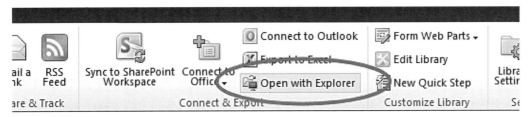

Figure 12.19   Opening a document library with Windows Explorer.

If your SharePoint environment and client workstation are properly configured to enable Explorer View, clicking the Open with Explorer button launches an instance of Windows Explorer and navigates to the document library.

To open a SharePoint resource directly via WebDAV, you must translate the resource's Share-Point URL into a Windows Explorer–friendly UNC path. You can accomplish this by copying the target URL into a text file. (Don't include the .aspx file name at the end of URL; focus only on the folder objects above that file so you can open the containing object for the resource and not an item within it.) Remove http:// at the beginning of the address and replace it with \\. Replace all forward slashes (/) with backslashes (\). Then copy the address, paste it into the address bar of a Windows Explorer window, and press Enter to load the address. The SharePoint resource now opens as a folder within Windows Explorer on your desktop.

Like sites and list templates, Explorer View and WebDAV let you easily copy the contents of a SharePoint list or document library to your local workstation for backup purposes and likewise restore them to the resource as needed. They use a familiar interface, and the commands to manage the files within them are simple and common to Windows operating systems. But, like site and list templates, end users must manually execute them, and they are better suited to one-time actions, whereby an end user wants to create a copy of crucial content.

Server and Workstation Configuration

One drawback with using both Explorer View and WebDAV is the difficulty associated with configuring SharePoint servers and client workstations to use them without issue on a consistent basis. Configuration on the server side of the equation is largely a nonissue thanks to the Share-Point 2010 prerequisites installer that runs when SharePoint is being set up initially. Client-side configuration, on the other hand, is another matter altogether.

An end user's ability to use Explorer View is greatly impacted by the combination of his oper-ating system, his Web browser, and the versions of both items. Even when those are configured optimally (which can be difficult in environments with a variety of workstation configurations), Explorer View can be slow, prone to crashing, or simply unusable at times.

Explorer View and WebDAV also suffer from additional dependencies on client configuration. For WebDAV to work, for example, the WebClient service must be running on the client workstation you're using to access the SharePoint resource. For most consumer operating systems, such as Windows 7, the WebClient service is running by default. If you want to use Explorer View from a server-based operating system, though, additional configuration steps are often necessary. On Windows Server 2008 and Windows Server 2008 R2, for example, the WebClient service only becomes available after enabling the Desktop Experience feature, as shown in Figure 12.20.

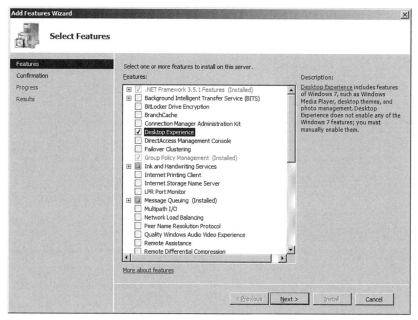

Figure 12.20   Enabling a server's Desktop Experience feature.

Failure to configure and enable the WebClient service is the most common reason for end users not being able to access a SharePoint list or document library through Explorer View and WebDAV. Until the WebClient service is running properly, SharePoint displays the dialog box shown in Figure 12.21 when attempts are made to launch Explorer View.

Figure 12.21   Message box indicating that a client can't connect using Explorer View.

Administrative Concerns

As stated already, most of the difficulty in getting Explorer View and WebDAV configured for use with SharePoint lies on the client side of the equation. Whether or not this impacts you depends on the scope of your duties as an administrator.

On the server side of things, there isn't much for you to do either except ensure that you install SharePoint properly and let the prerequisites installer do its thing during the initial setup process. There are no readily visible knobs and dials for the configuration of Explorer View and Web-DAV for SharePoint; SharePoint handles and controls its implementation internally.

Caution: Internet Information Server 7 (IIS7) includes its own WebDAV Publishing role service that does not get enabled by the SharePoint 2010 prerequisites installer. In actuality, SharePoint 2010 supplies its WebDAV functionality through a private internal implementation—not through IIS7. It is recommended that you avoid enabling the IIS7 WebDAV Publishing role service on servers running SharePoint 2010. The jury is still out on how the WebDAV Publishing role service might impact SharePoint 2010, but enabling the role service prevented WebDAV from working properly with SharePoint 2007.

SharePoint Workspace 2010

SharePoint Workspace 2010 (SPW) is the new kid on the block in the SharePoint product lineup —or rather, one of the existing products with a new name and some new tricks to match.

When the Office 2010 and SharePoint 2010 product lines were being fleshed out, Microsoft made the decision to take Microsoft Office Groove 2007, overhaul and add a number of Share-Point 2010–specific features to it, and rebrand the resultant product as SharePoint Workspace 2010. Although the product features that were part of Groove 2007 still exist in SPW, this section focuses specifically on the features that support SharePoint 2010. Groove and related functions, such as peer collaboration, are not discussed.

What Can It Do?

If you're familiar with Microsoft Exchange and e-mail, the easiest way to explain SPW is with an analogy. SPW's role with regard to SharePoint is analogous to the role that the Microsoft Outlook client serves for Exchange servers. Although you can access an Exchange e-mail account using the browser-based Outlook Web Access (OWA) client, using the Microsoft Outlook rich client on your workstation adds significant functionality and improves the usability over OWA alone.

The capability that is front and center in SPW is the ability it affords you to work with Share-Point content in an offline, rich client application setting. When SPW is installed and configured on your workstation, you have the option of creating offline SharePoint workspaces that are tied directly to SharePoint sites and subsites. An example of the SharePoint Workspace for the root Web of a team site is shown in Figure 12.22.

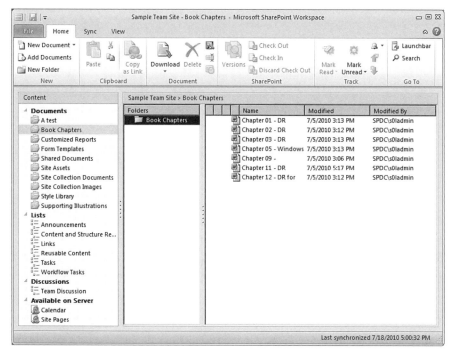

Figure 12.22   An offline workspace for a SharePoint team site.

You can use the SharePoint Workspace client to interact with SharePoint lists and libraries, check documents in and out, add new content, and perform most of the list and document-centric tasks you are used to using a browser to perform.

Note: SPW's SharePoint functions operate only with SharePoint 2010 sites. You cannot create workspaces that are tied to SharePoint 2007 sites.

Your ability to work with SharePoint content isn't limited to just the times you are online and connected. Behind the scenes, SPW uses the Office Documents Cache (ODC) to track changes you make while working offline. Once you eventually go back online and have access to the SharePoint sites associated with your changes, SPW performs bidirectional synchronization to ensure that both the SPW client ODC and the SharePoint sites are up-to-date with the latest changes, updates, and additions.

SPW isn't a complete replacement for browser-based access to SharePoint sites, though. SPW's ability to work with lists and libraries is tied to the content types that those lists and libraries implement. Lists and libraries that are based on some content types, such as the publishing content types, surveys, and events (calendars), for example, are clearly identified by SPW as content that the application cannot handle.

Administrative Concerns

SPW is the evolution of the Groove client, but to many users the product is new in the SharePoint 2010 landscape. Once end users learn about it and figure out how easily it works, you can expect adoption to grow quickly—something that didn't really happen with Groove. SPW's offline capabilities are compelling, and its ability to effectively replicate an entire SharePoint site from the server to a workstation is undoubtedly going to go a long way toward reassuring users that they are in control of their data.

These new capabilities afford end users a great deal of much-needed functionality, but there are some administrative aspects that you should understand.

Limiting the Use of SharePoint Workspace

Upon learning about SPW and how it works, the first question uttered by many administrators is "how do I turn it off?" This is a good question; by default, SPW can connect to every new site that is created within SharePoint 2010 for purposes of establishing a client-side workspace.

Disabling SPW support (and offline client support in general) can be accomplished at two different levels. The approach you take is driven by whether you need to lock out an entire site or just portions of it.

- **Site.** Preventing SPW and other offline client access to an entire SharePoint site involves changing the Offline Client Availability setting for the site to No. This setting is available on the Search and Offline Availability page that is available under the list of Site Administration links for a selected SharePoint site.

- **List or Document Library.** You can block the offline availability of a specific list or document library through the Offline Client Availability setting on the list's or library's Advanced Settings page. By default, the option is set to Yes to enable access to the list or library by SPW and other offline clients. Changing the option to No blocks offline client access for the list or library only; the rest of the site remains unaffected.

Caution: Changes that are made through each of the aforementioned settings take effect immediately. Changing the offline availability settings for a site or list/library that an end user already has a workspace for doesn't sever connections between SPW and the site and its lists/libraries, though. In fact, end users can continue to operate with a fair level of functionality. Operations become somewhat unpredictable, though, particularly when SPW launches another application (such as Microsoft Word) for editing. As a matter of policy, you should strive to set the offline policy for your sites and lists/libraries before end users begin using them. Changing them after the fact is seldom accomplished cleanly.

Configuration Items and Concerns

To support the operation of SPW, Microsoft actually created and implemented a new file synchronization specification called the "File Synchronization via SOAP over HTTP Protocol Specification," or MS-FSSHTTP. MS-FSSHTTP is a Web service-based protocol that allows for the efficient transfer and synchronization of files between two endpoints. The protocol supports a number of attractive capabilities in the offline editing of documents that are housed in SharePoint, such as incremental file synchronization, coauthoring of documents, and multiuser editing without synchronization/conflict concerns.

Note: Microsoft has published the MS-FSSHTTP specification, and you can download it free. If you want to learn more about the protocol and how it operates, check it out at http://msdn.microsoft.com/en-us/library/dd943623.aspx.

By and large, SPW's ability to take files offline and synchronize them with a SharePoint site is one of those things that simply "just works" from an administrator's perspective. Strictly speaking, there isn't really anything extra or special that you need to do to ensure that SPW can be employed by your end user base. That doesn't mean that you won't benefit from some additional insight, though.

First, Microsoft recommends that you enable the Remote Differential Compression (RDC) feature on Windows servers where offline clients are connecting. Although clients that employ the MS-FSSHTTP protocol for connections to the SharePoint environment support incremental file transfers and other benefits already mentioned, other offline clients such as older versions of Microsoft Office do not. RDC complements MS-FSSHTP and enables the efficient upload and download of incremental file changes on these other offline client types. Without RDC enabled, the upload and download of an entire file is needed when an older client type is performing an incremental change only.

RDC is not enabled by default on Windows Server 2008, and it isn't enabled by the SharePoint 2010 prerequisites installer. You must manually enable the RDC server feature from either the command line or using the Windows Server Add Features Wizard.

Offline Operations and Security

Another area you should be concerned about when allowing SPW usage is security. As an administrator, you need to address two specific areas:

- **Transport layer security.** By default, communications between SPW and the SharePoint environment take place through the URL endpoint that end users supply when setting up an SPW workspace on their workstations. If the URL that is supplied doesn't map to an endpoint that supports some form of transport layer security such as Secure Socket Layer (SSL) encryption, end users are going to be transmitting the contents of lists and libraries across the wire in unencrypted form. This really is no different from other forms of access to the SharePoint site through the endpoint specified, but the sheer volume of file traffic that occurs with SPW warrants this special mention.

- **Client storage security.** SPW uses the ODC for offline SharePoint list and library storage. Although SPW is capable of encrypting some Groove-related data, SharePoint file and nonfile data is not encrypted on end user workstations. This means that the contents of each SharePoint workspace (that is, the lists and libraries that are within the associated Share-Point site) reside on end user workstations in unencrypted form. The contents of these offline files aren't human readable, but the fact that they aren't encrypted won't stop someone determined to read them. If data protection is a concern, you must employ a secondary form of encryption (such as Windows BitLocker drive encryption).

Synchronizing Large Numbers of Documents

Although SharePoint synchronization with SPW simply works in the majority of cases, you need to be aware of a couple of thresholds when working with large numbers of client-side documents that are tied to SharePoint sites through workspaces.

The first threshold is hit when SPW attempts to synchronize approximately 500 or more documents between SharePoint sites and all client-side workspaces. When this threshold is hit, you are warned that you need to free up some space on your workstation. You can safely ignore this warning, but increasing the number of offline SharePoint documents yields increased synchronization overhead that may result in a degraded experience and poorer performance.

A more dramatic threshold is hit when the total number of offline documents across all workspaces exceeds 1800. At this point, SharePoint Workspace switches from regular synchronization of all document content and metadata to regular synchronization of document metadata only. Any time a document is targeted for action or modification, the document content is synchronized on demand to ensure that you have a valid copy. This on-demand content synchronization behavior allows SPW to limit what would otherwise be excessive overhead and performance degradation.

Bringing SPW back to a point that is below the document thresholds mentioned is as simple as discarding local SharePoint documents, deleting unused SharePoint workspaces, and disconnecting from unused or unneeded document libraries. As a general rule of thumb, the fewer the number of offline documents you have on your workstation, the better your performance will be with SPW synchronization.

Conclusion

SharePoint 2010 provides end users with a number of tools that provide some level of protection against data loss, undesired changes, and SharePoint site outage scenarios. Recycle Bins, versioning, the creation of templates, Explorer View, WebDAV, and SharePoint Workspace 2010 all meet different needs for different end users. Although none of these tools plays a significant role in the overall disaster recovery strategy that you are responsible for developing and maintaining, these tools can help promote end user self-sufficiency for some of the lesser data protection and recovery tasks you would be tasked with handling otherwise.

At a minimum, each of the end user tools and techniques that have been described in this chapter demands some level of operational awareness on your part. Some of the features, such as Recycle Bins and templates, require some actual administrative configuration on your part. Regardless of your own personal leanings, it is likely in your best interests as an administrator to understand what end users can do to protect and recover data in the SharePoint environment. The next support call you get may be resolved more quickly if you are able to direct users to one of the tools or techniques described in this chapter.

Having completed this chapter, you should now be able to answer the following questions. As with the other chapters, answers to the following questions appear in Appendix A, "Chapter Review Q&A," found on the Cengage Learning Web site at http://www.courseptr.com/downloads.

1. What are the maximum storage limits that are in place for the first and second stage Recycle Bins for a site collection created on a Web application with default settings?

2. How do you enable versioning on a list or library?

3. What is the primary security concern associated with site and list template creation?

4. What key service must be installed and functional for client-side WebDAV access to a SharePoint list or library?

5. How do you turn off SharePoint Workspace 2010 access to a SharePoint list or document library? To an entire SharePoint site?

13 Conclusion

You've finished the book, and hopefully you've preserved your sanity by reading chapters and sections here and there as needed. We packed an awful lot of information into this book, and it's hard to pull it all in at once and process it without coming up for air.

If you didn't pace yourself and you're one of those die-hard troopers who read the book from cover to cover, we salute you! You are indeed a rare breed—the type that probably winds down at night reading patent applications, instruction manuals, and a randomly selected book from the encyclopedia set on the shelf.

Regardless of how you identify yourself as a reader, we hope that you found each of the chapters between the covers to be helpful, informative, and referential. We spent many long hours writing and refining the content in this book. Our goal was to provide you, the administrator, with the material you would need to understand and carry out disaster recovery planning for your SharePoint environment in an informed and educated manner.

If we did our jobs properly, the structural integrity of your cranium is probably somewhat compromised from the constant drumming we have been doing throughout many of the chapters. Regardless of who you are or why you picked up this book, we made the reasonable assumption that you have at least some interest in SharePoint disaster recovery. With that in mind, we tried to drive home a handful of universal concepts whenever and wherever we could.

The most important concept we tried to drive home bears repeating one more time as a parting shot: there is no such thing as a one-size-fits-all SharePoint disaster recovery strategy. Although there are some patterns that do arise in SharePoint disaster recovery planning and implementation, your environment is unique. You may have some luck in starting with a template that was designed by someone else with disaster recovery needs that were similar to yours, but by now you should fully understand why any such template or prepackaged strategy is merely a starting point—not the end of the conversation.

You should also realize that disaster recovery is an awful lot more than just backup and restore. Some administrators fall into the habit of using "disaster recovery" and "backup/restore" interchangeably, but they are not synonymous. The latter is often a major facet of the former, but disaster recovery activities are driven primarily by business concerns—not technical concerns as in the case of backup/restore. If any of this sounds a little fuzzy, go back and reread the first few chapters of the book. It's okay, and we understand. The material was covered quite some time ago if you're one of the aforementioned die-hard, cover-to-cover readers.

Microsoft has packed some great new disaster recovery features and capabilities into the SharePoint 2010 platform, and we've attempted to cover as many of them as possible in this book. Much as there is no one-size-fits-all approach to disaster recovery in general, there is no magic bullet feature that is going to address your disaster recovery needs in every scenario. Every technology supporting disaster recovery comes with its own benefits and disadvantages, and we have tried to provide you with the information needed to compare the platform features and understand where each of them excels and comes up short.

After all the disaster recovery strategies have been plotted, the technologies have been selected, and the plans have been built, you still have to deal with the day-to-day operational concerns that remain in the disaster recovery bucket. Backups, restores, recoveries, and rebuilds are some of the activities that tend to get tossed into that bucket. We covered many of these concerns and operating scenarios in several of the chapters, and we tried to address the challenges and questions that we ourselves have seen in our SharePoint travels. We hope that you found the material to be useful in your role as an administrator.

Even though we managed to go on about SharePoint disaster recovery for more than 400 pages, we would be lying if we said that we were able to cover all the technologies, concerns, scenarios, and watch-outs that we would have liked. We had to make some compromises on coverage, and where we did, we attempted to call those out. If you found something particularly helpful, we would love to hear about it. At the same time, we want to hear about troubles you've had, technologies we should have covered, situations that have frustrated you, and anything else you want to share that is disaster recovery related.

We closed our 2007 version of this book with the following quote, and it remains just as applicable now as it did before. The following is attributed to Alan Lakein, an acknowledged expert on personal time management:

"Planning is bringing the future into the present so that you can do something about it now."

These words summarize the essence of disaster recovery planning in a nutshell. Disasters don't happen when it's organizationally convenient, and they strike without warning. The only reasonable course of action is to assume that a disaster *will* happen to your SharePoint environment at some point in the future and work to prepare for that disaster now. After all, hope and ignorance are not recognized as acceptable risk mitigation strategies in any technical group or organization.

Index